LIBRARIES IN THE TWENTY-FIRST CENTURY

Topics in Australasian Library and Information Studies

Series editors: Professor Ross Harvey and Dr Stuart Ferguson

This series provides detailed, formally refereed works on a wide range of topics and issues relevant to professionals and para-professionals in the library and information industry and to students of library and information studies. All titles are written from an Australasian perspective, drawing on professional experience and research in Australia, New Zealand and the wider Pacific region. Proposals for publications should be addressed to the series editors (rossharvey@csu.edu.au, sferguson@csu.edu.au).

Recent publications include:

Number 26
Collection management: A concise introduction. Revised edition
John Kennedy

Number 25
The other 51 weeks: A marketing handbook for librarians. Revised edition
Lee Welch

Number 24
Archives: Recordkeeping in society
Edited by Sue McKemmish, Michael Piggott, Barbara Reed and Frank Upward

Number 23
Organising knowledge in a global society: Principles and practice in libraries and information centres
Ross Harvey and Philip Hider

Number 22
Computers for librarians: An introduction to the electronic library. 3rd edition
Stuart Ferguson with Rodney Hebels

Number 21
Australian library supervision and management. 2nd edition
Roy Sanders

Number 20
Research methods for students, academics and professionals. 2nd edition
Kirsty Williamson et al.

LIBRARIES IN THE TWENTY-FIRST CENTURY

Charting new directions in information services

Edited by Stuart Ferguson

Topics in Australasian Library and Information Studies, Number 27

Centre for Information Studies

Charles Sturt University
Wagga Wagga New South Wales

ISBN 9781876938437 (pbk.)
ISBN 1 876938 43 9 (pbk.)
ISSN: 1030-5009

National Library of Australia cataloguing-in-publication data

---

Ferguson, Stuart, 1953- .
  Libraries in the twenty-first century : charting new directions in information services.

  Includes index.
  ISBN 9781876938437 (pbk.)

  ISBN 1 876938 43 9 (pbk.)

  1. Libraries and community - Australia. 2. Information services - Australia. 3. Information resources - Australia. I. Charles Sturt University. Centre for Information Studies. II. Title. (Series : Topics in Australasian library and information studies ; no. 27).

021.20994

Published in 2007

Series editor: R. Harvey
Copy editors: R. Crease, J. Harris
Indexer: S. Quinn
Cover designer: T. O'Neill
Typesetter: N. Anderson
Printer: Quick Print, Wagga Wagga

Centre for Information Studies
Locked Bag 660
Wagga Wagga NSW 2678
Australia
Phone: + 61 (0)2 6933 2325
Fax: +61 (0)2 6933 2733
Email: cis@csu.edu.au
http://www.csu.edu.au/cis

Contents

Acknowledgements

One of the reasons for embarking on a publication of this kind was the relative absence of a generic monograph of this kind on the profession of library and information management and the directions it is currently taking. The genesis of this collection lies in discussions with colleagues at Charles Sturt University, School of Information Studies, and with students of CSU's library and information management programs, who have not always been impressed with the readings to which they have been referred. My first acknowledgement therefore is to these two groups. I hope this monograph meets their needs.

There are many debts of gratitude in putting together a collaborative work on this scale. Below are the principal acknowledgements.

Chris Jones thanks Robert Knight, Director, Riverina Regional Library; Lyn Makin, CEO, Upper Murray Regional Library; and Jan Richards, Manager Library Services, Central West Libraries, for their input.

Alison O'Connor acknowledges the assistance of Jenelle Cleary, Client Support Librarian from the Victorian Parliamentary Library for her assistance with the parliamentary libraries section of Chapter 4.

Roxanne Missingham and Jasmine Cameron acknowledge input from Sandra Henderson, National Library of Australia, who compiled Appendix 1, 'The NSLA libraries: Some basic facts'.

Jan Houghton and Jennifer Berryman acknowledge with thanks the assistance of Carolyn Austin and Jo Orsatti in the preparation of Chapter 16.

As editor, I would like to thank the contributors, who put a great deal of effort into their chapters – all without remuneration – especially those who write for publication only occasionally and were less confident than the others about the outcome of their efforts. I would also like to acknowledge Susie Halverson, the ex-administrative officer of the CIS, whose assistance with the website we set up for this project was invaluable, and the principal copy editor, Rachel Crease, whose (apparently) unflappable attention to detail and to the needs of the potential reader are extremely reassuring for a hard-pressed editor. Finally, I thank my wife, Alice, for her forbearance and acknowledge her (no doubt) sound advice to 'stick to journal articles in future'.

Figures and tables

Introduction

Stuart Ferguson

A critic might say that a book called *Libraries in the twenty-first century* is bound to be a slim volume – after all, libraries and librarians are soon to be things of the past. Those who saw the 2002 film version of HG Wells's *The time machine* may recall the Vox System in the New York Public Library, a holographic cyber librarian from 2030 that can access every database on the planet and interact with library clients to provide any information they require. It even produces a treatise written by the time traveller himself (assumed to have died in 1903) on the creation of a time machine, although when the time traveller asks about the time machine he is referred to HG Wells's novel, in one of those frustrating logical loops with which users of the world wide web are all too familiar. This wonderful, if flawed, librarian of the future also remembers its customers. When the time traveller finds himself 800,000 years in the future, in the world of the Eloi and the Morlocks, he stumbles across a much diminished holograph, bemoaning the fact that it remembers everything – 'I even remember you', it comments, 'Time travel – practical applications' (2002). Despite the obvious limitations of the cyber librarian, the image is a powerful one – not simply on account of the near-omniscience of the cyber librarian, but also because of the personalised service.

It would be easy to dismiss the romanticised imagery as so much science fiction except that, as with some of the genre, the technology is not all that far away – at least it is not far removed from the screenplay (although the cyber librarian was not part of Wells's early twentieth-century vision). We do presently have holographic representations, after all, and we also have relatively easy computer access to a wide range of resources in digital formats that can be stored, manipulated and transferred across telecommunications networks by computers. Indeed, many pre-digital resources stored by libraries and other collecting institutions in paper and audio-visual formats are in the course of being digitised or converted into digital formats. In a recent symposium at the State Library of Victoria, for instance, Mary Jane Stannus of the Australian Broadcasting Corporation announced that the ABC would digitise 30,000 one-inch tapes in the space of three years, adding 'we won't have that format to deal with anymore, and then SP Beta Cam, SX Digi Beta Cam. So the problem that archives face with changing formats and having to keep them up to date' (2006).

There have also been a number of attempts to digitise print books, the most famous being Project Gutenberg, and, while this particular book is being written, Google has embarked on a project to digitise as many as fifteen million books, in association with the libraries of Harvard, Stanford, University of Michigan, University of Oxford and, yes, the iconic New York Public Library. Even before Google itself was started, says co-founder Larry Page, the vision was to make 'the incredible breadth of information that librarians so lovingly organize searchable online' ('Google checks out library books' 2004). Librarians, who make as much use of Google as anyone else, can hardly help but notice the patronising 'so lovingly'.

What of the cyber librarian, however? We do have what are occasionally called 'cybrarians' in some of our organisations. University of Queensland Library, for instance, did so, although its 'Ask a Cybrarian' link now takes clients to a more standard 'Ask a Librarian' service (University of Queensland 2007). These are human information professionals, however, working in a virtual environment, typically without face-to-face contact with clients. They are not computer programs and we are a long way from the New York Public Library's futuristic Vox System – not altogether surprising since science fiction does contain a strong element of the fictional. It is true to say that artificial intelligence (AI) – the already old-fashioned sounding area of computer science that includes 'intelligent' systems – has not developed to the level of interactivity demonstrated in the film, despite the promise of expert systems research in the early 1990s. Nonetheless, elements of AI have found their way into software developments in other fields of computing and we see increasing interactivity in our information retrieval systems. Take, for instance, the intelligent agent (sometimes also called AI agent or autonomous agent), which can make inferences based on its memory and on its previous contact with its environment (inputs), thus learning from its environment and from past inferences. An example with which some people will be familiar is the customer-service agent, which uses natural language to interact with customers and allows them to state their intentions instead of having to search for information themselves on an organisation's website (Barbuceanu et al. 2004, p.47).

Do librarians, or their 'cybrarian' counterparts, need to start retraining, before they go the way of the typesetter? In this collection the authors think not. Although there are examples of libraries being closed in the corporate sector and even in the school sector, the papers in this collection bear witness to a considerable role for libraries in the early twenty-first century. Anyone reading the chapter by Roxanne Missingham and Jasmine Cameron, for instance, cannot fail to be impressed by the fact that collecting institutions such as the National Library of Australia have harnessed information and communication technologies (ICTs) to create institutions that are far more 'national' in terms of delivery of service and sheer presence than ever their print-based predecessors could be. Their immediate future is certainly an exciting one. The public library described by Chris Jones in the opening chapter also remains a vibrant institution, which not only seeks to develop virtual resources and services, but also continues to provide an important physical space for local communities. Moreover, as Jake Wallis's chapter on the wider social environment eloquently demonstrates, libraries are significant players in any attempt to counter the so-called 'digital divide' between information 'haves' and have-nots' that some believe characterise our so-called 'information society'. James Herring's chapter on school libraries highlights the extent to which 'information literacy', which has been driven in the educational sector by librarians, is increasingly seen by educators as a central strand in the education of our children – and adults.

Libraries for the moment, then, seem highly relevant to their parent institutions and communities. This is in stark contrast to the vision of a senior library educator at Charles Sturt University, who in the early 1990s announced to a startled group of information technology (IT) lecturers that libraries would be dead by the year 2000, made redundant by the very ICTs they taught. Nothing could have been further from the truth. Is this a cause for complacency – yet another poor performance indicator for the profession of futurology? Library and information professionals are not rushing to retrain as futurologists but they are not complacent either. There are significant challenges facing them. The information environment in which they develop their services is growing ever more complex. They used to enjoy a *relatively* privileged position as major intermediaries (some would even say 'gatekeepers') between the individuals, organisations and communities they served and the world of (largely) print publications. This involved functions such as the following:

- analysing the information needs of clients, organisations and the community, whether these needs be educational, recreational or purely informational;
- developing collections of publications that meet their clients' information needs;
- assisting clients find publications they may find useful by describing them (using elements such as publication details, physical description or subject descriptors) and developing appropriate resource discovery tools, such as library catalogues;
- assisting clients access publications by developing information services, products and systems such as reference assistance, document delivery and inter-library loans;
- managing library collections, including their storage, organisation, dissemination and preservation;
- instructing clients on how they themselves can address their information needs and make best use of the resource discovery and delivery systems developed by the librarians (a function sometimes called information literacy instruction); and
- evaluating the information services, products and systems they have acquired or developed.

These functions are still central to what many library and information professionals do but the information landscape in which they perform them is much more complex, for instance:

- clients served may not have physical access to their libraries, for instance, distance learning students in the tertiary education sector or staff in multi-site and multi-national organisations;
- library collections may be a mixture of physical and electronic resources (sometimes called hybrid libraries) or completely electronic (variously referred to as electronic, digital or virtual libraries);
- library collections are based increasingly on subscription rather than acquisition, involving complex and expensive licensing arrangements and large datasets of resources that may be lost to libraries as soon as subscriptions cease and, almost invariably, include resources, such as runs of journals, that are of little interest to the client base;
- libraries have invested heavily in, what are called, 'legacy systems' (for instance, library catalogues and the standards used to develop them) that lag behind the web-based systems to which many people have become accustomed, and may need to adapt their systems (or perhaps even scrap them) instead of insisting that clients learn about their systems;
- many people feel that they can get enough in the way of information resources from the internet, and do not therefore have such a pressing need for the services, products and systems developed by librarians;
- there are so many players in the information industries, some of which encroach on the field (or 'turf') previously occupied principally by librarians (such as Google's digitisation of print resources, mentioned earlier);

- with many individuals and organisations getting into electronic publishing (for instance, university libraries developing digital institutional repositories of research and teaching resources), there is no longer a clearly identified 'information cycle', in which libraries constitute one of the main intermediaries between publishers and library clients; and
- there are so many different electronic resources and information providers that those searching for appropriate resources are faced with a variety of different search facilities and search interfaces (largely, the documentation on their computer screens that helps them find what they want).

These are merely a sample of the issues and challenges addressed in this book. One of the most interesting is the so-called interface between the individual, searching for information resources in an increasingly electronic environment, and the world of published resources. Librarians represent one of several information professions working to make that interface as transparent and as easily navigated as possible. There is a long way to go. Certainly there has been progress since the 1970s, when many of the resource discovery tools associated with library work, such as the library catalogue and the remote online bibliographic database, were command driven; that is, users needed to know the command language required to interrogate a computerised information retrieval (IR) system.

Interfaces are much easier to use in the early twenty-first century than in these early days, but they are still anything but intuitive, as witnessed by those who have tried using IR systems that offer users the opportunity to conduct a boolean search, in which the system searches for combinations of user-specified words (or parts of words or adjacency of words!) in documents and/or document descriptions in order to produce search results. Even assuming the occurrence of specified words in a document is a guide to its relevance to a user (a point many would question), is this a process that one really wants to inflict on the user of an IR system? Ideally, such processes are best left to the 'back-end' of IR systems, unseen by users, with intelligent front-ends providing the guidance, or even the prompts, to assist the user interrogate the system. Perhaps the cyber librarian described earlier is a worthwhile ideal to keep in mind.

It would be a mistake, however, to focus too much on the technology. While technological development may be one of the drivers of change in library and information services, it is by no means the only one. As a number of papers in this collection demonstrate, there are many more drivers, most of them socio-economic and/or political. There is nothing new about the idea of a global economy – Karl Marx, after all, wrote about it towards the end of the nineteenth century – but 'globalisation' is now spoken and written about as if it were a new phenomenon that has burst on the world's nation states like an irreversible force of nature. One of the many far-reaching effects of globalisation is the impact of competition on areas of the world's economy (or economies) that have hitherto enjoyed some protection, although some would question the notion that the powerful multi-national corporations are a force for competition and would see them as more of a barrier. Along with the economic pressures come political changes such as the challenge that the notion 'user pays' offers to library and information services in the public sector. Some library and information professionals need to learn what for many of them are new skills, such as political skills or the ability to put together successful grant applications – digitisation projects, for instance, don't come cheaply.

Accompanying the unforgiving forces of competition is a realisation that one of the factors that distinguishes the more successful organisations from the less successful ones is their information resource and how they 'leverage' it (or give value to it) – not just the technology component in IT but increasingly the *information* part. Moreover, since the mid-nineteen nineties, the library and information services sector, along with many others, including business and information technology, has taken considerable interest in knowledge management (one of the topics of Chapter 13) and how organisations can become more adaptive and innovative by becoming 'learning organisations', harnessing their corporate knowledge better in the pursuit of their strategic objectives. The interest in knowledge management and in what many call knowledge society reflects, in part, the realisation by many organisations of the value of people and their 'intellectual capital', especially in knowledge-intensive industries such as legal and financial companies, in which the knowledge leaders are worth more financially than corporate buildings and technology.

Finally, it is worth reflecting on the earlier point that many library and information services remain relevant to their parent bodies, funding authorities and/or communities at the beginning of the twenty-first century. One of the keys to this survival has been a knowledge of the informational and related needs of the organisations and/or communities they serve. In some communities in which there has been considerable investment in information and communication technologies (ICTs) one hears complaints if the service component of library and information services is put aside in the mistaken belief that the development of better ICTs is the sole priority.

While this book was being written, a revised edition of Lee Welch's *The other 51 weeks*, her invaluable work on marketing for librarians, was published. It is especially worth noting that the peculiar title – something that Lee pressed on her reluctant publisher – reflects the central idea that library marketing is not confined to Library and Information Week and, more important, is not confined to promotions. Marketing, she suggests (2006, p.8), is basically 'the process of identifying and meeting client needs' and 'a building block … in the process of managing and fostering our libraries'. In a key passage, she claims that 'librarians should have a head start in understanding the application of marketing practices because they are based simply on understanding clients and putting them first'. Marketing is indeed a building block in the development and management of our library and information services and, if there is a major theme emerging from recent research into information management, it is that this understanding of client needs is far more critical to organisational success than any amount of funding for ICT infrastructure. Can library and information professionals tap into the current development of 'social webs' – human groupings and networks that typically act as sources of information for their members – and look at ways of facilitating greater interactions with their users, such as allowing them to annotate services (Cameron 2006).

What *Libraries in the twenty-first century* sets out to do, then, is to provide a diverse and informed perspective on current developments in library and information service, the environment in which these developments take place and research on these developments, with the intention of charting current and future directions for the library and information profession. There are undoubtedly challenges for the profession but what is especially noteworthy, it is suggested here, is the way in which it has adapted to the changing environment. Organisational skills that were once devoted to library catalogues and bibliographic classification, for instance, are now being applied to website development, the building of electronic repositories and design of client-focused gateways into the anarchic virtual world of the internet.

This book does not purport to be a manual that spells out how to be a librarian. Such works as *Library practice: A manual and textbook* (Burkett, Ritchie & Standley 1977) and *The basics of librarianship* (Beenham & Harrison 1990) are *arguably* a thing of the past. Libraries and related information services have for many years gone through a far-reaching process of change and this process, according to the papers in this collection, is likely to continue for the foreseeable future. Library and information professionals have been adapting, and continue to adapt, to changing roles, to technologies that help push the boundaries of service delivery and, in many countries, to political economies (or should one say, a single global economy?) that challenge many of the services and values of the library and information profession. As the following chapters demonstrate, not least Gill Hallam's paper on educational issues, the knowledge and skills required in the contemporary library and information services sector are far too wide-ranging to be captured in a single book – a point to which the developers of educational programs for library and information services can attest.

The book's aim is to use the collective expertise and interests of its contributors to provide a scholarly but accessible overview of library and information management (LIM) at the beginning of the twenty-first century and to analyse the many issues facing the profession. If this collection provides a clear snapshot of where library and information services are, at the beginning of the twenty-first century, and gives a sense of the directions in which they are moving then it will have achieved its purpose.

Chapter outline

Unlike the many textbooks of LIM, which tend to start from general principles and work down to the specifics of how to implement them, this collection starts from the 'concrete' world of specific library and information agencies, identifying primary client bases and key functions, concerns, issues and changes, before moving out from these to a more general discussion, first, of functional and operational issues, such as the management of digital collections, and then of still more general issues, such as information ethics, management and the socio-political environment.

Part 1, 'Library and information agencies in the twenty-first century', focuses on specific types of library and information agency. Individual chapters may identify the communities or organisations served, outline the agencies' purpose or mission, examine the resources, staff, systems and services that help deliver specific types of information service, and reflect upon the main issues and concerns confronting information professionals in these particular sectors. In Chapter 1, for instance, Chris Jones draws on his experience as a public librarian in New South Wales to discuss trends and issues in the contemporary public library, including its developing role as a 'village square'. What is impressive, quite apart from the variety of public library collections and the range of services offered, is the sheer political challenge. As Jake Wallis underlines in Chapter 15, public libraries constitute a key resource for citizens in an 'information society'.

Chapter 2 provides a significantly different perspective because the focus is not so much school libraries as the dual-qualified teacher librarians who generally lead school library development in Australia (although not on the other side of the Tasman, in New Zealand, where the norm is the library and information management qualified school librarian). James Herring analyses the changing and multi-faceted role of teacher librarians and in particular their concern with information literacy, which is increasingly seen by educators as a central strand in school education and by many within and outside the sector as a key to lifelong learning.

The following chapter draws on the experience of Shirley Oakley and Jennifer Vaughan in different types of library in the higher education sector and demonstrates library services that have moved quickly to embrace the new information and communication technologies (ICTs) and the possibilities of moving services outside the traditional library walls. In some ways these libraries resemble school libraries, especially in the prominence given to the development of information literacy. What emerges strongly from this discussion, however, is the context in which library managers in the higher education sector operate and the main drivers of change – political, legal and regulatory, as well as technological. While libraries have positioned themselves for many years as information agencies, what has emerged in the last decade (and this is reflected in this chapter) is the tendency for higher education libraries to engage more directly as partners in the main business of higher education institutions – teaching and learning.

In Chapter 4, Alison O'Connor provides a radically different perspective on library and information services. Hers is described as a special library, which is a catch-all term used to describe library-type services that do not fall under the other categories of library discussed in this part of the book. Special libraries are typically, but not always, part of a larger organisation, such as a government department or a private company, which they serve, and special librarians generally take pride in their engagement with parent organisations. Some do not call themselves librarians, many seeing themselves as 'information managers'. In recent years some have even relabelled themselves 'knowledge managers', which carries different connotations for many in the profession. The account of this sector in Chapter 4 not only provides a useful discussion of an organisational culture that differs substantially from that found in many other types of library but also gives personal insight into the worlds of the law librarian and the parliamentary librarian and into the current challenges facing information services in the corporate sector.

The final chapter in Part 1, by Roxanne Missingham and Jasmine Cameron, discusses national, state and territory libraries. These, as the names suggest, cover a wider geographical area than public libraries. These are very often leading agencies in their sector and have used ICT development to move out of their capital cities to deliver resources and services directly to clients' computer desktops – a point taken up later. Many of them are also key supporters of the public library sector, as Chris Jones points out in Chapter 1, and in the case of the national libraries of Australia and New Zealand (Te Puna Mātauranga o Aotearoa) to the wider information infrastructures of their respective countries.

Part 2, 'Library and information services in the twenty-first century', takes a different approach from Part 1, examining specific aspects of library and information management, as distinct from specific sectors. In Chapter 6, John Mills examines changes in client and information services in the library environment. Whether developing face-to-face services or virtual services, he suggests, library managers need to understand the information needs of the communities they serve, whether these relate to educational curricula, support for organisational objectives, research or personal development. He also emphasises how important it is that library and information professionals study how their clients search for information or information resources, in order that managers can adapt their service delivery to ever-changing client understanding, behaviour and expectation, as distinct from expecting clients to adapt to library systems.

Chapter 7, by Alastair Smith, deals with the other side of information service provision – the enormous range of electronic, print and audio-visual resources that are the librarian's stock in trade. Knowing clients' needs is one thing, but being familiar with the databases, web-based resources, search engines, subject directories, web portals, 'ready-reference' resources, bibliographic tools, government publications and so on is one of the attributes that defines library and information professionals. Some of these resources are part of the 'invisible web', to which even Google has little or no access (at the time of writing!). What also defines a good information professional and sets him or her apart from many others in the community is their ability to *evaluate* information resources, an aspect of information work on which this chapter touches.

In Chapter 8, Paul Genoni focuses on one of the key areas of library and information management, namely, libraries as collecting agencies – a topic to which most of the preceding chapters have already referred. Traditionally, libraries consisted of collections of books, hence the name, derived from the Latin, *liber* or book. (Similarly French, in which *libraire* means bookshop, uses *bibliothèque*, from the Greek $\beta\iota\beta\lambda\iota o\upsilon$, or book, to denote a library.) A library collection today may consist almost entirely of weblinks or, in other words, a set of addresses or URLs (uniform resource locators) that identify resources on the world wide web. More typically, library collections are a 'hybrid' mixture of digital resources, provided by external agencies for a substantial subscription fee, electronic resources owned by the library itself, links to digital resources for which no charge is made and physical resources that the library owns, whether in print or audio-visual format. Just as the collections themselves are more complex than they used to be, so too the financial commitments, technological issues, licensing issues and policy decisions – issues with which this chapter deals. It also discusses some of the key functions associated with library collections, such as the selection of library information resources and collection assessment.

Chapter 9, by Philip Hider, focuses on another of the key areas of librarianship: information access, which refers to the means by which library and information professionals help clients find relevant resources by providing descriptions of resources – typically called metadata – that include given information (such as bibliographic and physical details of resources) and additional information that helps clients decide what a resource is 'about' (such as subject descriptors). Here standards are especially important. This chapter outlines the main standards used – some of them library specific and some with applications in the wider community – before discussing the importance of studying 'information architecture' and speculating on the future of information organisation, which is the name often given to this important area of information work.

Chapter 10, by Tom Denison, 'Library and information systems – a work in progress', covers the main types of ICTs supporting library and related fields of information work. This includes the information systems, networks, communications technologies and many standards (protocols) that enable the various systems to talk to each other and make possible the virtual library services discussed in earlier chapters. The chapter provides a wide-ranging overview of library technology development before focusing on integrated library management systems (ILMS), the key system in the management of library collections and increasingly their services; portals, which are an important integrative technology in information management; digital repositories; and the development of 'open source' software, which promises greater interoperability among the information systems being developed – one of the many works in progress reported here.

Part 3, 'The information environment in the twenty-first century', takes a broader approach than the two preceding sections, and places developments in library and information services in a number of different contexts. Chapter 11, by Michael Middleton, goes beyond the library environment to consider the wider field of information management and the changing role of the information manager. This chapter outlines the scope and history of information management – tracing its origins to attempts by the US Government in the 1970s to reduce paperwork – before focusing on the key tasks of an information manager. While some of these involve skills and understanding that are not always the stock-in-trade of all library and information professionals, this chapter demonstrates many commonalities between broader information management functions and those that characterise library and information management – for instance, the use of metadata standards, information resource evaluation and needs analysis.

In Chapter 12, Karen Anderson also moves beyond the library environment, in this case to examine developments in two related areas of information management – records and archives. Like libraries these are collecting agencies but they do not, by and large, handle the published information resources that make up most library collections. There are interesting commonalities with libraries, including the enthusiastic take-up of new ICTs, but there are issues that are quite specific to this sector, such as the development of highly evolved disposal schedules, in the case of records managers, or the need to address complex ethically-driven retention policies, in the case of archivists. As in the library environment, it has been felt necessary to develop standards to assist organisation of and access to the unique resources for which records managers and archivists are responsible, and these are outlined here.

The following chapter considers areas of information work that might best be categorised as information and knowledge management. Stuart Ferguson and Anne Lloyd discuss information literacy (IL), focusing on the higher education sector and on moves to integrate IL instruction into the more general curriculum. They go on to suggest, however, that it is necessary to look beyond IL instruction as a process by which library and information professionals teach clients how to find information using library systems, and to study IL in the context of workplace learning – an area in which Lloyd has done considerable research. The chapter argues for a broader definition of IL, based on issues of workplace learning, before discussing knowledge management (KM), a management paradigm built on theories of the 'Learning Organisation' and to a lesser extent on the information management principles outlined by Michael Middleton in Chapter 11. This chapter draws out some of the commonalities between workplace IL and KM, while recognising that which differentiates the two areas of study.

In Chapter 14, Ross Harvey looks at developments in library services from a historical perspective. This raises the question: why conduct research into our past, with all the pitfalls that involves, when the future of library and information services is so clearly going to involve a radical departure from previous practice? One reason is that by exploring the relationship between library history and wider socio-economic developments one may develop a more sound critical understanding of the current processes of change – if we understand where we have come from, we will have a clearer idea of where we are. The chapter discusses general issues such as these, before outlining the library history that has been published, providing a broad overview of library history and focusing on the evolution of public libraries in Australia, by way of example.

In Chapter 15, Jake Wallis picks up on some of the themes discussed by Harvey and provides a broad overview of the social and political environment that currently shapes the development of library and information services. Some in the profession are cheered by sociological studies that chart the development of a 'post-industrial society' into an information or knowledge society, and see the future for information professionals as a bright one, while others, Wallis included, focus on the need for the profession to be vigilant in the face of the growing gap between 'information rich' and 'information poor' – often referred to specifically in terms of a 'digital divide'. While recognising that libraries, like any other postmodern institution, need to adapt and change, Wallis suggests that they have a continuing role in support of what Habermas in 1962 called the public sphere – a point emphasised in the statements of the Australian Library and Information Association on information literacy, which it links to a set of social, economic and democratic goals.

Chapter 16, by Jan Houghton and Jennifer Berryman, focuses on two imposing sets of issues confronting information professionals in an 'information society', namely, ethical and legal issues. While some values may remain relatively constant, the preceding chapters (especially Wallis's overview) have demonstrated to some extent the global challenge to traditional values, especially in areas such as intellectual property, censorship, security and privacy – not to mention such basic values as freedom and equality. The library and information profession, like any other profession, is informed by a foundation of ethical practice – in its case, one that gives strong expression to freedom of information, equity of service and privacy rights. This chapter provides a general overview of professional ethics, a brief history of information ethics and a study of professional values and codes of practice. Also in this substantial and wide-ranging review – almost a chapter in its own right – is an account of information law, including intellectual property, censorship, privacy, national security and freedom of information, and an analysis of the sometimes complementary, sometimes conflicting demands of information ethics and legal obligation.

In Chapter 17, Damian Lodge and Bob Pymm deal with one of the most important resources in library and information work – people. If libraries are to implement the changes outlined above, they require a well-informed, innovative and skilled workforce. This chapter covers many of the management issues that have a major bearing on the development of information agencies, such as approaches to staffing information agencies, including staff training and induction, financial management, the evaluation of library and information services, change management and, more specifically, some of the management issues associated with the changing nature of library collections. The issue of marketing is prominent, as library and information agencies attempt to adapt to the greater availability of information resources, not least via the internet, and the growing number of information providers (including Google). While there are clearly challenges – outlined especially clearly in the two preceding chapters – this chapter provides a positive account of how library managers are responding to these challenges.

Chapter 18, by Gill Hallam, focuses on one particular area of human resources, namely, the education of library and information professionals. This includes not just the constantly evolving formal educational programs in the university and TAFE (Technical and Further Education) sectors, but also the role of professional associations and the growing importance of professional development in a changing profession that frequently requires new knowledge and skill sets. This is another area that is critical to the future of the profession. Some practitioners and educators worry that there are librarians who desperately want to hang on to their role as guardians of knowledge/resources and see delivery of resources directly to users as a threat. One of the themes to emerge from this collection is that librarians may need retraining in ways of thinking – a challenge for those involved in education and professional development. Issues covered in this chapter include the perennial ones such as the frequently alleged gap between the worlds of practitioners and educators, the relative lack of financial incentive to study higher degrees, the many demands placed on the curriculum and the relationship between library research and practice, plus some issues that are relatively new, including the ageing of library educators.

Some conclusions are provided by Alex Byrne, who has contributed to the profession here in Australia but also overseas, through his involvement in the International Federation of Library Associations (IFLA). He draws an interesting parallel between the nineteenth-century notion (at least in the English-speaking world) of the public library as the 'people's university' and the current drive to create an 'information society for all', providing in the process a global, societal context for the endeavours of the library and information professions mapped out in this collection.

For the benefit of relative novices to this field, there is also a glossary of terms. Readers could always be left to 'google' terms but it was believed that a glossary would be a useful 'ready-reference' resource, as would the appendices, which provide the reader with supplementary material, such as the factual data on national, state and territory libraries.

References

Barbuceanu, M, Fox, MS, Hong, L, Lallement, Y & Zhang, Z 2004, 'Building agents to serve customers', *AI Magazine*, vol.25, no.3, pp.47-60.

Beenham, R & Harrison, C 1990, *The basics of librarianship*, 3rd edn, Bingley, London.

Burkett, J, Ritchie, S & Standley, A 1977, *Library practice: A manual and textbook*, ELM Publications, Buckden, 1977.

Cameron, J 2006, Personal communication, 19 April 2006.

'Google checks out library books', Google press release, 14 December 2004, http://www.google.com/press/pressrel/print_library.html

Stannus, MJ 2006, Presentation to *Libraries and collaboration: Library of the 21st century symposium*, State Library of Victoria, 23 February 2006, http://www.slv.vic.gov.au/programs/events/2006/collaboration/stannus.html

The time machine 2002, motion picture, screenplay by John Logan, based on a screenplay by David Duncan, director Simon Wells, Warner Brothers and Dreamworks LLC.

University of Queensland 2007, *Help accessing databases and ejournals*, http://www.library.uq.edu.au/database/help.html

Welch, L 2006, *The other 51 weeks: A marketing handbook for librarians*, rev. edn, Centre for Information Studies, Wagga Wagga, NSW.

PART 1:

Library and information agencies in the twenty-first century: case studies

CHAPTER 1
The evolving public library

Chris Jones

The public library is there for everyone and the services it provides are in general free of charge. In Australia, this freedom of access is encapsulated in various state legislations and is embedded in the philosophies of national industry bodies like Public Libraries Australia (PLA) and the Australian Library and Information Association (ALIA). Such a broad scope with such a low price tag would suggest that everyone might be beating down the doors of public libraries. To some degree this is the case. People of all ages, all levels of ability, all ethnicity, all educational needs and with differing demands are walking through the doors of a public library somewhere.

There are, however, certain sectors of the community that traditionally are more regular library users than others. A group of particular importance considering its growing representation in the community is senior citizens. It is no coincidence that many of the busiest public libraries in Australia lie in communities that are popular retirement destinations. Coastal library services are a classic example of this. At the other end of the age spectrum, children and youth often appear as heavy users of public libraries. This use may take the form of leisure material (particularly in the non-print areas) or information related to studies. Of course, underlying usage of any public library are the demographics of its community. Public libraries with high ethnic representation certainly have extensive and often expensive demands placed on them to purchase non-English material. Other inner-city libraries experience high demand placed on them by a transient working population.

One common area in public library service lies in the online world. Every public library now has an online community. This means that virtually all public libraries have a web presence and increasingly are placing services such as reservations, catalogues and even reference services online. There is also an assumption that public libraries will provide computer access to the online environment.

Before exploring different aspects of the evolving public library, it would be worth considering the sheer scale of public library service and operations. The following figures represent the state of Australian public libraries as at June 2004 (Australian Bureau of Statistics 2005):

- There are 532 local government library organisations (up from 505 in 1999/2000).

- These operate out of 1,716 locations (up from 1,510 in 1999/2000).

- They employ 10,606 staff (1,000 more than in 1999/2000).

- They utilise 6,315 volunteers, equating to 55,746 hours worth of labour. The amount of voluntary labour used had risen dramatically from 30,647 hours of work done in 1999/2000.

- They cost $545.2 million to operate ($521.9 million of the funding to do so comes from government sources). This is up almost $90 million on 1999/2000 figures.

- There were 99.6 million visits to public libraries in 2003/04 (up more than 6 million from 1999/2000).

- They hold 42 million items (up 2 million from 1999/2000).

- They lent out 176 million items in 2003/04.

The public library mission

Defining the mission and role of public libraries in society is a challenge in itself. It is tempting to think of the public library as an information gateway for all, but those 'information-only' days are long gone. Certainly provision of information (along with the skilled staff to retrieve it) is a key service of public libraries, but this is not all they do. The modern public library also caters for the leisure needs of society – but this would hardly come as surprise (although the range of formats in which this occurs may do). What really has changed in the past decade has been the huge emphasis now put on public libraries being safe, comfortable and socially inclusive places to visit.

The vision statement of the Country Public Libraries Association of New South Wales underlines this shift (Country Public Libraries Association 2005, p.2): '*Every local public library will be a focal point and a public space for the community, and a gateway for residents of NSW to the information resources of the world*' (italics added). This developing role of the library as a 'village square' has resulted in public libraries broadening their missions. This can be clearly seen in the library strategy for the Great Lakes Library Service (Jones 2006, p.16): 'The library will endeavour to meet the community's need for information, education, culture, leisure and social interaction through the provision of an efficient and adequately resourced network of library services.' One of the most apt comments on the challenge of dealing with the scope of demand placed on public libraries comes from Alan Bundy (2003, p.6): 'no other agency in society has the breadth of role, the user range and diversity and the potential impact. In an age of specialization and community silos, public libraries are unique.'

It seems then that the modern public library must be all things for all people. This has its downside, but it certainly offers plenty of opportunities for variety. Those interested in the social role of public libraries are strongly recommend to read *A safe place to go: Libraries and social capital* (Cox 2000). This is based on a statewide survey and has some revealing and powerful information. It is also a strong theme in Chapter 15 of this book, which charts the social, political and cultural context of libraries in the twenty-first century.

Services offered and staff required

The demand for traditional services is strong in public libraries. Total loans for public libraries in NSW has risen steadily and reached more than forty-five million in 2002/03 (State Library of NSW 2004, p.x). Consequently, the issuing of items remains a central service of the library. Developments in self-check technology have meant that for some libraries the labour intensity has been reduced, but the simple issuing and returning of items is still core business. Public libraries also field reference enquiries on a daily basis and many libraries have dedicated reference staff. Some libraries even provide homework help for school students, which generally involves payment of an external tutor or tutors.

The area of starkest growth for public libraries has been in the online environment. It would be a rare public library that did not have some form of web presence or offer access (usually free) to the internet. It is common for libraries to place their catalogues online and to provide online access to reservations, loan renewals and so on. Online reference services are also becoming regular features of public libraries, though not necessarily based on immediate response. An interesting area of growth is in the provision of access to subscription databases via public libraries. In NSW, the state government supports a scheme known as NSW.net, which provides public libraries and their clients with access to a range of subscription databases free of charge. Victoria has a similar scheme, known as Gulliver. Tied in with the growth in demand for internet access has been a distinct community interest in training on using the internet. This presents its own challenges in providing the human resources needed to supply the training.

The online environment has had a substantial impact on inter-library loans (ILL) services. Gone are the days of sending out ILL request forms into the wider library community and hoping for the best. All public libraries now have access to quite sophisticated online networks and databases that enable the rapid identification of holdings for items. The client can expect to receive items within a comparatively short period of time. As a result of this, the ILL success rate in NSW has been rising steadily for a number of years, though interestingly total ILLs have dropped. This may reflect more of a 'do-it-yourself' approach among clients, particularly in tracking down information on the internet.

Public libraries also have staff dedicated to serving targeted sectors of the community. Many libraries have children's librarians; some even have the luxury of youth librarians. Older clients have quite specific needs and a library may have a home services librarian to meet these demands. Provision of access to local history and genealogical material is important to many libraries and a number employ staff specifically in this area.

In keeping with the developing role of public libraries as centres of social interaction there has been a distinct growth in public libraries holding community events. These can take the form of author talks, Higher School Certificate (HSC) workshops, creative arts exhibitions and workshops, book launches and even musical concerts. Associated with this is the provision of display space and notice boards for community use. The demand for such services has seen the emergence of positions such as marketing and events librarians.

Another area of growth in the modern public library is the shift towards entrepreneurial activities. It is not uncommon to find a library that provides food and drink vending machines. Coffee machines are all the vogue, or at least talking about them is. Some libraries act as outlets for booksellers and many sell varying forms of merchandise. Others rent out meeting space. Libraries are constantly seeking ways of meeting demand. If it generates revenue all the better.

The services many public libraries offer include (but are not limited to): lending of books and other material; enquiry assistance, including homework help and HSC workshops; online access to the library's collection and services; internet services (and possibly training in this area); access to online information; inter-library loans; children's and youth events/activities/services; home library services; mobile library services; genealogy/local history services; general events; displays and notice board space; sale point for various material and foodstuffs; and venue hire.

As can be seen from the services listed, the modern public library is a mixture of traditional and emerging roles. Consequently there is a wide range of roles and positions. These will vary from library to library, though many are virtually universal:

- *Circulation/loans services* – Even with the emergence of self-check technology this remains a mainstay for staffing. Often these positions will not require staff who hold qualifications. The need for these services to be coordinated in larger libraries means there will also be qualified positions associated with this area.

- *Reference/information services* – Another mainstay. Many libraries have staff dedicated to assisting clients in finding information. Changes in this area include delving into the online world and the development of reader services (involving advice to leisure readers on potentially interesting topics). Inter-library loans often fall under the brief of reference services.

- *Cataloguing/technical services* – This area varies in breadth from library to library and has undergone significant changes in some libraries. In its narrowest sense this means the cataloguing of material for lending, but for many libraries it also includes stock selection and weeding of stock. There is a trend towards this becoming a more holistic collection management area. A number of libraries have opted for much of this work to be done offsite, though there still remains a need for overall collection management.

- *Information technology* – The growth in the presence of computers connected to the internet in libraries has resulted in a greater staffing commitment to this area. Staff in these positions may have responsibility for technology, telecommunications, the website and often developments in library software. There may also be a public internet training component.

- *Children's/youth services* – The high use that children and youth make of libraries means there are often dedicated staff in these areas. Some libraries are lucky enough to have separate children's and youth positions. They may be diploma or degree qualified positions depending on the job description.

- *Home library/housebound services* – Some libraries may have staff that provide a selection and delivery service to homebound individuals and nursing home/retirement villages. This has particular relevance to the ageing of the Australian population. These positions are usually degree-qualified.

- *Local history/genealogy* – Most libraries have some form of local history collection and often a genealogy collection/service of some description. Larger libraries may have a professional staff member allocated to manage these aspects of the service. Again, this is likely to be a degree-qualified position.

- *Mobile library services* – Libraries that have clients in rural and remote locations may provide services via a mobile library.

- *Multicultural services* – A number of urban library services have a high proportion of residents from diverse cultural backgrounds and they may provide a service targeted at this demographic.

- *Marketing/promotions/events* – A position that is occurring more frequently in public libraries is in events/promotions/marketing as libraries seek to raise their profile in the community. These positions may be degree or diploma-qualified.

- *Indigenous services* – In areas of significant indigenous representation public libraries may have positions targeted to services to this community sector. It is quite possible that these positions are filled by staff of indigenous background.

- *Management* – Many of the above positions have management components but overseeing all of these will be a senior manager or managers. Smaller libraries are likely to have one manager who wears several hats. Larger organisations may well have a more extensive senior management structure. A number of library managers also have community services or art galleries under their portfolio.

Public library collections

The stock item of public libraries remains the book or its non-print equivalent. In the last decade this traditional format for information provision has been supplemented with access to online and electronic data. Typically many libraries provide access to various CD-ROM databases. These CDs may range in content from junior encyclopaedias to births, deaths and marriages data for genealogists. CD-ROM collections have been steadily growing in size in NSW, though the future of this format is likely to be a bit shaky as data increasingly becomes available through online sources. Public libraries have taken to online information access, though possibly more slowly then academic libraries. The limiting factor for public libraries has been the sheer cost of subscribing to many databases. Consortia purchasing arrangements such as those available through Gulliver and NSW.net have greatly increased the ability of smaller libraries to enter this realm.

Library collections are as diverse as the clientele they serve. Typically public libraries will hold: fiction books; non-fiction books; magazines; talking books (both tape and CD, with the tape collections rapidly disappearing – MP3 format is also emerging); music CDs; DVDs and videos (with video collections dwindling as DVD collections grow); large print items; reference material; local history (including maps, photographs and so on); genealogical material (in print, microfiche, microfilm, CD-ROM and online); and literacy material. Libraries may also hold: foreign language collections; disability-related collections (for instance, Braille). Other new collection formats emerging are electronic games and graphic novels. Electronic games are incredibly popular but they come with a word of caution. There is currently a licensing debate occurring that may make this provision somewhat more challenging (that is, expensive). In addition to physical collections, public libraries also provide access to what amounts to virtual collections. This virtual access could include: homepage links to other sites; online databases; photographic collections; and cataloguing online sites as part of the library catalogue.

The layout of physical collections has undergone some revision in recent years. As far as can be established, Australian public libraries universally use the Dewey Decimal Classification system (see Chapter 9 for an account of bibliographic classification) but this does have its drawbacks. For example, books on horses could be found in the zoological area (599.6655), under horse care (636.1) or in equestrian sports (798.2-798.6). Because Dewey can scatter related materials over a wide range of locations (as can the local supermarket), a number of public libraries have begun to place non-fiction material in broad subject categories and shelve them accordingly. Dewey is retained and it is the shelf locations that vary. This will be an interesting trend to follow.

A hybrid of the above is the creation of targeted separate collections. Because of their popularity, many public libraries have separate biography sections. While purists would suggest biographical material belongs under its related subject, many clients would appear to prefer having biographies shelved together. Other separate collections may include such topics as indigenous works.

In addition to grouping non-fiction, many public libraries also shelve fiction in genre collections such as romance, westerns and so on. Although this does present certain challenges, it is a relatively easy practice to implement. Anecdotal evidence suggests that it is quite popular but that there are clients who strongly dislike it. When it comes to non-fiction, some libraries have to separate larger (quarto) material from normal (octavo) books because of space considerations, though this is becoming less common. Another issue with non-fiction relates to interfiling junior and adult materials. This has advantages and disadvantages and generally libraries still keep these separated.

Library facilities

It is interesting to note the number of new library facilities being erected. At any given time there are around fifty new public libraries at a significant planning or construction phase in NSW alone. There are growing signs that local government is aware of the increasing role that public libraries play in their community and this has lead to the availability of funds to construct new buildings. This has enabled libraries to integrate client-friendly designs into these libraries. Alongside buildings, there are developments occurring with mobile libraries. Mobile libraries are going through a transition from a book drop facility to a library on wheels. With modern technology and telecommunications, these greatly enhanced mobile libraries play an important role in the lives of people in rural remote areas. For those local councils without access to the funding required to maintain and upgrade facilities, and this applies to many rural local government areas, there are opportunities to co-locate with other services. Often now public libraries are co-located with other council services, tourism, community technology centres (CTCs) and even schools. This makes good economic sense, though it requires a cooperative and clearly understood relationship between all parties involved.

Cataloguing and processing of material

This is an area of significant change for public libraries. A decade ago most public libraries managed their collection 'from cradle to grave' – selecting material, processing and cataloguing it on site and then culling it after its useful life had passed. This is still quite common, but external providers and access to online catalogue records have changed the landscape. For a price, material can be purchased shelf-ready with full catalogue records available to download directly into the library database. Indeed many suppliers now provide electronic records free of charge. This gives public libraries the scope to free up staff for other duties. In going down this path, libraries need to be aware that there is a cost to shelf-ready items and detailed specifications are required to ensure material is processed to a suitable standard. Some public libraries have taken a step further. These libraries have gone through the extensive process of developing a profile of their collection. Following a tendering process or its equivalent, a library supplier (or suppliers) is then chosen to purchase relevant material based on this profile (this is also discussed in Chapter 8). This frees up even more staff time, although there is still a need for the library to have staff managing the collection and reviewing selections.

The online world has provided excellent tools for the cataloguer. The Dewey Decimal Classification (see Chapter 9) is now available online and is updated monthly. Cataloguers have ready access to online records at such locations as the national database, Libraries Australia (discussed in Chapter 5). With the vast majority of library operational software now supporting the Z39.50 protocol, a data communications protocol for open system interconnection, there is also scope for effective transfer of MARC (machine-readable cataloguing) records (see Chapter 9) between library systems and even book suppliers. An interesting challenge that the online world presents for the cataloguer is the possibility of cataloguing online resources as part of the online catalogue. Although not necessarily widespread, this may become more common. The alternative is to provide access to this information via website links.

Funding of public libraries and their relationship to state and local government

The federal government in Australia provides no direct funding of public libraries. Occasionally project-based, non-recurrent funding becomes available (for instance, Networking the Nation), which public libraries may be able to access. Otherwise all direct government funding comes from the state and local levels. Funding of public libraries varies from state to state and is largely demographically driven. The denser the available rate-base the higher the role local government plays in funding public libraries. Arrangements for providing library services also differ according to the community needs of the state or territory (Table 1.1).

Trends and issues for public libraries

The modern public library environment is a volatile one. The image of a staid, relaxing place to work bears little relationship to reality. This environment presents its own challenges and opportunities, many of which are alluded to above. The matter of funding is one of the most pressing issues of all. Rising staff costs, increased client expectations and an expanding range of formats have all placed pressure on library budgets. With times generally difficult for local government – the major funding provider for many library services – public libraries have sought greater funding from other sources.

Table 1.1 Summary of state and territory arrangements for Australian public library services

State/territory	Funding and management
ACT	Centralised administration and funding.
New South Wales	Mixture of independent library services operated by a single local government authority and regional library services: local councils provide autonomous library services and the State Library funds public library services via an annual subsidy and a grants program.
Northern Territory	Public libraries are provided by local government but supported on a range of fronts by the Northern Territory Library.
Queensland	Library services to smaller local government areas (population less than 20,000) can be centrally provided by the State Library, with local government contributing building and staff – an arrangement known as the Country Lending Scheme (CLS). Larger libraries provide independent services, predominantly funded by local government. These independent libraries receive a per capita subsidy from the State Library. The State Library also provides grant funding.
South Australia	Cooperative arrangement between state and local government. The State (through the Libraries Board) provides a range of grants as well as the centralised Public Libraries Automated Information Network (PLAIN). For smaller communities there is a relationship for service provision through the Department of Education and Children's Services.
Tasmania	Public libraries are funded and managed on a state government level.
Victoria	Similar model to the one in New South Wales.
Western Australia	Centralised arrangement based upon a formal agreement between local and state government bodies.

Limited access to federal funding has led to the emergence of Public Libraries Australia (PLA). Although public libraries have been represented in the past by ALIA, the breadth of responsibility for ALIA (they represent all libraries) makes the lobbying required for public libraries at a federal level difficult. PLA is now pressing for funded partnerships that integrate with government policy and advance the capacity and provision of public library services, among other things, but it will be no easy road to travel. One of the major issues is that the federal government does not seem to see the relevance or potential of public libraries.

Awareness raising is another key function of PLA, though all public libraries should be striving to increase their community profile. A recent achievement of PLA has been its inclusion in the annual Read Aloud summit held by the federal government.

In addition to federal funding, there remains a need for public libraries to be taken more seriously by state governments. There have been some positive moves made, but in NSW the level of state funding remains at only around 10 per cent of overall operating costs. Public libraries should be seeking opportunities to enter into partnerships with government to provide enhanced access to information via the public library network instead of governments developing parallel information infrastructures.

The need for stronger representation of public libraries has begun to bring lobby groups such as 'friends of the library' organisations to the fore. Public libraries should give serious consideration to the development of their own 'friends' groups. These can be a powerful voice in the community, provided the right people with the right focus are involved.

Changes in community expectations are having an impact on the way libraries provide services. There is a move towards a more client-focused service. A visit to the public library should be an experience not just a transaction. This has seen a number of changes in public library service provision. Some libraries have moved away from a fixed reference desk to floor-walking staff and some libraries now even have drive-through services. Online provision of services will continue to develop, including a '24/7' approach to enquiries via multi-library networks. This client focus has seen some public libraries moving from a traditional technical services structure to a client service-based model. This is occurring, in part, as a result of cataloguing shifting to collection management with the potential for much of the processing work to be done offsite – for a price.

Technology is playing its part at the 'coal-face' of client service and many libraries have self-check systems to reduce client waiting times. At the circulation desk the development of sophisticated book processing technology and the emergence of radio frequency identification (RFID) systems has the potential to save staff time. This comes with a warning. It is important not to lose sight of the clients. Client/staff interaction is one of the great strengths of public libraries. Dealing with machines may not provide the experience that clients are seeking.

Public libraries increasingly are being designed, or redesigned, to create more comfort space for clients. Drink and food machines and coffee bars are now common in libraries and co-located coffee shops are being planned for new facilities. Those who see this as a divergence from the traditional role of libraries should look at trends in bookshop design. Co-location of food and drink outlets with bookshops is becoming more common as they strive for the client experience rather than a simple sale. These are real competitors for libraries and library professionals need to learn from the bookshop experience. One of the great challenges to this is the question of floor space. Many libraries are trying to create wider aisles and more relaxation space, and to lower (or raise) bookshelves. These competing demands place substantial pressure on existing floor space and on the budget projections for new facilities.

Another client service issue that is appearing in libraries is the layout of collections. One can expect to see more libraries experimenting with genre collections for fiction and a creative approach to the layout of non-fiction material. This has led to some libraries creating living-room style designs, with each room having a different theme and appearance.

In this push towards improved client service an interesting trend is emerging. Libraries traditionally have always seen themselves as storehouses of information. This is how they brand themselves and non-fiction information provision features very heavily in all tertiary library courses. For too long the provision of leisure material has come second to this, and yet lending of such material is a major part of public library service provision. In 2002–2003, fiction stock in public libraries had a turnover rate of 4.87 loans per annum. During the same period non-fiction material had a turnover rate of 1.71. Fiction is being lent out at nearly three times the rate of non-fiction, and there is evidence this gap is widening. Non-fiction lending may be what library and information services (LIS) professionals aspire to – especially given the demands of an 'information society' (see Chapter 15) – but it is fiction lending that pays the rent.

This is not to say that non-fiction loans are unimportant, but rather to say that more emphasis must be placed on fiction services. Libraries have long offered excellent reference services for non-fiction information enquiries – the time has now arrived for a similar amount of effort and thought to be put into supporting fiction/leisure reading enquiries. It is pleasing to note that many public libraries have realised this and are now developing their readers' advisory programs. This can only contribute to improved client services.

As client services develop, so does a move towards greater marketing of library services. This has resulted in libraries having far more sophisticated display arrangements designed in order to increase turnover and improve appearance. The move towards more attractive libraries is long overdue and being widely taken up. The marketing push has also seen libraries hold a much greater range of events to attract clients. A number of libraries, for instance, host regular musical concerts of differing styles.

Age is also having a significant impact on libraries and will continue to do so. The most obvious area of influence is on the changing nature of the community. People are getting older and this affects the library. There is good correlation between the age of the community and use of the library. This means that as the community ages library stock will wear out more rapidly through higher usage, placing greater burden on already tight budgets. Public libraries will also have to invest in more expensive formats such as large print material and talking books – another obvious cost impact. There may also be a need to dedicate staff to this area.

As well as placing a strain on resources, an ageing community presents another issue. Older people are often willing to assist libraries in a voluntary capacity. Many retirement destinations have libraries with a strong volunteer base. This presents opportunities to fill gaps in service, but it too comes at a price. Management of volunteers becomes an additional library task and different and lower expectations can be placed on volunteers. There is also the danger that paid positions may be lost to volunteers. One final risk in using volunteers lies in what appears to be a general decline in the number of people offering to volunteer for community groups and organisations right across Australia. A simple search via Google or other search engines will show a general concern in this area. Public libraries that rely on volunteers are likely to face future challenges.

The ageing of the community has one further impact on public libraries, although libraries are not alone on this front – library staff are getting older and at a rapid rate. Phil Teece (2005, p.6) provides the following data: 'Librarians are markedly older than the average for Australian occupations. Sixty per cent are 45 or older, compared to 35 per cent in the total workforce, 86 per cent are 35 or more [55 per cent in the total workforce]. Only 14 per cent are under 35 [42 per cent]. The median age is 46.' Although not directly related to service provision, this trend in the ageing of the library labour force is likely to have an impact. This may take the form of difficulties in attracting professional staff, particularly to remote areas. The other challenge it presents is that libraries increasingly will have older staff in senior positions. Whether this will present problems in a library environment where change is becoming commonplace remains to be seen.

Conclusion

Public libraries are places of regular and challenging change. The range of collections and the services public libraries provide seem only to be growing. This is occurring in a climate where funds and human resources are becoming harder to come by. The role of public libraries has also changed and they now play an important part in the well being of communities. Even the traditional services are constantly under review as librarians seek to make the best use of technology, telecommunications and library networks.

The modern public library and the staff involved in its management cannot remain insular. There needs to be interest and involvement in local, state and federal government and in its impact on public libraries. Public library staff will have to be opportunistic and creative in sourcing funds. They will need to monitor developments in other library services, interact professionally at every opportunity and be innovative in the provision of services.

References

Australian Bureau of Statistics (ABS) 2005, *Public libraries: 2003-04*, Cat. No. 8561.0., http://www.abs.gov.au/Ausstats/abs@.nsf/0/08CDEAE368A2A931CA256A780001D4DB?Open

Australian public libraries statistical report 2002–2003 2005, compiled by Public Library Services, State Library of Queensland, http://www.casl.org.au/papers/Aust%20Pub%20Lib%20Stats%20Report%202002-03.doc

Bundy, A 2003, 'Vision, mission, trumpets: Public libraries as social capita', NSW Country Public Libraries Association Conference 2003: *Public libraries light up lives*, held at Tweed Heads, NSW, 3 July 2003, http://www.lga.sa.gov.au/webdata/resources/Files/Conference_Paper_on_libraries_in_Australia___Dr_Alan_Bundy_2003_pdf1.pdf

Country Public Libraries Association 2005, *Draft strategic plan: 2005–07*, http://www.cpla.asn.au/misc/docs/strategic_plan05/draft_strategic_planII.doc

Cox, E 2000, *A safe place to go: Libraries and social capital*, University of Technology, Sydney, NSW.

Jones, C 2006, *Library strategy 2006*, Great Lakes Council, Forster, NSW, http://www.greatlakes.nsw.gov.au/Library/documents/LibraryStrategyJul01.pdf

State Library of New South Wales 2004, *Public library statistics 2002/03*, State Library of New South Wales, Sydney, NSW.

Teece, P 2005, 'Australia's library labour market', *Incite*, vol.19, p.6, http://www.alia.org.au/publishing/incite/2005/10/labour.market.html

CHAPTER 2
Teacher librarians and the school library

James Herring

In the economically developed countries of the world libraries are an integral part of most schools, but it is only in countries such as Australia and the USA that most schools, at primary and secondary level, have professional staff who are both teachers and librarians. 'School library' is the most common term used to refer to a school's library, but the school library is also referred to as 'library media center' (North America) and 'library resource centre' (UK). Professional staff in school libraries are referred to as teacher librarians in Australia and Canada, school library media specialists in the USA and school librarians in the UK and many other countries. This chapter will examine the learning and teaching context of the school library; the mission of the school library; standards for school libraries; the role of the teacher librarian; information literacy in schools; collection development in school libraries; information services for students and teachers; and the development of effective school library websites and school intranets.

The learning and teaching context of school libraries

School libraries do not exist in a vacuum and should not be seen as in any way separate from the school environment. In a school, the library and the teacher librarian are an integral part of the learning and teaching community that makes up the school. Thus school libraries do not, like many other libraries, merely support the community in which they exist, nor do they merely serve that community, but they are a vital *part* of the school. The school library should be seen as a centre of learning first and a centre of resources second. Teacher librarians in Australia and other countries need to be aware of the learning and teaching context in which they work because it is the learning and teaching that happens in the school which is at the heart of the school.

Herring (2004) reviews a number of learning theories that have influenced the development of learning in schools and notes that schools are now moving away from behaviourist theories, which tended to view school students as children who would learn best through passively listening to a teacher and repeating tasks to ensure reinforcement of learning, to more cognitive and constructivist theories. The most commonly known and used cognitive theory is Bloom's Taxonomy of Learning which identifies a range of skills of increasing complexity that students can apply to different tasks. The highest level of Bloom's taxonomy is *evaluation* in which students are able to make judgements on concepts or ideas (Thomas 1999). Constructivist theories of learning, which view knowledge not as some external block of ideas, concepts and information to be acquired, but as something constructed by individual learners, have become more accepted in schools. Carnell and Lodge (2002) argue that constructivism enables students to reflect more on their own learning and may make students more engaged in learning. How students learn in the school library will be influenced by how they are encouraged to learn in the school as a whole, and teacher librarians can influence student learning by working with teachers to develop learning opportunities that are challenging for students.

Teaching is also an activity that takes place in the school library, in the form of a classroom teacher bringing a group of students to the library, extending what has been taught in the classroom and allowing students to use library resources. Teaching students to develop information skills is done by teacher librarians in the library and this is integrated with classroom teaching. Effective teaching should include the creation of a supportive environment, challenges for students to produce quality work, the development of students as active learners and good feedback to students (Schunk 2000). The integration of information and communication technologies (ICTs) into teaching has encouraged the development of more active learning among students who increasingly use online resources for their coursework. Teachers also use different ICTs to enhance their presentations and recent developments such as interactive whiteboards (Becta 2006) have enabled teachers to encourage collaborative learning among students. School libraries exist within the school's learning and teaching context and teacher librarians aid the development of effective learning and teaching in the school. Using a school library well and learning from a teacher librarian can be a vital part of students' education.

The school library mission

The Australian School Library Association (ASLA) (2004a, paragraph 1) states that 'School library and information programs and services are integral to the goals of the school and the aims of the school curriculum' and thus the mission of any school library will be closely allied to that of the school. The mission of the school library should therefore be primarily focused on the development of effective learning and teaching in the school and statements about the provision of learning resources should follow this. The United Nations Educational, Scientific and Cultural Organization (UNESCO) School Library Manifesto states that 'The school library equips students with lifelong learning skills and develops the imagination, enabling them to live as responsible citizens' but it can be criticised for putting services before this in a preceding sentence (International Federation of Library Associations (IFLA) 2006, paragraph 1). Some school libraries emphasise the creation of a suitable learning environment – the mission of Beechmont State School (2006, paragraph 1) is 'to promote a supportive, effective and enjoyable information environment which will enhance lifelong learning and teaching opportunities for all members of the school community'.

Many school libraries include reading for enjoyment as well as for information in their mission statements. Beaconhills College (2006, paragraph 1) states that its mission is 'to ensure that students and staff members read for pleasure and develop the necessary skills to use information, ideas and technology ethically, creatively and critically to make intelligent judgements throughout their daily life'. Given that reading for pleasure is a small (but important) part of the school curriculum, it can be argued that this aspect is given unnecessary prominence in some school library mission statements.

One of the key elements of most school library mission statements relates to the development of information literate students, and the mission of the Springfield Township High School Library (2006, paragraph 1) is 'to ensure that students graduate as competent, critical and ethical users of information. It is our mission to prepare lifelong learners: information literate citizens able to determine their information needs, recognize relevant information, solve problems and effectively communicate the results of their research.' (This aspect of teacher librarianship is discussed below.)

Mission statements for school libraries should be brief statements that encapsulate the ethos of both the school and the library.

Standards for school libraries

Standards for school libraries are developed as a guide to what might be seen as ideal levels of staffing, funding, collection size and quality, organisation of materials, services and space, for schools in the country for which the standards were developed. Given the differences in the average education levels between economically developed and less developed countries, school library standards need to be viewed in the context of the country being considered. Although the standards developed by IFLA and UNESCO (2006) attempt to provide an international benchmark for school libraries, they may be seen as more useful to countries which are developing economically.

In Australia, the current standards are related to 'the professional knowledge, skills and commitment demonstrated by teacher librarians working at a level of excellence. It [statement on standards] represents the goals to which all Australian teacher librarians should aspire, and provides inspiration for quality teaching and ongoing professional practice' (ASLA 2004b, p.1). The standards include a definition of the teacher librarian and cover aspects of what an 'excellent' teacher librarian should have knowledge of, covering areas of 'the principles of lifelong learning', 'learning and teaching across curriculum areas', the school curriculum and 'library and information management' including the use of ICTs (ASLA 2004b, p.2). In terms of teacher librarians being excellent practitioners, the standards state that teacher librarians will 'engage and challenge learners', work collaboratively with teachers in developing information literacy, 'provide exemplary library and information services' and evaluate their own role and the services they provide. The standards state that excellent teacher librarians are committed professionals who are leaders in their school in developing learning and are active within the teacher librarian profession (ASLA 2004b, pp.3-4).

The best known standards for school libraries outside Australia are those incorporated in *Information power* (American Association of School Librarians (AASL) and Association for Educational Communications and Technology (AECT) 1998). These standards focus mainly on the development of information literacy in American schools but also cover 'the mission and goals of the school library media program', 'roles and responsibilities of the school library media specialist', 'collaboration, leadership and technology', as well as aspects of learning and teaching, information services and library management. In the UK, school library standards (School Libraries Group 2004) cover similar areas to those in *Information power* but include aspects such as marketing the school library and partnerships with organisations outside the school. In Canada, the current standards for school libraries (Canadian School Library Association 2003) focus mainly on the development of information literacy in a similar way to *Information power* and cover areas of policy, staffing, collection management and services. One notable feature of the Canadian standards is that standards for excellent, acceptable and unsatisfactory levels of service are given in the discussion of services provided by the school library.

Standards for school libraries can be very useful documents for teacher librarians who wish to influence their school management and advocate a stronger role for the school library and teacher librarian in the school, but standards are also documents which may be used *against* teacher librarians if the standards are not considered in the school context. For example, school principals cannot expect levels of excellence from teacher librarians who are poorly supported in terms of finance, staffing or school policy.

The role of the teacher librarian

The role of the teacher librarian is a multi-faceted one and *possible* roles for the teacher librarian can be seen in Figure 2.1.

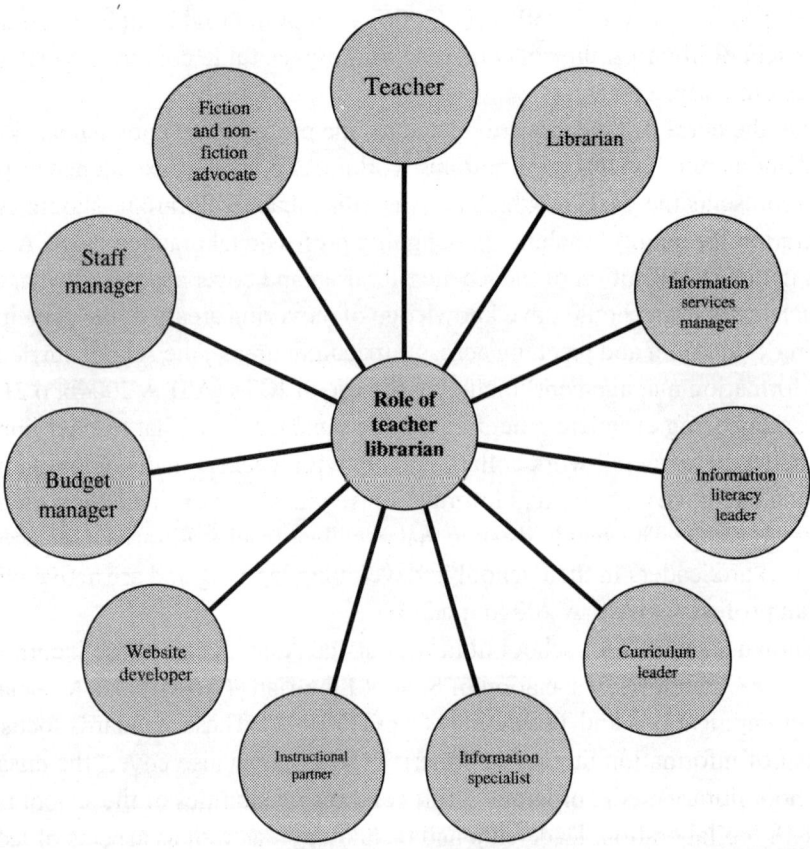

Figure 2.1 Multi-faceted role of the teacher librarian

It is clear that no teacher librarian could fulfil all of these roles at the same time and teacher librarians who manage their time effectively prioritise roles according to the current needs of students, staff and parents in the school community. In Australia, the influential document *Learning for the future* (ASLA 2003) focuses on three particular roles of the teacher librarian: curriculum leader, information specialist and information services manager. As curriculum leaders, teacher librarians are expected to 'work with school principals and senior staff to ensure information literacy outcomes are a major school focus', promote information literacy development in the schools, 'plan, teach and evaluate collaboratively with teachers to ensure the effective integration of information resources and technologies into student learning' and to promote reading 'for understanding and enjoyment' among students (ASLA 2003, p.61). As information specialists, teacher librarians organise information for effective retrieval, 'interpret information systems, and technologies for students and teachers in the context of curriculum programs', enable students to use learning resources within and outside the school, and encourage students to use the library for independent learning (ASLA 2003, p.61). As information service managers, teacher librarians should assess student and staff information needs and evaluate the library collection, develop collection management policies, manage the library's information services effectively, and 'provide a stimulating and helpful environment that is a focal point and showcase for students' learning achievements' (ASLA 2003, p.62).

While these guidelines encapsulate the role of the teacher librarian to some extent, there is an overlap between the roles of information specialist and information service manager. The guidelines are also rather vague on the use of information systems and technologies and there is a total absence of any reference to the internet or the web which make the guidelines appear dated. The role of the teacher librarian is considered in more detail by the School Library Association of South Australia (SLASA), which makes reference to managing the school library's automated system and recommends that teacher librarians 'contribute to the school web page or intranet' (SLASA 2003).

In the USA, *Information power* (AASL & AECT 1998) views the role of teacher librarian as being mainly that of a teacher, an instructional partner, an information specialist and a program administrator. As a teacher, the role encompasses collaborating 'with students and other members of the learning community to analyze learning and information needs, to locate and use resources that will meet those needs, and to understand and communicate the information the resources provide' (AASL & AECT 1998, 'Roles and responsibilities of the school library media specialist', paragraph 1), and developing information literacy in the school. As instructional partner, the teacher librarian 'works closely with individual teachers in the critical areas of designing authentic learning tasks and assessments and integrating the information and communication abilities required to meet subject matter standards' (AASL/AECT 1998, 'Roles and responsibilities of the school library media specialist', paragraph 1). This statement of role is much more explicit and closer to actual practice than the more general statements in the ASLA guidelines above, while the roles of information specialist and program administrator are similar to those of information specialists and information service managers in the ASLA guidelines.

One of the most up-to-date statements on the role of the teacher librarian is the Canadian-based Learning Resources Council's guidelines (2005, 'Role of the teacher librarian', paragraph 2), which view the role of the teacher librarian in terms of leadership in the areas of information literacy, ICT and teaching, 'needs assessment and goal setting, consultation and program planning', and collection management. The Canadian guidelines also focus on collaboration with teachers as a major role, in that this collaboration can enhance the development of information literacy in schools and ensure joint development of curricular subjects by incorporating learning resources into the curriculum as a whole . This role is extended to that of instructor in the guidelines, which reinforce the role of the teacher librarian in developing information literacy in the school and ensuring 'that the inquiry process is taught as a comprehensive process, systematically and developmentally, to all students in the school' (Learning Resources Council 2005, paragraph 3).

In the UK, Barrett (2004, 'Management of ICT', paragraph 2) comments on updated guidelines for school libraries and notes that the role of the teacher librarian is now affected by internet developments and states that 'The plethora of information available from the internet and other e-resources offers huge benefits to learners. However, it also raises questions that librarians need to be able to answer'. Barrett (2004) states that the new guidelines indicate an altered role for the teacher librarian in the UK and that this role means that teacher librarians must take a proactive role in influencing the development of innovations such as e-learning and ensure that information literacy skills are incorporated into curricular subject areas.

A number of impact studies have been carried out which demonstrate that an effective teacher librarian can make a significant difference to student learning in schools. Lance et al. (2005) report a study in Illinois which demonstrated that the teacher librarian's role in cooperative planning with teachers, development of information literacy in students, mediation of learning resources for students and teachers and other activities contributed to a higher standard of student learning and student performance in state tests. Other studies, including Todd and Kuhlthau's research (Ohio Educational Library Media Association 2003), also indicate that where schools have a qualified and active teacher librarian students recognise the value of the teacher librarian and students acknowledge the impact that the teacher librarian can have on their learning.

Herring (2005a) argues that while ICT developments such as the internet, school intranets and the development of learning and teaching websites may be seen as a threat to the role of the teacher librarian, 'Embracing, exploiting and sharing new technologies is an effective way for the teacher librarian to promote the position's vast contributions to the school' and to ensure that the role of the teacher librarian is a dynamic one which is regularly evaluated to ensure the teacher librarian's continued value in the school community (2005a, p.29).

The role of the teacher librarian continues to change and one key feature of this role is the ability of the teacher librarian to adapt to new pedagogies in schools, to new technologies used by students at school and at home, and to multiliterate students who will continue to make new demands on the teacher librarian. Smart information-using students need smart teacher librarians to help them learn.

Information literacy in schools

Developing information literate students is the key role of the teacher librarian in today's schools. It is an *educational* as opposed to an administrative role, and the increasing use of digital resources by students in the school and at home means that information literacy skills are now a vital part of a student's repertoire of learning skills. While there is no one agreed definition of information literacy in schools, Doyle (1994, p.40) defines information literacy as 'the ability to access, evaluate, and use information from a variety of sources, to recognize when information is needed, and to know how to learn' but also identifies some attributes of an information literate student and this definition is widely referred to. This definition, however, does not refer to the identification of a clear purpose for information, nor does it refer to self-reflection by students on their own learning. Abilock (2004, p.1) takes a wider view of information literacy stating that 'Information literacy is a transformational process in which the learner needs to find, understand, evaluate, and use information in various forms to create for personal, social or global purposes'. Williams (2001, p.1) takes a critical view of information literacy definitions, stating that 'Definitions of information literacy, drawn from many perspectives, seem to situate themselves *outside the actual learning process*' [italics added].

A number of definitions of information literacy in the school context claim that lifelong learning skills, transferable from school to the workplace and society in general, can be taught in schools. This may be true of skills used at university or in some professional contexts, but Lloyd (2005) clearly shows that in some workplaces different information skills and different information literacy attributes may be needed (see Chapter 13 for a discussion of this issue). Teacher librarians and teachers in schools need to clarify their views on information literacy in schools and decide whether it is a set of skills to be acquired by students, a list of attributes which an information literate student (and teacher) acquires, or a way of thinking about an individual's learning.

A number of information literacy models have been developed for use by teacher librarians, teachers and students, but only a limited number are designed to be used by students themselves. Kuhlthau's (2004) Information Search Process (ISP) developed in the 1980s and 1990s has been influential as it identified the affective aspects of students' use of information skills, such as feelings of anxiety at the start of assignment planning, and the ISP has been used in schools to develop in-house guidelines for students. In Australia, Capra and Ryan's Information Literacy Planning Overview (ILPO) (Ryan & Capra 2001) is the most commonly used model in both primary and high schools and the elements of the model, *Defining, Locating, Selecting/Analysing, Organising/Synthesising, Creating/Presenting, Evaluation,* can be seen on posters in these schools. In North America, the Big 6 (Eisenberg & Berkowitz 1990) is the most commonly used model. The model has an extensive website (www.big6.com) and posters, videos and workshops are available. The Big 6 elements are: *Task definition, Information seeking, Location and access, Use of information, Synthesis, Evaluation* and are similar to those in the ILPO model. In the UK, Herring's (2004) PLUS model (*Purpose, Location, Use* and *Self-evaluation*), developed in the 1990s, is also used directly by students. Teacher librarians often select certain elements from these models and use them to provide students with scaffolding when completing school assignments. The main criticism of these models is that they may not suit the individual learning styles of some students.

Research in information literacy in schools mainly has sought to examine how students cope with aspects of the information skills process when completing curriculum-related assignments, but it has not focused on the information literacy attributes of students. Thus, while attributes cited by Doyle (1994) and AASL/AECT (1998) stress that information literate students, for example, recognise the social, ethical and economic use of information, research has tended to be related less to information literacy principles than to students' use of information skills, and this reflects how information literacy skills are taught in schools.

Aspects of students' use of information were studied by Bilal (2004) who found that students were more successful in retrieving relevant information when they were engaged in tasks that included question formulation by students as opposed to the teacher. Bilal also stressed the need for students who used search engines to evaluate and understand the information found rather than seeking specific answers. McGregor and Williamson (2005) examined aspects of students' understanding of plagiarism in schools and found that not only did students plagiarise by copying parts of published works, but also that students' and some teachers' understanding of the extent of plagiarism was often lacking. McGregor and Williamson (2005) suggest ways of teaching students how to avoid plagiarism. Although plagiarism is covered in most information skills teaching in schools, it is often taught very superficially and given students' increasing use of digital resources, this aspect of information literacy needs more attention from teacher librarians.

The effective development of information literacy skills with school students is demonstrated by Ryan and Hudson's (2003) report on their programme developed in a Melbourne school. A key aim of this programme was to incorporate information skills into the school curriculum and not to teach information literacy skills as a separate 'subject' in the school library, something for which teacher librarians have often been criticised. Ryan and Hudson (2003) state that students in Year 7 were provided with information literacy scaffolds. These helped them to plan their curricular assignments in a structured way, from defining a clear purpose to locating information sources, reading for information and understanding, note-taking and writing/presenting. Ryan and Hudson (2003) asked students for feedback in the form of questionnaires and found that most students at first lacked a holistic view of the assignment process and tended to focus on their outcome and on finding information. With subsequent teaching of information literacy skills, Ryan and Hudson (2003) reported a marked improvement in students' understanding of the process and ability to use information effectively.

There has been limited research on the use of information literacy models in schools, but Wolf (2003) studied the use of the Big 6 model in order to establish whether it encouraged students to take a metacognitive view of information use. Wolf (2003, Conclusion, paragraph 3) concludes that models such as the Big 6 provide students with 'the elements for mental modelling so necessary in helping the novice construct a method to meet the information use tasks placed before him or her'. According to Wolf's (2003) findings, students showed some evidence of taking a metacognitive view of their task, for example, by being able to relate different parts of the process to one another. Herring (2006) examined the use of the PLUS model by students in a UK school and found that most students saw the model as a useful tool which provided them with support when using information sources for a school assignment. There was also evidence of metacognition by some students who could relate their use of brainstorming and concept mapping to later stages of the assignment process. In this study, Herring also examined the views of teachers and the teacher librarian in the school and teachers saw clear benefits from students using the PLUS model, in that their work was better structured and there was evidence that they made better use of learning resources, both print and digital, when completing assignments.

There has been considerable progress in teaching information literacy skills in schools. However, if the development of information literate students is a key aim for teacher librarians, new strategies will need to be developed to encourage students to take a wider view of information use and to examine how they might effectively recognise a need for information and then find and effectively use that information in all areas of their school work and in aspects of their lives outside school. The increasing use of mobile technologies by students will also have an impact on how they find and use information, and a preliminary study of smart information use by students (Hay & Eyre 2005) shows that schools may lag behind students in their appreciation of new technologies. Developing future information literate students will mean that teacher librarians and teachers will have to teach students how to apply their information literacy skills irrespective of what technology they are using and where they are finding and using information. Langford (2006) indicates a range of technologies that might become part of the pedagogical approach taken by teachers to encourage the development of students with multiliteracies and these include podcasting, mobile phones, voice over internet protocol (VoIP), personal response systems, e-games and augmented reality.

Collection development in school libraries

The materials held in the school library and the materials available for access via the school library constitute the school library collection. What was once a store of books is now a multi-format information centre with a collection that can be accessed and used from within the school, from home or from anywhere with online access. This has meant that teacher librarians have had to reappraise what they mean by collection management and collection development. Collection management focuses on the organisation of the collection and in some cases is interpreted as managing a collection for access, and includes aspects of cataloguing, classification and circulation. Hughes-Hassell and Mancall (2005) argue that *developing* a collection in a school primarily should focus on the needs of the school community, which includes students and staff as well as the wider school community. The emphasis is on ensuring that the school library collection is developed to meet the needs of learners and that managing the collection is a subsidiary part of collection development. Thus before collections can be managed effectively, the information needs of students have to be identified and this can be done via curriculum mapping but may also involve student surveys to identify the changing needs of particular groups of students (Hughes-Hassell & Mancall 2005).

Loertscher (1996) argues that the school library collection should not be seen narrowly as a collection existing within the school but should be seen as part of the total information system in which students and staff operate, both in school and outside school. The increase in home internet access for students in Australia and elsewhere has meant that teacher librarians need to consider not only how the school library collection is part of the global information system, given the ubiquity of internet access, but also how the school library can provide students with knowledge of and access to the myriad of other information sources available to them.

The key aspect of developing a school library collection lies in the selection of materials relevant to the needs of the school community and the acquisition or provision of access to those materials. It is important that this selection reflects the principles of the school, the goals of the school and the school curriculum. In too many schools, the collections developed reflect more the views and aspirations of the teacher librarian rather than that of the school. It is suggested here that a school library collection that has printed materials dominated by fiction is not reflecting the total curricular needs of the school community – a view that would be regarded as controversial in some schools. School libraries are not 'mini public libraries' but learning centres with varied collections which challenge students intellectually and widen their horizons. ASLA states that each school should have a collection development policy that 'ensures that the collection reflects the school's priorities and considers all information resources available to the school community' (ASLA 2003, p.26). There are now a number of collection development policies online that can provide guidance for teacher librarians developing a policy or revising a policy. Two good examples from Australia are provided by Horton (2004) and Braxton (2004). Dillon et al. (2001) state that a collection development policy should demonstrate the overall principles on which materials are acquired or access is provided, the criteria used for selection of materials, the acquisition *policies* (not procedures) of the school, the ways in which the collection will be regularly evaluated and policies to deal with disputed materials.

The selection of materials for the school library collection needs to consider a range of aspects of the school community but particularly the needs of students. Braxton (2004, 'General criteria for selection', paragraphs 2-9) states that the main general criteria for selection of materials should include 'authority … physical format and technical quality … arrangement of material … appropriateness … cost … availability … format … currency'. Hughes-Hassell and Mancall (2005) stress that the needs of the widest range of students in the school should be taken into account and selection criteria should include aspects of the level of language used in print or digital resources. As many school library collections now include websites, the criteria for selecting websites need to be clear in the collection development policy. Schrock (2002) is recognised as an expert in this field and recommends that teacher librarians examine the authority of the site, in terms of the author or the institution, how up to date the site is, whether the site is unreasonably biased and whether the site contains misinformation. Herring (2004, p.50) poses questions such as 'Can I trust this site because I recognise the author or organisation as a reliable source of information?'

Other aspects of collection development include the need for maintenance of the collection. This includes weeding of out-of-date or damaged print materials and keeping a regular check on whether links to websites are still operable. The teacher librarian's task is to provide the school community with access – physical or digital – to a wide range of learning resources and to keep track of the increasing number of new digital resources available. For example, Lu (2004) examines the criteria for selecting online magazines or journals (e-zines) for children and states that while the number of youth-related e-zines is regularly increasing, many are of dubious value and that teacher librarians should only select those that are appropriate. Lu (2004) includes a range of criteria and indicates that, for example, e-zines which seek personal information from students should not be selected. As the formats of potentially relevant digital learning resources constantly increase, teacher librarians need to be aware of what is available.

Information services to students and teachers

ASLA (2004b, p.3) states that excellent teacher librarians 'provide exemplary reference and information services to the school community' but does not explain the nature of these services. The Department of Education Tasmania (2003) states there is no definitive list of information services that can be provided in a school but provides a list of potential services, which include information to support professional development in the school, information and displays relating to national book week, information relating to copyright in the school and in online and face-to-face reference services, and advice on purchasing learning materials, developing lists of resources for teachers and students and developing subject-related resource kits for use in the class or the library. Information services in schools should be related closely to the information needs of students and teachers. Student information needs will include:

- Information literacy skills to make effective use of learning resources.

- Information on print and digital sources within and outside the school.

- Access to specialist information sources in subject areas.

- Access to and guidance on the use of the web.

- Individual advice from the teacher librarian via reference interviews.

- Awareness of new fiction and non-fiction (print and digital) resources held in or accessed by the school library.

Teachers' information needs will include:

- Information to support curriculum planning.

- Information on a subject area to keep up to date.

- Information on ICT use in the curriculum.

- Information on print and digital learning resources available in or accessed by the school library.

- Current awareness and selective dissemination of information services.

- Individual advice from the teacher librarian via reference interviews.

Lanning and Bryner (2004, p.45) emphasise the importance of the reference interview which is 'sometimes overlooked with the wealth of resources we all have to learn, but it is at the heart of being a good librarian'. The reference interview in a school library is, according to Lanning and Bryner (2004, p.49), 'when we find out what the student or teacher really wants so we can devise a strategy to help them'. They advise teacher librarians that they need to be careful not to intimidate students by providing answers that are too technical or provide over-simplified solutions to a student problem. Reference interviews should enable students to help themselves, following advice from the teacher librarian.

Tilke (2002, p.183) provides an example of selective dissemination of information (SDI) in a school which takes the form of the teacher librarian identifying the subject needs of a group of teachers and regularly emailing them information extracted from relevant journals 'based on a knowledge of the curriculum and important issues for the school'. Teacher librarians also provide current awareness services which often take the form of the contents pages of new issues of journals relevant to the needs of teachers. For example, a teacher librarian in Queensland might circulate the contents of *The History Teacher* (http://www.qhta.com.au/resources.htm) to interested teachers as each issue appears online. Information services provided by teacher librarians can be very proactive in keeping teachers up to date with developments in their own fields.

Reference services for students can include the use of pathfinders which guide them to resources that have been mediated by the teacher librarian and chosen to meet a range of student needs and abilities in a particular subject area. Figure 2.2 shows an example from Adelaide High School. A key aspect of pathfinders is that they are actively promoted by the teacher librarian, either directly to students or by their inclusion in assignment specifications given to students in particular subject areas.

Adelaide High School

www.adelaidehs.sa.edu.au/ahsintranet/subjects/index.htm

This subject links page includes pathfinders, hotlists and online assignments for students in a wide range of learning areas and topics. Pathfinder examples include:

- Animal Adaptation in Arid Areas [Science]

- Fitness [Health Education]

- IT in Tourism [Information Technology]

- Lifestyle, Diet and Disease [Home Economics]

- Surrealism [Art]

Figure 2.2 Sample school library pathfinder from Adelaide High School website at www.adelaidehs.sa.edu.au

Information services in school libraries will vary in each school but a good service will combine aspects of the availability of print and digital reference sources, effective reference interviews with students and teachers, the use of interesting and informative displays in the library, well-promoted and timely digital reference services, including current awareness and selective dissemination of information, with all these services linked to the development of information literate students in the school.

The school library website and school intranet

Valenza (2005, 'Introduction') encapsulates the value of a well-designed, well-used and effective school library website and states that, for teacher librarians:

> Your library Web page is your second front door. It meets your students where they live, play, and work! It creates signage for students and staff. The effective library Web page pulls together, in one unified interface, all of a library's resources – print and electronic. It offers guidance while it fosters independent learning. It models careful selection. It offers valuable public service and can redefine 'community'. It can even lead users back to print. A good library Web page offers implicit instruction and projects an important image of the librarian as an information professional.

The most successful school library websites are those which are closely linked to and are visible as part of the school website. This indicates the value which the school places on the school library. School library websites can be used for a range of purposes, including:

- promotion of the school library and of the services offered by the teacher librarian;

- provision of links to digital and print resources and to the local community;

- provision of specific, mediated learning resources in curricular areas (e.g., history, geography or science) or in areas related to student assignments (e.g., the local environment); and

- provision of information literacy guidelines or scaffolds which students can access at any time and from any where.

Warlick (2005) advises teacher librarians that they need to be clear about their purpose in having a website and might usefully identify barriers to information access in the school library that might be removed by use of the website. Warlick (2005) also emphasises the need for teacher librarians to ensure that the school library website is actively used by students and staff in the school and from outside the school. Key ways of ensuring use, according to Warlick (2005), include having teachers put a link on their own web pages to the school library site and including the school library URL in all school library documentation. It is suggested here that teacher librarians encourage teachers to put the library URL on all assignment specifications; collaborate with teachers to ensure that using the school library website is a part of all research work done by students; encourage students to participate in the design and content of the library website, for instance, by including examples of student work on the site; and encourage teachers to provide content for the site in the form of potential learning resources, assignment specifications and information literacy advice to students. Excellent examples of school library websites are highlighted by Braxton (2003), who provides a list of links to school library websites in different parts of the world.

Teacher librarians increasingly are involved in developing school intranets and often play a key role in the creation or maintenance of the school intranet. Carter (2002) identified a number of roles for the teacher librarian in relation to the school intranet, which included 'intranet builder' (taking a key role in establishing the school intranet); 'intranet manager' (gathering information for the intranet, organising and editing content); 'intranet mediator' (identifying and evaluating online links to be included in the intranet); and 'content creator' (creating materials for the intranet such as learning and teaching websites). Herring (2005b) examined the creation of learning and teaching websites for a school intranet and suggested that a key value of those websites created by the teacher librarian and teachers lay in the collaboration between the teacher librarian and the teachers. Benefits to students included online access to curricular work, assignment specifications and information literacy guidance. Teachers valued the sites because when used by students their use of both print and online resources and the structure of their written assignments improved.

Conclusion

School libraries are integral to today's schools and teacher librarians will continue to have a key role in the education of their school's students if they are seen to be adaptable to developments in learning, such as e-learning, in teaching, such as distance education for some schools, in technology, such as mobile internet technologies, in the internet, such as the use of visual search engines, and in librarianship, such as the increasing availability of digital information in a range of formats. While the physical environment of the school library may contract, the information and knowledge environments created by teacher librarians in collaboration with teachers will greatly expand. If student learning is to benefit, then this new information and knowledge environment in the school will need to be carefully managed.

References

Abilock, D 2004, *Information literacy: An overview of design, process and outcomes*, http://www.noodletools.com/debbie/literacies/information/1over/infolit1.html

American Association of School Librarians (AASL) & Association for Educational Communications and Technology (AECT) 1998, *Information power: Building partnerships for learning*, American Library Association, Chicago, IL.

Australian School Library Association (ASLA) 2003, *Learning for the future*, 2nd edn, Curriculum Corporation, Carlton, Vic.

Australian School Library Association (ASLA) 2004a, *Policy statement – ALIA/ASLA joint statement on library and information services in schools*, http://www.asla.org.au/policy/p_services_ in_schools.htm

Australian School Library Association (ASLA) 2004b, *Standards of professional excellence for teacher librarians*, Australian School Library Association/Australian Library and Information Association, Zillmere, Qld.

Barrett, L 2004, 'New guidelines, new challenges in schools', *Update*, September, http://www.cilip.org.uk/publications/updatemagazine/archive/archive2004/september/article2.htm

Beaconhills College 2006, *Beaconhills College Valley Campus mission statement*, http://www.beaconhills.vic.edu.au/valleysite/library/library.htm

Becta (British educational technology service for schools) 2006, 'What the research says about interactive whiteboards' http://www.becta.org.uk/page_documents/research/wtrs_whiteboards.pdf

Beechmont State School 2006, *Beechmont State School Library Resource Centre mission statement*, http://www.beechmontss.eq.edu.au/web/index.php?id=215

Bilal, D 2004, 'Research on children's information seeking on the web' in *Youth information-seeking behaviour: Theories, models and issues*, Chelton, M & Cool, C 2004, Scarecrow Press, Lanham, MD.

Braxton, B 2003, *School library websites*, http://www.palmdps.act.edu.au/resource_centre/inside_out/library_websites.htm

Braxton, B 2004, *General criteria for selection*, viewed 15 May 2006, http://www.palmdps.act.edu.au/resource_centre/policies/collection_dvpt.htm

Canadian School Library Association 2003, *Achieving information literacy: Standards for school library programs in Canada*, Canadian Library Association, Ottawa, Canada.

Carnell, E & Lodge, C 2002, *Supporting effective learning*, Paul Chapman, London.

Carter, M 2002, 'The connecting school and the intranet librarian', *School Libraries Worldwide*, vol.8, no.2, pp.51-64.

Department of Education Tasmania 2003, *Developing information services*, http://www.education.tas.gov.au/delic/school-lib-guidelines/section4/adevelopinginfoservices.htm

Dillon, K, Henri, J & McGregor, J (eds) 2001, *Providing more with less: Collection management for school libraries*, Centre for Information Studies, Charles Sturt University, Wagga Wagga, NSW.

Doyle, C 1994, *Information literacy in an information society: A concept for the information age*, ERIC Clearing House on Information & Technology, Syracuse, NY.

Eisenberg M & Berkowitz R 1990, *Information problem-solving: The big six skills approach to library and information skills instruction*, Ablex, Norwood, NJ.

Hay, L & Eyre, G 2005, 'Smart information use: An exploration of research and practice', *Access*, vol.19, no.2, pp.27-33.

Herring, J 2004, *The internet and information skills: A guide for teachers and school librarians*, Facet Publishing, London.

Herring, J 2005a, 'The end of the teacher librarian', *Teacher Librarian*, vol.33, no.1,pp.26-29.

Herring, J 2005b, 'The instructional website as a focus for teacher librarian and teacher collaboration: A research study', *Synergy*, vol.3, no.1, pp.29-38.

Herring, J 2006, 'A critical investigation of students' and teachers' views of the use of information literacy skills in school assignments', *School Library Media Research*, vol.9.

Horton, R 2004, *Policy for PL Duffy Resource Centre, Trinity College*, http://www.trinity.wa.edu.au/plduffyrc/library/lib/phil.htm

Hughes-Hassell, S & Mancall, J 2005, *Collection management for youth: Responding to the needs of learners*, American Library Association, Chicago, IL.

International Federation of Library Associations (IFLA) & United Nations Educational, Scientific and Cultural Organization (UNESCO) 2006, *School library manifesto*, latest revision, http://www.ifla.org/VII/s11/pubs/manifest.htm

Kuhlthau, C 2004, *Seeking meaning: A process approach to library and information services*, 2nd edn, Libraries Unlimited, Westport, CT.

Lance, K, Rodney, M & Hamilton-Pennell, C 2005, *Powerful libraries make powerful learners: The Illinois study*, http://www.alliancelibrarysystem.com/illinoisstudy/TheStudy.pdf

Langford, L 2006, 'Knowledge-rich kids: Innovate and be bold!' in *Visions of Learning: ASLA Online II conference*, http://www.cybertext.net.au/acell_06/papers/paper7_06.htm

Lanning, S & Bryner, J 2004, *Essential reference services for today's school media specialists*, Libraries Unlimited, Westport, CT.

Learning Resources Council 2005, R*ole of the teacher-librarian*, http://www.learningresources.ab.ca/pdf/role.pdf

Lloyd, A 2005, 'Information literacy: Different concepts, different contexts, different truths?', *Journal of Library and Information Science*, vol.37, no.2, pp.82-88.

Loertscher, D 1996, 'Take heart, you already know how!' *School Library Media Quarterly*, vol.24, no.2, pp.71-72.

Lu, M-Y 2004, 'Evaluating and selecting online magazines for children', http://www.indiana.edu/~reading/ieo/digests/d180.html

McGregor, J & Williamson, K 2005, 'Appropriate use of information at the secondary school level: Understanding and avoiding plagiarism', *Library & Information Science Research*, vol.27, pp.496-512.

Ohio Educational Library Media Association 2003, *Student learning through Ohio school libraries*, http://www.oelma.org/StudentLearning/documents/OELMAResearchStudy8page.pdf

Ryan, S & Capra, J 2001, 'Information literacy planning for educators: The ILPO approach', *School Libraries Worldwide*, vol.7, no.1, pp.1-10.

Ryan S & Hudson V 2003, 'Evidence-based practice, transformational leadership and information literacy at Santa Maria College', *Synergy*, vol.1, no.1, pp.29-41.

School Libraries Group 2004, *CILIP guidelines for secondary school libraries*, Facet Publishing, London.

Schrock, K 2002, *The ABCs of website evaluation*, http://school.discovery.com/schrockguide/pdf/weval_02.pdf

Schunk, D 2000, *Learning theories: An educational perspective*, 3rd edn, Prentice Hall, Upper Saddle River, NJ.

School Library Association of South Australia (SLASA) 2003, 'Teacher librarian role statement', http://www.slasa.asn.au/rolestatement.html

Springfield Township High School 2006, *Springfield Township High School Library mission statement*, http://mciunix.mciu.k12.pa.us/~spjvweb/missionmaster.html

Thomas, N 1999, *Information literacy and information skills instruction*, Libraries Unlimited, Westport, CT.

Tilke, A 2002, *Managing your school library and information service: A practical handbook*, Facet Publishing, London.

Valenza, J 2005, 'A WebQuest about school library websites' http://mciunix.mciu.k12.pa.us/~spjvweb/evallib.html

Warlick, D 2005, 'Building websites that work for your media center', *Knowledge Quest*, vol.33, no.3, http://www.ala.org/ala/aasl/aaslpubsandjournals/kqweb/kqarchives/v33/warlick.pdf

Williams, D 2001, 'Information literacy and learning on-line' In *SCROLLA Networked Learning Symposium*, University of Glasgow, 14 November 2001, http://www.scrolla.ac.uk/resources/s1/williams_paper.pdf

Wolf, S 2003 'The Big Six information skills as a metacognitive scaffold: A case study', *School Library Media Research*, vol.6, article 3, http://www.ala.org/ala/aasl/aaslpubsandjournals/slmrb/slmrcontents/volume62003/bigsixinformation.htm

CHAPTER 3
Higher education libraries

Shirley Oakley and Jennifer Vaughan

Higher education in Australia spans both the university and the vocational education and training (VET) sectors. Universities provide academic and professional education and conduct research. Public universities dominate the sector. They receive most of their funding from the federal (commonwealth) government, although non-government funding is increasing in both quantity and importance as the funding models, particularly for research, are changing. Administration of public universities operates at both state and federal levels. Technical and Further Education (TAFE) institutes provide most of the VET services. TAFE institutes are funded and administered at the state and territory level, although the federal government provides a minority of funding and has recently entered the VET sector more directly.

The boundary between the university and VET sectors is not easily defined (West 1998, p.3). As well as their traditional specialisation in trades, TAFE institutes provide qualifications in a range of disciplines at certificate levels 1–4, diploma and advanced diploma levels, spanning age ranges from fifteen years and upwards, and overlapping the upper secondary school and undergraduate university education systems. Universities provide education at bachelor degree and other undergraduate qualification levels, and postgraduate education at graduate certificate, graduate diploma, masters and doctoral levels, spanning the age ranges from eighteen years and upwards, and overlapping to some extent the TAFE advanced diploma level.

The higher education sector contributes more than $4 billion to the national economy (Australian Vice-Chancellors' Committee (AVCC) 2002) and is the eighth largest source of export income (AVCC 2003). Statistics for the university sector in 2004 (DEST 2005) showed forty-four institutions (more than two thirds of them multi-campus) employed 87,658 staff, enrolled 944,977 students (228,555 overseas), received Australian government grants totalling $11.9 billion, and expended $3.4 billion on research and development. Statistics for the VET sector (National Centre for Vocational Education Research (NCVER) 2005) showed sixty-eight institutions (with more than 1100 campuses) enrolled 1.7 million students and received total recurrent public funding of $4,887 million. Eleven per cent of Australia's working age population access TAFE courses.

Mission of higher education libraries

Higher education libraries have a relatively simple mission: to support the learning, teaching and (where applicable) research of their parent institutions. However, the complexity of the higher education environment in which they operate complicates the carriage of this simple mission. The Council of Australian University Librarians (CAUL) in its strategic plan (2003a) describes the university environment as being characterised by:

- A changing student population, including increasing numbers of students who are time-poor.

- Changes in research practices facilitated by technology.

- Changes in teaching and learning practices facilitated by technology.

- A developing policy environment that puts research activity in a national perspective.

- Increasing requirements to demonstrate quality processes and outcomes.

- The steady maturing of alternative approaches to academic publishing.

- Continuing financial stringency.

Within this environment, CAUL (2003a, p.1) recognises that 'No individual university library can meet the needs of its users by standing alone.' Collaboration and partnerships at local, regional and national level are necessary to support the advancement of learning, teaching and research.

TAFE libraries operate in an equally dynamic environment. To support the teaching methodologies, commercial training and courses currently offered by their institutes, they must empower staff and students with a range of information and information literacy skills geared to lifelong learning. Unlike the research and archival role played by university libraries, or the cradle-to-grave role of the public library, this role provides a highly focused framework for library operations in an environment of exponential change.

TAFE Libraries Australia (TLA) is a peak national library group of state and territory representatives that actively promotes an integrated approach to the delivery of library and information services, which advances and supports VET outcomes and the emerging changes in learning and teaching. The key focus areas are to:

- Provide expert and informed advice on TAFE libraries to relevant bodies.

- Monitor trends and developments in learning strategies and information technologies.

- Develop and disseminate national guidelines and performance measures for TAFE libraries.

- Collect and distribute national TAFE library statistics.

- Provide strategies on the development of information literacy skills within the VET sector.

- Promote the sharing of information and resources, including consortia.

- Encourage and support the development of best practice in TAFE libraries.

- Promote future directions for TAFE libraries.

- Promote discussion of library and information issues in the VET sector.

- Propose and manage research projects that relate to the work undertaken by information professionals within TAFE.

- Encourage cross-sectoral library cooperation.

The most significant environmental factors of higher education libraries are the ongoing and significant changes in policy and regulation, the student population, learning and teaching practice, quality assurance requirements, financially-driven resource sharing requirements, and, in the university sector, changes in research and academic publishing. Workforce planning is also an important facet of higher education library strategy.

Policy and regulation

The current Unified National System (UNS) of universities exists as a result of Commonwealth Government policy outlined in the Dawkins White Paper (Dawkins 1988). The UNS replaced the binary system of universities and colleges of advanced education (CAEs). The UNS introduced a competitive and commercialised funding environment, requiring universities to become more entrepreneurial in diversifying their income stream and at the same time holding them more accountable for the effective and efficient use of public funding. 'The dual pressures of funding diversity and public accountability are a source of a number of tensions within higher education' (Meek & Wood 1997, ch.3, p.1). Full fee-paying overseas students, taught onshore and offshore, provide substantial funds to Australian universities, increasing the level of competition between them.

A new package of policy reforms Our Universities: Backing Australia's Future is being progressively implemented from 2005. The reforms are structured around four key policy principles: sustainability, quality and accountability, equity of access and diversity. Achievement of these policy objectives significantly affects funding outcomes and introduces greater levels of competition between universities in both teaching and research. Policy focus on diversity between universities will transform the current UNS landscape, although outcomes are not yet clearly defined.

Research funding is more competitive, and the degree of competition will increase under the proposed Research Quality Framework (RQF) currently being developed (DEST 2006a). The RQF places particular pressures on the newer UNS universities which are still building research capacity. Proposed changes to the accreditation framework will allow a wider distribution of university status, including single discipline universities and foreign universities, again increasing competition for student numbers and funding, particularly in the full-fee market.

The founders of vocational education in Australia believed that education should enrich society not just train unskilled convicts and labourers for life in a new country. Financial responsibility for vocational education was assumed by the state in NSW in 1878, and provided free training to returned servicemen following the First World War, and later met the needs of industry during and after the Second World War. The Report of the Australian Committee on Technical and Further Education (Kangan 1974) redefined TAFE to meet the needs of people who had to cope with recession and changing job requirements.

Major policy and regulatory reform occurred in the 1990s when several reports (Deveson 1990; Finn 1991; Carmichael 1992; Mayer 1992) highlighted consensus on the need for change. In 1992, the Australian National Training Authority (ANTA) was established and with the Australian National Qualification Framework provided a coordinated national approach to training, with emphasis on flexible delivery of courses. Influenced by the reports of the 1990s, the current vocational education and training system emphasises user choice and best practice, state accreditation and endorsed standards, VET in schools, new apprenticeships, training packages, and strong industry involvement.

Evaluation of the impact on the VET sector of market reforms of the 1990s indicates positive outcomes occurred in the form of greater diversity, responsiveness, flexibility and innovation. Negative outcomes resulted from greater complexity, affecting efficiency, responsiveness, quality, and access and equity. As reflected in the title of his paper, Anderson (2005) found that TAFE and private training companies were 'trading places', as private companies became more dependent on government funding and TAFE institutes became less reliant. Anderson argues for more creative planning to serve the interests of all stakeholders and public interest objectives (2005).

A recent political decision to deregulate the vocational education and training industry requires TAFE institutes to compete in an open commercial environment. Federal government funding represents 30 per cent of the annual TAFE operational budget and is now conditional on Australian workplace agreements being offered to all staff. The federal government has introduced stringent regulatory and reporting obligations based on the requirements of the Skilling Australia's Workforce Act 2005 and the associated VET Plan and Bilateral Agreement, as implemented through output-based results and services plans (RSP) negotiated with TAFE institutes in each state and territory.

A federal budget of $343 million over the period of 2005–2009 has been made available to establish Australian technical colleges which are designed to provide vocational education for students at secondary school level in regional areas with identified skills shortages. State and territory governments are expected to provide recurrent funding to each college at current per-student rates (DEST 2006b). The federal government has also committed $22.9 million to the establishment of the Institute of Trade Skills Excellence to 'promote and advance the quality and industry relevance of vocational and technical education for all the trades in Australia'. Industry stakeholders, the Australian Chamber of Commerce and Industry, Australian Industry Group and the National Farmers Federation agreed in principle that the Institute will be established as a public company (Hardgrave 2005).

The competitive outcomes of higher education policy place particular pressures on libraries in the sector. Libraries have always cooperated in providing access to information resources for their client groups. This is particularly important today when no single library can provide all the resources required to support its mission. However, cooperation between libraries must now recognise increasing competition between educational institutions for both funding and students.

Student population

The characteristics of the student population have changed over the last ten years. Students are less likely to have gone to university directly from school and are more likely to juggle study with work and family responsibilities than was the case ten years ago. The number of students in paid employment has increased by 8 per cent since 1994. The majority of students use online teaching methods, access learning resources electronically and use email to contact peers and staff. Students have fewer contact hours and spend fewer hours on campus (Krause et al. 2005). Students pay fees through the Higher Education Contribution Scheme for (federal) commonwealth funded places, and full-fee places are available to both local and international students. Student expectations for service quality are very high.

Two-way student traffic between the university and VET sectors is significant and growing. Employment prospects and personal development are complementary drivers that motivate these student movements (Harris et al. 2005).

School leavers entering university are 'Millennials', members of the Net-generation (Oblinger 2003) who have grown up with computers and the internet and take connectivity for granted. For these students, staying in touch is essential; they multi-task, they use multiple methods of communication, they study, shop and socialise online. They have an expectation of service support whenever they need it, and they have low tolerance of delay. Similarly, mature-age students bring expectations for service provision based on their life experiences: they are time-poor and they want services that are convenient to them. Both groups of students expect self-help, seamlessness in both access to information and between work, study and socialisation, and are satisfied with the results of their online activities (Wilson 2003).

These expectations have significant implications for the provision of library services. Students expect to communicate online. They want instant service anytime, anywhere. Libraries respond through web-based services, and the use of technologies such as chat and weblogs. Requests for services such as document delivery and reference assistance are available through online request forms and email. All higher education libraries have some kind of online 'Ask a Librarian' service which utilises a variety of access methods: real-time chat, talk online, email, telephone and frequently asked questions (FAQs) on common requests for assistance. Most of these services are available during set hours, but some libraries are moving to collaborative reference services with partner institutions in different time zones to provide twenty-four hour coverage. Self-help services are provided via the library website through 'how to ...' information on topics required by significant numbers of students. Although predominantly text-based, these self-help services increasingly use multimedia technologies.

Learning and teaching

Both the way students learn and the way they are taught have changed significantly over the last ten years. Students are 'time-poor', have fewer contact hours and spend fewer hours on campus (Krause et al. 2005). They are social and team orientated, comfortable with multi-tasking, and have a learn-by-doing approach facilitated by technology. They are comfortable in virtual spaces – synchronous (chat, blogs, wikis) and asynchronous (email, forums). They want integrated access to all their information needs (Wyndham 2005). The focus in higher education has moved from teaching to learning. There is an emphasis on core attributes that facilitate lifelong learning. Problem-based learning is a major pedagogy in some disciplines. Flexible delivery through online course materials is important in higher education. All of these factors impinge on the way libraries support learning and teaching.

Information literacy skills (discussed in Chapter 2) underpin most graduate attributes defined by the institution. CAUL and TLA endorse the information literacy framework developed by the Australian and New Zealand Institute for Information Literacy (Bundy 2004) which aims to embed information literacy within the total educational process. Libraries now work with educational designers and academic staff to integrate information literacy concepts into course materials, particularly online course materials.

The spaces in which learning takes place are no longer those of the traditional classroom or library. Learning spaces are both physical and virtual, enabled by portable technologies and wireless access (Brown 2005). Students prefer experiential learning activities and enjoy social interaction. The boundaries between learning and socialising are indistinct. The pattern of use of libraries has already changed dramatically – physical activity is down (loans, reserve loans, visits) but electronic activity is expanding exponentially. Group work and social interaction characterise student library use.

Libraries are developing their spaces to meet these needs. The library is becoming the 'learning commons', a student-centred, social, collaborative learning space outside the formal classroom that provides access to a range of materials, learning spaces and the technologies needed to continue the learning process. As student ownership of laptop computers increases, the need to provide formal workstations declines and the learning commons becomes a space that can be reconfigured by students according to need. Access is provided to library resources and to a wide range of applications software. These convergent technologies require different service models, providing technology support and increasingly learning skills support as well as traditional reference support. They are very highly utilised and rapidly become the preferred access point to library resources and services (Anderson & Rigby 2006).

Distance education requires high levels of support by the library, much of it still print based, but the virtual learning commons experience is important for off-campus students as well as for those on campus. Electronic books and electronic document delivery are providing access to resources in parallel with online help. These services extend to offshore students as well as onshore students. CAUL's principles for library services to offshore students acknowledge the importance of support for the quality of the student experience and educational outcomes (CAUL 2004a).

Quality assurance

Quality assurance processes for higher education courses follow national frameworks agreed by the Ministerial Council on Education, Employment, Training and Youth Affairs (MCEETYA) which span federal, state and territory jurisdictions (Australian Qualifications Framework (AQF) 2006). Courses in both sectors are accredited under the AQF, a unified system of national qualifications.

Under the AQF, TAFE courses are accredited by state and territory bodies applying standards and required competencies developed under the Australian Quality Training Framework (AQTF). To issue an AQF qualification in the VET sector, the institutions must be registered by a state or territory government recognition authority as a registered training organisation (RTO). RTOs must comply with national standards as well as all relevant local legislative and regulatory requirements. Courses are assessed against sets of industry competency standards defined in training packages, or course accreditation where no training package exists. National consistency in assessment is mandated. RTOs are audited within the registration cycle under the AQTF external review protocol. Reregistration requires quality compliance. Many TAFE institutes use international standard ISO9001:2000 accredited management systems to demonstrate ability to consistently provide product that meets client satisfaction and applicable regulatory requirements, and processes for continual improvement. Institutes are audited regularly to maintain their quality standard accreditation.

Universities are authorised to accredit their own courses and academic standards. They must have appropriate quality assurance processes in place, including peer assessment processes, external examination of higher degrees and the involvement of professional bodies in the accreditation of particular courses. The states and territories exercise control over recognition of a 'university', the right to use the name 'university' and the capacity to accredit courses leading to degrees. The Australian Universities Quality Agency (AUQA) monitors, audits and publicly reports on quality assurance in self-accrediting institutions. In addition, the commonwealth Department of Education, Science and Training (DEST) publishes a range of comparative data to inform both students and institutions about the characteristics and performance of universities. The adequacy of information resources to support learning and teaching (in other words, the library collection and services) are assessed in this way.

CAUL provides a range of data and tools to assist Australian university libraries to compare outcomes using standardised performance indicators including client satisfaction and the quality of service delivery. CAUL's Best Practice Working Group has developed a range of performance indicator kits to allow the collection of standardised data to facilitate benchmarking across the sector. Libraries share these tools under agreed benchmarking protocols (CAUL 2003b). CAUL statistics provide longitudinal benchmarking data from 1992 to the present (http://www.caul.edu.au/stats/).

Resource sharing

Libraries in the higher education sector are committed to resource sharing: 'Access to information is a core value of libraries and librarians. It builds informed communities, lowers barriers to learning, and contributes to the elimination of social and economic disadvantage' (CAUL 2004b, p.1). With declining budgets and increasing prices, no single library can meet all the needs of its users from its own resources: cooperation is essential at the practical level.

Higher education libraries contribute their holdings to Libraries Australia, which provides end user access to the national bibliographic database managed by the National Library of Australia (see Chapter 5) and both CAUL and TLA are represented on the National Resource Sharing Working Group. University libraries operate a national reciprocal borrowing scheme through CAUL's University Library Australia, under which students and staff of member universities of the Australian Vice-Chancellors' Committee are eligible to borrow from any other member university. The TAFE libraries' national reciprocal borrowing scheme (NRBS) is designed to assist students and staff borrow materials in person from any other host library as a means of improving access to library resources close to home if participating in a course in another state. The individual reciprocal borrowing arrangements between TAFE libraries within a state are not affected by this scheme.

Consortial purchasing of both monographs and serials extends buying power for individual libraries. CAUL's Electronic Information Resources Committee (CEIRC), for example, facilitates consortial purchasing of electronic datasets across the university and research sectors in Australia and New Zealand. In 2002, ANTA funded a milestone project to support resource sharing and government initiatives to encourage lifelong learning and to address the lack of TAFE access to consortial purchase infrastructure similar to CEIRC, Council of Australian State Librarians (CASL) and public libraries' Gulliver Project. The ANTA project allowed for the national consortial purchase of electronic databases to provide students and staff at Australian TAFE institutions with cost effective and equitable access to a range of electronic resources regardless of geographic location (Barnett 2002).

Research

Libraries maintain their traditional role in supporting research, but the changing research environment changes the way support is provided. Electronic access to search tools, indexing and abstracting databases and content have reduced reliance on large physical collections of research journals but increased the complexity of access pathways. Different aggregations of content have different search interfaces, and multiple logins, adding complexity to the library's task in assisting researchers to use them. The demand for seamless discovery of and access to content over multiple platforms has led to the provision of search portals which provide a single search interface with direct links to content on many platforms. The Australian Academic and Research Library Network (AARLIN) is one such portal. AARLIN aims to provide a collaborative research information infrastructure that will:

- Streamline information access through targeted search options.

- Offer a choice of targeted services at the point of need on the research desktop.

- Share processes and workloads to maximise electronic resource discovery & delivery.

- Provide a portal for these services.

- Expedite access through use of single-sign-on and authentication technology (http://www.aarlin.edu.au/about.shtml).

Research is increasingly multidisciplinary, with research teams working across institutional and national boundaries. E-science, 'large scale science that will increasingly be carried out through distributed global collaborations enabled by the internet' (Research Councils UK 2006), requires new types of support infrastructure. Research data and research results produced electronically offer opportunities for improved access by researchers to information, but also require new methods of preservation. The Australian Research Information Infrastructure Committee (ARIIC) funds projects which will improve the access of Australian researchers to the information they need to carry out their research and make the results of Australian research widely available and easily accessible. Libraries are directly involved in funded infrastructure projects: Australian Research Repositories Online to the World (ARROW); Australian Digital Theses Program Expansion (ADT); Australian Partnership for Sustainable Repositories (APSR); and Regional Universities Building Research Infrastructure Collaboratively (RUBRIC). New initiatives in e-Science which facilitate researcher collaboration, data sharing and data preservation offer new challenges for libraries. The Dataset Acquisition, Accessibility and Annotation e-Research Technologies (DART) project, for example, builds on ARROW by storing datasets as well as the published research, making it possible to include annotations on datasets and publications.

Increased competition for research funding under the proposed Research Quality Framework (RQF) (DEST 2006c) places a significant value on the ability of university libraries to support researchers. There is increased pressure on libraries in the 'Dawkins' universities which do not have a long history of collecting for research support. The ability of the library to support researchers is considered a competitive advantage in the RQF funding regime.

Academic publishing

Traditional access to scholarly information through research collections of peer-reviewed print materials has been eroded as libraries reduce subscriptions under the pressures of increasing costs and static budgets. University libraries are moving rapidly to electronic collections of journals which enable scholars to access content at their desktop; however, electronic subscriptions are not yet significantly cheaper than print. On the one hand, licensing models that require subscriptions to discipline-based sets increase the breadth of coverage for an individual library, but, on the other, they limit the ability to buy only those titles which are relevant to the research needs of the institution.

The electronic subscription model limits access in the case of those scholars not affiliated with a subscribing university. Walk-in access may be allowed by license but prevented by university network security, and document delivery is often prohibited. CEIRC defines model clauses for licenses which aim to allow content to be accessed and used in the same ways libraries provided access to print. Electronic subscriptions introduce the problem of long-term access when subscriptions cease. Long-term preservation of electronic content is not assured.

The open access movement proposes a different access model from the subscription-based model, facilitated by digital technologies and networked access. Open access provides the end user with free access to content. CAUL's statement on open access (CAUL 2004b) endorses the Budapest Open Access Initiative and declares that CAUL will work towards:

- Building the infrastructure, such as institutional repositories, that will advance open access.

- Collaborating with researchers, research institutions and publishers to raise awareness of the principles and practice of open access publishing within CAUL institutions.

- The generation and implementation of public policies that ensure fair use of copyrighted information for educational and research purposes.

- Cooperation with the Australian government to improve access to scholarly information, and to maximise the amount of information in the public domain, or otherwise available without economic restriction.

University libraries consequently are involved not only in providing access to content, but also in providing the content itself through institutional repositories for the research output of their own university, and through commonwealth-funded projects such as ARROW, ADT, RUBRIC, and through APSR, which seeks to sustain content.

Workforce planning

The changing nature of the workplace requires new skills and new job types. There is a lack of match between what is needed and what is available in the existing workforce and indeed in the types of students entering the sector from library education programs. Australian higher education libraries face challenges similar to the library sector internationally. Workforce planning must encompass the ageing workforce, sector recruitment disadvantages, and the changing nature of the library workplace (Institute for Museum and Library Science 2006; Ingles 2003).

Core skills identified (Australian Library and Information Association (ALIA) 2005; Fisher, 2004) include not only knowledge and skills, but also the aptitudes and personal attributes required to 'future-proof' services in a rapidly changing, service-orientated environment. The principle underlying ALIA's core skills (2005) states: 'The library and information sector has a distinctive area of knowledge and skills which is required for effective professional practice. Library and information professionals need to acquire the relevant disciplinary expertise, demonstrate employment-related skills and be prepared for a challenging and dynamic future.'

Significant recruitment disadvantages in the sector (Whitmell 2004) include low salaries; poor reward systems for good performance; bureaucratic hierarchies and processes; positions with limited functional diversity; and promotion systems based on increasing responsibility rather than professional excellence. These factors particularly discourage younger workers of the 'Millennium' generation. Regional higher education organisations experience additional difficulties in the recruitment and retention of appropriately qualified and experienced professional staff because of the perceived career and economic disadvantage in moving out of metropolitan areas (TAFE Directors Australia 2004). In Australian libraries, 52 per cent of the workforce is over forty-five years and 20 per cent is over fifty-five years, which is older than the general workforce (34 per cent and 12 per cent respectively). Libraries face a significant loss of skills and experience as the existing workforce retires.

Higher education libraries are beginning to address workforce planning issues both individually and collectively. University Libraries in the Australian Technology Network jointly commissioned advice on workforce planning matters (Whitmell 2004). Libraries collaborate on specific competencies for the sector and share generic position descriptions. The Queensland University Libraries Office of Cooperation (2006), for example, shares workforce planning data, competencies and position descriptions openly on its website.

Higher education libraries in regional Australia: a case study

Government policy, federal, state and territory, in both the university and TAFE sectors, places emphasis on education and training in regional Australia to overcome severe skills shortages. Creation of university campuses in regional areas and the commonwealth government's new funding initiative for Australian technical colleges are both manifestations of policy initiatives addressing rural and regional disadvantage. A recent study (Alloway et al. 2004) showed that students in rural, regional and remote areas have high aspirations. They are very aware of changing economic and social structures and recognise that the end of school signals a transition point to further education and training, not an end of study. Economic realities in the regions, particularly as a result of prolonged drought, reduce opportunities for students from disadvantaged areas to relocate in order to pursue higher education. Universities and TAFE institutes located in regional areas recognise the needs of these students and increasingly are providing courses thats allow articulation from TAFE certificate to bachelor degree. Teaching methods using flexible delivery and distance education programs also provide education and training opportunities for these students.

Charles Sturt University (CSU) and the Riverina Institute of TAFE (RI), for instance, operate in regional NSW and are subject to the pressures of the policy environment, the local economies and student aspirations. Both are multi-campus institutions spread over large geographical areas.

In response to the western Riverina higher education needs analysis conducted for the Riverina Regional Development Board (Alston et al. 2001), CSU and RI collaborate to provide educational services and opportunities in their regions to address higher education disadvantage and the skills shortages that constrain economic development in the region. Articulated courses are offered to allow students to move seamlessly from RI certificates and diplomas to CSU degrees in only three years. Using the TAFE Griffith campus infrastructure the initial co-enrolled students successfully completed their business course with a TAFE certificate and diploma, and a CSU Bachelor of Business degree. Joint courses are now also offered at CSU and RI campuses at Albury and Wagga Wagga in business studies, information technology and fine arts.

The libraries operate collaboratively to provide coordinated collection development and support services to their co-enrolled students, and induction programs to raise awareness of the combined library resources and services available. The CSU and RI reciprocal agreement spans all libraries across the geographic spread of their respective organisations. In alignment with the university's mandate to provide services to the communities in its region, CSU offers access and borrowing rights to teachers and senior students in local high schools and community borrowing memberships to members of the public. RI libraries offer similar access to community users. Riverina is the only TAFE institute in NSW to offer library access to teachers and senior high school students. A strong professional network exists to share staff development activities and to consult on library strategies to integrate assistive technologies for students with special needs.

Information literacy instruction is a priority to prepare students for the academic demands of university and lifelong learning. CSU and RI librarians were active participants in the Australian and New Zealand Institute for Information Literacy (ANZIIL) forum, Information Literacy – Strategies for Success, held in Canberra in 2004, at which the focus was on sharing information literacy strategies and developing a regional information literacy network.

Support services for flexible delivery of learning and distance education are provided in a region of highly variable technological infrastructure. Services must take account of student access to the internet and available bandwidth. CSU Library provides an online forum where library users can communicate with each other on topics relating to library services. The forum is moderated by a librarian, and in addition to meeting student information needs it provides valuable feedback to the library on services and self-help resources that may be required.

Online services are particularly important in institutions like CSU and RI which span large geographic areas and have significant cohorts of students studying off campus. At CSU, 71 per cent of students study via distance education; at RI 5.75 per cent of students study totally online but this figure does not capture the online activity of students using flexible delivery and blended learning methodologies to complete their courses. To be effective, librarians require skills in designing online learning materials for adult learners. At the same time, design must take into account that internet access is often difficult in small regional centres and bandwidth does not accommodate high volumes of data.

Conclusion

The current higher education legislative and regulatory environment presents immediate challenges in meeting professional goals of service and the essential educational role of empowering students with skills for lifelong learning for a future of exponential change. Evolving teaching and learning methodologies require appropriate new resources and services to support students and academic staff.

Communication technologies and the internet have not of themselves delivered the answers in how to manage these technologies and the proliferation of information. Instead of the role of the librarian becoming devalued, as was prophesised in the 1990s, the need is greater than ever for reflection on our underpinning professional philosophy and involvement in the development of user friendly online content and the information literacy skills necessary to optimise available information.

An ageing workforce and profession is not all doom and gloom. Managed wisely this represents an unprecedented opportunity for creating the new professionals uniquely placed to excel in a workplace that is intensely networked and is at once integrated and devolved. The changing political, economic and demographic environment provides the impetus for creative and innovative responses to resource development, access and delivery. The role of the higher education librarian has never been more challenging and filled with promise for the sort of fulfilling and exciting career that is appealing to the best and the brightest of the next generation who can recognise that times of change are times of opportunity.

References

Alloway, N, Gilbert, P, Gilbert, R & Muspratt, S 2004, *Factors impacting on student aspirations and expectations in regional Australia,* EIP 04/01, Evaluations and Investigations Programme, Department of Education, Science and Training, Canberra, ACT, http://www.dest.gov.au/NR/rdonlyres/01B35FAF-F5D5-4346-A2B8-9EF75DA58FBA/816/eip_04_01.pdf

Alston, M, Pawar, M & Bell, K 2001, *The western Riverina higher education needs analysis*, The Centre for Rural Social Research, Charles Sturt University, Wagga Wagga, NSW.

Anderson, D 2005, *Trading places: The impact and outcomes of market reform in vocational education and training*, National Centre for Vocational Education Research, Adelaide, SA.

Anderson, G & Rigby, A 2006, 'Internet café or learning environment? The University of Newcastle's information common after the first 18 months', *Connecting with users: VALA 2006 13th Biennial Conference and Exhibition,* Melbourne, held at the Crown Towers, 8-10 February, 2006, http://www.valaconf.org/vala2006/papers2006/77_Anderson_Final.pdf

Australian Library and Information Association (ALIA) 2005, *The library and information sector: Core knowledge, skills and attributes*, http://alia.org.au/policies/core.knowledge.html

Australian Qualifications Framework (AQF) 2006, *The AQF and quality assurance processes in Australian education and training*, http://www.aqf.edu.au/quality.htm#theaqf

Australian Vice-Chancellors' Committee (AVCC) 2002, *Positioning Australia's universities for 2020: An AVCC policy statement*, Canberra, ACT, http://www.avcc.edu.au/documents/policies_programs/statements/2020.pdf

Australian Vice-Chancellors' Committee (AVCC) 2003, *Integrity of higher education a must [media release]*, http://www.avcc.edu.au/content.asp?page=/news/media_releases/2003/avcc_media_05_03.htm.

Barnett, S 2002, Information access VET Australia: A consortia approach to electronic resource purchase by Australian TAFE library services, viewed 6 May 2006, http://library.swantafe.wa.edu.au/tla/Documents/National%20TAFE%20Database%20Consortia%20Project%20Final%20report.doc

Brown, M 2005 'Learning Spaces' in *Educating the Net Generation*, eds Oblinger, DG & Oblinger, JL, EDUCAUSE, pp.12.1-12.22, http://www.educause.edu/ir/library/pdf/pub7101l.pdf

Bundy, A (ed.) 2004, *Australian and New Zealand information literacy framework: Principles, standards and practice*, 2nd edn, Australian and New Zealand Institute for Information Literacy, Adelaide, http://www.anziil.org/resources/Info%20lit%202nd%20edition.pdf

Carmichael, L 1992, *The Australian vocational certificate training system*, National Board of Employment, Education and Training, Canberra, ACT.

Council of Australian University Librarians (CAUL) 2003a, *Strategic plan 2003-2004*, http://www.caul.edu.au/caul-doc/StrategicPlan.html

Council of Australian University Librarians (CAUL) 2003b, *Benchmarking protocols – A guide for CAUL*, http://www.caul.edu.au/best-practice/policies.html

Council of Australian University Librarians (CAUL) 2004a, *CAUL principles for library services to offshore students*, http://www.caul.edu.au/best-practice/offshore.html

Council of Australian University Librarians (CAUL) 2004b, *Statement on open access*, http://www.caul.edu.au/scholcomm/

Dawkins, JS 1988, *Higher education: A policy statement* [White Paper], AGPS, Canberra, ACT.

Department of Education Science and Training (DEST) 2005, *Higher education report 2004–05*, viewed 6 May 2006, http://www.dest.gov.au/NR/rdonlyres/136CDC4E-9770-464D-BDCF-72E56B031C6A/8092/highered_report_fullversion11.pdf

Department of Education Science and Training (DEST) 2006a, *Research quality framework: Assessing the quality and impact of research in Australia – Final advice on the preferred RQF model*, viewed 5 May 2006, http://www.dest.gov.au/sectors/research_sector/policies_issues_reviews/key_issues/research_quality_framework/final_advice_on_preferred_rqf_model.htm.

Department of Education Science and Training (DEST) 2006b, *Australian technical colleges*, viewed 7 May 2006, http://www.australiantechnicalcolleges.gov.au/

Department of Education Science and Training (DEST) 2006c, *Higher education equity support programme*, viewed 10 May 2006, http://www.dest.gov.au/sectors/higher_education/programmes_funding/programme_categories/special_needs_disadvantage/higher_education_equity_support_program.htm

Deveson, I 1990, *Training costs of award restructuring: Report of the training costs review committee*, AGPS, Canberra, ACT.

Finn, B 1991, *Young people's participation in post-compulsory education and training: Report of the Australian Education Council Review Committee*, AGPS, Canberra, ACT.

Fisher, B 2004, 'Workforce skills development: The professional imperative for information services in the United Kingdom', *Challenging ideas: ALIA 2004 Biennial Conference*, Gold Coast, held at the Gold Coast Convention & Exhibition Centre, 21-24 September 2004, http://conferences.alia.org.au/ alia2004/pdfs/fisher.b.paper.pdf

Hardgrave, G 2005, 'Institute for trade skills excellence established' [media release], http://www.dest.gov.au/ministers/media/hardgrave/2005/12/h001211205.asp

Harris, R, Sumner, R & Rainey, L 2005, *Student traffic: Two-way movement between vocational education and training and higher education*, http://www.ncver.edu.au/research/proj/nr3003.pdf

Ingles, E 2003, *Canadian library human resource study*, http://www.ls.ualberta.ca/8rs/8rsresearch propNov14A.pdf

Institute for Museum and Library Science 2006, *The future of librarians in the workforce*, http://libraryworkforce.org/

Kangan, M 1974, *TAFE in Australia: Report on needs in technical and further education*, Australian Committee on Technical and Further Education, AGPS, Canberra, ACT.

Krause, KL, Hartley, R, James, R & McInnis, C 2005 *The first year experience in Australian universities: Findings from a decade of national studies*, Department of Education, Science and Training, Canberra, ACT, http://www.dest.gov.au/NR/rdonlyres/1B0F1A03-E7BC-4BE4-B45C-735F95BC67CB/5885/FYEFinalReportforWebsiteMay06.pdf.

Mayer, E 1992, *Putting general education to work: The key competencies*, The Australian Education Council and Ministers for Vocational Education and Training, Melbourne, Vic.

Meek, VL & Wood, FQ 1997, *Higher education governance and management: An Australian study*, Department of Employment, Education and Youth Affairs, http://www.dest.gov.au/archive/ highered/eippubs/eip9701/front.htm

National Centre for Vocational Education Research (NCVER) 2005, *Australian vocational education and training statistics: Pocket guide*, http://www.ncver.edu.au/publications/1633.html

Oblinger, D 2003, *Boomers, Gen-Xers and Millennials: Understanding the new students*, EDUCAUSE, http://www.educause.edu/ir/library/pdf/ERM0342.pdf

Queensland University Libraries Office of Cooperation 2006, *Staffing issues – reports and presentations*, http://www.quloc.org.au/

Research Councils UK 2006, *e-Science: About the UK e-science program*, http://www.rcuk.ac.uk/ escience/

TAFE Directors Australia 2004, *The role of TAFE in regional and remote Australia: a TDA position paper*, http://www.tda.edu.au/download_files/position_papers/TDA%20Regional%20TAFE%20 Position%20Paper.pdf

West, R et al. 1998, *Learning for life: Final report of the Review of Higher Education Financing and Policy*, Department of Employment, Education and Youth Affairs, http://www.dest.gov.au/ archive/highered/hereview/herr.pdf

Whitmell, V 2004, *Workforce and succession planning in the libraries of the Australian Technology Network: Preparing for demographic change*, http://www.atn.edu.au/docs/LATN%20Workforce%20 and%20Succession%20Planning%20.pdf

Wilson, A (ed.) 2003, *The 2003 OCLC environmental scan: Pattern recognition*, Online Computer Library Centre Inc. (OCLC), Dublin, OH, http://www.oclc.org/reports/escan/downloads/introduction.pdf

Wyndham, C 2005, 'The student's perspective', in *Educating the Net generation*, eds DG Oblinger & JL Oblinger, *EDUCAUSE*, pp.5.1-5.16, http://www.educause.edu/ir/library/pdf/pub7101e.pdf

CHAPTER 4
Special libraries and information services

Alison O'Connor

This chapter discusses the world of the 'specials' – those library and information services that do not fit into any of the other categories of library discussed in the preceding three chapters or in the following one. It provides a brief overview of special libraries in Australia before focusing on the core competencies of special librarians – however they describe themselves. It also presents two 'case studies', with a more in-depth analysis of the worlds of law libraries and parliamentary libraries. Each of these case studies covers the role of the library, collections, clients of the library and staffing skills required. The chapter ends by considering the main challenges facing special libraries and drawing some general conclusions about the sector.

It could be argued, of course, that all libraries are special, but the term 'special libraries' is generally taken to refer specifically to a segment of the library sector that has the following defining features:

- The library is usually devoted to a particular subject area.

- Users of the library are a well-defined group, often with highly specialised needs.

Special libraries are usually attached to a parent organisation or body, and their main role is to meet the information needs of that organisation. The special libraries sector is further segmented into the type or subject area of libraries including health, law, government, scientific, art/music, professional bodies, corporate libraries and so on. Indeed, libraries are likely to define themselves by subject area, rather than the generic term of 'special library'. A library in a hospital, for instance, will describe itself as a health library, and a library at a court will classify itself as a law library.

The overarching term of special library appeared with the creation of the Special Libraries Association (SLA) at the Bretton Woods meeting of the American Library Association in July 1909. The SLA was created in recognition of the growth in these types of libraries. The president, John Cotton Dana, from the Newark Free Public Library, defined special libraries as 'the library of a modern man of affairs' (Special Libraries Association 1910, p.4). At the first meeting of the association he commented that 'the habit is growing among men of affairs to look to books and periodicals and printed materials in general for direct help in the solution of the questions that are continually confronting them' (Special Libraries Association 1910, p.4). Special libraries were seen as differing from traditional libraries in that their purpose was to meet the needs of specialised situations. The libraries soon developed from being traditional collecting libraries to focusing on up-to-date current information and the provision of research services.

Special libraries in Australia

Throughout the twentieth century, the number of special libraries grew dramatically. The tenth edition of the *Directory of special libraries in Australia* (Eames 1999) lists 1,125 special libraries, divided among the following states and territories: Australian Capital Territory, 92; New South Wales, 341; Northern Territory, 34; Queensland, 155; South Australia, 87; Tasmania, 44; Victoria, 252; and Western Australia, 120. This has grown significantly from the 384 libraries listed in the first edition, published in 1952. The subjects covered by these libraries range across abattoirs, cement, earth sciences, international law, navy, photography, religion, soils, zoos and many others.

Peter Biskup (1994) records that the first special library in Australia dates back to 1821 in Sydney and was the Philosophical Society of Australasia (now the Royal Society of New South Wales). At that time each member of the society would have provided the secretary with an alphabetical catalogue of the books in his private library, and these were available for loan to other members.

The function of this library was very different from the role of the special library as perceived by the founders of the SLA. Over the years, special libraries have evolved, moving away from merely gathering information (the collection era), as described in the example above, and into the era of access, where distributing timely and, most important, relevant information to users is the main goal of the library service.

Competencies of special librarians

Special librarianship according to White (1989, p.24) is a state of mind and an attitude. It is 'putting knowledge to work', and is not defined by the type of library in which the information professional works but by the value system that is brought to the information interaction with the client. Traditional library skills apply to the sphere of special librarianship, but there is an increased emphasis on two key attributes: knowledge of the business and partnership with the clients. These two attributes will be discussed in conjunction with the Special Libraries Association's *Competencies for information professionals of the 21st century* (2003). In the 1990s, the SLA developed this set of competencies for special librarians, revising them in 2003. They are divided into core, professional and personal competencies.

Core competencies

The core competencies relate to the information professional's commitment to the profession, the ethics of the industry and the ongoing development of their knowledge, and can be applied to any librarian or information professional. A commitment to knowledge sharing has always been at the heart of the library and information profession, long before it became popular for businesses and organisations to talk about developing 'knowledge sharing cultures'. In a special library environment this sharing of knowledge and the networks and professional activities developed to enable knowledge sharing are essential for the ongoing development of the profession. Unlike other library sectors, special libraries are only one department (usually a small component) of a larger business or organisation. This can be quite isolating for the information professionals working in the organisation. They have fewer library colleagues to associate with, to mentor them and to share ideas. Library associations and networks become a lifeline to the outside world, particularly to those special librarians who are operating in a one-person library. The SLA core competencies recognise that in order for the profession to grow and develop, those working in special libraries have to be committed to lifelong learning, and to the development of their own skills and those of their colleagues in other special library environments.

Professional competencies

The professional competencies identified by the SLA are divided into the following categories: 'Managing information organisations'; 'Managing information resources'; 'Managing information services'; and 'Applying information tools and technologies' (Abels et al. 2003).

Managing information organisations is essentially the management of the information function, library, knowledge centre or similar service within an organisation or business. In order for special librarians to succeed in this role it is imperative that they understand the wider business in which they are operating. They cannot operate in isolation. The goals, objectives and very reason for the information service existing must relate to the wider purpose and goals of the organisation. A health library, for example, is not in the business of libraries, but in the business of provision of health services, just as the libraries discussed in the two preceding chapters are in the business of teaching and learning.

While it is not necessary to have formal qualifications in the subject area of the special library, it does help, and special librarians do need a commitment to keep up to date with the developments in the industry in which they are operating. Their professional reading should include industry as well as library and information profession publications.

In order to prevent the library service from being marginalised, special librarians need to use every opportunity they can to overcome the traditional or old-fashioned perception of libraries. They need to 'talk the talk' of senior management, where possible displaying their business nous, and identify opportunities outside the traditional role of a library. It is crucial in today's environment that they can develop business plans, project plans or business cases; demonstrate return on investment; demonstrate sound financial skills; conduct benchmarking studies; demonstrate reporting skills; and market and communicate the value of their services and resources to clients and key stakeholders.

The 'Managing information resources' competencies are carried out by all librarians across all sectors and include the identifying, acquisition, cataloguing, provision and evaluation of relevant information resources. Special librarians need to use the information they have obtained about the industry in which they work to ensure that the collection and resources meet the changing needs of their organisation.

'Managing information services' for special librarians involves an acute awareness of the library's business and the needs of their users. Bender (1998a, p.198) explains that constant assessment of clients' needs is vital in order to ensure that the special library or information resource centre is user driven. He goes on to say that the packaging or re-packaging of information based upon a client's needs or product analysis and evaluation were once seen as 'value-added services'. There is, however, an expectation that this analysis and evaluation is now a core part of a special library's service. This has meant that special librarians now have to be even more resourceful and innovative in identifying new opportunities and demonstrating their value or return on investment.

In an environment in which 'information overload' is a common complaint, the ability to analyse and synthesise information is a key skill for special librarians. In an ideal special library setting, the information professional would be enlisted as a consultant or adviser, rather than just being seen as a service expense.

Bender (1998b) talks about special libraries evolving through the following stages:

- 'Just in case'.

- 'Just in time' information delivery, where special librarians became information consultants and information employers – they listened to the clientele describe what they needed then provided it 'just in time'.

- 'Just for you', where information professionals analyse, interpret, customise and provide information to each individual and his/her needs.

One of the challenges facing special libraries is to advance the provision of information services to the next level:

- 'Just with you', where special librarians are being brought in at the strategic-planning level of business. Bender talks about special librarians sitting next to the decision makers at the senior level to provide critical information in areas of crisis management, competitive business strategy and bottom-line driven decision making.

The final professional competency listed by the SLA, 'Applying information tools and technologies', essentially refers to the need for special librarians to stay abreast of emerging technologies, and to look for opportunities to harness and use them to benefit their own organisations. Once again there is an emphasis on forming partnerships, but this time with vendors and the IT (information technology) department. These close relationships are vital for all information professionals, but particularly in special libraries where in the past technology has been seen as a way in which the library resources and staff can be reduced. Fortunately senior managers are now starting to realise that introducing the latest technology will not resolve the information needs of their organisations on its own.

Special librarians need to be champions for new technology, not see it as a threat. They need to be able to communicate its value to senior management, in particular the value add-ons it may allow the library service to provide to clients. They need to be part of the project teams for roll-outs in their organisations and if possible become leaders of technology initiatives.

Personal competencies

The SLA has also prepared a list of personal competencies which relate to the skills, attitudes, and mindset required to be a special librarian. Like the core and professional competencies, many of these are also relevant to other library sectors. A full list of these competencies is provided on the SLA website (http://www.sla.org). For the purposes of this chapter a selection has been made of those which are particularly pertinent to special libraries.

'Sees the big picture'

Seeing the big picture is looking outside the library to the challenges and opportunities facing the business or parent organisation and also the wider industry in which the library operates. As mentioned previously, it is about recognising that the special librarian is not solely in the business of libraries and information but in the business of the wider industry in which they operate, such as health, law, mining and financial services. It is not only being aware of the environment, but monitoring industry trends to help senior management realign its business or organisation and also to help the library realign its services.

'Seeks out challenges and capitalizes on new opportunities' and 'Thinks creatively and innovatively; seeks new or "reinvents" opportunities'

These two competencies recognise that special librarians need to expand upon the traditional role of librarians and become information leaders in the organisation. Libraries used to operate in a monopoly environment. Now there are other businesses and options for clients. Not to develop the services and resources provided would be to become a bystander to the main game and even to face extinction. This competency involves being aware of developments in other library sectors and how these can be applied to one's own environment.

'Remains flexible and positive in a time of continuing change'

The one constant for any business or organisation today is change. Because of the need for special libraries to align the information service closely to the parent body, any change to the structure or management of the organisation profoundly affects the library. Special libraries need to have a structure that is flexible and managers who can lead their staff through periods of change, whether that is technological change, changes to the structure of the parent body or changes to the resources and services provided by the library.

'Presents ideas clearly; negotiates confidently and persuasively' and 'Communicates effectively'

These skills are imperative in the special library environment where often the library manager is reporting to someone who may not understand libraries or the services they provide. The library manager could be reporting, for instance, to someone in IT or finance and these people may not have an understanding of what the library is doing for the organisation's employees or members. In these cases, it is important to speak their language and not get caught up in library jargon. Another of the SLA competencies (Abels et al. 2003) talks about working closely with those in power who may say 'no' in order to understand clearly what's required to arrive at 'yes'. This involves learning what their pressures and concerns are, and addressing these in any proposals. It also involves recognising that every time special librarians talk to someone outside the library, in a meeting, or by the drink cooler, they are promoting the library and its services.

'Creates partnerships and alliances'

There are two parts to this competency. First, there is the need to create strategic partnerships within the organisation, to develop champions at the senior level who can promote and if necessary defend the library and information service. There is also the need to create excellent working relationships with similar support functions within the organisation such as IT and HR (human resources). Second, there is the need to create partnerships and alliances with similar libraries and information services, and to develop relationships with vendors of information products. An excellent relationship with vendors can assist with pricing and licensing negotiation, and also assist in the development and customisation of information solutions to the library's clients.

Law libraries

The law library sector is itself quite diverse with law libraries found in courts and tribunals, law firms, universities and law societies. There are also criminology and police libraries, and some government departments and companies have legal collections for their in-house counsel.

Although their user groups and needs may differ, the above libraries do have one underlining similarity, and that is their collections. Law library collections comprise primary materials (legislation, case law, patents, treaties) and secondary materials (text books, loose-leaf material, journals, legal dictionaries, directories and encyclopedias). There is also a number of legal citators, indexes and digests, which assist in the legal research process. Historical volumes and publications are also important in law libraries. Often it will be an 1800s volume of a law report that will contain a case on point. At other times it is necessary to consult legislation amendments, parliamentary debates, reports and explanatory notes to be able to interpret the intention of a section of legislation. The online information environment has led to an explosion in the number of tools and services available to keep legal professionals up to date with new legislation, cases and other legal developments.

The importance of the doctrine of precedent in law means that research services are a crucial activity of law libraries. The doctrine of precedent is an underlying principle of the Australian legal system, and is where a decision of a court on a particular matter of law is binding on all lower courts in the court hierarchy. Sometimes a British case from 150 years ago may actually be the precedent or leading case for a particular area of law. Most legal problems that lawyers deal with are not straightforward. Extensive research is often required which involves: 'analysing the facts; determining the legal issues involved; researching the legal issues thoroughly; and evaluating the results' (Cook et al. 2005, p.294).

Sometimes the legal professionals complete this research with assistance from the law library. The librarians may direct them to relevant resources or perhaps assist with use of legal databases. Increasingly, however, this research is being delegated to the library to complete and in some law firms the librarians bill their research time to the clients, in the same manner as the lawyers bill for their services, although law firm libraries charging for legal research is perhaps more prevalent overseas, particularly in the United States. Research in law libraries is not strictly confined to legal principles. Law librarians will often be required to conduct industry-based research. If, for example, the parties are involved in the diamond industry, the research may involve searching mining resources. If the case is in relation to a medical issue, the research may involve obtaining journal articles outlining the latest research or medical developments. This diversity makes working in law libraries interesting, but also a challenge, as the firm's own collection will often not have the industry resources needed.

The time available to complete the research is another challenge for law librarians. There are often court-imposed or client-imposed deadlines, and one of the most important questions in the reference interview process (discussed in Chapter 6) is 'when do you need this information?' It is unlikely the answer will be by the end of the week. It is more likely to be in the hour, now or yesterday! Because of these deadlines the library is often confronted by anxious and rather stressed clients. Frequent communication is needed to update library clients on progress and advise them of any delays. Law libraries are one of those rare sectors where the user often is prepared to pay whatever it costs in order to get the information as quickly as possible.

The hierarchical structure of the legal profession means that research tasks are usually delegated to juniors, therefore there can be several layers between the librarian and the person actually asking the question and directing the matter. In a law firm setting, a partner will be responsible for a matter, a senior associate may be acting on the matter, there will be lawyers and below that a graduate who is undertaking the research and who comes to the library for assistance. These layers pose several challenges for law librarians, who may have someone seeking assistance from the library who does not understand the question or problem they have been asked to research. Reference interview skills are vital to try to clarify the problem. Often what the clients initially ask for is not what they actually need. The first part of the interaction with the user may be helping them formulate what further information they need from their supervisors. With libraries conducting most of their work for the juniors, there is also a danger that the library's work is going unnoticed by senior bodies in the organisation or by those who control the 'purse strings'.

For information professionals working in law libraries it is critical to have strong analytical and evaluation skills. The assessment of the accuracy, currency and authoritativeness of a work is an important skill for all information professionals, but for law librarians it is crucial. Increasingly, primary materials such as cases and legislation are freely available from the internet, but these versions are not yet authoritative, and the legislation is not always up to date. In the near future the electronic versions of legislation will become the official versions, but for now it is necessary to refer to the paper, and preference is still given to those cases which have been reported in the authorised series of law reports.

Law libraries, more than any other type of special library, are stuck in the middle of the transition from print to online resources. The legal publishers have made great strides in providing their material in electronic format, but in many instances it is the hardcopy version of the material that is authorised for use in court, so for now law libraries are required to maintain the hardcopy versions but also feel pressured to provide electronic versions because of the advantages the online version offers in terms of access. This situation is putting a lot of stress on the acquisition budgets of law libraries.

The emphasis being placed on information literacy is another similarity across the law sector libraries. In law firms, courts and universities there is universal acknowledgment that more is required than an overview of the library catalogue, an introduction to the electronic resources and a tour of the library. The teaching function in law libraries has developed to a stage where many libraries have a structured information literacy program, which involves having staff whose responsibility it is to coordinate the training program and to develop training plans and guides. Training sessions have progressed from being product based, to covering legal research methodologies. In the university sector there is often a legal research subject or component in the law degree, and gradually legal research skills are being integrated into the curriculum. As outlined above, research is an important component of practicing law, and students who do not grasp basic research methodologies during the course of their studies will struggle when they enter the professional arena. The challenge for university law libraries is to make students see the relevance of developing legal research skills, when they are under pressure to complete essays and lists of recommended reading, which they often see as the quickest and easiest way to get the resources they need.

Court sittings and other commitments of the judiciary make scheduling training sessions difficult in the court sector. In law firms there is the pressure of the 'billable' hour and client deadlines that can make it difficult to attend training sessions. In this setting, 'time is money' and training sessions need to be directly related to the work of the participants for them to see the value in attending. Traditional group training sessions may not be appropriate, as senior legal professionals often will not want to demonstrate their lack of knowledge in a group setting. To combat this, libraries conduct one-on-one sessions. They also attend group meetings and look at how each interaction they have with their users can become a teaching opportunity.

Contributing to the development of the skills and expertise of legal professionals is one very clear way that law libraries demonstrate their worth to their organisation or business. As well as empowering the user, being so involved in teaching demonstrates the knowledge and expertise of the library staff. Rather than library use decreasing due to training, a professional information literacy program is excellent promotion for the research services that law libraries provide and is leading libraries to be more involved in 'high-end' research.

Parliamentary libraries

Australia's parliamentary libraries have changed significantly since the first parliamentary library was established in 1840 by the New South Wales Legislative Council. The original parliamentary libraries could best be described as gentlemen's libraries. Biskup (1994, p.280) describes them as little more than well-appointed clubs where members could read their favourite newspapers and find the occasional literary allusion or a quotation for their speeches.

The early parliamentary libraries were, however, developing some of the most remarkable collections in the country. Russell Cope (2000, p.321) explains that the large general collections developed by the early parliamentary libraries reflect the intellectual perspectives and curiosity of the times. He points out that it was the age of self-education, and the presence of good holdings of monographs, journals and newspapers from overseas and Australia provided members with ready access to information about world events and the British empire. At the federal level, the Australian Parliamentary Library was also the National Library for the first sixty years of its existence.

The development of these general collections has been criticised for as long as Australia has had parliamentary libraries. Biskup (1994, p.281) reports that Munn and Pitt (1935), McColvin (1947) and Tauber (1962) all questioned the purpose of Australia's parliamentary libraries, in particular whether they should be competing with other institutions in building general collections. There was some resistance to these comments at the time, but Australia's eight parliamentary libraries have indeed moved away from this collection era and now provide a wide ranging service for their clients that focuses on reference and research services. This change has largely been a result of the changing nature of Australian society. The institution of parliament is now operating in a very different world, and libraries have had to adapt to the new environment in which members operate, and to their different information requirements. Cope

(2000, p.314) notes that parliaments themselves have shown little commitment to the fine heritage collections that have been assembled.

For many years parliamentary libraries have had competing priorities of preservation of their unique collections and development of new information services. One of the challenges that many of the libraries have faced has been collection space. Some of Australia's parliamentary libraries are in spectacular buildings, but because of the heritage issues of the buildings they are restricted in what they can do with the space. The Victorian Library, for example, has floor to ceiling wooden shelving, with wooden ladders, but has removed the material from the top shelves for reasons of occupational health and safety. As a result of accommodation issues, some of the parliamentary libraries have been forced to cull their collections significantly, move material off site and transfer much of their nineteenth-century material to academic or state library collections. Other parliamentary libraries continue to maintain this collection role by being the legal deposit libraries for their state's publications.

Staffing numbers and the library structure of Australia's parliamentary libraries differ in each jurisdiction, but all exist to provide reference, research and information services to assist members in objective legislative decision making, and other electoral and parliamentary duties associated with representing their constituents. The libraries' biggest users tend to be the opposition members of parliament, because they are without the luxury of staff and information resources of the bureaucracy. Parliamentary libraries also provide library services to ministerial staff, past MPs and electoral offices. They receive enquiries from government departments, which have increased in those jurisdictions where there have been cutbacks to government libraries. Most parliamentary libraries do not provide services to the public, but they often receive calls from members of the public covering everything from contact details of MPs to people seeking assistance in finding the correct department in the government for their enquiry.

At first glance it looks as if parliamentary libraries have quite a distinct and easily defined client base. In reality they are dealing with people with diverse backgrounds in such areas as education level, information literacy and technology skills. A member of parliament may, for example, have a background in business, professional sport, farming or the bureaucracy. Not all members will have encountered such a specialised library service and may have little understanding of what the parliamentary library service can offer them. The libraries therefore put a lot of effort into developing induction programs which promote their services.

Parliamentary librarians working in the area of reference need to be able to work quickly, prioritise and cope well with pressure. They need to deliver their work within the constraints set by the deadlines of parliament. The library may receive an enquiry which would normally take half a day to research, for example, but instead it has to provide a response for a speech being presented in fifteen minutes. Parliamentary librarians also find themselves being called on to research across the broad range of topics covered by pubic policy. The days on which parliament meets, sitting days, are usually the most busy for reference staff, and sometimes they have to work long days and even into the night. The library remains staffed until parliament finishes sitting. So if parliament is debating a bill to 1.00 or 2.00 am, the library also remains open until this time.

In today's world the media play an important part in politics, and parliamentary libraries have developed specialised services to meet the needs of the members. One of the traditional services provided by the parliamentary libraries has been the clipping of newspaper articles. These indexed files continue to be extremely valuable as they date back to before the advent of media databases. Even with the provision of commercial media databases, the libraries continue their clipping service and have developed in-house databases of scanned newspaper articles. This clipping service is still undertaken because the commercial services are not comprehensive enough. Most of the commercial services are also text based and cannot demonstrate the size and location of the article in the newspaper, the size of the heading or any associated pictures. Unlike other special libraries, the parliamentary libraries are exempt from the copyright restrictions that would prevent other libraries creating these in-house databases. As well as covering the print media, the libraries also tape relevant radio and television programs.

An extra dimension to parliamentary libraries is the highly specialised research service they provide. This is quite separate from the reference service provided by librarians. The research service falls under the umbrella of the library but is staffed by non-librarians with subject experts such as academics, lawyers and statisticians. The Commonwealth Parliamentary Library first established a research service in 1966 to provide in-depth analysis and advice on legislation, policy and other federal issues. The Research Branch now has approximately eighty staff and is divided into the areas of economics; foreign affairs, defence and trade; laws and bills digest; politics and public administration; science, technology, environment and resources; social policy; and statistics and mapping. The branch prepares and releases a wide range of publications, such as the Bills digests, which provide an independent summary of the Bills, research briefs, research notes, chronologies and e-briefs, many of which are released to the public and made available on the parliament's web page (http://www.aph.gov.au/). The Research Branch also conducts specially commissioned research work. The state parliamentary libraries have also introduced research services, albeit on a much smaller scale.

Confidentiality is a crucial element of parliamentary librarianship. The library needs to be seen as providing a bi-partisan service, and parliamentary librarians have to put aside their own political ideologies to provide a truly independent service. This independence is something that over the years has been challenged. A recent controversial example was the Bills digest prepared by the Australian Parliamentary Library for the Medibank Private Sale Bill. The digest contradicted the legal advice that had been provided to the government and the government announced that the Parliamentary Library advice was wrong. Members of the Opposition, however, pounced on the advice with the Hon. Martin Ferguson stating in Hansard:

> I praise the library's courage in making this advice available. We must always defend the integrity and independence of the library. As far as I am concerned, that is a fundamental requirement of all members of this House, irrespective of their political persuasion. This advice clearly proves why the library is doing a great and valuable service for the Australian community (Commonwealth of Australia 2006).

The issue of which advice was correct may not have been resolved, but the situation is an example of how the work of parliamentary libraries contributes to objective legislative decision making and the parliamentary process.

Challenges for special libraries

Special libraries can be a dynamic environment in which to work, but, like many library sectors, special libraries are struggling to find their place, to establish their territory and define their services in a new information world. In an article about the closure of a large corporate library in Melbourne in the early 1990s, it was noted by Jill Nicholls (1992) that in a climate of unpredictable management decisions it was imperative that special librarians do not become complacent and assume that their services are recognised and indispensable.

The funding and resources afforded to a special library are often directly related to the success and financial position of its parent company or organisation. Many special libraries are a support service. They support the overall goals of the organisation and assist in providing employees/members with the information they need to complete their jobs or roles. From an accounting point of view, when it comes down to the bottom line, however, they are essentially an organisational expense, an overhead. Unfortunately, one of the first areas to be looked at when an organisation is not performing is the cost of its overheads.

Another challenge facing special libraries is the view that 'everything is on the internet, why do we need a library anymore?' This is actually a challenge for all library sectors, but more so for special libraries where the existence of a library is perhaps not as secure. As mentioned previously, libraries used to operate in a monopoly environment, but now there are other businesses and options for their clients. It is imperative, therefore, that special libraries demonstrate their worth. Glockner (2004) argues that special libraries and information services need to do this through accountability and accreditation and they should apply the following three levels of accountability:

- Fiscal – proving how we spend our budgets.

- Process – explaining why we bought certain resources for our libraries.

- Program – showing that those resources are used and useful to our clients.

Hendricks and Wooler (2006, p.14) maintain that being good at what one does and the services one provides is no longer good enough. They assert that very good information centres will be cut, and may be outsourced or 'off-shored', not because of their inability to provide good services, but because of their inability to demonstrate a return on investment (ROI) or provide evidence of the impact they make on their organisations.

Interestingly, there does not appear to be a universally accepted method for measuring value. Woldring (2001, p.294) provides a summary of the literature and methods for measuring the value of special libraries. He warns that special librarians currently hold the key to using the vast array of online databases, but this professional niche increasingly will be challenged by clients conducting searches themselves as end-users at their desks.

The next challenge for special libraries is to get management and their users to look outside the traditional view of what libraries and librarians can do. This involves promotion and marketing of the library services to demonstrate to potential clients 'what's in it' for them. Special libraries need to identify new opportunities and to continue to move away from the perception that they are the gatekeepers of information, looking instead to be partners with their clients. As long ago as 1989, Herbert White (p.24) argued that the profession of special librarianship was at a crossroads and that it was in danger of committing suicide. At that time he was calling for special librarians to remain professionals, rather than falling into the clerical trap and focusing on tasks that could easily be computerised. Today the profession faces another crossroads, but this time it needs to choose whether to remain a service provider or move to the role of consultant and advisor.

The question of where special libraries fit into the wider organisation and what role they will play is perhaps the biggest challenge. Libraries need to make strategic decisions about the areas of the business or organisation with which they wish to align themselves. Many special libraries received considerable kudos from their organisations for driving the implementation of intranets. Some lost this mantle as the intranets outgrew their resources and responsibility was given to others within the organisations. In some cases this is the right business decision for the library, since they focus their resources and efforts elsewhere, but in other organisations it may be important from a political point of view that the library remain involved. Special libraries have to be aware that the environment in which they are operating is constantly changing, and they need to make wise strategic decisions about the initiatives on which they are going to focus. For some organisations at the moment it may be knowledge management, for others, evidence-based research or perhaps web 2.0 applications.

Finally, there is the challenge for special librarians to step back and see themselves first and foremost as employees of the wider organisation and second as librarians. They must continue to look for ways in which the library and information service can assist the business or organisation achieve its goals and objectives.

Conclusion

In researching this chapter, it has been extremely difficult to obtain current statistics on the special library sector in Australia. The last directory of special libraries (1999) lists 1,125 special libraries but anecdotal evidence seems to indicate that a number of special libraries have downsized, faced restructures or closed in the last ten years. A number of high profile corporate and government libraries in particular did not make it through the 1990s.

So is the golden age of special libraries over? With the empowerment of end users, are special libraries on a downward spiral to insignificance? Talk of a downsize in the sector is contradicted by the number of special libraries listed in the Australian Libraries Gateway. There are 1,813 special libraries listed in the free web-based directory – this number includes art, corporate/business, cultural, defence, government, health/medical, law, local/family history, music, parliamentary, religious and science/technology libraries.

The numbers, however, give little insight into whether these libraries have experienced growth or downsizing as a result of developments in technology, the change in the way in which people search for and obtain their information, and the other challenges facing special libraries today.

It could be argued that to a certain extent all of the challenges and the competencies discussed in this chapter are relevant to all library sectors, not just special libraries. Meg Paul and Sandra Crabtree (1994, p.2) talk about the four constants faced by special librarians:

1. People want solutions to their problems, not the books journals and search results that contain the information. Information must be evaluated and packaged to this end.

2. The information provided by the library can make or break the host organization. By incorporating value added information and filtering out the irrelevant mass, the management should be able to make informed decisions that will play a significant role in the success of the organization.

3. The service provided must be as near to perfect as defined by the clients, and as efficient and cost effective as librarians can make it.

4. As the service provided improves, the demands the clients make on it will increase.

Special libraries have developed significantly since the creation of the Special Libraries Association in 1909. They have moved successfully from the collection era to an environment in which they are linking the library user with the right information at the right time. Rather than being gatekeepers to knowledge they are empowering users and providing them with the information edge. The next step for special libraries will be to invent themselves again to become more closely aligned to the industries or businesses in which they are operating and to look to developing partnerships, rather than just providing a service.

References

Abels, E, Jones, R, Latham, J, Magnoni D & Marshall, J 2003, 'Competencies for information professionals of the 21st century, http://www.sla.org/content/learn/comp2003/index.cfm

Bender, D 1998a, 'What's special about special libraries? – SLA and the continuous education challenge', *INSPEL*, vol.32, no.4, pp.197-204, http://www.ifla.org/VII/d2/inspel/98-4bend.pdf

Bender, D 1998b, 'What's special about special libraries?', *64th IFLA General Conference August 16-August 21, 1998*, http://www.ifla.org/IV/ifla64/134-88e.htm

Biskup, P 1994, 'Special libraries' in *Libraries in Australia*, Centre for Information Studies, Charles Sturt University, Wagga Wagga, NSW, pp.279-325.

Commonwealth of Australia 2006, *House of Representatives votes and proceedings Hansard, Wednesday, 1 November 2006*, http://parlinfoweb.aph.gov.au/piweb/Repository/Chamber/Hansardr/Linked/5102-1.PDF

Cook, C, Creyke, R, Geddes, R & Hamer, D 2005, *Laying down the law*, LexisNexis Butterworths, Chatswood, NSW.

Cope, R 2000, 'If special libraries are disappearing, why are parliamentary libraries surviving? Contradictory currents and changing perceptions', *The Australian Library Journal*, vol.49, no.4 pp.307-326.

Eames B, ed. 1999, *Directory of special libraries in Australia*, Australian Library and Information Association, Special Libraries Section, Kingston, ACT.

Glockner, B 2004, 'Accountability and accreditation for special libraries: It can be done!', *The Australian Library Journal,* vol.53, no.3, Aug, http://www.alia.org.au/publishing/alj/53.3/full.text/glockner.html

Hendricks, B & Wooler, I 2006, 'Establishing the return on investment for information and knowledge services', *Business Information Review*, SAGE Publications, London.

McColvin, L 1947, *Public libraries in Australia: Present conditions and future possibilities*, Melbourne University Press for ACER, Melbourne, Vic.

Munn, R & Pitt, E 1935, *Australian libraries*, Melbourne, Vic.

Nicholls, J, 1992, 'Closure of the BHP corporate library', *Vic Specials*, vol.9 no.4, Dec 1992, pp.8.

Paul, M & Crabtree S 1994, *Strategies for special libraries*, Freelance Library and Information Services, Camberwell, Vic.

Special Libraries Association 1910, 'First meeting of Special Libraries Association', *Special Libraries,* vol.1, no.1, p.4, http://www.sla.org/content/shop/speclibs.cfm#1910

Special Libraries Association 2003, *Competencies for information professionals of the 21st century*, rev. edn, http://www.sla.org/content/learn/comp2003/index.cfm

Tauber, MF 1962, *Resources of Australian libraries*, Australian Advisory Council on Bibliographical Services (AACOBS), Canberra, ACT.

White, H 1989, 'The "quiet revolution": A profession at the crossroads', *Special Libraries*, vol.80, no.1, Winter, pp.24-30, http://www.sla.org/speciallibraries/ISSN00386723V80N1.PDF

Woldring, E 2001 'Strategies to measure the value of special libraries', *Australian Law Librarian* vol.9, no.4, pp284-295.

CHAPTER 5
National, state and territory libraries: information for the nation

Roxanne Missingham and Jasmine Cameron

'It is the golden age in providing truly *national* access to our collections', according to the National Library of Australia's director general, Jan Fullerton (2005). Australians now have unrivalled access to library collections and services through their national, state and territory libraries, which provide services to people everywhere, supporting their study, research, work, business and leisure activities.

While the National Library has its origins in the Commonwealth Parliamentary Library, which was established in 1901, most state libraries emerged from the early public libraries. Other countries have state libraries, but generally these fulfil quite different roles from those in Australia. In the United States, for example, they are usually small libraries that serve the legislature primarily. The State Library of Victoria grew out of the first state-supported public reference library, the Melbourne Public Library, established in 1854, and the State Library of New South Wales evolved from the Free Public Library, Sydney, which was founded in 1869. Other libraries emerged over the following decades. Based in capital cities, these 'deposit libraries' offer extensive onsite services for the public, including access to more than eleven million collection items (Australian Bureau of Statistics 2005) and a vast array of digital resources. In 2003–2004 more than five million visits were made to the national, state and territory libraries. The deposit libraries also offer remote online access to a wide range of services enabling people living in rural and regional areas to take advantage of the important Australiana and many unique collections held by the national, state and territory libraries.

A major role of the deposit libraries is collecting and preserving Australia's documentary heritage. Under national, state and territory legislation, publishers are required to supply (deposit) a copy of their publications to the designated deposit library in that state or territory and to the National Library, and in some cases copies must be forwarded to other libraries as well. This ensures that Australia's research and creative output is available to all now and in the future. The national, state and territory libraries have a combined collection strength of more than twenty-five million items when Australian and overseas collections are taken into account. The collections include printed and online publications, pictures, maps, manuscripts, oral histories, sheet music and sound recordings. They form a significant information resource for the Australian community.

Another major role of the deposit libraries is providing leadership on key issues of importance at the national and state level respectively. A high level of cooperation exists among the libraries, in particular through the organisation National & State Libraries Australasia (NSLA).

National & State Libraries Australasia (NSLA)

The national, state and territory libraries collaborate on a wide range of services and projects in order to provide the Australian public with world-class access to information. Under the auspices of NSLA, the deposit libraries meet four times a year to develop policies, share information and agree on actions to achieve their strategic plan. The group adopted the name National & State Libraries Australasia in July 2006. Until then it had been called the Council of Australian State Libraries (CASL). The name was changed to more clearly represent the increase in membership since 2000 to include the national libraries of Australia and New Zealand.

Between meetings, activities are progressed through eleven working groups. In 2005, the National Library of New Zealand joined NSLA, after attending as an observer for several years. This broadening of the group enables Australian and New Zealand libraries to work on common issues more effectively. Recent collaborative activities include a major national travelling exhibition, National Treasures From Australia's Great Libraries, the NSLA consortium for purchasing electronic journals and the highly successful online chat reference service, AskNow! NSLA's key priorities are to:

1. Promote and advance the provision, awareness and use of library and information services by promoting the role of libraries in lifelong learning, particularly literacy; enhancing partnerships between the library, education and cultural sectors; demonstrating the value of libraries in the economic, social and intellectual development of the nation; and articulating the role and direction of libraries for community and government.
2. Strengthen the national information infrastructure and promote cross-sectoral collaboration to improve access to information services for Australians by enhancing access to selected Australian cultural collections, for example, Australian newspapers; extending the range of online information resources to the community through collaboration; promoting the use of open standards to improve access to information; and improving library services for indigenous people through the support of the National Policy Framework for Indigenous Library Services.
3. Represent member libraries in relevant matters of public interest by presenting a single voice to government and other relevant bodies.

For facts about the national, state and territory libraries see Appendix 1.

Collections: building and preserving

National, state and territory libraries have a legislated mandate to collect and preserve a comprehensive collection of Australian documentary resources. The National Library Act 1960 sets out the National Library's core functions, the first of which is 'to maintain and develop a national collection of library material, including a comprehensive collection of library material relating to Australia and the Australian people' (National Library Act 1960, section 2). To assist the National Library with its collecting function, the Copyright Act 1968 has a section on legal deposit which (as already noted) requires publishers of printed publications to give the Library a gratis copy for its collection. The state and territory libraries have similar state-based legislation. To fulfil its mandate, the National Library is committed to working with the state and territory libraries to ensure that 'a significant record of Australia and Australians is collected and safeguarded' (National Library of Australia 2006). While formal collecting agreements do not exist, there is an understanding among the deposit libraries that the National Library will leave some collecting areas to the state and territory libraries, for example, the publications of local associations and schools, and will not aim to collect as comprehensively in some other areas, such as state, regional and local government publications.

State library mandates are contained in state legislation, except for Western Australia where there is no legislation at present. The state library acts outline the role of the libraries in supporting their community and often contain provision for legal deposit. In South Australia, for example, the Library's role is:

> (a) to achieve and maintain a coordinated system of libraries and library services that adequately meets the needs of the whole community;
> (b) to promote and facilitate the establishment and maintenance of libraries and library services by councils and other appropriate bodies;
> (c) to promote a cooperative approach to the provision of library services;
> (d) to ensure that the community has available to it adequate research and information services providing access to library materials and information stored in libraries and other institutions both within and outside the State (Libraries Act 1982, section 7).

In the area of collecting original materials such as maps, manuscripts, pictures and the commissioning of oral history recordings, there is close cooperation among national, territory and state libraries. This cooperation is based on an understanding of the state, territory and national significance of people, places and events. Developing and preserving a national collection of documentary resources is a core function of the national, state and territory libraries and will continue to be a top priority for them in the twenty-first century.

The collections have developed in no small part due the acquisition by gift and purchase from the great collectors of the nineteenth and twentieth centuries. In Sydney, for instance, the Mitchell Library's manuscript and printed book collection is based on the collection of David Scott Mitchell (1836–1907), Australia's first significant collector of Australiana. Mitchell bequeathed more than 67,000 items to the State Library of New South Wales (at that time known as the Public Library of New South Wales) in 1907. The Dixson Library printed book collection of more than 20,000 printed items acquired by Sir William Dixson (1870–1952) was another very significant donation. The collection contains material relating to Australia, New Zealand and the Pacific with particular strengths in early navigation, geography, voyages of discovery and the spread of European settlement in the region. These two collections provide the basis for an outstanding historical collection for Australian research and scholarship.

In South Australia, John Andrew Tennant Mortlock (1894–1950), the eldest son of a wealthy pastoralist family, was a major benefactor. When he died in 1950 his estate was left jointly to his beneficiaries, the University of Adelaide and the Libraries Board of South Australia. His wife continued to support the State Library, annually donating children's books and providing funds that were used to purchase many rare books. The Mortlock Library of

South Australiana is named after these major donors. Collection strengths include rare books, children's literature, wine literature, shipping, maps, indigenous materials and family history.

Queensland has also benefited from the donation or purchase of the collections of individuals and corporations. The State Library of Queensland had its origins in the Brisbane Public Library, which was established in 1896 when the Queensland Government purchased the private collection of Mr Justice Harding. A century later, in 1988, James Hardie Industries Limited donated their library containing an extensive collection of Australian fine arts to the State Library of Queensland. The Australian Library of Art created from this donation includes books, exhibition catalogues, ephemera, posters and broadsides, manuscripts, artists' books and private press publications.

The State Library of Tasmania's WL Crowther Library recognises the donations of Sir William Crowther from 1964 to 1981. It is a rich collection of books, pamphlets, maps, manuscripts, photographs, works of art and museum objects, largely relating to Tasmania. The collection includes approximately 15,000 printed works, 4,000 photographs, 300 works of art and 400 objects. Subjects covered in the collection include whaling, the history of medicine, book-collecting and works printed in Pacific Island languages.

The State Library of Victoria's La Trobe collection encompasses a number of small collections focusing on Victoria and covering history, literature, culture, biography, travel and indigenous studies. The collection boasts 150,000 items published about or by Australians, with two special interest collections of theatre programmes and political ephemera.

In Western Australia, James Sykes Battye, Chief Librarian of the Victoria Public Library (later to become the State Library of Western Australia), began building a significant collection of Western Australian documentary heritage material in 1894. Battye is responsible for the acquisition of the *Pelsaert journal* and many other early newspapers, manuscripts and government records.

The National Library's Australiana collection has benefited from the acquisition of several major collections and significant individual items, many of which were purchased before the National Library had formally separated from the Commonwealth Parliamentary Library. The desire to build a national collection and to record and preserve the nation's documentary heritage was present very early on. In 1907, the speaker of the House of Representatives and chairman of the Library Committee, Sir Frederick Holder, eulogised about developing 'a great Public Library on the lines of the world-famous Library of Congress of Washington, such a library, indeed, as shall be worthy of the Australian nation' (Osborn & Osborn 1989, p.12).

The Petherick collection of Australian and Pacific material was acquired by the National Library in 1911. It consists of approximately 10,000 books, 6,500 pamphlets, maps, manuscripts and pictures. Sir John Ferguson's collection was acquired in stages from 1946 to 1969. An extraordinary collection, it contains more than 34,000 books, manuscripts and paintings and is the largest private collection in the Library's possession. Subjects covered include areas relating to Australia and the Pacific, such as sociology, publishing history, poetry and economics. The collection of Sir Rex de Charembac Nan Kivell which comprises more than 15,000 early maps, manuscripts, books, oil paintings, watercolours, prints and photographs relating to Australia, New Zealand and the Pacific was acquired by the Australian Government in two instalments in 1948 and 1962. Other items were acquired individually, the most famous being the purchase in

1923 of Captain James Cook's *Endeavour journal* (see http://www.nla.gov.au/pub/endeavour/index.html). It is significant that it was shortly after this purchase that the decision was made to adopt the title Commonwealth National Library.

In New Zealand, the National Library's collection had a similarly strong foundation of donations, in addition to an active acquisition program. The Alexander Turnbull collections commenced with a bequest from Alexander Horsburgh Turnbull in 1918. The Turnbull collection contains original material such as photographs, drawings and prints, oral histories, manuscripts and archives, and printed material – books, newspapers, maps, magazines and ephemera relating to New Zealand and the Pacific. It also contains the largest collection of early printed books in New Zealand, including early voyages, works relating to John Milton and the seventeenth century, and examples of fine printing from around the world.

Preservation of this vast array of material has always been an area of great strength and commitment for the deposit libraries. Each library routinely undertakes preservation work including rebinding, treatment of damaged materials and treatment of special format material such as maps and pictures. The National Library of Australia is committed to undertaking 'a leadership role in sharing our expertise' (National Library of Australia 2006) in preservation and it works with the NSLA libraries on a number of major preservation projects. Recent prominent examples of this are the National Plan for Newspapers (NPLAN 2005) and the Australian Network for Information on Cellulose Acetate (ANICA 2005) – the management of collections on cellulose acetate, which are under threat of deterioration from vinegar syndrome.

Digital collecting and preservation

The emergence of information resources in digital format has presented the deposit libraries with a significant new collecting and preservation challenge. The internet has provided governments, researchers, businesses, special interest and community groups, and indeed anyone with an interest in creating and disseminating information, with a cheap and effective means of publishing. Collecting and preserving resources in digital format, however, is vastly more complex and costly than managing the equivalent collections in print (Sweeney 2001).

The National Library of Australia was one of the first national libraries to commence collecting digital resources and remains a leader in this field. In 1995, the National Library established Pandora: Australia's online web archive. It supports the collaborative collecting of selected Australian digital resources and the provision of access to those resources. The state and territory libraries are partners in this venture. Pandora hosts a significant collection of Australian electronic journals and selected websites documenting topical subjects such as Australian intervention in East Timor and the 2004 Asian Tsunami. In 2005, the archive held copies of more than 10,000 Australian digital resources. More than 20 per cent of these resources no longer exist in the public domain of the internet. The State Library of Tasmania manages its own digital archive known as Our Digital Island, but it works closely with the National Library on many aspects of digital collecting and preservation.

Since 1998, the National Library, in partnership with the National Film and Sound Archive, has been actively seeking the extension of legal deposit to cover Australian digital resources. While this is still being pursued at the national level, several state and territory libraries have successfully sought amendments to their legislation and instructions/guidelines for the state and territory public sector. The National Library believes that the fundamental principles and objectives that underpin traditional legal deposit apply equally to digital resources and will continue to seek a legal underpinning of the Library's digital collecting role (Gatenby 2002).

In 2005, the National Library sought to extend its collecting of digital resources through its first 'whole-of-domain' harvest of Australian websites. More than 185 million unique documents were collected and archived from 811,000 sites, yielding 6.69 terabytes of content. The National Library aims to supplement the selective collecting undertaken for Pandora with periodic snapshots of the Australian internet domain (Koerbin 2005).

As it develops new strategies and directions for the twenty-first century, the National Library recognises the importance of working collaboratively, not only across the Australian library sector, but across the cultural and collecting sectors in general, and with other government agencies, publishers, academics and creators. The concept of the distributed national collection has assumed renewed relevance in the digital age, and the National Library is seeking new partners in recognition of the fact that in a networked digital environment many resources that once would have been available through libraries are now available via other organisations. Many Australian Government agencies and other institutions are investing heavily in the creation of digital information resources and information services based on these resources. To bring these groups together, the National Library has initiated a National Coalition on Maintaining Access to Australia's Digital Information Resources. The National Library of Australia, National Archives of Australia, the Australian Government Information Management Office, Australian Bureau of Statistics and Geoscience Australia are the initial members of the consortium, the aim of which is to develop a whole-of-government response to managing digital resources and to stimulate community advocacy of the case for managing and sustaining digital collections for the benefit of all Australians.

Access to collections and information services

National, state and territory libraries provide extensive access to collections and services through their websites. Libraries provide access through their catalogues and other resource discovery services to material in their physical collections and digital resources including digitised copies of collection material.

Since 2000, following user feedback on its website and other online services, the National Library has been developing a new user-centred service model. This is a fundamental shift in direction away from services that traditionally have been developed by librarians for library staff and experienced researchers (Missingham 2004). Significant barriers to access were identified during the evaluation in 2000, including the fact that users did not understand the distinction between the website and the catalogue when searching for information and were confused by many different services whose names did not reveal to the user what the service was offering. The National Library's website has evolved over time from a place where users find information about the Library to a primary means of online service delivery. An opportunity to improve service to users came in 2002 when the National Library commenced a project to replace its integrated library management system, allowing significant improvements and flexibility in delivering the online public access catalogue. The redesign of the website and catalogue was undertaken holistically and features a 'one-search' option which allows users to search across the catalogue, all web information pages and the other resource discovery services provided via the website. It also includes new service delivery options such as a remote access online book request facility and a service called Copies Direct which provides a single online point for ordering copies of items held in the National Library's collection.

The need to increase the effectiveness of resource discovery and delivery services for the public is also being addressed by NSLA through its Information Access Plan. The aim of the plan is to improve public access to information resources by simplifying service interfaces and integrating searches for resources where possible. The public library sector is integral to the success of the Information Access Plan and NSLA is working closely with public libraries to develop a workable and practical application of the plan. Initially, work is concentrating on areas where some immediate improvement to existing services can be made, for example, streamlining access to the indexes and databases created by NSLA libraries, and developing a single core set of internet subject guides. The National Library is taking the lead on the NSLA Information Access Plan initiative because it believes that if libraries do not make their services more user friendly and accessible then people increasingly will seek their information resources elsewhere. One of the more ambitious aspects of the plan involves the NSLA libraries investigating how they can expose Libraries Australia to their user community. The National Library is assisting with this by examining how its own users might benefit if it were to make the Australian National Bibliographic Database within the Libraries Australia service the primary search target for users instead of the Library's own online public access catalogue. The importance of moving forward in this way has been clearly articulated for the library sector by Jan Fullerton, Director General, National Library of Australia.

> As a sector we need to look at the services we are providing to our users from the user perspective. We must move away from systems and services that can be used comfortably by library staff but that leave our users bamboozled and ultimately dependent on the mediation of library staff to find and get information resources (Fullerton 2003).

Reference services increasingly are being provided online. Such services have been offered by the national and state libraries since the mid 1990s, primarily through email and web forms. In 2002, NSLA launched a collaborative virtual reference service, AskNow! Answers are provided immediately by operators using chat software and searching the internet and library resources. All state and territory libraries, the national libraries of Australia, New Zealand and Singapore and fifteen public libraries collaborate to resource the service. The service is available from Monday to Friday, 9am to 7pm Australian Eastern Standard Time, with three operators (seats) answering questions simultaneously. More than 100,000 questions had been answered by August 2005, reaching those in metropolitan areas (60 per cent) and rural areas (40 per cent).

In addition to offering reference services online, deposit libraries are creating new spaces on the web for individuals to share information and create communities of interest. The State Library of Victoria's Centre for Youth Literature launched a youth literature blog in May 2005, Read Alert (http://www.slv.vic.gov.au/about/centreforyouthliterature/youthlit.html). It creates a lively interactive space where people can keep up to date with the latest information, current thinking and issues in youth literature.

Australia's national infrastructure

The National Library plays a major role in the development of Australia's national information infrastructure. The work undertaken by the National Library in this area is fundamental to the achievement of the Library's key goal 'to provide rapid and easy access to the wealth of information resources that reside in libraries and other cultural institutions – and to break down the barriers that work against this' (National Library of Australia 2006). In pursuing this goal, the National Library has extended the concept of resource sharing and collaboration beyond the library sector to embrace a broad range of Australian cultural and collecting institutions. The National Library is now extending its services directly to individuals in recognition of the growing preference of many Australians using the internet for unmediated access to information resources. Infrastructure developments that support a high degree of access to national, state and territory library collections include Libraries Australia and PictureAustralia.

Libraries Australia: national access to forty million resources

The National Library provides access to the nation's library collections through Libraries Australia, which replaced the Kinetica service in December 2005. Australian libraries have a long tradition of sharing their collections for the benefit of their users and Libraries Australia is the fundamental building block for resource sharing and collaboration among Australian libraries (Boston et al. 2005). It is an essential tool for the Australian library sector and supports resource discovery; cataloguing, through supply of records for overseas and Australian resources; and an online interlibrary loan system. In spite of the increasing number of resources available in digital format, a significant proportion of the collections of the deposit libraries and many other Australian libraries will continue to exist in physical form (Pearce & Gatenby 2005). Libraries Australia provides a simple, free search interface to forty million resources held by 1,100 Australian libraries. It is one of the most significant research tools available to Australian researchers and has been designed for ease of use by individuals who are accustomed to using search engines for resource discovery. The service offers searching across twelve databases, including the Australian National Bibliographic Database (ANBD). Records of catalogued resources held in the national, state and public library collections are held on the ANBD and are accessible through Libraries Australia.

In addition to providing a simple federated search facility, the National Library aims to provide users with the most direct form of access possible to the information resources they find through Libraries Australia. Although considerable work remains to be done in this area, Libraries Australia is providing users with direct online access to increasing numbers of digital resources. It also provides access to a range of options that allow users to seek a copy of other resources through the National Library's Copies Direct service, through standard inter-library loan or from online bookshops. And, where technically possible, users are alerted to resources held within their own local library. The most significant achievement, however, is the provision of a free search facility that provides all Australians with access to the combined collections of the Australian library sector and other collecting institutions such as that of the National Film and Sound Archive. The importance of free public access to Libraries Australia was acknowledged as one of the key recommendations of *Libraries in the online environment*, the report tabled in 2003 by the Senate Environment, Communications, Information Technology and the Arts References Committee.

PictureAustralia

PictureAustralia is a digital image service provided by the National Library that enables the digitised images of cultural institutions to be searched simultaneously. With more than 1.2 million images, the service commenced in 1998 as a pilot project called ImageSearch, involving the Australian War Memorial, the National Library of Australia and the state libraries of New South Wales, Tasmania and Victoria. Metadata are collected regularly and shared through a central repository. (Metadata are a major topic in Chapter 9.) All state and territory libraries now participate in the service and are experiencing significant growth in the use of their digital images as a consequence.

In 2006, PictureAustralia launched a new collaboration with Flickr, a popular digital image sharing space managed by Yahoo! The partnership enables individuals to contribute images to PictureAustralia by placing them in Flickr under two categories: 'PictureAustralia: Australia Day' and 'PictureAustralia: People, Places and Events'. The addition of photos from Flickr enhances the value of PictureAustralia to researchers and the general public by significantly expanding the number of contemporary images available through the service.

Other collaborative resource discovery services

Access to resources in other subjects and formats is similarly available through collaborative online resource discovery services. MusicAustralia, launched in early 2005, has enjoyed considerable success in providing access to online and print music resources held in the national, state and territory library collections. Over 1.3 million page views were recorded in the first quarter of its release, from March to June 2005. The State Library of Queensland has also developed its own state-based version of the service, Music Queensland. In partnership with the Queensland Conservatorium of Music, the State Library of Queensland is recording versions of digitised sheet music which users can listen to online.

Relationship with public libraries

State and territory libraries also support access to information and collections for residents of their states through their support for the public library network, as demonstrated already in Chris Jones' short summary in Chapter 1. Because state libraries are funded by state governments, the interconnection with public libraries is a critical part of providing effective library services to the public in each state. The National Library does not usually have a direct relationship with public libraries, but is committed through its work with NSLA to continually improving the public's access to information through the public library sector.

In Tasmania and the Northern Territory, public libraries are integrated with the state and territory systems. In the Northern Territory, public library services are delivered in partnership with the Department of Education, Employment and Training (DEET), communities and local government. The Northern Territory Library provides support for professional development of staff in public libraries and directly manages two joint-use libraries, Taminmin Community Library at Humpty Doo and Nhulunbuy Community Library. It also provides services to remote communities through a series of libraries and knowledge centres. The State Library of Tasmania delivers services through a network of libraries including forty-eight public libraries, the State Reference Service and the Heritage Collections. This model enables the public to access significant collections through integrated resource discovery services and state-wide subscriptions to electronic resources.

In other states, public libraries are supported through a range of programs including grants, circulating book collections, purchasing and training and development programs. The State Library of Western Australia supports a vast network of 239 public libraries spread across the state. It provides public libraries with collections of catalogued books and other materials. It also facilitates the provision of a wide range of information services to the people of Western Australia through the state-wide network of public libraries managed by local government. This gives people in remote locations access to regularly changing library resources and to online resources.

In South Australia, the State Library supports public libraries through Public Library Services, previously known as the Public Library Automated Information Network. It provides support for selection, acquisition, cataloguing and purchase of electronic resources, and runs a state-based catalogue, among other services. Major successful collaborative projects with public libraries in recent years include the '@yourlibrary' promotion, the Big Book Club and the Little Big Book Club (see http://www.thebigbookclub.com.au/).

The State Library of New South Wales provides support through Public Library Services with an advisory service on all aspects of public library provision for state and local governments. Subsidies and library development grants are also available for public libraries. Quality research and evaluation occurs through the State Library's Public Library Network Research Program, established in July 2002 to inform the promotion, planning, development and review of the NSW Public Library Network. Recent research projects include investigating the contribution public libraries make to sustainable communities and providing a means of quantifying that contribution; an assessment of the role public libraries play in supporting egovernment initiatives and a guide for public library buildings in New South Wales.

Relationships between Victoria's forty-three public library services and the Library Board of Victoria and the State Library of Victoria reached a milestone with agreement on a new framework in 2004. It recognises commitment to delivering information services to the whole Victorian community. It proposes a new focus for collaboration in order to achieve increased community and government understanding of and engagement with libraries and greater efficiency and effectiveness of library services. The first phase will focus on the funds allocated to the Statewide Public Library Development Projects, the resources of the Public Libraries Unit and further development of Victoria's Virtual Library.

More than 330 Queensland public libraries are supported by the State Library through collection support, planning and specialist services including Community Services, Multicultural Services, Readers Services, Interlibrary Loans, Indigenous Services, Young People's Services, Local Studies, Family History, Mobile Libraries and Training. The State Library leads and facilitates the Smart Library Network, including the development and dissemination of models of best practice.

Development of closer relationships with public libraries, particularly through activities focused on creating a greater public awareness of libraries, such as the '@ your library' campaign, is a growing trend. The framework adopted in Victoria provides a basis for extending access to services and creating new funding opportunities and is a model for the way forward for other state libraries.

Development of digital collections for national access

The world wide web and other developments in technology have provided libraries with a highly effective mechanism for overcoming the barriers of distance that have constrained national access to its vast collections. This has been assisted by the fact that Australians have rapidly adopted the internet and other new technologies (Australian Bureau of Statistics 2003). In this environment, one of the most effective strategies to provide users with simple, direct and unmediated access to information is the provision of information resources in digital form. To support this, the national, state and territory libraries all have digitisation programs in place.

Creating digital versions of resources in the National Library's original Australian collections is an important way of improving national access to the collections and meeting the growing demand for access to online resources. In May 2005, the number of items digitised in the National Library's collection reached 100,000. The Library is responding to user demand for increased access to digital resources by seeking to supplement its selective digitisation of original resources with large-scale digitisation projects encompassing resources such as out-of-copyright Australian newspapers and journals.

The State Library of New South Wales has launched a major digitisation program with their 'atmitchell.com' initiative (http://www.atmitchell.com/). The site won the Standard of Excellence, Government Category in the 2005 International Web Awards. It provides access to digitised collection material and interpretive content for educational use. Atmitchell.com builds on an already extensive image digitisation program that encompasses thousands of early photographs, manuscripts and maps.

The State Library of Victoria's 'slv21.com' also demonstrates the move to a service model based on access to digital information. The new model enables all users freely to access information, increasingly in digital format, when and where they want it. It aims to open up access to collections, digitise resources and provide a new range of interpretative materials. Connections with educational environments, Years 6-12 and tertiary, enable the libraries to make a significant contribution to learning. The development is also underpinned by new financial models – offering opportunities to interact with other government organisations, donors and commercial organisations.

Supporting research at the national level

National, state and territory libraries make a significant contribution to the provision of services and infrastructure to support research and scholarship in Australia. The national and state libraries are major research libraries in their own right and they have a vested interest in working with the research sector on infrastructure projects that will allow the Australian public to find and use Australia's research output. The National Library's role in this area has been recognised by membership of the Australian Research Information Infrastructure Committee, which advises the Minister for Science, Education and Training on the medium term infrastructure needs of the research sector. The change brought about by documenting research and scholarship in the digital environment has created important strategic issues for research libraries and has led to the establishment within universities of institutional repositories as the means for long-term management of research output in digital form (Cathro 2005).

The National Library's role in three major infrastructure projects funded by the Department of Education, Science and Training (DEST) as part of the Government's Backing Australia's Ability program is an example of its support for the research sector in areas where Library staff can offer significant professional expertise. In 2005–2006, the National Library participated in the ARROW project (Australian Research Repositories Online to the World), led by Monash University, testing software for institutional repositories and developing a federated search service (Campbell 2005); the APSR project (Australian Partnership for Sustainable Repositories), led by the Australian National University Centre for Cross Cultural Research (2004), supporting long-term sustainability of research output in digital form, including research datasets; and the MAMS project (Meta Access Management Systems), led by Macquarie University, which is developing a new conceptual architecture capable of supporting multiple, independent models for the authentication and authorisation of users accessing institutional and other repositories.

National, state and territory libraries are also involved with a wide range of activities supporting the creation of research. Some are funded by the Australian Research Council, for example, the State Library of New South Wales is a partner in the Dictionary of Sydney project which will develop digital multimedia resources about Sydney. The State Library of Western Australian has been a partner in the research project on the East Perth Power Station and the Electrification of Western Australia, creating scholarly outputs in print and digital form of historic heritage interpretation. In Victoria, the project Copyright and Cultural Institutions: Digitising Collections in Public Museums, Galleries and Libraries has been developing guidelines for cultural institutions. Primarily funded by the Australian Research Council, six cultural institutions, including the State Library of Victoria, have contributed to the project. In 2006, the National Library was a partner in the Ballets Russes and Australian Dictionary of Biography projects.

Support for scholarship also occurs through fellowships and awards. The National Library offers Harold White Fellowships for scholars and writers using the collection – covering a wide range of subject areas and resource materials. In addition, the McCann Summer Scholarships in Australian History and Literature support younger scholars undertaking research in Australian history and literature, and the National Library of Australia Folk Festival Fellowship funds a folk performer to research original source materials in the National Library folklore archives. State libraries in New South Wales and Victoria also fund research through fellowships such as the CH Currey Memorial Fellowship (for the writing of Australian history from original sources, preferably using the State Library of New South Wales' resources), the Nancy Keesing Fellowship (for research into aspects of Australian life and culture using the resources of the State Library of New South Wales), the National Biography Award (for a published work of biographical or autobiographical writing) and Creative Fellowships (for original artistic work using the resources of the State Library of Victoria).

National planning: Peak Bodies Forum and a national agenda

Coordination of all Australian library representative bodies is an activity that has recently moved to a more formal phase. The National Library has a long history of developing strategic alliances and partnerships for the benefit of the Australian library sector. A number of strong sectoral bodies exist that represent the interests of particular library sectors such as schools, universities, government, law, health and public libraries. The National Library brings these groups together annually at the Peak Bodies Forum to identify significant issues facing the Australian library sector. The aim of the forum is to develop a national plan of action to address those issues that representatives of the Australian library sector determine can be successfully managed at the national level.

Perhaps the most significant document on library issues and services in recent years is the October 2003 report of the Senate Environment, Communications, Information Technology and the Arts References Committee, *Libraries in the online environment*. The report contains eleven recommendations which reflect the key issues that emerged during the enquiry. Members of the community, libraries and associations were active in outlining major issues of access, funding and services.

The Australian Government responded to the report in June 2004. There was strong support for the principles espoused in the report relating to 'national information strategies'. The National Library in collaboration with the Australian library sector has made good progress on achieving the key recommendations. In particular, the National Library has revised its business model for Libraries Australia and now provides a free search interface for users to access through their local libraries or directly from their home, work or place of study; discussions have been held with the Australian Government Information Management Office about increasing access to government publications – a seminar, Digital Amnesia, was held in April 2005 highlighting issues of long-term access to government online publications and information services; and the Library hosted two national forums on site licensing (8 December 2004 and 12 October 2005) which has resulted in an agreement between peak library bodies and existing consortia to proceed with developing a national licence for a core set of databases. A national survey has been conducted to determine the most useful set of products for a national licence. Future work is planned on governance, costing and acquisition of products.

Delivering services to users in the twenty-first century

At the launch of the free public interface to Libraries Australia in February 2006, Jan Fullerton, director general, National Library of Australia encapsulated service delivery to users in the twenty-first century when she said that 'Libraries Australia puts information into the users' space rather than the user having to come into the libraries' space.' The national, state and territory libraries will continue to work together to make their services and collections central to all Australians seeking information. However, the NSLA libraries will work increasingly with new partners both within and beyond the library sector in order to exploit new technologies and infrastructure that will enhance the visibility and accessibility of their vast resources. Anne-Marie Schwirtlich, chief executive officer and state librarian, State Library of Victoria, has posed the question 'Why use the library when I could Google?' (State Library of Victoria 2004) The response of the NSLA libraries in the twenty-first century is to ensure that Australians are in fact finding and using library resources when they 'google'. It is important that NSLA libraries continue to develop services that connect their collections and services directly with users, and provide innovative spaces for individuals and communities of interest to interact with them.

One of the major areas of activity for state and territory libraries for the future is to build on activities addressing the information needs of indigenous Australians. In 2004, the State Library of New South Wales held a National Colloquium on Libraries and Indigenous Knowledge. Participants identified the key issues associated with understanding the intersection of indigenous and western knowledge systems. A national strategy to deal with the issues is being developed. Both the Northern Territory and Queensland have developed centres in indigenous communities to assist with knowledge development and further activities to assist community knowledge recording and sharing are planned, involving community consultation, volunteers and education agencies.

The national, state and territory libraries provide services to all Australians regardless of their location. The highly collaborative approach taken by the NSLA libraries provides a sound basis for continued success in the twenty-first century.

References

Australian Bureau of Statistics (ABS) 2003, *Measures of a knowledge based economy and society: Australia information and communications technology indicators*, ABS, Canberra, ACT.

Australian Bureau of Statistics (ABS) 2005, *Public libraries, Australia*, cat no. 8561.0, ABS, Canberra, ACT, http://www.abs.gov.au/ausstats/abs@.nsf/Lookup/08CDEAE368A2A931CA256A78 0001D4DB

Australian National University Centre for Cross Cultural Research 2004, *South Seas project*, http://southseas.nla.gov.au/

Australian Network for Information on Cellulose Acetate (ANICA) 2005, http://www.nla.gov.au/anica/about-anica.html

Boston, T, Rajapatirana, B & Missingham, R 2005, 'Libraries Australia: Simplifying the search experience', http://www.nla.gov.au/nla/staffpaper/2005/boston1.html

Campbell, D 2005, 'Public funding, public knowledge, public access', http://www.nla.gov.au/pub/gateways/archive/76/Campbell-ArrowProject.html

Cathro, W 2005, 'Submission to the National Collaborative Research Infrastructure Strategy', http://www.dest.gov.au/.../key_issues/ncris/documents/172_national_library_of_australia_rtf.htm

Fullerton, J 2003, 'Opening address', *National Resource Sharing Forum*, 11 November 2003, Canberra, ACT.

Gatenby, P 2002, 'Legal deposit, electronic publications and digital archiving: The National Library of Australia's experience', http://www.nla.gov.au/nla/staffpaper/2002/gatenby1.html

Koerbin, P 2005, *Report on the crawl and harvest of the whole Australian web undertaken during June and July 2005*, http://pandora.nla.gov.au/documents/domain_harvest_report_public.pdf

Libraries Act 1982 (South Australia), http://www.austlii.edu.au/au/legis/sa/consol_act/la1982105/

Missingham, R 2004, 'A new strategic direction for the National Library of Australia', http://www.nla.gov.au/nla/staffpaper/2004/missingham3.html

National Library Act 1960, http://scaletext.law.gov.au/html/pasteact/1/761/top.htm

National Library of Australia 2006, *Directions for 2006–2008*, http://www.nla.gov.au/library/directions.html

NPLAN (National Plan for Newspapers) 2005, http://www.nla.gov.au/preserve/nplan.html

Osborn, A & Osborn, M 1989, *The Commonwealth Parliamentary Library, 1901–27 and the origins of the National Library of Australia*, Department of the Parliamentary Library, in association with the National Library of Australia, Canberra, ACT.

Pearce, J & Gatenby, J 2005, 'New frameworks for resource discovery', http://www.nla.gov.au/nla/staffpaper/2005/pearce.html

Senate Environment, Communications, Information Technology and the Arts References Committee 2003, *Libraries in the online environment*, http://www.aph.gov.au/Senate/committee/ecita_ctte/online_libraries/report/index.htm

State Library of Victoria 2004, *Framework for collaborative action*, http://www.slv.vic.gov.au/pdfs/aboutus/lbv_vpln.pdf

Sweeney, J 2001, 'Cost/performance comparison of print vs. licensed electronic journal titles in UC Davis Libraries', paper presented to the *4th Northumbria International Conference on Performance Measurement in Libraries & Information Services*, http://www.arl.org/stats/north/powerpoints/sweeney.ppt

PART 2:

Library and information services in the twenty-first century

PART 2.
Library and information services in the twenty-first century

CHAPTER 6
Creating desire: bringing the library client and the librarian together

John Mills

Without users there is little point in libraries providing access to their collections, and now more than ever it is vital that users are encouraged and attracted to use library services. At the centre of library service is the interaction that takes place between the user and the librarian in order to answer a question and/or solve an information need. This interaction may be called a meeting, interchange, or transaction but the most commonly used term for it is the reference interview. This interview can take many forms and be of variable length; it may be a series of questions and answers to solve an information need, in other words what an individual wants to know, or a simple answer to one question. The reference interview is a two-way process in the sense that it should reveal what the user wants both to the librarian and to the user. Theoretically, every interchange between the library staff and a user that relates to solving an information need could be called a 'reference interview'.

Ross (2003, p.38) calls the reference interview:

> A creative, problem-solving process that is collaborative … A well-conducted reference interview usually is a very short exchange. The librarian may start with an acknowledgement ('Health information, uh-huh.') followed by one or two strategic open questions ('What particular aspect of health information are you interested in?' or 'What would you like to find out?'). And of course a lot of hard listening. But through the questions they answer during this brief process, people are able to clarify in their own minds what their question really is.

Historically, the reference interview has often been the term that refers to the face-to-face interview between the user and the librarian rather than the evolving online interview from computer to computer, although as Ross (2003, p.38) says: 'Few library users, even experienced ones, have ever heard of the reference interview or know that they are being interviewed.' Yet the online interview is becoming more common. Users are 'gradually becoming more independent in their information-seeking behaviour as internet access becomes more widespread, resources are increasingly available in electronic format, and search engines make information easier to locate' (Boyd 2005, p.234). Nonetheless, most of the characteristics of the 'traditional' face-to-face interview are also relevant in these other forms, such as the telephone, with its emphasis on listening and using tone and positive questioning to make the user feel at ease, and the more remote, impersonal chat or email reference interview. Each form requires attention on the part of the librarian to really get to the core of the user's information need.

Information seekers and their information needs

In the literature on library and information management, the users of libraries are often portrayed as information seekers and the information they are seeking may be anything from advice on a good crime novel to read to questions on how to operate library systems and computers, use the children's services, browse the shelves or the web, or read the newspapers or journals. Not all users are seeking help to find information, however, and not all need to ask library staff for assistance. Self service has become much more common and it is often the case that the only staff member the user may see is the one who checks out library materials for borrowing (although there are now a number of self-checking machines available in libraries, further reducing the need to talk to or use library staff members). The increasing use of the internet, to access library collections and to ask librarians questions via email, for example, has also expanded the options for information seeking without a face-to-face encounter with library staff. It could be asked whether the librarian today has a continuing role in dealing with users face to face. The short answer is yes, and this changing role for the librarian is explored below.

The information seeker – using the broad definition of information seeking, according to which information is everything the library client considers it to be – is guided by a number of principles. These can be identified as:

- Information needs arise from the help seeker's situation.
- The decision to seek help or not to seek help is affected by many factors.
- People tend to seek information that is most accessible.
- People tend to first seek help or information from interpersonal sources, especially from people like themselves.
- Information seekers expect emotional support.
- People follow habitual patterns in seeking information (Harris & Dewdney 1994, pp.20-27).

These principles can also be used to provide guidance as to how the information professional or librarian can best help the information seeker. Some understanding of users and their information-seeking habits can provide a template for ways to achieve successful librarian–user interaction.

Information needs and the Information seeker's situation

Depending on the needs of the information (or help) seeker, the means chosen to answer a question or fulfil the requirements of an information need might be an information source or sources, or it might be instruction or education in operating library systems such as databases or catalogues.

Factors affecting the decision whether or not to seek help

Not all information needs are articulated as questions to a librarian or asked of a system such as an online catalogue or the world wide web. Answers to many information needs are found without recourse to formal help organisations such as libraries. Users can be motivated or, indeed, demotivated to ask librarians for assistance. These reasons may include any or some of the following:

- Attitudes, feelings, beliefs about the type of assistance the librarian or library can provide.

- Attitudes, feelings, beliefs about the librarian or library. Past experience in using library services may have not been successful and people tend to use the most successful experiences as guidance for current actions.

- The library services are difficult to access – this may involve physical travel to the library or require a user to negotiate online access.

The approach used by a library or the image presented by a website can act as a key motivator as to whether the users go ahead and ask their questions.

Seeking of information that is most accessible

Harris and Dewdney (1994, p.22) suggest:

> Given a choice, people tend to prefer to find a solution easily, without a great expenditure of time or effort and without loss of self-esteem or other emotional costs. This might explain, then, why people sometimes accept information from more convenient, although possibly less reliable, sources, and why they may abandon the search if it becomes too costly in terms of time or trouble.

Relevant to seeking solutions from librarians are the often quoted words of Mooers (1960) who said that 'An information retrieval system [the catalogue, for example] will tend not to be used whenever it is more painful and troublesome for a customer to have information than for him not to have it.' Adding to this law, Austin (2001, p.609) proposed two additional laws relating to information access. These focus on the ease of access of the information retrieval system and are stated as:

> In an environment in which it is absolutely critical for a customer to have information, an IR system, no matter how poorly designed, will tend to be used ... [and] In an environment in which the trouble of having information vs that of not having it are fairly evenly balanced, system design and performance tend to be the deciding factors in whether or not an IR system will be used.

The link between information retrieval (IR) systems and the user is the librarian – that part of the reference interview instructing users how to use library systems is important. The librarian can only provide the link if these systems are seen as accessible and available.

The information seeker's preference for interpersonal sources

Libraries are not necessarily the first choice to find solutions to information needs or the questions that come out of them. For academic staff in the higher education sector the colleague in the room next door is often the first choice and for school children it may be an older brother or sister or a parent or friend. People prefer personal sources of information for a variety of reasons, as Grosser (1989, pp.18-21) suggests:

- A natural human need for social interaction, for developing meaningful relationships with others.

- A desire to establish or promote a conducive and mutually supportive working climate, to nurture personal links through frequent interaction.

- Laziness: when it seems easier to call out and ask someone rather than spend time and effort locating the answer personally.

- The quickest means of procuring the desired information.

- The most efficient means of procuring the desired information, avoiding problems of information overload required in the process of identifying, sifting and evaluating information sources.

- Expert advice from someone who is more familiar with the area than you are.

- They may provide more up to date information than is available in physical sources.

- They add value to information, interpret its meaning and significance in a particular context.

Information seekers and the need for emotional support

People often want to feel that the person to whom they are asking questions is interested in answering their question and even interested in their question. It may well be difficult to remain interested in all questions asked, but easier to remain interested in the person asking the question. An individual's self-esteem can be affected if they feel incompetent in undertaking a task or action, or if they fear looking incompetent, especially if the assistance of another person such as a librarian is needed. Few people want to be perceived as incompetent in seeking assistance. Many students and adults have reported this concern, and the term 'library anxiety' is one that has received increasing attention in recent years.

People follow habitual patterns in seeking information

It is often easier to follow the most successful path for seeking solutions to information needs than to try new paths. Prior experience is a major determinant of the action people take.

Motivating the information seeker

Choosing the source

In order to take the first step in information-seeking behaviour, the client needs to be motivated to choose the library and/or librarian as an information source. Motivation provides the driving force for behaviour, and motivators or demotivators can be considered the positive and negative aspects of this force. It is not enough for librarians, except perhaps those working in educational institutions, to be confident that because they have electronic access to vast amounts of information clients will choose them as an information source. Clients need to be motivated to use library staff and through them the resources to which libraries provide access.

One does not have to look far in the literature on motivation in psychology or social psychology to see that the whole area of motivation is complex, diverse and representative of many viewpoints, and that it is extremely relevant in the library setting. According to Zimbardo, 'Psychologists have advanced many different theoretical views to understand the nature of motivated behavior, but none have been completely satisfactory … The dynamic aspects of motivation are being investigated at many different levels from the genetic and biological to the behavioral, cognitive, social and cultural' (1992, pp.435, 455).

Motivation is generally thought of as the process that energises and directs behaviour, or as Zimbardo (1992, p.424) puts it: 'Motivation is the general term for all the processes involved in starting, directing, and maintaining physical and psychological activities.'

Some psychologists see it arising out of 'instincts, drives and other biological forces which underlie behaviour' while others look at psychological aspects of the individual and aspects of the environment (Avery & Baker 1990, p.374). According to Avery and Baker, 'our understanding of human motivation is incomplete if we do not consider sources which stem from the environment and from the individual's personality, experiences and ways of viewing the world' (1990, p.375). It is also important to note that 'significant human motivation comes not from objective realities but from our subjective interpretation of them. What we do now is often controlled by what we think was responsible for our past successes and failures, by what we believe is possible for us to do, and by what we anticipate the outcome of the action will be (Zimbardo 1992, p.434).

It therefore seems appropriate that the perception of what was responsible for the success or lack of success in information-seeking behaviour could be thought of in terms of motivating or demotivating factors that would either encourage or discourage such behaviour in the future. We need to limit demotivating factors (often called barriers) and maximise motivating factors. It is part of the role of information professionals to facilitate the needs of their customers or users so that the users will return. The role of perceptions as motivating or demotivating influences, and the role they may play in librarian–user interaction can be seen in the following comment from a participant in research on the information-seeking behaviour of academics:

> They [the librarians] came here and introduced themselves, they would maintain regular contact … If the librarian was really keen and enthusiastic and working in with us and sort of discussing with us what we thought was best for the students and what we would like them to do. That was really an enjoyable task and then I came across one that was a little bit stroppy or felt that we were imposing too much work I felt … that that wasn't such a pleasant experience … because of that I probably don't ring that person as often if I would have another librarian to ask for something … I always had the feeling that that person would much rather not be involved … several experiences like that would cause me to not ring up in the future; I'd try to find another way to get the information (Mills 2003, pp.140-141).

Librarians do not have control over all of the reasons why a user may or may not approach them. They can, however, minimise the reasons that could demotivate an approach and maximise the reasons that could influence or motivate an approach.

Asking for help

The second step in information-seeking behaviour is motivation to seek assistance of library staff and to engage the librarian by asking questions relating to the client's information need. This refers to both face-to-face and remote (telephone or electronic) encounters. Once clients have made the choice to use library sources, either in person or through a computer or telephone, they need to feel that they can ask the questions they want and that their information need will be dealt with. This is assuming in the first place that they have a clear idea of their information needs and what library staff can do to assist.

As mentioned earlier in this chapter, the essence of librarian–client interaction traditionally has been seen as the starting point, where the librarian meets the client in a reference encounter or interview to work through the 'information need' of the client. This information need is what the client wants answered or fulfilled. In the process, the librarian seeks to understand the information need of the client and to answer that need. At the reference encounter or interview, the librarian, by using standard communication techniques, identifies what the user wants. In the most desirable situations, the librarian either links the user with sources that could lead to the required information or finds the information for the user.

Receiving the desired answer

The third step in information-seeking behaviour is motivation to seek the desired answer. Before the client leaves the library, the librarian ideally checks whether the client has the information required. Librarians consider themselves the link between the information retrieval (IR) system and the client, and between the sources available and the user. The key to this process going smoothly, and to the three steps being successfully achieved, lies in the communication ability of the library staff to identify what is needed, identify the sources to meet the information need and either to provide the answer, or sources that might provide it, or to recommend alternative sources of information.

Not all interaction between the client and the library has a happy ending. There are many demotivators or barriers that prevent successful completion of the reference encounter. These barriers often relate not to the location of sources to meet the information need but to communication problems between the user and the librarian (Mount 1966; Crum 1969; Swope & Katzer 1972; Taylor 1968).

Communication and the reference interview

In an early study of what he called 'communication barriers' between clients and reference librarians, Mount (1966, pp.576-578) pointed to the following:

> An inquirer lacks knowledge of the depth and quality of the collection … knowledge of the reference tools available … knowledge of the vocabulary used by a particular set of tools … An inquirer does not willingly reveal his reason for needing the information … hasn't decided what he really wants … is not at ease in asking his question … feels that he cannot reveal the true question because it is of a sensitive nature … dislikes reference staff members (or vice versa) and consequently avoids giving a true picture of his needs … lacks confidence in the ability of the reference staff.

In a later paper, Crum (1969) identified physical, personality, psychological, communications and professional barriers in the 'librarian–customer' relationship. Swope and Katzer (1972, p.164) in their paper, 'Why don't they ask questions?', found that 'through words and actions librarians are reinforcing the user's feelings that he is a bother or he is stupid' and 'it does not appear that familiarity with the library (high use) helps overcome those barriers which inhibit user-initiated interaction with the librarian'. They concluded by pointing out that librarians must become aware of the image they have acquired in the eyes of the client and that a client-centred point of view of library service is needed.

In an early seminal paper on information seeking, Taylor (1968, p.82) went some way towards trying to conceptualise the reference process from the client's point of view rather than from the librarian's perspective. He identified four stages in formulating questions that many users experienced: 'the actual, but unexpressed need for information (the visceral need); the conscious, within-brain description of the need (the conscious need); the formal statement of the need (the formalised need); the question as presented to the information system (the compromised need)'. He concluded that the decision on whether or not to ask a librarian for assistance is based upon factors such as 'the inquirer's image of the personnel, their effectiveness, and his previous experience with this or any other library or librarian'.

More recently, Wilson (1999, p.257), in a model of information-seeking behaviour, drew attention to what are called intervening variables between the information need as asked and the resolution of that need. These variables have the potential to affect the interview process and are seen as arising out of the following areas: psychological, demographic, role-related or interpersonal, environmental or source characteristics. In a study of the information-seeking behaviour of university academic staff, Mills (2003) found that many potential clients were reluctant to seek assistance from librarians because of concerns about showing their ignorance about libraries and library systems. Some librarians were also considered unapproachable, and if academics did not feel confident about approaching library staff they would either not ask a question or they would use online access to the library's resources.

In research on information-seeking behaviour of students for completion of assignments, Kuhlthau (2004, p.52) found that they went through several stages in the search process:

> In each stage various feelings, thoughts, actions, strategies and moods were identified. In many cases students' expectations of the process and the tasks did not match their experience. Uncertainty and the more formulative task of the early stages were frequently met with impatience and a sense of inadequacy. An additional problem was students' limited perception of librarians as merely locators of sources. Such a perception was inadequate to mediate in the dynamic process of the search.

In the days of Mount (1966), Crum (1969), Swope and Katzer (1972) and Taylor (1968), the main means to use library services were in person or by telephone or letter. A major change since their time is that electronic access is now often the preferred first means of access to library services, either by choice or for convenience. Librarians cannot rely on getting clients through the door to justify their existence. They need to motivate clients and potential clients to use their libraries, their sources, their systems and themselves as people – either in person or electronically.

According to Church (2005), school librarians need to recognise that they live in a digital, online environment and that:

> Periodicals, general non-fiction, and reference works are readily available and widely accepted in electronic format. Our patrons like this electronic environment. Library media specialists who ignore the fact that students prefer information in electronic format will be left behind. To survive and thrive in the 21st century, school librarians must rethink collections and services. Collections must include electronic resources, and services must be designed to reach patrons who are outside of the physical library walls.

Tenopir (2000, p.30) says of change in accessibility to resources that new technology allows librarians 'to play "information missionary" ... We can reach our users wherever they may be hiding – [in] their dormitories, their offices, or at home ... We can "compel" the reader to "enter" in virtual ways as well as physical.'

How then might library and information professionals in the online/digital setting take into account the points of commentators such as Taylor (1968) relating to personal communication in librarian–client interaction? Tenopir (2000, p.30) says, 'between OPACs, indexes, pathfinders and search engines, we've tried as best we can to inform individuals about the many resources they can now access, but there has been little personalization.' Is lack of personalisation an issue for the future of librarian–client interaction and are clients still in need of interaction with information intermediaries? After all, information seekers have access to greater amounts of information in a wider variety of formats than ever before, with access more easily available than ever before, without necessary interaction with a librarian.

More often than not the literature of library science is dominated by the viewpoint of the academic library, in which personal assistance to users has always philosophically and practically taken a second place to user instruction in library and resource use – a consequence of having to cope with large numbers of clients at the one time. More recently, user instruction has been subsumed into the much broader area of information literacy instruction, in which the client is also taught to evaluate and filter the information available (a point taken up in Chapter 13). While goals of information literacy for all are promoted in all types of libraries, school and academic libraries remain the key bastion of this approach where clients are primarily seen as needing to take charge of their own information seeking (see Chapters 2 and 3). In other types of library, such as special and public libraries, the personal assistance given to users in finding information has always been considered the primary aim, in preference to information literacy for independent information seeking.

As Tenopir (2000, p.32) reports, however, 'Online resources allow us to turn much of the intermediary role over to the end user … Technology both enables and requires librarians to be educators – patrons need instruction in techniques and, more importantly, in analysis and evaluation.' Tenopir's view of this changing role accepts the increasing need for the information professional to play a more significant role in filtering and evaluating a greater range and amount of information in a greater range of formats than ever before.

It could be suggested that such a role might make client–librarian interaction skills redundant and that the importance of this interaction is reduced by the change in emphasis from face-to-face to online encounters, with verbal and non-verbal communication skills contributing to the success of the former interaction. However, Taylor's points (1968, p.82) on the decision about whether or not to ask a librarian for assistance and its relationship to factors such as 'the inquirer's image of the personnel, their effectiveness, and his previous experience with this or any other library or librarian' remain relevant in the online setting. In the email or chat interview, interaction is still required even though the participants are physically invisible to each other.

Does this invisibility reduce the problems referred to by Taylor (1968) and Kuhlthau (2004)? Some observations on the characteristics of email or chat reference interaction include:

Lack of nonverbal cues, such as body language or gestures.
Lack of voice intonation or accents.
Language more like spoken than written.
Conducted at a fast pace.
Writing, spelling, typing skills important.

Fluid identity of user and librarian.
Reduced inhibitions (Ronan 2003, p.43).

The outcomes of an online interaction should ideally be the same as one conducted face to face – that is, a successful resolution of the information need.

Ensuring successful librarian–user interaction

The *Guidelines for behavioral performance of reference and information service providers*, produced by the American Library Association (2004 p.1), state that:

> In all forms of reference services, the success of the transaction is measured not only by the information conveyed, but also by the positive or negative impact of the patron/staff interaction. The positive or negative behaviour of the reference staff member (as observed by the patron) becomes a significant factor in perceived success or failure.

Discussing positive behaviour attributes to facilitate successful librarian–client interaction the guidelines identify the following factors as important to the success of the reference transaction: 'Approachability, Interest, Listening/Inquiring, Searching and Follow-up'. These are fairly standard measures that can be used as guides to how the librarian should approach interaction with clients, and are explored below.

Approachability

It seems obvious that a librarian should be approachable, but what is approachable may depend upon one's viewpoint. In this case, the important view is that of the client approaching the librarian. Perhaps the following may be considered key approachability signals for many in the face-to-face environment:

- Facing client when they approach a very visible information desk where the librarian is seated (assuming the library has an information desk).

- Not looking distracted or busy when the client approaches the desk.

- Smiling and welcoming the client.

- Maintaining eye contact with the client.

- Involving the client in the search for information either by looking at the computer screen together or going to the shelves together.

The client must feel motivated to approach the librarian and these signals are important steps in creating motivation.

For the remote client, who is likely to be looking at a computer screen, key approachability and motivating factors that will encourage them to present an information need may involve:

- Easy identification of the available chat or email service from a library's web page.

- Easy-to-understand instructions on how to proceed to present an information need.

Figure 6.1 shows the web page that greets users of the National Library of Australia's AskNow! online chat service. The clear list of 'AskUs' enquiry options provides a good example of an approachable information service. The positive message it conveys precedes the more cautionary 'Before You Ask' instructions.

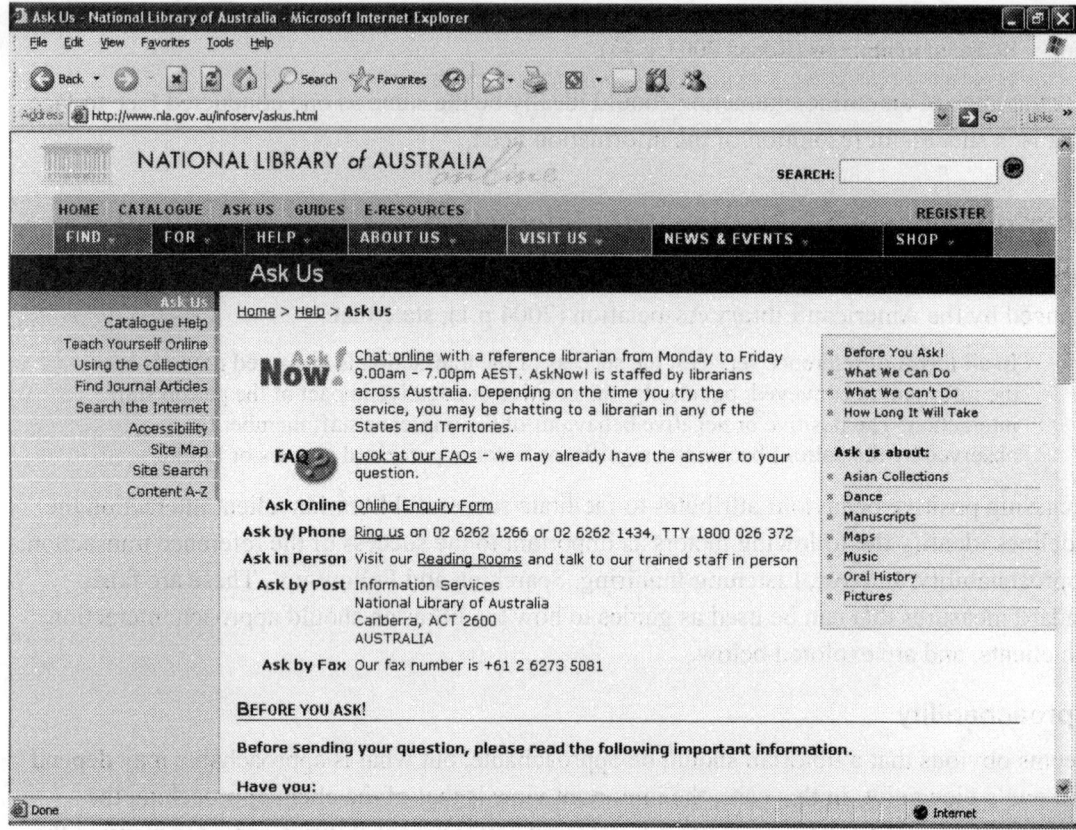

Figure 6.1 The National Library of Australia's AskNow! website, http://www.nla.gov.au/infoserv/askus.html

Interest

It is also obvious that a librarian should appear interested in both the client and their information need. Interest is evident when the approachability factors mentioned earlier are adhered to, in addition to 'signalling understanding of the client's needs through verbal or non-verbal cues such as nodding of the head or questions to the client to clarify points' (ALA 2004, p.2). Similar principles apply in the case of the remote client. For instance, acknowledgement of the request is necessary with a welcoming message, such as 'thank you for your request, we are attending to it', as are questions to clarify points relating to the information need, where appropriate. Time taken to answer online requests is a necessary indicator that must be given to the client.

Listening and enquiring

It is often difficult to be a good listener, but this is a key requirement of the reference librarian. It is easy to assume one knows what the client wants and to go off searching for the answer. Care must be taken not to jump to conclusions. What has sometimes been called 'premature diagnosis' of a client's information need is demonstrated in the following real-life scenario.

> A chat email service is asked for information on purchasing commercial quantities of cinnamon. The information seeker is given a list of suppliers of condiments when in

fact a list of spice suppliers would have been much more useful. The information provider should always aim for the most correct answer rather than an answer that is only partially correct. Had the librarian in this case checked the list supplied to the client, the problem could have been identified. To be fair to the librarian, the chat session did include an indication that more information could be obtained by sending another email, but the information seeker did not feel confident that this would achieve the desired outcome so he identified another source – the local library, as it happened – explained his information need there and clarified terms before they could be misinterpreted and lead to the supply of further inappropriate information.

The following key strategies would help to avoid the problem outlined here.

- Use of open-ended questions rather than closed questions: for example, 'Tell me more about what you want this information for' rather than 'Do you want this information for...?'

- Asking what level of information is required? Is it for a layperson, child or a specialist in the area?

- Asking if the client already has any information on the subject.

- Asking how much information the client wants – a book, a few articles and so on.

These strategies are equally effective for live (synchronous) information chat services, emailed (asynchronous) information services or face-to-face information services.

Searching

The librarian may carry out the search with the client present or the client may leave the librarian to conduct the search and wait to be notified when the information is available. As indicated in the example above, it is essential for the librarian to match the information need of the client with appropriate sources. The degree of assistance by the librarian in meeting the need may be influenced by the type of library (discussed below) in which the information need was received. The maximum level of service would be one in which the answer to the question is given in full. This may be simple, such as the number of people in Poland, or more complex, such as recent articles on natural treatments for acne in teenage boys for a parent. The remote client can be notified of answers to simple questions online, but more detailed responses may require attachments to online messages, such as scanned images of articles, or even print material.

Follow-up

When the client is happy with the response to their information need (or in turn breaks off the search for information) it is desirable that there is agreement between the client and the librarian that the information need has been met and that no further interaction is required.

Reference service in different library settings

As indicated earlier, the type of information service offered to clients differs markedly according to the type of library. It was suggested that academic libraries, whether in the school or higher education sector, tend to believe that clients need to take charge of their own information seeking, focusing as a consequence on information literacy, whereas other types of library tend to place greater emphasis on providing clients with personal assistance in finding information. Information service needs to be understood, therefore, in terms of the function a library performs within its organisation or community.

As is demonstrated in Chapter 2, the reference or information service in school libraries is dictated by the curriculum. The collection is designed to assist in responding to the needs of the curriculum and to the types of information need that arise, and it reflects the tasks and assignments that students are given to complete. In Australia, this type of library is often staffed by only one or two teacher librarians who service the requirements of hundreds of students. A key responsibility of the teacher librarian is to ensure that students are equipped with information literacy skills. The overall objective is not so much to answer the information needs of students as to facilitate their information-seeking behaviour in order that they can become independent and efficient information seekers and learners.

The information service in other academic libraries is generally designed to facilitate independent information seeking and to encourage the development of independent learners. The collection reflects the demands of the courses taught and the institution's research profile, and information service is organised to meet the needs of the students, the academics and researchers. Considerable time is spent on delivering classes in information skills to all clients and facilitating the meeting of information needs by a combination of training clients in independent information seeking and assisting them to 'commence' their searches. Libraries in the higher education sector have gone to great efforts during the past ten years or more to deliver information literacy instruction online – an aspect of service provision that is discussed in Chapter 13.

In research or special libraries, the emphasis is placed on serving a group of clients who have things in common. As discussed in Chapter 4, these may include common subject interests such as departments of the environment, road safety or agriculture, or organisations like the CSIRO; common organisational objectives (these are often training organisations) such as health (hospitals), religious organisations or mining companies; and common interests such as statistics or archives.

Information services in these libraries are characterised by the need to provide solutions to information needs – answers to questions rather than precise directions as to where an answer can be found. While it is also desirable to engage in information skills training to assist clients find their own information – often the case in subject areas of high demand such as genealogical enquiries – this is not a primary aim as it is in school and academic libraries.

In public libraries, the appeal of the collections must be broad and must reflect the information needs of all members of the community, including senior citizens, children, homebound, ethnic groups, hobby groups and sporting clubs. Collections may not be as specialised as in research or special libraries, or even school and academic libraries, but should be representative of the detail that could be expected to be requested from the average client. Most public libraries, however, also have special collections, typically in the form of local history and genealogy collections. As the account of public library service in Chapter 1 indicated, the information service that is required of public library staff is in many ways the most challenging. Responding to information needs in a wide range of subjects and from varying types of clients – from school students to educated laypersons, specialists in particular areas, and hobby, sport and recreation enthusiasts – is demanding.

While the public library has a local and/or regional perspective, the national and state libraries' collections represent the national and state perspectives. Often at the forefront of recent developments in the field, their role in Australia includes supporting library networks, and the state libraries have varying responsibilities for supporting public library networks. As is demonstrated in Chapter 5, other key responsibilities include preserving the history of the state or nation, as well as ensuring the literature of the nation is recorded and made available to its people.

Future of librarian–user interaction

A recurring theme in this book is the increasing availability of electronic access, especially in western industrialised nations. This raises the question of whether there is still a need for a library building to serve clients or for a librarian to be on duty. The view taken here is that there is. The rationale for this view is outlined below.

- Not all clients are able or willing to use library collections electronically.

- Not all clients can articulate their needs easily using, say, online chat sessions with library staff.

- Not all clients want to search for information themselves or, indeed, have any idea how to do so.

- The increasing amount of information available, especially on the internet and via library collections, raises issues of access and whether information seekers actually have the ability to find it.

- Human beings are social animals and often prefer to deal with another human being in their information seeking.

- Information seekers are not limited to one type of source; combinations of personal sources (librarians) and electronic sources are quite natural and indeed the use of one source can often initiate use of other sources.

- Library staff are being driven to evaluate and filter the ever increasing amount of information available electronically – it may be available but it is not always easy to access or identify.

- Because successful and efficient use of information is not easy, information literacy instruction is a key role of the librarian.

- As Curry articulates (2005 p.6), 'while patrons may be more technologically savvy, computer literate, they still are not sophisticated in navigating their way through the maze of computer interfaces, selection of "best" reference tools for their needs and the management of information overload'.

- Access to online/real-time reference services may direct information seekers to sources that answer their questions rather than answer the specific question asked.

The AskNow! chat reference service, discussed earlier, demonstrates this last point. It operates in conjunction with the collaboration of several contributing libraries and works something like this:

> Reference librarians from each of the libraries work shifts to man the service from their own libraries, to answer questions in real time via a logged in session on the web. The main function is to direct readers to appropriate online resources to answer their questions, and the quality and quantity of such resources is increasing all the time. The service is assessed from a link on the web sites of all the participating libraries, as well as from the web sites of some educational institutions (Tillotson 2005, p.8

If, as noted above, it cannot be assumed that people have the ability to access information online then there is a continuing need for librarians to be available. In a well-publicised Online Computer Library Center (OCLC) report, *Perceptions of libraries and information resources* (2005, pp.6-4), it is suggested that there are opportunities for librarians to assist users make sense of the vast array of resources that libraries have at their disposal:

> the majority of information seekers are not making much use of the array of electronic resources (online magazines, databases and reference assistance, for example) libraries make available to their communities. Very few respondents use such resources regularly and the majority of respondents are not aware that their libraries have these electronic resources. Most do not use the library web site where access to electronic resources is made available. College students are the exception.

Care should be taken, however. The librarian in the reference interview or encounter or transaction or interaction (the preferred term here) can control clients and their information experience, but this power should only be exercised to the benefit of the client, not to control the dynamics of the interview. Misuse of this position can only damage the role of the librarian in the eyes of clients and motivate them to use one of the many other information-seeking paths available. The following quote from Cohen (1993 cited in Curry 2005, p.4) encapsulates the dilemma of the client in seeking assistance, whether this assistance is sought in a face-to-face encounter or via email or in a chat session:

> Human beings are creatures of emotion ... and as soon as a word is created through the mouth of the speaker, then that speaker places himself at the mercy of the other. The speaker becomes immediately vulnerable and so exposes his inner self to the other half of the partnership. Even the simplest of reference questions is an offering, to some degree, of oneself to another. For many that involves a great deal of personal pain and even for the strongest of us, it exposes a degree of weakness which screams out against our need for survival. We never want to display our personal vulnerabilities to others and always have a strong tendency to mask our true selves. Part of the reference librarian's task is to go behind the mask to meet the client at a truly personal level.

Conclusion

This chapter has promoted the view that assistance given to clients is the most important activity performed in libraries, but the level of this assistance is tempered by the type of library and the availability of staff to provide assistance. Valid reasons are often provided as to why a reference service to clients may be reduced or limited at times – this reflects the reality of the pressured working environment. Library and information professionals need to be careful, however, not to become invisible or information phantoms. There are alternative non-library sources of information that are less threatening, more engaging and friendly, while perhaps providing less useful information. One of the conclusions of the *Perceptions of libraries and information resources* study (OCLC 2005) pointed to dissatisfaction, even though they found that clients were generally satisfied with libraries and librarians, and with some aspects of the service experience of the libraries they frequented: *'Poor signage, inhospitable surroundings, unfriendly staff, lack of parking ... hard to use systems and inconvenient hours were mentioned ...'* (p.6; italics added). Such comments need to be absorbed and used positively for improvement if the rich resources of staff and materials available through libraries are to be used to their capacity.

References

American Library Association (ALA) 2004, *Guidelines for behavioral performance of reference and information service providers*, American Library Association, Chicago, http://www.ala.org/ala/rusa/rusaprotools/referenceguide/guidelinesbehavioral.htm

Austin, B 2001, 'Mooers' law: in and out of context', *Journal of the American Society for Information Science*, vol.52, no.8, pp.607-609.

Avery, G & Baker, E 1990, *Psychology at work*, Prentice-Hall, New York.

Boyd, RS 2005, 'Assessing the true nature of information transactions at a suburban library', *Public Libraries*, vol.44, no.4, pp.234-239.

Church, AP 2005, 'Virtual school libraries – the time is now!', *MultiMedia & Internet@Schools*, vol.12, no.2, pp.8-12.

Cohen, J 1993, 'The hermeneutics of the reference question', *Australian Library Journal*, vol.42, pp.182-189.

Crum, NJ 1969, 'The librarian-customer relationship: Dynamics of filling requests for information,' *Special Libraries*, vol.60, pp.269-277.

Curry, EL 2005, 'The reference interview revisited: Librarian–patron interaction in the virtual environment,' *Simile*, vol.5, no.1, http://web31.epnet.com/citation.asp?tb=1&_ug=sid+8166 B4B6%2D5E57%2D49A8

Grosser, K 1989, 'Human aspects of organisational information processing: Implications for educating information professionals', *The information investment: Proceedings of the 3rd Asian Pacific Special and Law Librarians Conference*, ALIA, Canberra, ACT, pp.18-21.

Harris, RM & Dewdney, P 1994, *Barriers to information: How formal systems fail battered women*, Greenwood Press, Westport, CT.

Kuhlthau, C 2004, *Seeking meaning*, 2nd edn, Libraries Unlimited, Westport, CT.

Mills, JJ 2003, 'Information-seeking behaviour of university academics', PhD thesis, Charles Sturt University, Wagga Wagga, NSW.

Mooers, CN 1960, 'Mooers' law, or why some information systems are used and others are not', *American Documentation*, vol.11, no.3, editorial.

Mount, E 1966, 'Communication barriers and the reference question', *Special Libraries*, vol.57, no.8, pp.575-578.

Online Computer Library Center (OCLC) 2005, *Perceptions of libraries and information resources*, OCLC, Columbus, OH, http://www.oclc.org/reports/2005perceptions.htm

Ronan, J 2003, 'The reference interview online', *Reference & User Services Quarterly*, vol.43, no.1 pp.43-47.

Ross, CS 2003, 'The reference interview: Why it needs to be used in every (well, almost every) reference transaction', *Reference & User Services Quarterly*, vol.43, no.1, pp.38-42.

Swope, MJ & Katzer, J 1972, 'Why don't they ask questions?', *RQ*, vol.12, pp.161-166.

Taylor, RS 1968, 'Question-negotiation and information seeking in libraries,' *College and Research Libraries*, vol.29, pp.178-194.

Tenopir, C 2000, 'Online goals before there was online', *Library Journal*, vol.15, no.8, pp.30-31.

Tillotson, D 2005, 'AskNow! Again', *Online Currents*, vol.20, no.5, pp.8-10.

Wilson, TD 1999, 'Models in information behaviour research', *Journal of Documentation*, vol.55, no.3, pp.249-270.

Zimbardo, PG 1992, *Psychology and life*, 13th edn, Harper Collins, New York.

CHAPTER 7
Information sources

Alastair Smith

At the start of the twenty-first century, it is tempting to suggest that for most people there is one information source – Google or a similar internet search engine. A survey by the Pew Internet & American Life Project (2006) suggests that 38 per cent of American internet users will use a search engine on any given day. In contrast, until relatively recently the most common information source in an American household was the Bible (Katz 2002). For an information professional, however, a more varied range of sources and a more sophisticated understanding of the structures of information sources are essential. It is clear that not all information is in forms that can be accessed by an internet search engine, and not all information is on the open web and accessible to anyone with a web browser and an internet connection. Much information is accessed through the internet, but is only available to subscribers or members of specific organisations.

In this chapter, 'information source' refers to a tool that can be used to find information. This information may be contained within the information source (for example, in an encyclopaedia) or the information source may lead the information seeker (through a bibliographic reference, for example), to a document that contains the information. A 'document' in this case may be a book, a journal article, a website or any similar resource. The first case is often called a 'direct' information source, because the information is found directly from the source, and the second case is called an 'indirect' source. In practice this distinction may blur, particularly in the hypertext environment of the web, where a website may link seamlessly to information at other sites.

In the twentieth century, categorisation of print-based sources was along the lines of bibliographies, indexes and abstracts, guides to the literature, directories of organisations, encyclopedias, dictionaries, biographical sources, geographic sources and almanacs. In addition, certain types of information sources that required special access have been dealt with separately, for example, government publications and audiovisual materials. With the growth of digital information in the late twentieth century, resources also began to be classified according to format: print, digital offline (for instance, CD-ROM) and digital online (online indexing and abstracting databases and so on).

Now, most (but not all) information sources are available in digital format so it is not useful to treat print and digital separately. In fact most users access the digital online form, even in libraries where the print versions are available. A survey of sources used by reference librarians in a US tertiary library showed that only 9 per cent of information sources used were in print, even though the librarians were situated next to a print reference collection (Bradford et al. 2005).

Another aspect of digital delivery is the growth of digital full text, in which resources contain not just the bibliographic details of works, but the works themselves in digital format. This has changed the way people use information sources, from a model in which they might consult one information source to obtain bibliographic details of a document, then undertake a separate process (consulting library catalogues, interlibrary loan systems and so on) to obtain the document itself. Now it is much more common for there to be a direct link from the details of the document to the document itself. As a result, the distinction noted above between direct and indirect information sources is blurring.

There are two main types of search tool used to find information sources on the internet:

- Internet directories, for which information resources have been selected and classified by human beings.
- Search engines, which have automatically word indexed information resources and made the information available in a database.

Because these two types of information sources have become so important, they are discussed first, before attention turns to more specific types of information sources, such as indexing and abstracting databases.

Internet directories

Internet directories (sometimes called subject directories, subject guides, subject portals, resource guides or subject gateways) provide links to internet documents – websites and so on – that have been selected and organised by people. Librarians have been at the forefront of developing internet directories, such as subject directories on library websites, tailored to the needs of their libraries' users. Features of internet directories include:

- The documents have been selected according to some criteria (which may or may not be stated on the internet directory website) by people, rather than by software.
- The directory listing will often provide a brief annotation describing the document, and its strengths and weaknesses.
- The directory listings are arranged according to a categorisation scheme, allowing the user to navigate from broad classifications to specific groups of documents relating to a topic.
- There will usually be access by keyword searching, to find directory listings where the keywords appear in the title or description of the document.

Examples of general internet directories include: BUBL Link (http://bubl.ac.uk/); Yahoo! (http://www.yahoo.com/); Librarian's Index to the Internet (http://lii.org/); Te Puna Web Directory (http://webdirectory.natlib.govt.nz/) and Social Science Information Gateway (http://www.sosig.ac.uk).

BUBL Link (Williamson 2000) is based at the Centre for Digital Library Research at Strathclyde University, and indexes resources that are useful for the UK higher education community. Sites are indexed from all over the world, however, and BUBL Link can be useful for general internet searches. BUBL Link uses the Dewey Decimal Classification (discussed in Chapter 9) as its main categorisation system, so the structure is familiar to many library clients, particularly users of public libraries. Someone interested in astronomical observatories, for example, could navigate through:

- 500 Natural sciences and mathematics
  - o 520 Astronomy and allied sciences
    - ▪ 522 Astronomy techniques, procedures, apparatus, equipment, materials

In this category they would find descriptions of websites such as the Bradford Robotic Telescope (http://www.telescope.org/). BUBL Link also has subject headings, with the Bradford Robotic Telescope listed under 'Robotics' along with other headings. It is also possible to do a keyword search for any words in the title or description of listed sites, so a search on 'Bradford' would bring up the entry for the Bradford Robotic Telescope. There are also many specialised internet directories, for example the Australian e-Humanities gateway (http://www.ehum.edu.au/) and the Health and Life Sciences Resource Discovery Network BIOME (http://biome.ac.uk/).

The strengths of internet directories are that the documents listed have been selected as having some value and relevance to the subject and that documents are grouped according to topic. However, maintenance of internet directories does take time which means listings may not be up to date and the number of documents that can be listed will be limited by the resources available. Also the categories may reflect the indexer's view of the subject and documents may not be listed in the categories that users of the directory expect.

When searching an internet directory, it is important to note that what is sought is a site that may contain the answer, not the answer itself. If a search for information on kiwifruit was being made on BUBL Link, for instance, no listings that specifically mention kiwifruit would be found, but a search for sites that discuss fruit would find 'Kiwifruit and Related Species' in section 634, Orchards and Fruits, where there is an entry for 'Fruits of Warm Climates' (http://www.hort.purdue.edu/newcrop/morton/).

Search engines

Search engines are created automatically by software programs (variously called 'robots', 'bots' or 'spiders') which index the words on web pages. While there are many search engines, the process by which they are built is similar. First the robot visits a web page and sends back to its database a list of the words on the page and the URL (uniform resource locator) of the page at which they were found. Then the robot follows any links from the page and repeats the indexing process at those pages. Over time, the robot should visit most pages on the internet, and the resulting database should contain the URLs of every word on those pages. A user searches the database for a combination of words, and gets a listing of pages where that specified combination occurs. Results are ordered by a relevance algorithm that uses factors such as the frequency of search terms, links made to the sites, and so on. As a result, although a simple search may produce tens of thousands of hits, it is likely that some relevant documents will appear in the first screen of results.

The three main advantages of search engines are that they require no human intervention, which means they can be updated continuously and are relatively cheap to build; they cover a significant proportion of websites; and they are fast and easy to use. The problems are as follows. Because search engines are built automatically, there is no selection of the sites returned. Also, the search is of a 'snapshot' of the internet – the information about a page reflects the page as it was when the robot visited it, and new pages and changes to pages will not appear in the database until the robot next visits the page. Outdated links are a further problem and unless steps are taken to remove them there may be pages listed in the database that no longer exist. Finally, pages that are not directly linked may not be found by the robot. In fact, research indicates that only 60 per cent of websites are linked from other sites (Broder et al. 2000). Pages generated from databases, or that require authentication (for example, subscription databases) may also not be found.

Because not all websites are found by the search engine robot, people refer to the 'hidden web' of sites that can not be found directly by using search engines. Of course, these sites are not necessarily hidden; it is just that alternative information sources, such as internet directories, need to be used to find them.

Currently Google (http://www.google.com/) is one of the most popular internet search engines, but there are many others. Research indicates that there is a low degree of overlap between search engines, and anything approaching a comprehensive search requires the use of several search engines (Jacsó 2005a). There are country-specific search engines, such as SearchNZ (http://www.searchnz.co.nz/), but these tend to be less effective than global search engines, and in any case many sites with information about a specific country, such as NZ or Australia, are not in the relevant country domain (Smith 2003).

While internet directories and search engines have been discussed separately, in practice they have converged. Google, for example, includes the Google Directory (http://www.google.com/dirhp) and Yahoo!, one of the original internet directories, is now putting more emphasis on its search engine facility (http://www.yahoo.com/).

In order to use search engines effectively, it is important to make use of the 'relevancy ranking' facility. It helps, for instance, if users:

- Include as many relevant words as possible in their search statements.
- Use the most specific words possible and use alternative spellings, for instance, 'aluminum OR aluminium'
- Think about words that are likely to appear in a site with the answer to the question, rather than words that appear in the question: for instance, 'search engine optimization OR optimisation' rather than 'information about improving my website results'.
- Examine the 'hits' (search results) to identify extra words that could be included in the search.
- Look for sites in the results that may link to relevant sites – the answer to a question may not appear in the results immediately, but there may be sites that provide a link to the answer.

While internet directories and search engines provide access to information on the open web, much important information is still only in print or in online sources that have controlled access. Some of the more traditional tools are now examined.

Bibliographies

Access to the world of published documents (books, periodicals, conference proceedings and so on) has traditionally been provided by bibliographies. These fall into two groups:

- Subject bibliographies, generally one-off works that list documents relating to a specific topic (which might be a person, a geographic area or a historical period).
- General bibliographies that list documents published on an ongoing basis. The most important of these are now the bibliographic databases maintained by national libraries (see Chapter 5).

During the twentieth century, librarians worked towards 'Universal Bibliographic Control' – the idea that the details of any published document would appear in the combined bibliographic databases maintained through cooperation among the national library systems. To a large extent this ideal has been achieved, at least in the English-speaking developed world. A book published in most developed countries will be recorded in a national bibliography of the country of publication and the bibliographic record will, through a process of exchanges of MARC records, appear in bibliographic databases such as that of the Library of Congress (http://catalog.loc.gov/), Libraries Australia (http://librariesaustralia.nla.gov.au/), or Te Puna, the New Zealand National Bibliographic Database (http://tepuna.natlib.govt.nz/). Thus a library user in Australia or New Zealand is able to access details of virtually all works published by conventional means in the English-speaking developed world. The irony is that just as this was being achieved at the end of the twentieth century, the internet changed the meaning of 'published', opening up a web of documents that is proving impossible to bring into the orderly world of universal bibliographic control.

Indexing and abstracting databases

Accessing information in documents such as periodicals and conference proceedings has been a challenge for libraries. While general bibliographic databases such as Libraries Australia record, for example, the details of a periodical, say, *New Scientist*, they do not list the specific articles within the periodical. This is the role of indexing and abstracting databases. Indexing and abstracting databases have a long history, particularly in the sciences where much information appears in journals. Information in journal articles and conference proceedings is indexed and, in abstracting databases, a short summary or abstract is provided (see Chapter 9 for an account of indexing). An example of a long running indexing and abstracting service is *Chemical Abstracts*, started in 1907 by the American Chemical Society and indexing journal articles, conference papers and patents in pure and applied chemistry.

Originally indexes were produced manually, but with the advent of computer typesetting the printed indexes began to be generated from a computer database. The next stage was for the computer database itself to be searched, initially in batch mode – a program would be run overnight that would scan the database for particular combinations of keywords – but by the 1970s it became common for searches to be done in real time from remote computer terminals. Several 'database vendors' emerged, for example, Dialog (http://www.dialog.com/). A database vendor acquires indexing and abstracting databases from a number of producers and mounts them on a server with a common search interface, charging users for access and paying a royalty to the producer.

A key to effective searching of databases is use of the subject descriptors attached to the computer records. These are generally drawn from a thesaurus or subject headings list. An example of this is the medical subject headings (MeSH) that provide the descriptors in the Medline database, which is the main database in the medical and health sciences, available on the open web as PubMed (http://www.pubmed.gov/). In order to search effectively for 'cancer', for instance, it is necessary to use the MeSH term 'neoplasm'. Another example of the use of specialised descriptors is Chemical Abstracts Registry Numbers (RNs) – if one wants to search for 'aspirin' in a database using Registry Numbers, one can search on 50-78-2 (the RN for aspirin) rather than all the alternative brand and chemical names for the material.

Citation databases are a specialised type of indexing database and work on the principle that scientific papers cite related, previous papers. To take an example, a searcher interested in the impact of rabbits on grazing and aware of Cooke's 1987 paper on the subject in the *Australian Journal of Ecology* can trace papers that cite Cooke's article, using a citation database, and have access to more recent information. Law case citation indexes had been compiled manually for a long time (from 1873 in the case of Shepards), but Eugene Garfield realised the advantages of computers in the creation of citation indexes for scientific information and in 1964 Garfield's Institute for Scientific Information (ISI) launched Science Citation Index. Initially a computer database was used to produce printed citation indexes but the index is now available as the web-based database, Web of Knowledge (http://isiwebofknowledge.com/), with coverage of social sciences, arts and humanities, as well as the conventional sciences. While ISI was for a long time the only general citation database vendor, competitors have appeared in the twenty-first century, such as Elsevier's *Scopus* (http://www.scopus.com/).

Until the 1990s, most database vendors were geared to information professionals. Databases charged by time spent online and had sophisticated interfaces that required people to be trained to use them effectively. Databases gave only bibliographic details, and library skills were required to locate the actual documents and obtain them by inter-library loan or using a commercial document delivery service. In the 1990s, however, it became increasingly common to link full text of articles with the indexing and abstracting databases, and with the growth of web-based user-friendly search interfaces, it has become common for library users, particularly in academic libraries, to access databases that allow seamless movement from an indexing function to a document supply function. Database vendors have been joined by journal publishers such as Elsevier and MCB in providing online access to the full text of journals.

The 'open access movement' has facilitated the availability of research material on the open web through electronic journals, authors websites and institutional repositories. As a result it has become common to search for research material through internet directories and search engines. Google has taken this a step further with Google Scholar (http://scholar.google.com/) – an extension of the Google database, which indexes research writing on the open web. Despite scepticism that Google Scholar has the consistency and accuracy of more conventional indexing and abstracting databases (Jacsó 2005b), web search engines are likely to play an increased role in searching for research material.

The value of searching indexing and abstracting databases is that they access a much greater depth and authority of information than is available on the open web. Despite the open access movement, much research writing appears only in proprietary databases and is available only to members of subscribing institutions such as universities or research institutes. A valuable function of libraries in the twenty-first century is managing the availability of these proprietary databases to their clients both inside the library building and remotely from their home or workplace.

'Ready reference' information sources

Librarians use the term 'ready reference' for requests for relatively simple facts ('where was Joh Bjelke-Petersen born?') and overviews of topics ('what were the Punic wars?'). Ready reference information sources include almanacs and yearbooks, encyclopedias, dictionaries, biographical sources, geographical sources and directories of organisations. Traditionally available in print, and in libraries kept in a designated 'reference' area , most of the ready reference sources now have online equivalents, which give information seekers the freedom of consulting them away from a physical library. While many are available on the open web, many are proprietary and may only be available in their full versions online through subscription. Even when the online version is available, the nature of ready reference queries can mean that accessing information may be easier in print. Determining the spelling of a word from a desk dictionary may be easier than logging on to an online dictionary, for instance. While there are justifiable concerns about the accuracy of web-based resources, a systematic assessment of the results of ready reference queries using search engines showed a high degree of accuracy (Frick & Fallis 2003).

A twenty-first century trend is for search engines to be used for ready reference functions, for example, as dictionaries. Web search engines are in effect large scale dictionaries and can be used to find context for recently coined words. This is facilitated by Google's 'define:' command, for example, 'define: kangaroo' will produce a range of definitions from online dictionaries and glossaries. While many ready reference sources have open web equivalents, information seekers need to be aware that for copyright reasons the web version may not be the latest edition. The online *Bartlett's Dictionary of Quotations* (http://www.bartleby.com/100/), is (at the time of writing) the 1919 edition, despite the fact that far more recent editions are available in print.

Almanacs and yearbooks

In their print form, almanacs and yearbooks are one-volume compendiums of facts – the ultimate ready reference tool. Almanacs are usually revised on an annual basis and contain statistics, significant dates, country overviews, summaries of recent events, conversion tables, lists of government bodies, and so on. *Whitaker's almanack* is the prime example in the British world. The north American *Information please almanac* is also available on the open web at http://www.infoplease.com/.

Yearbooks are similar tools to almanacs, but tend to have a national focus. *Statesman's yearbook* has key summaries of every country in the world, along with details of international organisations and so on. Official yearbooks are often issued by the national statistical bureau of a specific country. *Yearbook Australia*, for example, is issued annually by the Australian Bureau of Statistics and summarises census and statistical information relating to the country, along with overviews of the government structure, society and industry.

Encyclopedias

Encyclopedias attempt to summarise knowledge in relatively short articles. As well as providing basic overviews of topics and answers to simple facts, encyclopedias perform the function of providing context, in other words, identifying where the topic fits in the overall scheme of knowledge. Articles often contain references to further reading so they can be a starting point for more detailed research. Possibly the best known encyclopedia of the English-speaking world is the *Encyclopaedia Britannica*, started in 1768 in Britain but for many years based in the USA. While still sold and used in libraries in its multi-volume paper-based version, it is also available on CD-ROM and online by subscription (http://www.britannica.com/). Conventional encyclopedias such as the Britannica have moved to digital format, not just to reduce production and distribution costs, but also because the digital format allows detailed keyword searching and the incorporation of multimedia.

On the web, the encyclopedia model has been developed by Wikipedia (http://www.wikipedia.org/) by incorporating the wiki model of a collaborative website. Anyone can contribute information to the site, either by expanding or correcting existing articles, or creating new articles. While information professionals have expressed scepticism about the accuracy and authority of this model (Wallace & Van Fleet 2005), Wikipedia has proved to be surprisingly effective and resilient against deliberate attempts to introduce errors, which in most cases are rapidly corrected by interested users. Wikipedia has the advantage of being far more up to date than established encyclopedias. The death of the noted feminist Andrea Dworkin, for example, was recorded in her Wikipedia entry before being reported in the conventional media. Wikipedia is becoming a useful ready reference source complementing traditional encyclopedias, as well as performing the function of an internet directory, in that articles provide links to key websites related to the topic.

As well as general encyclopedias such as *Britannica* and Wikipedia, there are encyclopedias that summarise knowledge in a particular subject, for instance, the *Encyclopedia of library and information science* and the *McGraw Hill encyclopedia of science and technology*, or relating to a particular country, such as the *Australian encyclopedia*. New Zealand's Ministry for Culture and Heritage has recently undertaken a project to develop a national encyclopedia accessible from the open web, *Te ara* (http://www.teara.govt.nz/).

Dictionaries

Dictionaries have a role as ready reference sources, not just for determining the spelling and meaning of words, but also their history, pronunciation and so on. There is some difference of opinion about whether dictionaries should be prescriptive, in other words, defining how a language should be used, or whether they should be descriptive and simply recording the evolving use of the language. In practice most modern dictionaries, such as the benchmark *Oxford English dictionary* (OED), are descriptive. Most are now generated from databases. The OED is now an output of the Oxford English Corpus, a database of words as recorded throughout the English-speaking world. The Corpus is used to create the OED, smaller versions, such as the *Concise Oxford English dictionary*, and national versions such as the *New Zealand*

Oxford dictionary. The variations of 'standard' English mean that many English-speaking countries have their own national dictionary, for example Australia's *Macquarie dictionary.*

A number of dictionaries are available on the web. Some are subscription based, such as the OED Online (http://www.oed.com/), and others are freely accessible, such as the *American heritage dictionary of the English language* (http://www.bartleby.com/61). The term 'dictionary' can also apply to specialised dictionaries, such as the *Penguin dictionary of sociology*, multilingual dictionaries such as *A comprehensive Indonesian-English dictionary*, and dictionaries of quotations such as the *Oxford dictionary of quotations.*

Biographical sources

Biographical sources tend to be divided into two types – dictionaries of biography, which record the lives of people who are dead, and 'who's who' compilations, which record prominent living people. Both types tend to be national in scope – the *Australian dictionary of biography* (1976–2005) for prominent dead Australians, for example, and *Who's who in Australia* for currently alive Australians. The division is partly because a definitive summation of a person's life is only possible after that person has died. *Who's who* entries are generally based on information provided by the subject –which does not make them accurate – while dictionary of biography entries are based on obituaries, biographies and similar sources. Biographical sources on the open web have tended to lack the editorial control and depth of conventional sources. An interesting experiment is Biography Center (http://search.biography-center.com/), an internet directory that provides links to open web biographical information on individuals, both dead and alive.

New Zealand's *Dictionary of New Zealand biography* (DNZB), originally published in print, is notable for two reasons. An editorial decision was made to include women, workers and Māori; counteracting a bias of more traditional biographic sources towards male European members of the upper classes. Also, the DNZB has been made available on the open web (http://www.dnzb.govt.nz/).

Geographical sources

Geographical sources include atlases and gazetteers. World atlases can range from relatively simple school atlases to the benchmark *Times comprehensive atlas of the world.* While people tend to associate atlases with maps, they contain more than just cartographic information. The *Times atlas*, for example, includes statistical, geological and climate information. Regional and country atlases give greater detail, for example *Atlas of the South Pacific* has detailed maps of small South Pacific islands. Themed atlases include historical atlases, which show history through maps that indicate political and social changes: for example, the *Bateman New Zealand historical atlas.* Gazetteers such as the *Gazetteer of New Zealand place names* provide information about places, their location, population, origins of names and so forth.

On the open web, mapping tools such as MapQuest (http://www.mapquest.com/) provide maps of most of the world, although the best coverage tends to be of North America and Europe. Web-based mapping tools often search by street address, and provide driving directions from one location to another. Google Earth (http://earth.google.com/) provides high resolution satellite images of all of the earth's surface, overlaid with geographic information such as roads and place names. Online mapping tools are very effective for providing detailed information. A print atlas, however, is often better for giving an overview of the geography of a region. Online mapping tools provide interesting potential for interactivity. When Hurricane Katrina struck the southern US in 2005, users posted information about the impact of the hurricane at specific locations to Google Earth, providing a continuously updated picture of the hurricane and its aftermath.

Directories of organisations

Directories of organisations are key business information sources. They can be used to find background information about a company or organisation, to compare companies (for instance, by turnover) and to identify companies that produce a particular product. The *Kompass* directories, for example, provide company profiles with information such as turnover, executive names and products. The print *Kompass* directories are produced in regional and country editions, and are available online (http://www.kompass.com), although full details of companies are only available to subscribers. The *Europa directory of international organizations* provides details on international organisations such as leading officials, membership and finance. In the twenty-first century, another important source of information about organisations is their websites, which may have more detail than a directory entry and be more up to date. Directories have the advantage of presenting information in a standard format, however, enabling more efficient and accurate comparisons, and putting the information in context.

Government publications

Government publications tend to be dealt with separately from other sources of information, largely because of the specialised structures used to convey legislation and statistical information, and because the forms vary from country to country. In federated countries such as Australia and the USA, government publications appear at the national and at the state level. Specific forms of government information include legal information, proceedings of legislative bodies such as Parliament or Congress, annual reports of government bodies, reports of commissions of enquiry and so on, and statistics.

Legal information generally has four forms, although the terminology varies from country to country. First, there are laws that have been proposed and debated in the legislative body (called 'bills' in parliamentary systems). Second, there are laws that have been passed and have become part of the country's legal framework (called 'acts' in parliamentary systems). Laws can appear in two forms – sequential, as passed by the legislature, and consolidated, where subsequent amendments have been incorporated into the text of the laws. It is important for users to know whether they are consulting sequential or consolidated versions of laws. Third, there are regulations, in which the government fills in the detail of the legislation – for example, the Transport Act gives the government power to set speed limits on roads but the Transport Regulations set the speed limit in urban areas to be 50km/hr. Fourth, there is case law, consisting of court decisions that interpret the law. Case law can be difficult to identify due to the many different courts and tribunals that can produce decisions that affect the interpretation of the law. Identifying case law generally requires the use of specialised legal databases and law reporting services.

The records of the legislative bodies ('Hansard' in parliamentary systems, the Congressional Record in the USA) are an important source of political information, and also provide background to the decisions of the government. In most countries, government bodies are required to provide an annual report, and these provide information about their activities, and the area of society for which they are responsible. The annual report of the government department responsible for employment, for example, is generally a useful source of information on trends in unemployment and the labour market. Annual reports are also important sources of historical information – sometimes in unlikely areas. The annual reports of the New Zealand Tourist Department for the early 1900s, for instance, include lists of climbers who reached the summit of Mt Cook/Aoraki.

Reports of commissions of enquiry are usually in high demand immediately after their release, but are also an important part of the historical record. Identifying commissions of enquiry can be complicated by a tendency to refer to them by names other than their formal one. The *Report of the Royal Commission to inquire into the crash on Mount Erebus, Antarctica of a DC10 aircraft operated by Air New Zealand Limited*, for example, is generally known as the 'Mahon Report', after the judge who headed the enquiry.

While official yearbooks, mentioned earlier, provide overviews of statistics for a country, detailed statistical information from censuses and other sources is generally produced by the Government statistics agency. In the twenty-first century this is most easily accessible online. The Australian Bureau of Statistics website (http://www.abs.gov.au) provides detailed census information as downloadable spreadsheets which can be manipulated and analysed in detail.

In order to provide access to print-based government information, many governments have depository schemes (similar to the legal deposit schemes discussed in Chapter 5), which require copies of government documents to be placed in designated public libraries. Today, much government information is provided on the open web, and most governments provide a portal site which links to web-based information provided by its agencies. For example, the Australian Government portal at http://www.gov.au/ provides links to government information at the federal, state and local government levels.

Audiovisual materials

Audiovisual materials, such as videotapes, DVDs, audio tapes, audio CDs and microforms, can be difficult to identify and access. Unlike books and journals, which are covered by regular bibliographic tools, audiovisual materials are not systematically covered. Audiovisual materials are particularly important in educational environments, with university and school libraries generally holding strong audiovisual collections. Increasingly, audiovisual materials are available through the open web, although much material has been placed on the open web without the copyright owners' permission, and users have to be cautious about downloading and using material, and particularly about passing audiovisual materials on to third parties, such as students in a class.

Microforms (microfilm and microfiche) are a means of preserving and distributing copies of information sources. Many libraries hold backruns of newspapers in microform in order to save space and because microforms are less likely to degrade than newsprint. In the twentieth century many libraries undertook microfilming projects in order to preserve valuable materials, although in the twenty-first century digitisation is becoming an alternative way to provide access to materials without the risks associated with users handling the originals.

Evaluation of sources

It has always been important to evaluate information before relying on it, but in the twenty-first century the increasing use of information from the open web has made evaluation of information even more critical. Conventionally published material has generally been through an editorial process of factual checking, and it is usually fairly easy to determine the author of the material. But information can be placed on the open web by an individual with no editorial input and it can be hard to determine the source of the material. An example of a site that appears to be offering reliable information, but on closer examination is completely fraudulent, is the Dihydrogen Monoxide Research Division (http://www.dhmo.org/). This site expands on the dangers of this chemical, for example, the number of deaths caused by it each year, particularly in marine industries, and creates the impression of a serious environmental danger. However, most people will realise from their school chemistry that dihydrogen monoxide is simply another name for – water!

Criteria used to evaluate information include:

- Authority – this refers to the qualification of the author (whether personal or corporate) to provide information on the topic. In the case of a medical topic, for instance, does the author have a medical qualification? Has the author published articles on the topic in reputable journals? Does he or she work for an official body in the subject area?

- Accuracy – this can be tested by checking known facts (an Australian assessing an atlas might look at the map of Melbourne and see if the latest freeway extensions appear) or by comparing several information sources to see if they give the same answer.

- Currency – the extent to which the source is up to date. In a historical source this may not be an issue, but for a news source currency is vital. Dates of updates should appear in sources – publication dates in the case of books, dates of last update for websites.

- Objectivity – the measure of the extent to which the source is unbiased about the topic. In most cases an objective view is required, for example, on the effectiveness of herbal remedies in treating cancer, although advocacy websites perform a valuable role, provided the biases are stated clearly.

- Usability – the ease of use of a source. Are the sections in a print source logically arranged and are there useful indexes? Can a web-based source be easily navigated, are the meanings of links clear, do the pages download in a reasonable time and can the site be used by the visually impaired?

One of the qualities required in an information professional is the ability to look critically at information sources. To take the first criterion listed above, it is important to assess the authority of web resources, which makes it necessary for the information professional to determine the responsibility for the information. Often this may not be made clear and may require research through tools such as *WhoIs* (http://www.whois.net/) to check the ownership of a domain name. The Martin Luther King website (http://martinlutherking.org/), for instance, which provides information about the Afro-American civil rights leader, is at a domain name owned by a white supremacist organisation and, on close examination, contains inaccurate and biased information.

Conclusion: the future of information sources

A brief survey like this can only indicate the broad range of information sources. Despite the increasing reliance on web search engines, a sophisticated user of information still needs to be aware of the variety of sources available and of the fact that not all information is available through Google. Sophistication in information use also means being critical of information sources, and judging the authority, accuracy, currency, objectivity and usability of information received, and its relevance to the information need. At the start of the twenty-first century the nature of information sources is changing dramatically, but some trends seem clear.

First, online web-based information sources are clearly replacing print for locating specific information, except in some specialist areas. Print, nonetheless, will still have a future for absorbing large 'chunks' of information, so physical books will continue, at least until there is a major breakthrough in computer display such as digital paper or virtual retinal projection. A trend worth noting, however, is that many people's everyday information gathering is now conducted through multimedia – increasingly people get their news through television and radio rather than newspapers, so it is likely that information sources will increasingly be multimedia rather than text based. Mobile information provision is also a likely trend with the increasing use of WiFi and mobile phone technology. Librarians who think of the internet as leading-edge technology should be aware that for teenagers email is what one uses to keep in touch with old people (Lenhart et al. 2005).

Interactive, user-contributed reference tools, such as Wikipedia and the interactive features of Google Earth, will become important information sources. While these will not replace traditional authoritative published sources, it is more likely that user contributed sources and authoritative sources will complement each other. Open access research publishing will result in more authoritative research material becoming available on the open web, meaning that selective web search engines such as Google Scholar will complement the traditional indexing and abstracting databases.

Being information literate – at a basic level, knowing how to find and assess information – will be an important attribute for the twenty-first century information seeker. While using most information sources will not require a visit to a physical library, libraries will still have important roles in facilitating access to information sources through training, advice and subscriptions. Libraries will also have an increasing role in creating and maintaining information sources, through initiatives such as institutional repositories and digitisation programmes.

While these developments pose obvious challenges in information provision, they also offer some fascinating possibilities for both information users and for the library and information service professions.

References

Abercrombie, N, Hill, S & Turner, BS 2006, *The Penguin dictionary of sociology*, Penguin, London.

Atlas of the South Pacific 1986, 2nd edn, Government Printing Office, Wellington.

Australian dictionary of biography 1976–2005, Melbourne University Press, Carlton, Vic.

The Australian encyclopedia, 1996, 6th edn, Australian Geographic Pty Ltd, Terrey Hills, NSW.

Bradford, JT, Costello, B & Lenholt, R 2005, 'Reference service in the digital age: An analysis of sources used to answer reference questions', *Journal of Academic Librarianship*, vol.31, no.3, pp.263-72.

Broder, A, Kumar, R, Maghoul, F, Raghavan, P, Rajagopalan, S, Stata, R, Tomkins, A & Wiener, J 2000, 'Graph structure in the web', paper presented to *Ninth International World Wide Web Conference*, held in Amsterdam, 15-19 May 2000, http://www.www9.org/w9cdrom/160/160.html

The dictionary of New Zealand biography, 1990–2000, Auckland University Press, Aukland; Dept. of Internal Affairs, Wellington.

Drake, MA (ed.) 2003, *Encyclopedia of library and information science*, Marcel Dekker, New York.

Encyclopaedia Britannica 2005, Encyclopaedia Britannica, Chicago, IL.

The Europa directory of international organizations 2006, 2006, Routledge, London.

Frick, M & Fallis, D 2003, 'Indicators of accuracy for answers to ready reference questions on the internet', *Journal of the American Society for Information Science and Technology*, vol.55, no.3, pp.238-45.

Gazetteer of New Zealand place names 1969, Department of Lands & Survey, Wellington.

Information please almanac 1947- , Information Please LLC, Boston.

Jacsó, P 2005a, 'Visualizing overlap and rank differences among web-wide search engines: Some free tools and services', *Online Information Review*, vol.29, no.5, pp.554-60.

Jacsó, P 2005b, 'Google scholar: The pros and the cons', *Online Information Review*, vol.29, no.2, pp.208-14.

Katz, WA 2002, *Introduction to reference work*, 8th edn, McGraw-Hill, Boston.

Kennedy, GD & Deverson, T (eds) 2005, *The New Zealand Oxford dictionary*, Oxford University Press, Auckland.

Knowles, EM (ed.) 2004, *The Oxford dictionary of quotations*, Oxford University Press, Oxford.

Lenhart, A, Madden, M & Hilting, P 2005, *Teens and technology: Youth are leading the transition to a fully wired and mobile nation*, Pew Internet & American Life Project, Washington, DC.

McGraw-Hill encyclopedia of science & technology : An international reference work in twenty volumes including an index, 2002, 9th edn, McGraw-Hill, New York.

McKinnon, M (ed.) 1997, *Bateman New Zealand historical atlas: Ko papatuanuku e takoto nei*, David Bateman in association with Historical Branch, Department of Internal Affairs, Auckland.

Pew Internet & American Life Project 2006, *Daily internet activities*, http://www.pewinternet.org/trends/ Daily_Internet_Activities_4.26.06.htm

Smith, AG 2003, 'Think local, search global? Comparing search engines for searching geographically specific information', *Online Information Review*, vol.27, no.2, pp.102-9.

Soanes, C & Stevenson, A (eds) 2004, *Concise Oxford English dictionary*, Oxford University Press, Oxford.

Statesman's year-book 1864-, Palgrave, London.

Stevens, AM & Schmidgall Tellings, AE 2004, *A comprehensive Indonesian-English dictionary*, Ohio University Press, Athens.

The Times comprehensive atlas of the world 2003, 11th edn, Times Books, London.

Wallace, DP & Van Fleet, C 2005, 'The democratization of information? Wikipedia as a reference resource', *Reference & User Services Quarterly*, vol.45 no.2, pp.100-103.

Whitaker's almanack 1869-, J Whitaker, London.

Who's who in Australia 2006 2005, 42nd edn, Crown Content Pty Ltd, Melbourne.

Williamson, AP 2000, 'BUBL LINK/5:15: Smarter than the average search engine', *Serials Librarian*, vol.37, no.4, pp.37-50.

Yallop, C (ed.) 2005, *Macquarie dictionary*, 4th edn, Macquarie Library, North Ryde, NSW.

Yearbook Australia 1901- , Australian Bureau of Statistics, Canberra.

CHAPTER 8
Current issues in library collecting

Paul Genoni

Collections are at the very heart of libraries. Without the human desire to compile and maintain collections of information in the variety of formats in which it has been distributed over many centuries, there would be no such institutions as libraries, and no such profession as librarianship. Indeed, the term 'library' has two principal meanings. It refers of course to the building that houses a collection and acts as a service point uniting library staff with information users. A 'library' also refers, however, to the collection itself – to the books, journals, databases, maps, pictures and so on that constitute a repository of information. In the former meaning a library remains intractably physical – a matter of bricks and mortar – but in the latter meaning libraries have recently been relieved of much of their physicality. The extent of the revolution engendered by the digital storage and transfer of information is almost impossible to overstate – comparisons with the invention of alphabetic scripts and moveable type are not unwarranted. Certainly it has a deep impact upon almost every aspect of library and information work, just as it affects profoundly the professional, business and recreational lives of most people in developed nations.

The purpose of this chapter is to address some of the issues currently confronting libraries in their role as collectors and keepers of information in all its forms. To do so is to consider the most 'traditional' of library functions, yet the tasks of developing, managing and maintaining collections remain core activities for the transformed library. It is a library's role as a collecting agency that forms the critical link between the great libraries of the ancient world and the digital library of the twenty-first century.

Libraries and collection management policy

Collection management is the term most commonly used to describe the area of librarianship that deals with collections. Collection management incorporates the variety of functions involved in selecting, acquiring, storing and maintaining collections in a cost-effective manner. There has been some challenge to the use of this term in a time when library 'collections' incorporate a great deal of content that is not physically owned by the library, but generally the term has retained its currency. Collection management needs to be distinguished from the related term of 'collection development'. Although the two terms may be used interchangeably in some of the library and information studies literature, collection development is usually considered to be a narrower function in that it specifically refers to that part of collection management in which librarians identify and select content (in whatever format) to be added to the collection.

Given that collection management incorporates a variety of library functions, it is often said to constitute a program. A critical component of a collection management program is a written collection development policy. This is a document that stipulates in some detail the basic principles upon which a library collection is founded, developed and maintained. Such a document can be relevant to the collecting activity of any library, from the largest publicly funded library to the smallest privately funded collection.

Collection development activity has long been conducted according to some form of 'policy', but this has often been unwritten or recorded. It was held as part of the personal or corporate memory of collections librarians or other long-serving staff. During the 1980s, in particular, a trend emerged towards recording such policy in documents that could be easily shared with library staff, users, funding agencies and other libraries. For most libraries, the preparation of such documents should necessitate consultation with each of these groups in order to ensure that collecting activity represents their various – and sometimes conflicting – interests. Certainly for many libraries the preparation of a written document was the first time they had undertaken a comprehensive and orderly review of their collecting activities. It should be noted that documents referred to as 'collection development policies' often include matters that more rightly belong to collection management, such as storage, preservation and disaster management.

By undertaking reviews of collection-related policy and then distributing the results, libraries hope to ensure that decisions made in relation to the collection are equitable, consistent and transparent. In this way, written collection development policies have become integral to the accountability function of libraries. It is common for libraries to spend more than 50 per cent of their budget on content, and it is important that this expenditure is accounted for in a manner that demonstrates that it is planned, prudent and consistent with institutional objectives.

Questions have been raised, however, as to the relevance of 'collection' development policies at a time when much library content is leased in digital format rather than owned (Kennedy 2005), but such documents remain central to the management process of many libraries. The current challenge, therefore, is to ensure they remain relevant by finding ways in which to integrate the various categories of owned, leased and accessed material into a meaningful statement. The concept of what constitutes a collection *has* changed, and this must be reflected in a library's planning, policy and accountability documents. It is for this reason that they now often carry names such as 'collections and access policy' or 'resources access policy', which indicate that they are concerned with more than just ownership.

Libraries and other collecting agencies

Libraries are not alone in their collecting activities. Museums, art galleries and archives stand out as other examples of publicly funded collecting agencies. Indeed, the distinctions between these various collecting agencies are difficult to state categorically. It is not a simple matter of libraries collecting print-based material such as books and journals, galleries collecting art objects such as painting and sculpture and museums collecting items of natural history and realia. The libraries of Australia, for example, hold non print-based collections of substantial national and international importance, including many items such as paintings, prints, photographs, maps, sound recordings and realia that the public might associate with other types of institutions.

Much of this material is held in major 'research libraries', including the National Library of Australia, the various state and territory libraries (see Chapter 5) and university libraries. It is also increasingly likely, however, that public or community libraries – often serving a community without its own museum or gallery – will collect non print-based items of local or regional importance.

One distinction that might exist in the public mind between libraries and other collecting institutions is that museums and galleries have an exhibition-based culture. That is, they attract public attention and visitors by mounting exhibitions derived from their own collections or borrowed from the collections of similar cooperating institutions. In contrast, libraries have typically drawn most of their visitors from regular readers or information users who are attracted by the desire to *use* a library's collection. Many libraries do, however, have a record of mounting exhibitions – often derived from their own collections and sometimes drawing upon other library collections. Recent major and successful exhibitions mounted by libraries in Australia, include the 'Treasures of the Great Libraries of the World' (National Library of Australia, 2001–2002; http://www.nla.gov.au/worldtreasures/index.html), and 'National Treasures from Australia's Great Libraries' (National Library of Australia and other venues, 2005–2007; http://nationaltreasures.nla.gov.au/). Events such as these impress upon the public both the importance and range of material and artefacts held in library collections, and establish libraries as significant exhibiting institutions.

The major collecting agencies, including libraries, are now often grouped together by commentators and government funding bodies as examples of 'memory institutions' (Dempsey 2000). Recognition of the overlap between the national collecting agencies came with the creation in 2004 of the Collections Council of Australia (http://www.collectionscouncil. com.au/), a body charged with overseeing the coordination of long-term policies for the coordination of collections held by libraries, museums, galleries and archives. It is certainly the case that these institutions face many similar issues and challenges related to their roles in developing and managing collections.

Collection assessment

Fundamental to collection management is the belief that collections can be assessed in some way. That is, it is possible to achieve an objective understanding of how 'good' a collection is. Some form of assessment is held to be necessary if the money spent on collection development is to be put to optimum use in meeting users' needs (Agee 2005). In its very crudest form, collection assessment (or 'collection evaluation' or 'collection measurement') may mean no more than counting volumes. The size of collections has long been held as an indicator of their worth, based on the simple assumption that the more titles and volumes in a collection the more information it can provide. Not surprisingly, library managers have found this measure wanting. Not only does it fail to address the issue of how well the items in the collection are matched to the users, but it has also begun to look increasingly inadequate as electronic access has made the counting of physical volumes almost meaningless.

Various methods have been developed to produce more sophisticated assessments. Some of these methods, referred to as 'collection based', still rely on volume counts. The difference is that an attempt is now made to test the holdings of the assessed collection against 'lists' that represent the totality of publishing activity in a particular discipline These lists might be sourced from standard bibliographies, or even from the catalogues of libraries known to have outstanding collections. A variation on this form of evaluation is the 'citation study', which is based on measuring the number of citations from reputable sources (namely, scholarly journals) that could be located in a particular collection.

Other forms of assessment are centred on trying to determine how well a collection is meeting users' needs. These may be either 'use-based' studies, that measure collection usage based on circulation statistics and 'in-house' usage studies of non-circulating material; or 'user-based' studies, that rely on obtaining feedback from users (by survey, interview or focus group) on how well a collection is meeting their needs.

All of these methods are flawed in that they produce fragmentary data at best. For example, all lists available for comparison have their own limitations, flaws and biases; usage figures may reflect borrowing activity but reveal little about the 'value' the borrower gains from that item; user surveys are often hampered by the user's limited knowledge of the publishing activity in a given subject. The effectiveness of all assessment methods is also crucially dependent on good research design and the appropriateness of the selected method to the collection being assessed. For example, the assessment methods used in a public library may be quite different from those applied in an academic library. As a result, for most libraries a good understanding of a collection will only be reached by the use of several methods and the correlation of the various data they gather. Good collection assessment may therefore be time-consuming and expensive in planning, implementing and evaluating.

The advent of digital storage and access to collections has complicated the task of assessment. In particular, it is not always clear when an item constitutes part of a 'collection'. Should 'ownership' be the test for inclusion? Should a leased item also be included? What about material freely available on the internet? Should this be included only if it has been in some way incorporated into the library's catalogue? Technology has helped address many of these collection assessment challenges. In particular, automated circulation systems can supply much more precise circulation data, and, more recently, the advent of large databases of e-journals has for the first time provided a means by which journal usage can be accurately measured.

Collection assessment remains a vexed issue. As Sheila Intner has concluded, 'To make collections work pay off for a library and its users, librarians need to gain profound knowledge of their collections and know how they are used' (Intner 2003).

Selection of library resources

Central to the process of collection management – and collection development in particular – is the act of selection. Selection involves the choice of content, in either physical or digital formats, for adding to collections. It includes choosing items that require a one-time purchase, such as books; other material which is purchased for retention by an ongoing subscription payment until such time as it is cancelled, such as printed journals or monographic series; or digital content to which access is provided by payment of a subscription and for the duration specified by a 'lease' agreement. Selection may also in some cases require no payment at all. That is, librarians will select freely available internet sites or electronic journals for recording and linking via catalogues and subject portals.

It is through the act of selection that practical expression is given to many of the policy decisions recorded in a collection development policy. The priorities that have been established for subject content, and the criteria that have been expressed by way of preferred format, language, geographic origin, price and so on, should be manifest in a library's selection practice.

While a well-prepared collection development policy will guide selection it will by no means resolve issues as to exactly which individual books, journals, databases or other information sources should be added to a collection. To a large extent these decisions still need to be made by librarians relying upon their skills and experience.

Many of the skills involved in good selection go to the heart of a librarian's professional expertise. These include knowing which sources to rely upon for information about new and forthcoming publications; where to find reliable reviews; how to anticipate demand that may not yet be apparent; how to engage users in the process while retaining responsibility; how to use the services provided by library suppliers and subscription agencies to assist with selection (see below); and how to balance the need for an independent collection while also relying upon inter-library loan and document delivery.

To a large extent, selection also gives librarians a chance to exercise their 'values'. Selection librarians make decisions that reflect their commitment to the type of collection they are trying to build. Will it be a collection that is primarily responsive to immediate needs, or will it be one that exhibits a commitment to longer-term goals? How much of a public library's acquisition budget, for example, should be used to provide multiple copies of items that are currently 'hot', and how much should be set aside for items for which there is little immediate demand but which in the librarian's judgement may have greater long-term value for the collection? This debate, sometimes expressed as a difference between meeting users' 'wants' as opposed to their 'needs', runs deeply through the literature of collection development.

The 'political' nature of selection should also be noted. Library acquisitions budgets are frequently divided among different interest groups. This is equally true if it is an academic or special library budget that is allocated between different departments within the parent institution, or a public library budget that is allocated to adult, young adult and children's material, or to fiction and non-fiction. In each case there will be pressure groups that seek to maximise the dollars available to acquire material meeting their own interests. It may be a matter of some sensitivity as to how a budget is divided, and to what extent the resulting decisions will be reported to users.

Pressure groups will also form around other aspects of library selection. There are few libraries that are not at least occasionally asked to justify the selection of material that might be deemed offensive. The issue of censorship is addressed in Chapter 16.

Suppliers and subscription agents

Libraries do not work alone in their collection development tasks. They are frequently assisted by library suppliers and subscription agents (also sometimes referred to as 'vendors' and in North America as 'jobbers'). Library suppliers and subscription agents serve as intermediaries between libraries and publishers. Their use is necessary in order to simplify the task libraries will otherwise face in dealing with a multitude of publishers in different continents and time zones and operating in different currencies. There are many suppliers and subscription agencies offering services to libraries. Some specialise in working with particular types of libraries; some deal with books only while others (subscription agents) will handle periodicals only; some are generalists while others specialise in certain subject areas. An important task for the collections librarian is to select suppliers who can best represent their interests. While small libraries may be able to depend on one supplier, it is likely that larger libraries will need to use several, including some suppliers who can represent them domestically, and others who act internationally.

While many of the tasks performed by library suppliers are of a routine or administrative nature (ordering titles, following up undelivered orders, making payments, producing expenditure reports, preparing items in a 'shelf-ready' form), and more to do with 'acquisitions' rather than 'collection development', they are also able to assist librarians with their selection work. This is often achieved by a library producing a detailed collection development 'profile', which describes their subject-based collecting priorities, plus other criteria they have set in terms of format, price, language and so on. The supplier will then undertake to provide information about new items – or copies of the items themselves – that meet the library's profile. In this way, librarians are relieved of the task of routinely searching through the vast amount of information relating to new publications.

Library suppliers also assist collection development by putting in place different levels of 'automatic ordering' that mean libraries do not need to order items individually (Mueller 2005). For example, under the terms of a 'blanket order' a supplier will automatically provide a library with a copy of all items that match their profile. A variation is the 'approval plan', under which a library is provided with items for their consideration, but usually with a limited right to return items that are not required. A further option is the 'standing order', which is used to establish an ongoing order for all parts of a series of books (Langendorfer & Hurst 2003). These various plans not only save libraries time but also can provide libraries with a substantial discount (perhaps as much as 30 per cent), because large orders can be placed, thus reducing overheads for the supplier and publisher.

The issue immediately facing libraries is the extent to which crucial collection development tasks and decisions should be 'outsourced'. One outcome of increased electronic publishing has been for library suppliers to find new and imaginative ways of marketing both product and services to libraries (a point discussed below). Indeed, suppliers have developed their services to a point where, once a collecting profile and relationship with a reliable supplier is established, it is feasible for many libraries to relinquish almost all of their daily involvement in selection activity. To do so might bring significant efficiencies, but these come at the cost of abandoning direct control over a key professional activity.

Whatever decision is made with regard to outsourcing, building a good relationship with suppliers is an important component of collection development work. It is, however, a very competitive market place, and librarians' business skills are tested as both parties are forced to negotiate in order to achieve the best deal (Flowers 2004).

Cooperative collecting

There has long been interest in the idea that libraries could cooperate in their collecting activity. The basic principle is that libraries within reasonable geographic reach of each other could coordinate their selection in order to minimise the overlap between the collections. Supported by preferred treatment in terms of access by users of cooperating libraries, the total pool of material available to the users of those libraries is thereby increased. It should be noted that less coordinated efforts at cooperation have existed successfully for many years, with inter-library loan networks allowing libraries to acquire items on short-term loan from other libraries. The difference with cooperative collecting is that the cooperation occurs prior to rather than after selection. Successful cooperative collecting programs have existed since at least the first half of the twentieth century (Dominguez & Swindler 1993).

There has been an increased interest in cooperative collecting since the 1980s. This interest was driven by what became known as the 'scholarly publishing crisis'. Although the crisis has to some extent abated, it needs to be understood in order to comprehend some of the imperatives that have driven cooperative collecting activity for the past two decades. In simple terms, the crisis was the result of ongoing and excessive rises in the price of published material, particularly scholarly journals, which commenced in the 1980s and continued throughout the 1990s. These price rises regularly outstripped increases in the general cost of living. The reasons for this are complex, but certainly related to the shift of scholarly publishing away from not-for-profit organisations such as universities and professional associations and into the hands of large, commercially driven international publishing houses. The impact of these price rises was made worse by the ongoing growth in publishing output that had been gaining momentum since the end of the Second World War. As a result, many libraries – and research libraries in particular – found that they were able to acquire an increasingly smaller percentage of the total published output. As libraries felt the pressure to buy more with less, the implementation of cooperative collecting agreements seemed like a natural means of protecting existing levels of access to material.

Although the scholarly publishing crisis (perhaps more accurately the 'scholarly purchasing crisis') was felt internationally, its impact was exacerbated in Australia because of the decline in the value of the Australian dollar in the corresponding period. Australia purchases the bulk of its scholarly publishing from North America and Europe, and the steady downward shift in the value of the dollar during this period resulted in a particularly severe erosion of purchasing power.

Libraries in Australia therefore developed a very singular response to the problem, a cooperative collecting program known as the Distributed National Collection (DNC). Led by the National Library, the DNC was devised at the Australian Libraries Summit in October 1988, and was basically an attempt to get all Australian libraries (and particularly the research-based national, state and university libraries) to manage their collecting in a cooperative fashion on a national scale. Australia was well placed for this 'experiment' in that it had in place much of the necessary bibliographic infrastructure in the form of the Australian Bibliographic Network/Kinetica; a comparatively small number of libraries that would be required to cooperate; and a source of leadership in the National Library and the (then) Australian Council of Library and Information Services (ACLIS).

Despite some initial progress, the DNC did not succeed to the extent that had been hoped, and by the mid 1990s it had largely been abandoned. There are a number of reasons for this (Genoni 2001), although at heart there may have been reluctance on the part of library managers to be seen to be surrendering autonomy over their own collection development programs. There was also a growing uncertainty in Australia and elsewhere as to whether the changing information environment may not render cooperative collecting programs obsolete. Sceptics were beginning to suggest that cooperative collecting was a solution devised for a predominantly print environment, but with the advent of the digital library and increasing reliance on copy sourced internationally from commercial document delivery services, there may be limited need for future cooperation in collection building (Shreeves 1997). Certainly some of the emphasis in cooperation has now shifted to agreements reached by consortia to acquire shared access to digital content (see below).

Cooperation in the building of physical collections is not, however, an idea that has died easily. Many programs continue to function. Some of these may be informal understandings between public libraries located in the same region, or between public and school libraries seeking to provide services to school children. Many of them remain far more ambitious, involving state-wide programs in the USA (Potter 1997; Richards 2001), or networks of academic libraries in a particular city. And while the push for a DNC may have receded in Australia, a similar solution – modified for an electronic environment – has been proposed for the United Kingdom under the auspices of the Research Support Libraries Program (Genoni 2002; Milne 2002).

Libraries of all types will continue to be challenged by the desirability of finding the right forms of cooperation in developing and sharing their collections. The issues include selecting the right partners, deciding the types of formats and content that will be the focus of cooperative activity, and negotiating a set of terms and conditions that make the arrangement beneficial to all parties.

Digital collections, including e-journals

Of the impacts that digitisation has had upon library collections and services none has been more profound than the electronic journal, or e-journal. It needs to be acknowledged that this has not affected all libraries equally. Public libraries, in particular, continue to receive the bulk of their journals (including magazines) in print format, but for libraries that rely upon scholarly journals it is clear that the electronic format is prevailing (Galvin 2004; Ware 2005).

E-journals began to make a serious impact in academic and special libraries in the mid 1990s. Although initially they were clumsy for users to access, with many different interfaces, they rapidly moved beyond being a novelty as libraries and users alike began to embrace their advantages. For libraries these advantages included streamlined acquisitions and processing, a reduction in storage and maintenance requirements and the elimination of binding and reshelving costs. For users the great advantage was improved accessibility. E-journals could be accessed remotely from a user's desktop and outside library opening hours. There was also removal of the frustration of finding that required volumes were 'off the shelves' or 'at the bindery'.

Libraries and publishers were reluctant to embrace the new technology absolutely during the 'start up' phase, as users began to make the transition from print to electronic. During this period, many libraries maintained dual print and electronic subscriptions (Rupp-Serrano et al. 2002). The important developments that hastened the shift were the introduction of large databases of journals that could be accessed via a common interface, and the acceptance of the internet as the standard delivery platform.

Another phenomenon that occurred at the same time was the introduction of journals that were made freely available on the internet. As an extension of the concept of open-access publishing some important journals have been created without any commercial aims whatsoever, and are available to anybody with internet access. More than 2,000 such journals are listed in the Directory of Open Access Journals (http://www.doaj.org/). For the collection development librarian, the task is to identify which of these journals might be relevant to library users and integrate them with other library content by recording them in catalogues and relevant subject portals.

In recent years, considerable research has been devoted to assessing readers' acceptance of e-journals (De Groote & Dorsch 2001; Tenopir & King 2002; Aerni et al. 2003; Vaughan 2003). Although initial reluctance was apparent, mounting evidence indicates that users have accepted and embraced the advantages of e-journals, although there is some evidence suggesting that the adoption of e-journals is not consistent across disciplines (Maula & Talja 2003).

The advent of e-journals and other electronic content has led to some significant changes in what is now meant by a 'collection', and in the relationships between librarians, publishers and library suppliers. In large part these changes result from the shift from a model of 'ownership' to one of 'leasing'. That is, access to e-journals is often negotiated for the duration covered by a contract or lease only, and if the lease is not renewed then the library loses access to the material. In these circumstances, a library does not build a permanent collection of back-sets in the same way as when they owned material that they had purchased.

A related matter is that, for the first time, content, be it in e-journals or some other form of electronic publishing, does not come with a virtually fixed price. Previously, libraries of various sizes would pay the same amount for the same item, but in an electronic environment, in which content is uncoupled from the fixed costs associated with printing and distribution, pricing has become flexible and negotiable. Collection development librarians have been put in a position of having to learn new business skills as they are required to negotiate leases covering both price and conditions of access. This factor has been partially responsible for the increased reliance on consortia-based deals.

Another important component of the shift to electronic content is the emergence of the e-book. E-books have been slower to gain acceptance by both libraries and users than have e-journals. This is at least partly the result of the array of e-book technologies that are available, each with a different level of utility for the various types of content that might conceivably be acquired, and therefore with varying levels of attractiveness for libraries and users. There is a particular problem with e-books that will need to be read outside of a library.

There are, however, two main technologies that provide access to e-books. The first is the delivery of text to the user's desktop via the internet. Many academic libraries are now using the internet to deliver copies of e-books to users. In addition, a number of internet sites have been developed to make available the text of books that are out of copyright. Perhaps the best known of these sites is Project Gutenberg (http://www.gutenberg.org/), which also includes an Australian arm of the project (http://gutenberg.net.au/). The second technology – and this is the subject of much development – features the use of hand-held storage devices to enable users to 'download' or 'borrow' text from a library. There are various such readers now on the market. One of the frequently noted issues with these devices is the reluctance of readers to absorb large amounts of text from a screen rather than a page. There is undoubtedly user resistance to technologies which are still regarded as less comfortable than a physical book, despite the many other advantages they may have in terms of storage, accessibility and retrieval of text (Mercieca 2004).

Despite the slow initial uptake of e-books, there remains a great deal of optimism about their future (Abbott & Kelly 2004; Cox 2004). The challenge for librarians is to find the e-book technology that suits their users' needs, and to normalise the handling of e-books within their workflows and collection management practices (Armstrong & Lonsdale 2005; Christianson & Aucoin 2005).

The 'big deal' and consortia

As libraries and users struggled to come to terms with the advent of e-journals, there emerged developments that made them considerably more palatable to both parties. Providers of e-journals determined that it was in the best interest of all parties if subscriptions to e-journals were 'bundled'. That is, rather than libraries subscribing on a title-by-title basis as they had with print journals, they would acquire sets of e-journals that had been pre-packaged by a publisher or other supplier. These bundles of journals became known as 'aggregations' or 'big-deals'.

Aggregations have been compiled in different sizes and for different reasons. Some are put together to represent the output of a single publisher, but many compile titles from a range of publishers. Some attempt to focus on particular disciplines, while others are multi-disciplinary. Some have been compiled by publishers or information suppliers of long standing, while others have been created by companies formed specifically for the purpose. Some of the major aggregations include EBSCOhost, Science Direct, Swetswise, ABI/Inform and InfoTrac OneFile. A major source of Australian e-journals is Australian Public Affairs Full Text (APA-FT), which offers the full text of more than 300 journals.

The attractions of these packages for libraries are two-fold. First, they enable libraries to acquire e-journals on a scale and in a format that make them easier to promote to users. Second, they are priced such that by subscribing to the package the cost of individual titles within the package is substantially reduced. This second advantage is crucial. After a decade or more of cancelling journal titles in response to rapidly increasing prices, libraries could now reverse this trend and add content (Nabe 2001; Quinn 2001).

These 'big-deals' are, however, by no means without their problems (Frazier 2001, Friend 2003, Ball 2004). In particular, the 'all-or-nothing' aspect presents librarians with a dilemma in that it requires them to give up some of their responsibility for collection content, with selection for journals being shifted from a title-by-title proposition, to a choice between competing aggregations. A further issue is that within aggregations there are inevitably titles that would not previously have been within the scope of a collection and, in some cases, the costs of the aggregation can only be met by cancelling other titles to which a library may have long subscribed. Moreover, there is frequently duplication between aggregations, which means a library in effect pays for the same title twice or more. It is also the practice of publishers to impose 'embargoes' on titles in aggregations. In order to protect the market for direct subscriptions (to either print or electronic versions of a journal) a publisher may licence a title to an aggregator, but not for the most recent issues. It is frustrating for library users to have access to a journal, but not to the last six months or year of that title (Brooks 2003). Another frustration for librarians and users is that titles may be dropped from an aggregation without any forewarning.

Nevertheless, the advantages in terms of additional content have resulted in the widespread acceptance of aggregations. This has in turn led to another important development in terms of collection management practice – the frequent use of consortia for the purpose of negotiating access to aggregations. A consortium can be described as a cooperative arrangement reached between two or more libraries for the purpose of sharing the costs and benefits associated with acquiring information, often in the form of large aggregated databases of e-journals. The case for consortia has become particularly compelling in terms of cost, with libraries finding the more combined users they could deliver, the cheaper the subscription paid by each participating library. Consortia have also become an important means of reducing the workload involved in negotiating with publishers and aggregators as they allow libraries to share their negotiating, technical and legal expertise. Examples of major Australian consortia include the university-based CAUL Electronic Information Resources Committee (CEIRC) (http://www.caul.edu.au/datasets/ceirc.htm) and the National and State Libraries Australasia (http://www.caslconsortium.org/), which includes the National Library of New Zealand.

A significant development in consortia activity has been the move towards implementing national site licences for core sets of electronic resources. Such licences have the potential to provide a basic collection of electronic texts to all participating libraries. In September 2006, the National Library of Australia announced that it was proceeding with plans for a national site licence that would deliver a core collection of electronic texts to all public libraries. New Zealand has implemented a national site licensing program, Electronic Purchasing in Collaboration (EPIC) (http://epic.org.nz/nl/epic.html), which provides the full text of 16,000 journals to public, academic and special libraries.

Consortia, though, are not without their own problems (Peters 2003). It can sometimes be as difficult and time consuming negotiating with consortia partners as with aggregators (Dorner 2004), and for some smaller libraries in particular it may mean a further erosion of their collection autonomy.

One outcome of the use of consortia to provide access to the aggregated databases is that this form of cooperation has led to an outcome quite opposite to that intended by cooperation in a print environment. That is, whereas cooperative collecting had been envisioned as a means of reducing duplication and providing access to a broader range of material between cooperating libraries, consortia-based access to databases has the aim of providing libraries with access to the same range of titles. As participation in consortia may be funded by cancellation of marginal titles, the outcome may be homogeneity rather than diversity between collections, and a threat to the existence of titles that remain outside the 'big deals' (Prosser 2004).

Institutional repositories

One of the outcomes of the development of digital libraries is that libraries now find themselves acting as quasi-publishers. As discussed elsewhere in this chapter, libraries will frequently make decisions that part of their existing collection should be digitised and made accessible ('published') via the internet. A related development is that many libraries are becoming actively engaged in providing access to digital copies of various documents generated by their parent institution. This is particularly true within libraries serving universities and other research institutions, but it is likely that this will be the case for other types of libraries. These digital collections of institutionally sourced content are commonly referred to as 'institutional repositories' and they are increasingly seen as being a core library function (Lynch 2003; Smith 2004). Institutional repositories have been described as having four key attributes:

- Institutionally defined
- Scholarly
- Cumulative and perpetual
- Open and interoperable (Johnson 2002).

The precedents for institutional repositories are found in the subject-based repositories that became popular, particularly in the sciences, during the 1990s. These repositories were loosely based on the model endowed by the creators of ArXiv.org (http://arXiv.org/), a repository based at Cornell University and offering content derived from physics, mathematics, computer science and biology.

There remain differences between institutions with regard to what they decide is appropriate for inclusion in institutional repositories, but often the criteria are set by libraries in consultation with depositors. For many libraries, the selection of material for adding to institutional repositories has now become part of their ongoing collection development activity (Genoni 2004). This has obvious resource implications for the many libraries that are operating under the pressure created by the need to manage both electronic and print material. It has, however, given libraries an important new role as collecting agencies and increased their visibility within their parent organisation.

Institutional repositories can also be seen a further reaction to the scholarly publishing crisis referred to previously, in that individuals and institutions began to seek ways of making research output available free of charge in competition with highly priced scholarly journals. The period since the late 1990s has seen the formation of a number of coalitions of librarians and researchers dedicated to what is commonly referred to as 'open access' or 'open archive' publishing (Willinsky 2005). The open access movement is dedicated to ensuring that as much scholarly content as possible is distributed free of charge, irrespective of whether it is also made available through commercial publishing channels. The key international organisation is the US-based Scholarly Publishing and Academic Resources Coalition (http://www.arl.org/sparc/), and the International Federation of Library Associations has lent important support with its 'Statement on open access to scholarly literature and research documentation' (IFLA 2004). The success or otherwise of the open access movement will have a critical impact on future collection management activities for many libraries.

Care of library material

Having acquired a collection, usually at great expense, it is clearly in the best interests of libraries to maintain that collection in a useable condition for as long as possible. It is the case, however, that all library material, whatever its format, is prone to deterioration because of use and handling, or simply ageing. It is a responsibility of libraries to manage their collection with a view to minimising damage and enhancing the longevity of individual items. This area of library practice is often referred to generically as 'conservation and preservation'. These are in fact two distinct tasks. 'Conservation' refers to the maintenance of an item in a form as near as possible to its original state, and 'preservation' refers to the steps taken to keep the content of an item in a useable condition. It is therefore possible that in preserving an item one may take action that is contrary to good conservation practice (such as rebinding a book). The degree of priority given to these two tasks will vary considerably between libraries. Libraries serving an archival function, such as state or national libraries, may emphasise conservation, while those serving more immediate needs, such as public or school libraries, are likely to emphasis preservation.

Good conservation and preservation practice is a substantial and complex task. In part this is a result of the sheer number of possible types of damage that can occur to library materials. Just some of the more common forms of damage include:

- wear and tear associated with normal reading or other use;
- (mis)handling by library staff in the course of shelving and other library functions;
- heat, humidity, light, dust and other environmental problems;
- rodent and insect activity;
- use of unsuitable materials such as acidic papers;
- catastrophic events such as fire, flood and earthquake;
- poorly maintained or operated library equipment; and
- theft and deliberate mutilation.

Nearly all of these factors can be prepared for and prevented to some extent. The first onus on a library is to provide a suitable environment. This is again a complex and multi-faceted task, ranging from control of air temperature and humidity, to providing proper storage, to maintaining a program of insect control and to minimising the risk of major adverse events such as flooding.

Proper staff training is another important element of good conservation and preservation. Staff should be aware of the need to anticipate and where possible avoid damage, but also of the importance of taking prompt and appropriate action to repair damage when it is noticed. A collection development policy statement can be an important training tool in this regard. It should include a clear statement of a library's commitment to a high standard of conservation and preservation, and guidance to staff regarding their particular responsibilities. For some libraries it is also appropriate to have a document dealing with disaster preparedness (Fullerton 2004). Such a document should include a guide to precautions put in place to prevent disaster, plus steps that can be taken to recover the collection if the worst eventuates.

It should be apparent from the distinction made above between conservation and preservation that, while physical items require both conservation and preservation, items that are 'born digital' will usually require preservation only. Few issues, however, have exercised the minds of librarians in recent years as much as that of the preservation of digital material (Hodge 2000; Chapman 2003; Ross & Hedstrom 2005). The problem as stated by the UK-based Joint Information Systems Committee (JISC) is that:

> There is growing realisation that ... investment (in) and future access to digital resources, are threatened by technology obsolescence and to a lesser degree by the fragility of digital media. The rate of change in computing technologies is such that information can be rendered inaccessible within a decade. Preservation is therefore a more immediate issue for digital than for traditional resources. Digital resources will not survive or remain accessible by accident: pro-active preservation is needed (JISC 2002).

As JISC point out, digital libraries must be actively managed if they are to achieve a high level of preservation. In a digital environment it is not possible to treat preservation as a low priority or an afterthought as has sometimes been the case in an analogue environment. Whereas analogue material can be left on library shelves with the risk of slow deterioration, digital material that is left in an 'unmanaged' state will be subject to rapid obsolescence due to developments in technology.

Many libraries currently are challenged by dual conservation and preservation tasks. They must care for both 'traditional' library materials and digital material, thereby placing substantial demands on resources and staff skills. Australia has a major resource available to assist in this task in the National Library's Preserving Access to Digital Information (PADI) website (http://www.nla.gov.au/padi/index.html). It would appear likely, however, that many libraries continue to ignore the pressing issue of digital preservation. It is understandable why this is the case – it can be expensive and time consuming, and the solutions may not be permanent.

National libraries, charged with the responsibility of forming comprehensive collections of their nation's publishing output, face particular challenges in their attempt to identify and preserve the ever-increasing amount of digital content that has no print equivalent. In Australia, this task is addressed by the Pandora program, which is responsible for archiving a representative sample of Australia's digital content (http://pandora.nla.gov.au/about.html) (Phillips 2005). Pandora was established by the National Library in 1996, and is now maintained by a network of ten national and state government libraries (see Chapter 5; see also Chapter 11 for a discussion of preservation in the wider information management environment).

Special collections

Many libraries maintain collections that they designate to be 'special'. They might be considered special for one of a number of reasons, but what they have in common is that a decision has been made that they need a level of care and attention that could not be afforded to the bulk of the collection. Some of the reasons that a collection might be considered special are that it consists of items that:

- are considered to be 'rare' or irreplaceable, such as early imprints, significant first editions and manuscripts;
- have considerable monetary value, including limited editions and major art books;
- are physically fragile or vulnerable to theft in whole or part, including books with loose inserts, fine art prints and maps;

- are of a controversial nature that makes them a target for deliberate damage;
- have some particular association with the library that houses them or the institution it serves;
- have a strong personal association, such as copies signed by authors, or including marginalia in a notable hand, or associated with a noteworthy previous owner;
- form a subject-based collection of particular interest to the collecting library; or
- are in a format that makes them prone to theft or damage and that might be difficult to integrate into the broader collection, such as computer software, ephemera, videos or slides.

Special collections are most commonly associated with the 'rare books' housed in major research libraries, but there are very few libraries that do not have at least a small collection of material set aside because it falls into one or more of the above categories. The recent emphasis on developing local studies or local history collections (in other words, collections of items containing information relevant to the immediate region) in public libraries is an example of how an item may not necessarily have great rarity or monetary value to make it worthy of entry into a special collection.

Placing items into a special collections area is a decision that needs to be made carefully. It has implications for the ongoing cost of maintaining that item, given that special collections areas are usually intensive in terms of staff and resources and have higher standards of environmental control. It also has implications in terms of accessibility for users and other libraries, as items are often no longer available for browsing or lending and their use may be limited only to individuals with particular credentials or authority (Hyland 2004). For libraries with special collections, it is appropriate to use their collection development policy to stipulate the criteria that will be used when assessing material for those collections.

Digital technology has also had a significant impact on special collections. Libraries have found that digitising material in special collections and making images available on the internet has several advantages. In particular, it allows for the wide dissemination of items that have limits placed on their physical use, because of their rarity or physical fragility. This both makes the content available to anyone with internet access and prevents further use of the original. Examples of the use of digitisation to expand access to special format materials include the National Library of Australia's websites for MusicAustralia (http://www.musicaustralia.org/) and PictureAustralia (http://www.pictureaustralia.org/index.html) (see Chapter 5).

It is likely that the place of special collections will become more problematic, and for some libraries they may become more important. As collections become increasingly homogenised by shared access to large databases, collection development librarians will seek out those items that are distinguished by their local or personal associations, or because of their rarity and intrinsic merit, in order to differentiate or add value to the collection of a particular library. They will be justified in doing so, because the ability to digitise this material will in turn mean that the benefits of these collections are potentially distributed to an international audience. Other librarians, however, might take a contrary view, believing that increasing digitisation will ensure that these specialised research materials will be increasingly retrievable in their surrogate form, and that therefore there is little incentive to take on the many issues associated with managing a local special collection.

Deselection

Just as the selection of material is an integral part of a library's collecting function, so to is the process that occurs at the opposite end of the information cycle – deselection. This is the process of identifying material that should be removed from the library collection. Good collection management practice requires that a collection be periodically reviewed in order to identify material that no longer merits inclusion (Divelko & Gottlieb 2003). In practice, many libraries defer undertaking deselection until an impending storage crisis makes this absolutely necessary. Proper deselection entails staff time and resources and it is one of those tasks that is often deferred for as long as possible. There are, however, reasons why libraries should engage in regular deselection. In particular, there is evidence that once a deselection exercise has been conducted, the circulation of the remaining stock will increase, as 'tired' stock is removed and browsing becomes more rewarding for library users.

In order to identify the material that should be deselected the collection is subjected to a process that is usually referred to as 'weeding'. The exact purpose for weeding and the procedures it entails will vary between different types of libraries. In very general terms, the intention is to identify material of reduced information value that has little likelihood of future use. The complicating factor is that 'reduced information value' and 'little likelihood of future use' are judgements that will vary between libraries, and between individual librarians.

In simple terms, a public library, which will place a high value on an appealing, up-to-date collection consisting of items with a high likelihood of circulation (Chelton 2001), will assess material differently from an academic library that appreciates that it is in the nature of a research collection to include some items that may be physically unattractive, dated and likely to be used infrequently. Having made that general distinction, however, there are still some categories of material that are prone to deselection in all types of libraries. These include items that:

- have no record of recent circulation;
- contain dated or misleading information, or have been replaced by new editions;
- have physically deteriorated and require maintenance; or
- are duplicate copies that are no longer justified by high demand.

Even in using these criteria, however, there are complicating factors. Many library materials (in particular journals), do not circulate and therefore require some other form of assessment of usage. And in some libraries, information may be valued *because* it has dated and therefore reflects the state of knowledge as it was at a particular point in time. Some important considerations when weeding lie outside the immediate library. These include the clients. Weeding is potentially a very 'political' process, and it is sensible to ensure that clients are consulted before removing items from the collection. It is also important to ensure that there is guaranteed continued access through alternative sources to deselected items. No library should be responsible for discarding what might be a 'last copy' of possible use to a particular region, or indeed the nation. Even this issue has become somewhat blurred, however. It is often no longer easy to identify what is meant by 'last copy', when so much material is obtainable in digital format from sources that are difficult to pinpoint physically (Banks 2002).

Once a collection has been weeded, there remains the matter of what becomes of items that do not justify retention. Most libraries will have no alternative but to permanently deselect or discard them, but in some cases, in particular research libraries, there will be access to high-density (frequently 'off-site') storage facilities. In these cases, a library may 'relegate' rather than discard and users thereby retain limited access to the material. Items may not be available for browsing, but they can be retrieved for the user, although inevitably with a delay that might be a matter of several hours or several days.

Space and storage

One of the great benefits of the shift towards the digitisation of library collections has been the reduced demand for physical space. Of all the collection-related expenses facing libraries and their funding institutions, there has been none larger or more persistent than the unavoidable need to provide space in which to house the collection. Some aspects of digitisation have consumed space – for example, the need to provide users with access to multiple computer terminals – but these have been offset by the reduction in demand for collection storage space. Reference and journal collections in particular have been transferred to digital formats, and this has had an immediately beneficial impact on the ongoing space crisis that besets many – perhaps most – libraries.

For the foreseeable future, however, substantial components of collections will remain physical, and it is the nature of these collections to grow in a manner that cannot be offset by relying on deselection alone. Librarians will therefore need to continue to find creative solutions that enable them to retain material while engaged in the often futile wait for additional space.

The issue of space is closely connected with that of storage, and in many cases issues of storage are intimately connected with issues of access. In an ideal world, all material would be retained indefinitely, with ready user access, and under state-of-the-art conditions. In the real world, however, librarians must often make the greatest use of the space at their disposal, and this will inevitably have some detrimental effect on users' access to the collection.

In the absence of the finances needed to acquire additional floor space, a library has three options when facing a space crisis. These are to use some form of cheaper, usually remote off-site storage area; acquire high-density on-site storage, such as compactus shelving; or displace other uses within the primary library site. All of these 'solutions' will in turn create a new set of problems. Off-site storage severely restricts users' access and invariably means using facilities that have lesser conservation and preservation standards than the primary library site (Seeds 2000). Selecting material appropriate for off-site storage is also a matter requiring some careful and potentially resource intensive planning (Hazen 2000; Shlomo 2003). High-density on-site storage is itself expensive, and is likely to entail loss of access and the facility to browse. Displacing other space uses will usually have a detrimental impact upon staff, users and other library services. It should also be noted that for many libraries options such as off-site storage and high-density on-site storage simply do not exist. Their cost, coupled with their effect on accessibility, is sufficient to make them largely the preserve of academic and research libraries.

The solution to space problems for many libraries is left to good planning. This is likely to entail a creative mix of careful discarding combined with space management that maximises both the space available for shelving and the volume of material that can be accommodated in that space, without placing staff or user safety at risk. In recent years, there has been increased interest in the use of combined storage facilities to house unwanted library material. This has been driven by both the practical need to solve the immediate storage problems of individual libraries, plus a concern that space pressures might even lead to 'last copies' being discarded. Some of these combined storage facilities function on a local or regional level, but in some countries – especially in Europe (Vattulainen 2004; Henden 2005) – there are moves to create national repositories for little-used research material in particular. Australia has a major repository in the CARM store (http://www.caval.edu.au/carm/pst/) located in outer Melbourne (O'Connor 2004).

Conclusion

Despite the prodigious impact that digitisation of content has had upon library collections in recent years, there is little reason to believe that the revolution has run its course. From our current perspective it may seem that library collections enjoyed several hundred years of relative stability before the onset of massive change in recent decades. It has, though, always been the case that library collections have been subject to the changes brought about by technological innovation, changing social and political climates and fluctuations in economic conditions. Moreover, while there is little doubt the word 'revolution' does not overstate the impact of digitisation, the challenge for librarians with responsibility for collections remains largely as it always has been – to be flexible and responsive in their practice in order to optimise access to content that is selected, stored and maintained for the clients' benefit.

References

Abbott, W & Kelly K 2004, 'Sooner or later! – Have e-books turned the page?' *VALA 2004: Breaking boundaries: Integration and interoperability. 12th Biennial Conference and Exhibition*, 3-5 February 2004, held in Melbourne, http://www.vala.org.au/vala2004/2004pdfs/46AbbKel.PDF

Aerni, SE, King, DW, Montgomery, CH & Tenopir, C 2003, 'Patterns of journal use by faculty at three diverse universities, *D-Lib Magazine*, vol.9, no.10, http://www.dlib.org/dlib/october03/king/10king.html

Agee, J 2005, 'Collection evaluation: A foundation for collection development', *Collection Building*, vol.24, no.3, pp.92-95.

Armstrong, C & Lonsdale R 2005, 'Challenges in managing e-books collections in UK academic libraries', *Library Collections, Acquisitions and Technical Services*, vol.29, no.1, pp.33-50.

Ball, D 2004, 'What's the "big deal", and why is it a bad deal for universities?', *Interlending & Document Supply*, vol.32, no.2, pp.117-125.

Banks, J 2002, 'Weeding book collections in the age of the internet', *Collection Building*, vol.21, no.3, pp.113-119.

Brooks, S 2003, 'Academic journal embargoes and full text databases', *The Library Quarterly*, vol.73, no.3, pp.243-260.

Chapman, S 2003, 'Counting the costs of digital preservation: Is repository storage affordable?', *Journal of Digital Information*, vol. 4, no. 2, http://jodi.ecs.soton.ac.uk/Articles/v04/i02/Chapman/chapman-final.pdf

Chelton, M 2001, 'Weeding the fiction collection: Or should I dump Peyton Place? *Reference & User Services Quarterly*, vol.40, no.3, pp.234-239.

Christianson, M & Aucoin, M 2005, 'Electronic or print books: Which are used?', *Library Collections, Acquisitions and Technical Services*, vol.29, no.1, pp.71-81.

Cox, J 2004, 'E-books: Challenges and opportunities', *D-Lib Magazine*, vol.10, no.10, http://www.dlib.org/dlib/october04/cox/10cox.html

De Groote, SL & Dorsch, JL 2001, 'Online journals: Impact on print usage', *Bulletin of the Medical Library Association*, vol.89, no.4, pp.372-378.

Dempsey L 2000, 'Scientific, industrial, and cultural heritage: A shared approach. A research framework for digital libraries, museums and archives', *Ariadne*, vol.22, http://www.ariadne.ac.uk/issue22/dempsey/intro.html

Divelko, J & Gottlieb, L 2003, 'Weed to achieve: A fundamental part of the public library mission?', *Library Collections, Acquisitions and Technical Services*, vol.27, no.1, pp.73-96.

Dominguez, PB & Swindler, L 1993, 'Cooperative collection development in the Research Triangle University Libraries: A model for the nation', *College & Research Libraries*, vol.54, pp.470-496.

Dorner, D 2004, 'The impact of digital information resources on the roles of collection managers in research libraries', *Library Collections, Acquisitions, and Technical Services*, vol.28, no.3, pp.249-274.

Flowers JL 2004, 'Specific tips for negotiations with library materials vendors depending upon acquisitions method', *Library Collections, Acquisitions, and Technical Services*, vol.28, no.4, pp.433-448.

Frazier, K 2001, 'The librarians' dilemma: contemplating the cost of the "big deal"', *D-Lib Magazine*, vol.7, no.3, http://www.dlib.org/dlib/march01/frazier/03frazier.html

Friend, FJ 2003, 'Big deal – good deal? Or is there a better deal?', *Learned Publishing*, vol.16, no.2, pp.153-155.

Fullerton, J 2004, 'Disaster preparedness at the National Library of Australia', *70th IFLA General Council and Conference,* Buenos Aires, http://www.ifla.org/IV/ifla70/papers/144e-Fullerton.pdf

Galvin, J 2004, 'The next step in scholarly communication: Is the traditional journal dead?', *Electronic Journal of Academic and Special Librarianship*, vol.5, no.1, http://southernlibrarianship.icaap.org/content/v05n01/galvin_j01.htm

Genoni, P 2001, 'Slouching towards Calvary: Whereto the national collection?', *Australian Academic and Research Libraries*, vol.32, no.2, pp.69-81.

Genoni, P 2002, 'Distributed national collection: Concept and reality in two countries', *Alexandria*, vol.14, no.3, pp.103-115.

Genoni, P 2004, 'Content in institutional repositories: A collection management issue', *Library Management,* vol.25, no.6/7, pp.300-306.

Hazen, D 2000, 'Selecting for storage: Local problems, local responses and an emerging common challenge', *Library Resources & Technical Services*, vol.44, no.4, pp.176-183.

Henden, J 2005, 'The Norwegian Repository Library', *Library Management*, vol.26, no.1/2, pp.73-78.

Hodge, GM 2000, 'Best practices for digital archiving: An information life cycle approach', *D-Lib Magazine*, vol.6, no.1, http://www.dlib.org/dlib/january00/01hodge.html

Hyland, A 2004, 'Providing access to atypical items in an academic library', *Collection Management*, vol.29, no.1, pp.57-72.

International Federation of Library Associations (IFLA) 2004, 'Statement on open access to scholarly literature and research documentation', http://www.ifla.org/V/cdoc/open-access04.html

Intner, SS 2003, 'Making your collections work for you: Collection evaluation myths and realities', *Library Collections, Acquisitions and Technical Services*, vol.27, no.3, pp.339-350.

Joint Information Systems Committee (JISC) 2002, 'Why digital preservation?', http://www.jisc.ac.uk/index.cfm?name=pres_why

Johnson, R 2002, 'Institutional repositories: Partnering with faculty to enhance scholarly communication', *D-Lib Magazine*, vol.8, no.11, http://www.dlib.org/dlib/november02/johnson/11johnson.html

Kennedy, J 2005, 'A collection development policy for digital information resources?', *The Australian Library Journal*, vol.54, no.3, pp.238-244.

Langendorfer, JM & Hurst, ML 2003, 'Comparison shopping: Purchasing continuations as standing orders or on approval', *Library Collections, Acquisitions and Technical Services*, vol.27, no.2, pp.169-172.

Lynch, CA 2003, 'Institutional repositories: Essential infrastructure for scholarship in the digital age', *ARL Bimonthly Report*, no.226, http://www.arl.org/newsltr/226/ir.html

Maula, H & Talja, S 2003, 'Reasons for the use and non-use of electronic journals and databases: A domain analytic study in four scholarly disciplines', *Journal of Documentation*, vol. 59, no. 6, pp. 673-691.

Mercieca, P 2004, 'E-book acceptance: What will make users read on screen?', *VALA 2004: Challenging Ideas*: 12th Biennial VALA Conference and Exhibition, Melbourne, http://www.vala.org.au/vala2004/2004pdfs/32Merci.PDF

Milne, R 2002, 'The "Distributed National Collection" access, and cross-sectoral collection: The Research Support Libraries program', *Ariadne*, vol.31, http://www.ariadne.ac.uk/issue31/rslp

Mueller, S 2005, 'Approval plans and faculty selection: Are they compatible?', *Library Collections, Acquisitions and Technical Services*, vol.21, no.2, pp.61-70.

Nabe, J 2001, 'E-journal bundling and its impact on academic libraries: Some early results', *Issues in Science and Technology Librarianship*, vol.30, http://www.istl.org/01-spring/article3.html

O'Connor, S 2004, 'Collaborative strategies for low-use research materials', *Library Collections, Acquisitions and Technical Services*, vol.28, no.1, pp.51-57.

Peters, T 2003, 'Consortia and their discontents', *Journal of Academic Librarianship*, vol.29, no.2, pp.111-114.

Phillips, M 2005, 'What should we preserve? The question for heritage libraries in a digital world', *Library Trends*, vol.54, pp.57-72.

Potter, WG 1997, 'Recent trends in statewide academic library consortia', *Library Trends*, vol.45, no.3, pp.416-434.

Prosser, DC 2004, 'Between a rock and a hard place: The big squeeze for small publishers', *Learned Publishing*, vol.17, pp.17-22.

Quinn, B 2001, 'The impact of aggregator packages on collection management', *Collection Management*, vol.25, no.3, pp.53-74.

Richards, D 2001, 'Making one size fit all: Minnesota state colleges and universities manage a legislative mandate for cooperative collection development', *Library Collections, Acquisitions & Technical Services*, vol.25, pp.93-112.

Ross, S & Hedstrom M 2005, 'Preservation research and sustainable digital libraries', *International Journal of Digital Libraries*, http://www.dpc.delos.info/private/output/ross_hedstrom_Int_j_Digit_Libr_2005.pdf

Rupp-Serrano, K, Robbins, S & Cain, D 2002, 'Canceling print serials in favour of electronic: Criteria for decision making', *Library Collections, Acquisitions, and Technical Services*, vol.26, no.4, pp.369-378.

Seeds, R 2000, 'The impact of remote storage on information consumers: Sophie's choice?', *Collection Building*, vol.19, no.3, pp.105-109.

Shlomo, ET 2003, 'Nicholson Baker wasn't all wrong: A collection development policy for remote storage', *The Acquisitions Librarian*, vol.30, pp.117-130.

Shreeves, E 1997, 'Is there a future for cooperative collection development in the digital age?', *Library Trends*, vol.45, no.3, pp.373-390.

Smith, M 2004, 'Libraries in the lead: The institutional repository phenomenon', *Breaking Boundaries: Integration and Interoperability: VALA 2004, 12th Biennial Conference and Exhibition*, Melbourne, http://www.vala.org.au/vala2004/2004pprs/prgm2004.htm

Tenopir, C & King DW 2002, 'Reading behaviour and electronic journals', *Learned Publishing*, vol.15, no.4, pp.259-265.

Vattulainen, P 2004, 'National repository initiatives in Europe', *Library Collections, Acquisitions, and Technical Services*, vol.28, no.1, pp.39-50.

Vaughan, KTL 2003, 'Changing use patterns of print journals in the digital age: Impacts of electronic equivalents on print chemistry journal use', *Journal of the American Society for Information Science and Technology*, vol.54, no.12, pp.1149-1152.

Ware, W 2005, 'E-journals only: Is it time to drop the print?', *Learned Publishing*, vol.18, pp.193-199.

Willinsky, J 2205, *The access principle: The case for open access to research and scholarship*, MIT Press, Boston, http://mtpress.mit.edu/catalog/item/default.asp?ttype=2&tid=10611

Rubio Serrano, F., Robbins, S. & Cliett, D. 2009. 'Consaline price increase in favour of electronic Options for decision making', Library Club from, Acquisitions and Technical Services, vol. 20, pp. 263-276.

Scott, R. 2004. 'The impact of single-storage on information consumers', Scoltec's choices', Collection Building, vol. 23, no. 3-4, pp. 102-110.

Stewart, L. 2000. 'Scholarly communication', in G. Baker & W. Fachendam (eds), Libraries as a synergic environment, Academic Press, New York, pp. 111-135.

Sweetman, B. 1991. 'Inclusive estate subscription mitigation and amortization in the digital age', Library Resources and Technical Services, vol. 35, no. 2, pp. 173-176.

Task, M. 2001. 'Information services and the collaboration repository project', IFLA Online, Australian Library and Information Association and University of Melbourne Library, viewed 30 April 2010, <http://www.ala.org/ala/...>.

Tenopir, C. & King, D. 2002. 'Electronic journals and scholarly publishing', D-Lib Magazine, <http://dlib.org/...>.

Vattimo, J., Rix, J. 'National repository initiatives in Europe', Library Collections, Acquisitions, and Technical Services, vol. 23, no. 1, pp. 35-50.

Vaughan, K. T. L. 2007. 'Changing use patterns of print journals in the digital age: Impacts of electronic equivalents on print chemistry journal use', Journal of the American Society for Information Science and Technology, vol. 34, no. 12, pp. 1149-1152.

Ware, W. 2006. 'E-Journals: only if it is free to drop the print?', Serials Publishing, vol. 19, pp. 199.

Wilbraham, E. 2006. 'The crisis paradigm: The new dumplex access to research and scholarship', MIT Press, Boston, <http://mitpress.mit.edu/...>.

CHAPTER 9
Information access

Philip Hider

Developments in information sources and services were outlined in Chapters 6 and 7. The focus of this chapter is the means by which information is made accessible and thus retrievable through various kinds of system. Nowadays, one tends to associate information retrieval (IR) systems with computers but there are still plenty of manual ones, such as shelving systems based on bibliographic classification schemes. Furthermore, many automated IR systems are only semi-automated, in that the information they make accessible is indexed by humans. The chapter begins with a brief discussion of terminology, before looking at various types of IR system. After this, it examines the key processes involved in providing information access – indexing and description – and considers how agencies provide subject access to resources. It goes on to discuss the concept of 'metadata' and its impact on traditional information organisation practices, ending with some thoughts on the future of this core area of librarianship and information management.

Organisation and retrieval

A key part of managing recorded information has always been to make it readily available by providing organised access to it. This may mean organising the information itself – or at least organising the carriers of the information (in other words, documents). Librarians, for instance, arrange books on shelves in a particular order. Or it may mean organising, and usually creating, bibliographic information or metadata to represent the documents. Cataloguers, for instance, create records for books and other items that are indexed by author's name, title, subject and so on. Both kinds of 'organising' represent what is often referred to as bibliographic organisation in librarianship, and what more generally may be referred to as information organisation (IO). This field of work aims to provide intellectual access to documents. A catalogue record should provide users with a shelf mark or some 'address' that points them in the direction of the information they require. However, the item itself may be out on loan; the equivalent scenario in the online information world might be a broken web link. Thus *physical* access is not always guaranteed, but fixing the link or arranging for the item to be returned to the shelf is really a subsidiary matter. The core activity of information organisation is the provision of intellectual – that is, bibliographic – access.

'IR systems' have already been mentioned. Information retrieval and information organisation are essentially two sides of the same coin. In order to retrieve information users want, systems need to organise the information in the ways described above. If an online IR system is offering full text (or any other type of document), then files need to be organised by the computer so that they can be retrieved. If the system is not offering the documents themselves, records still need to be organised, and this is usually done by constructing indexes. The difference between the fields of information retrieval and information organisation is primarily one of perspective. Information organisation focuses on the information and processing it in a way that facilitates retrieval, whereas information retrieval focuses on users and facilitating their searching. This is achieved not only by organising the information, but also by creating more user-friendly search interfaces, by processing the searches (for instance, translating search terms) and by analysing relationships between the searches and the information (through complex computer algorithms, for example). One may argue that information organisation is a subset of information retrieval, though those who profess to specialise in IR tend to focus on the non-IO aspects. At any rate, there is clearly a great deal of overlap. This chapter covers both fields.

Online and hybrid IR systems

Many online IR systems direct users to physical as well as virtual resources, and as such might be termed 'hybrid' systems in the same way that libraries offering a mix of physical and digital information resources are sometimes referred to as hybrid libraries. Indeed, there are some online IR systems that direct users only to physical collections, particularly in the archival field (see Chapter 12) – these are also hybrid in the sense that the metadata (the data used to describe the information resources) not the data themselves, are digital. However, there are also many systems that provide *only* online information (of course, such information can usually be printed out, if desired). A range of full-text, numerical and image databases exists in CD-ROM and DVD-ROM formats, but most fully online IR systems are now networked on intranets, or on the internet. These systems are discussed first, before a few of the hybrid varieties are mentioned. There are three main types of online IR system: the directory, the database and the search engine.

Directories

The directory or 'gateway' was discussed at some length in Chapter 7. It is especially common as it can be constructed in the same way as any other web resource, that is, as a website (or as one section of a website). The directory is the online equivalent of the traditional bibliography. It brings together resources, in this case online resources, on a particular basis – usually subject – through hyperlinks. The resources listed may be hosted on the same site (they might be archived copies), but more often they are linked from other sites. It could be argued that the online directory dissolves the distinction between the bibliography – a list of resources based on subject but not access – and the catalogue – a list of resources based primarily on access rather than on subject. The resources of an online directory may not be 'collected' in the sense of being acquisitions, but access to them may be said to be collected, in that the information specialist collects links to them. Examples of online directories and subject gateways are provided in Chapter 7.

Databases

Another prevalent online IR system is the database. There are now very many databases freely accessible on the web. Those that provide only bibliographic information, rather than links to the information itself, are often referred to as bibliographic databases. However, almost all databases that store information resources also store (and organise) some bibliographic data as well. For instance, users may be able to search on titles, author names, perhaps even subject terms. Even if the only type of search available is a 'keyword' search, this is usually a search on an index. All indexes are ultimately metadata (information about information), even if this is just each word of a text.

Whatever information is stored in the database, this information is not normally accessible via search engines such as Google, and is thus part of what is termed the 'hidden web'. The challenge for the search engines is to uncover more of this information – it is technically possible for databases to be searched from outside of their own websites, but only if they allow this to happen and implement certain standards. A good example of cooperation between a search engine and a database is Open WorldCat (http://www.oclc.org/worldcat/open), which allows libraries that are members of the OCLC network to have their catalogues accessible via Google. Examples of fully online database systems include CELT (http://curia.ucc.ie), the US Department of Agriculture's Plants Database (http://plants.usda.gov) and ChessBase's Online Database (http://www.chesslive.de).

Search engines

Whereas directories and databases have offline equivalents, the third type of online IR system, the search engine, is uniquely online. It is in some ways an extension of the database, but instead of being based on indexes relating to a fairly stable and bounded set of resources (such as journal publications in a specific subject field), the search engine aims to provide access to a much less stable and less bounded set of resources, although they may be bounded within a certain site (such as an intranet) or group of sites. While a search engine may store a copy of the information resource as well as the metadata for the resource, it does not store the original resource, but only a link to it (which one hopes has not been broken). In order to keep up to date, the search engine has to periodically re-index the intranet or internet content as it changes, and if it stores copies it has to take new copies of each resource.

Another difference between the database and the search engine is that many search engines rely more on analysis of what Rasmussen (2004) refers to as 'bags of words', in other words, the text of the resource itself, than on metadata, though most do take some account of embedded metadata, which may be marked up (encoded) by machine or author/editor. This means more than simply providing a keyword search on every word. Rather, it entails analysing the relationship between the words in the text and across texts, in order to find as good a 'match' as possible with the search query. The key concept here is *relevance*: some resources are more relevant to a given query than others. Most search engines (and some databases) attempt to rank resources in relevance order, so that the most relevant are listed first – clearly this would provide the user with the most efficient access to the information, particularly if there are thousands, if not millions, of 'hits' (resources or links to resources that may be of *some* relevance).

There is, however, no magic solution to relevance ranking, and search engines have different formulae (called algorithms), based on the way they analyse the 'bags of words'. It is not simply a matter of counting how many times a word occurs in a text, or how many times it occurs in a text in comparison with its frequency across texts. Sophisticated search engines – and some of them are very sophisticated – also look at where words occur in the text, in relation to other words, and various kinds of word. Of course, all of this is done by means of very powerful computer processing. The even more 'intelligent' search engines can also analyse the user's search query, by means of what is called natural language processing (NLP).

Statistics and computational linguistics have been gradually improving search engine algorithms for the past three decades. It appears that a performance plateau has now been reached when it comes to basic text retrieval – the experimental retrieval systems have not been able to improve the accuracy of their relevance rankings much in recent years. However, this does not signal the end of the information retrieval road. Far from it, there are several other areas in which systems are currently making giant strides, such as multimedia retrieval (retrieval of non-textual as well as textual resources), cross-language retrieval and web retrieval. This last category features some of the great success stories of contemporary information retrieval, including commercial search engines such as Google, which has proven so effective through an algorithm based on the nuts and bolts of the world wide web, in other words, its hyperlinks. Google's basic assumption is that the more links a particular site has from other sites to its own site, the more 'useful' the site is by the average searcher, and so ranks it more highly. Of course, it also makes use of the other statistical and linguistic work produced by the field of information retrieval, as do its competitors. Search Engine Watch (http://searchenginewatch.com) is a worthwhile resource with which to begin investigating web search engines.

Computerisation and human indexers

To a large extent, the development of information retrieval mirrors the development of computing in the second half of the last century, and it would be fair to say that IR remains very computer-oriented. Indeed, an aim of IR might be said to be the elimination of manual indexing. So far, this aim has not been fully realised, but there are many IR systems that minimise the use of metadata constructed by humans. Apart from being very costly (human wages are on the rise, whereas computing power is increasingly cheap), human indexing is not always very reliable – particularly if done by the author of the resource, rather than a specialist. Not only do authors of websites not always have a very broad perspective, sometimes they deliberately misrepresent their site, in order to gain for it a higher relevance ranking than it might deserve. (This type of metadata creation is known as index spamming – comparable to email spamming.) Hence, search engines pay less attention to metadata attached to web resources than they otherwise might.

Intervention by human indexers does, however, greatly increase the retrievability of some types of resource – particularly those in the physical realm (see below). The text of physical resources cannot be analysed by computer (unless it is digitised). In the case of journal articles, authors may offer keywords and abstracts, but in the case of books, it is still usually up to the information professional to create the metadata that forms the basis of that age-old means of information access – the library catalogue. This is perhaps the most well-known and most used hybrid IR system. Whereas most library catalogues are now online, at least in the developed world, there are still millions of library resources yet to be digitised. Only through the detailed indexing of these resources can library users easily pinpoint those particular resources – be they books, maps, videos or whatever – that will help (or entertain) them. Browsing through each book on each shelf might be more pleasurable, but a lot more time-consuming. Library catalogues, sometimes referred to as OPACs (online public access catalogues), thus provide much more efficient access to information, just as does relevance ranking by search engines.

A hundred years ago or so, the detailed indexing and metadata creation that built these catalogues developed into a specialism – *library cataloguing*. Ultimately, cataloguing – whether done in a library, museum or archives – is a form of indexing. Indeed, the component of library cataloguing that provides the chief form of subject access to library resources is known as *subject indexing*. Along with back-of-the-book indexers and archival cataloguers, library cataloguers represent the archetypal information organisation professional, and remain the most common breed – although, as discussed later, a breed that will need to evolve. The various elements involved in library cataloguing will be discussed further in the course of this chapter.

Other hybrid IR systems include other types of online catalogue, such as those used by archives, often referred to as finding aids (discussed in Chapter 12), and indexes to print journals.

Manual IR systems

Information organisation, and bibliographic organisation in particular, has a long history. It certainly did not start with computers, although they revolutionised the field. Even today, there are purely manual systems doing very useful work. For instance, shelf arrangements in libraries are usually based on a system of subject classification. Any sort of arrangement, or order, is in fact a system, enabling users to find items more easily (the most primitive being an alphabetic one). The classification systems are also known as schemes, as in the Dewey Decimal Classification scheme.

There are, of course, also manual systems based on bibliographic information, rather than the resources themselves. Bibliographies and catalogues date back a long time before the computer. Indeed, they date back before the time of printing, but came into their own as libraries grew rapidly in the eighteenth and nineteenth centuries. The first library catalogues were written or printed on sheets of paper, but card catalogues became *de rigour* for many libraries at the beginning of the twentieth century. Although card catalogues were gradually superseded by online catalogues in the 1970s and 1980s, some libraries, even in the West, still have operational card catalogues, which may be used as back-up (unlike online catalogues, they do not go 'down') or to cover older items or material in non-roman script.

Whether the catalogue or bibliography is on paper, card or microfilm, some kind of order is needed to enable users to look things up. A classified order, similar to that in which books are usually arranged on library shelves, may be employed. Alternatively, an alphabetical order based on the author's name or title, may be used. In the alphabetically ordered catalogue especially, multiple records may be used to represent a single item, so that, for instance, three record cards may be entered into the catalogue for a particular book, two under different co-authors, and one under the title. Records may also be entered under particular subject headings. (Catalogues which interfile headings for authors and titles, and also subjects, are known as *dictionary* catalogues.) A perennial debate among earlier generations of librarians was whether (subject) classified or author catalogues were 'better'. Fortunately, computers have made this debate obsolete, as authors, titles, subject terms and other bibliographic elements can be systematically indexed so that they can be readily looked up through keyword searches (as well as alphabetical browses).

Even though libraries have mostly moved on from the card catalogue, many pre-computer cataloguing principles still apply, while standards such as the Anglo-American Cataloguing Rules (AACR) still accommodate non-computerised catalogues. Indeed, AACR still refers to access points – the terms the user looks up on the catalogue – as 'headings,' even though they are not really located at the head of a computer record. Similarly, the main list of subject terms used in English-based libraries comprises the Library of Congress Subject Headings (LCSH). However, there are signs that the terminology, if not necessarily the principles, is beginning to move on – the new AACR (to be called Resource Description and Access) will probably use 'access point' instead of 'heading'.

Perhaps in part because of the nature of their material, archives have been a little slower than libraries to automate their information organisation. Archivists commonly refer to the process of information organisation as archival description, instead of cataloguing or bibliographic description. This is discussed briefly later on.

Indexing

Most information retrieval systems, whether online or manual, are based on some form of indexing. The library catalogue is really a kind of index, albeit often a rather sophisticated one. It refers the user to particular shelf numbers (those numbers used to place and locate books and other physical information resources on the shelves) or to particular files on the world wide web. Similarly, an index at the back of a book refers the reader to page numbers.

Other indexing systems refer not to physically whole items nor to single pages, but to a series of pages that comprise a particular article – they index articles from journals and other forms of serial publication. Nowadays, most of these systems are online, and many constitute very large databases covering hundreds or thousands of serials; many also provide links to online versions of some of the articles they index. Along with the usual types of bibliographic element such as title, author's name, subject descriptors, many systems include abstracts, or short summaries, of some or all of the articles indexed. Hence these systems are often referred to as indexing and abstracting services. Prominent examples include MEDLINE, LexisNexis, Chemical Abstracts and LISTA (Library, Information Science & Technology Abstracts) – see Chapter 7.

Many libraries and information resource centres provide access to a range of these services as they also house (either physically or virtually) many of the corresponding serials. Conventionally, the databases are not integrated with the library catalogue, but increasingly libraries are offering users a *federated search* facility. This allows them to search on multiple databases, including the library catalogue, simultaneously. Nevertheless, the bibliographic data are still stored in separate databases. There are several reasons for this. First, most indexing and abstracting services are commercial concerns – their proprietors need to keep control of the (meta)data. Second, users may wish to limit their search to one particular database with one particular kind of resource. Third, the indexing performed varies across databases, so that different databases use different subject terms, and include different bibliographic elements, according to the nature of material being indexed. Library catalogues are based on standards such as the Anglo-American Cataloguing Rules (see the following section) but these are usually not applied by indexing and abstracting services.

Although the product of any index is metadata, this does not mean that all metadata are indexed (and therefore used as access points). Some types of information may be deemed worth recording, but not considered to be what users would normally search on – such as the number of pages a book has. Thus, library cataloguing distinguishes between description and indexing. Bibliographic description is set out in a particular way to be *read*, once the record has been retrieved via the index. Not all of this description would necessarily be indexed, indeed, most will usually not be, but users may want to read it, in order to select or deselect an item – they may be interested in how long a book is or when it was published, for instance.

It may also be that the information is represented in a way that makes it less appropriate for indexing, for instance, it may be in whole sentences rather than a few key terms. Nowadays, many IR systems can retrieve on any word (or number), but this does not mean that everything should be indexed. Words such as 'a' and 'the' are too common, as well as almost meaningless, to be of much use, and are often not indexed (these are referred to as stop words). The fewer terms indexed, the more likely it is the system will retrieve relevant documents (and less irrelevant ones). The more terms indexed the more likely it is that the system will retrieve more documents that are relevant, but also more irrelevant ones. This brings up a key issue in indexing – vocabulary control.

Vocabulary control

The more control an IR system has over which words it indexes and which words it does not, the greater the *precision* it is likely to offer and the more relevant the search results will be. Indexers thus often used a tightly controlled vocabulary from which to select index terms – particularly subject index terms. Examples of these vocabularies are examined later in the chapter. Each of them is maintained according to the principles of vocabulary control, so that terms are added or revised on a systematic basis.

One should note from the outset, however, that vocabulary control has disadvantages, and that these have meant that in some IR situations, it may not be considered worthwhile. First, vocabulary control may increase precision, but it is also likely to decrease recall. This means that fewer semi-relevant documents will be retrieved because the indexers were restricted in the way they represented these documents. If there is no reference from a term the user employs in their search query to the term used in the controlled vocabulary, then relevant documents may not be retrieved. Second, controlled vocabularies are usually employed by *human* indexers, for whom they are normally designed. Human indexers do not cover every meaningful word in a document as a computer might, but rather attempt to identify the main topics and assign controlled terms to represent those. Again, this will have a significant effect on recall.

Third, and this is usually the biggest consideration, a major drawback of vocabulary control is its expense. Human indexers do not come cheap (even though many cataloguers would not consider themselves particularly well paid). While there have been attempts to automate indexing based on controlled vocabularies, most of these have not proven to be especially reliable. The power of keyword searching, however, coupled with sophisticated algorithms and huge pools of documents, have meant that in many online searching environments, users are able to find *some* documents of interest despite a lack of vocabulary control. The question then is whether this is enough. If precision is not so important – as it might not be for the average Google user – then indexing using controlled vocabularies might not be deemed value for money. For the more serious researcher, precision may be critical – and the costs of using and maintaining a controlled vocabulary may be something users are prepared to pay for, either directly or indirectly.

Descriptive cataloguing and bibliographic description

Library cataloguing has conventionally been divided into two processes: descriptive cataloguing and subject cataloguing/classification. The second process is examined in the next two sections, but here the focus is the first – cataloguing the non-subject aspects of a resource. Within descriptive cataloguing, there are two main sub-processes: bibliographic description and the assignment of non-subject access points.

It has been noted already that metadata are not always indexed – they may instead serve the purpose of describing a resource in order to help the information seeker select or deselect it from a results set. Furthermore, while some bibliographic elements, such as abstracts, may be indexed, they are also there to guide users as they look for the most relevant materials. Indeed, the indexed metadata, at least when it comes to descriptive cataloguing, is generally based on the description, rather than the other way around.

The Anglo-American Cataloguing Rules, the main set of rules for descriptive cataloguing in the English-speaking world, are currently split into two parts: the first part covers description; the second part covers access points (or 'headings'). Of the eight AACR areas of description, which is based on the International Standard Bibliographic Description (ISBD), only three include elements that are necessarily indexed according to Part 2 of AACR, although in reality (with the use of MARC21 exchange format, discussed later) several other elements are almost always indexed (and thus searchable) in online library catalogues. Those elements covered by Part 2 of AACR include names of persons and corporate bodies (organisations), titles and series titles.

AACR, and the application of AACR, cannot be learnt in a day; only experienced cataloguers can hope to apply them fully. Following them fully is also time-consuming, so many libraries have settled for applying only some of them, particularly with respect to the description. Fortunately, in AACR2 (2 stands for second edition) there are three *levels* of description, so libraries may elect to provide a minimal amount of detail (the first level), or more (the second or third levels), and still follow AACR.

On many occasions, a library will not need to follow AACR at all, since it can instead download an existing record for the resource needing to be described – this procedure is known as copy cataloguing. However, those libraries which need to do substantial amounts of original (as opposed to copy) cataloguing tend to be those that are better resourced and have more 'serious' types of user – especially, national and state libraries, large university libraries and libraries of research institutes. Many of these libraries do not consider first level description sufficient (not for all materials, anyway). Indeed, some take an approach that is not necessarily 'third level,' but might be termed a 'sophisticated second level'. That is, they describe their resources according to second level, in general terms, but also adhere (or try to adhere) to supplementary standards, in particular, the Library of Congress Rule Interpretations (LCRI), which are essentially a gloss on AACR (some would say a reinterpretation on occasion). While LCRI are more important in North American cataloguing (which tends to be relatively legalistic), they are by no means restricted to that continent. The Libraries Australia network (formerly Kinetica, and before that Australian Bibliographic Network), for instance, prescribes most of the LCRI.

Given that more rules and guidelines mean more to learn and more to do, this would not appear to be a good way of saving staff time and money, particularly if they are compiled by a library on another continent. So why do libraries follow them? They do so for the same reasons that they follow the basic AACR code, the principal one being that the more they follow them, the easier it is for them to accept record copy from other libraries and the less editing that is required. It is no coincidence that the Library of Congress is both the leading rule-maker in descriptive and subject cataloguing in the English-speaking world and the leading source of catalogue records.

While LCRI-based record copy might be accepted, however, this does not mean that libraries will necessarily apply all these rules and interpretations in their original cataloguing, even though theoretically it would be best to do so from a consistency standpoint. It may just be too expensive in terms of staff time and resources. Indeed, libraries may not have the expertise on their staff. Even the Library of Congress is beginning to support moves towards simplification, displaying an increasing desire to trim its LCRI, with a view to possibly discontinuing them altogether. The AACR rules themselves are currently being re-examined in light of the emergence of alternative, simpler standards and practices, which are especially popular among digital libraries. AACR's treatment of online resources has been criticised for being somewhat dated. The proposed AACR3, or Resource Description & Access (RDA) as it has been provisionally called, aims to address this complaint. RDA also aims to be less library-centric, no longer directly linked to ISBD (International Standard Bibliographic Description), and more compatible with a range of format standards, both inside and outside of the library world. Its theoretical foundations are also being strengthened, by underpinning it with the principles propounded in Fundamental Requirements of Bibliographic Records (FRBR) and Fundamental Requirements of Authority Records (FRAR). Perhaps most fundamental, rules are being revised with reference to the basic catalogue functions as determined by FRBR: to identify, to find, and to select.

Archival description

The focus so far has been on how libraries describe their resources and the sophisticated standards they have developed over the past hundred years or so. It is worth noting, however, that other information professionals, including archivists and museum curators, also have well-established traditions of resource description. In fact, description of archival documents and museum objects tends to be more detailed than librarians' bibliographic description. It also tends to be less standardised, mainly because of the nature of their material, which is typically unique. Economy that might be gained through copy cataloguing is thus much less of a driver. Nevertheless, a degree of standardisation has become increasingly desirable from a users' perspective, since it facilitates the searching of materials across collections, particularly via online databases. In recent years, consequently, archivists have endeavoured to find common ground, culminating in the General International Standard Archival Description, (ISAD(G)). This is in fact partly modelled on the librarians' ISBD, even though archivists generally work at a broader, collection level (for example, collections of papers) rather than with individual documents, to which ISBD is primarily geared. The museums community has not been left behind either, developing, among other standards, its International Guidelines for Museum Object Information: The CIDOC Information Categories, produced by the International Committee for Documentation (CIDOC) of the International Council of Museums (ICOM).

Authority control

Returning to AACR and RDA, it is worth noting that another important part of the proposed revision is the inclusion of new guidelines on the creation of authority records (hence FRAR, mentioned above). Authority records are not records of resources, but records of what AACR2 calls *headings* and what are otherwise known as access points. AACR2 differentiates headings from elements of description, as their form may be different, even if they might represent the same entity. For example, headings for authors' names should start with the family name, but in the description, author's names appear as they are presented on the resource (usually family name last, at least in Western publications). Generally, the principle for description is to *transcribe* elements from the resource; whereas the principle for headings and other access points is one discussed already – vocabulary control. In cataloguing, particularly descriptive cataloguing, this is otherwise known as authority control. As already mentioned, index entries are controlled when indexers and cataloguers are limited in which ones they can use. The goal of authority control is to eliminate all choice, so that only one heading can be used for one entity or concept. Thus, an author's name may occur in various forms on different publications, but only one particular form can be used for any heading for that particular author. The same for subjects: one heading is established for synonyms such as football and soccer. All cataloguers must use the same heading, say 'Soccer,' and never use 'Football'.

The mechanism for controlling names and subjects, and also titles, is the authority file. This complements the bibliographic file, where the bibliographic records sit. The authority file comprises authority records, each one of which represents an authorised heading – be it the name of a person or organisation, the title of a resource or series title, or a subject term – and references (otherwise known as cross-references) to these authority records from 'unauthorised' variants of the authorised headings. Thus, to use the above example, there might be an authority record for the authorised heading 'Soccer', and a reference from 'Football' to 'Soccer'. Those involved in authority control work are responsible for the maintenance of the authority file. In theory, at least, every heading in all the bibliographic records should be linked to an authority record – perfect vocabulary control. In practice, the situation may be somewhat different. While authority control is generally regarded as a good thing for library cataloguers to perform, it is *very* expensive and not as essential as is the creation of the basic bibliographic record. Although RDA probably should add guidelines on authority records, the issue of whether they will be needed by many libraries is another matter – nowadays only an 'elite' group of libraries undertake systematic authority control work on their catalogues (generally those with the largest cataloguing departments) and the trend does not appear to be an upward one.

Subject indexing

It has already been pointed out that indexing and abstracting services often use a controlled vocabulary to index the subjects of journal articles. Library cataloguers also often use such a vocabulary for subject indexing, most commonly in the English-speaking world the list of Library of Congress Subject Headings (LCSH). Some indexing services use this list as well but many use thesauri instead. The difference between a list of subject headings and a subject thesaurus is not really absolute, but, broadly speaking, the former does not include a systematic reference structure from one term to another, whereas the latter does. (LCSH is in fact a headings list which does include a fairly systematic reference structure, though not a comprehensive one). Subject thesauri, as their name might suggest, cover particular subjects; lists of subject headings can do so too, but others (like LCSH) are intended to cover everything. The terms used in thesauri are not called headings, but *descriptors*. This relates to the purpose of thesauri – they are employed mainly by indexers of databases, not by cataloguers.

Another difference is that subject headings are more often made up of strings of terms, such as 'Cricket – Australia – History – 19th century'. Descriptors generally are not strung together, so that the four concepts represented above might constitute four separate descriptors instead of one heading. The strings of LCSH and other subject heading systems are the products of what is called *pre-coordinated* indexing. This means that the indexer coordinates the different terms for a multi-concept subject into a single string, at the indexing stage. The opposite of this is *post-coordinated* indexing, whereby the indexer simply assigns different descriptors for each of the concepts represented in a multi-concept subject and leaves the searcher to coordinate the terms in their query. The advent of boolean search functionality on early computer databases made post-coordination not only feasible but the preferred approach in many cases – the boolean operators of AND, OR and NOT enable the user to combine separate terms in their query and retrieve those records which include the combination of terms, even if they are in separate fields. Whereas the terms in pre-coordinated strings are in a set order – so that the catalogue user would need to search under 'Cricket' in the above example (they would not find the same set of terms under 'Australia') – the order of terms in post-coordinated boolean retrieval is irrelevant. This flexibility usually makes things easier for both user and indexer, although pre-coordinated systems still have advantages – most notably for when users wish to browse subjects.

There are quite a number of thesauri available covering a wide range of subjects. Prominent examples include the Getty Trust's Art & Architecture Thesaurus, the UNESCO Thesaurus, and APAIS Thesaurus (Australian Public Affairs Information Service). There are also alternatives to LCSH, apart from lists in other languages, such as Sears (from the HW Wilson Company), MeSH (Medical Subject Headings from the National Library of Medicine (NLM)), and SCIS

Subject Headings (used in many Australian and New Zealand school libraries). LCSH also has a supplementary list of headings for the indexing of children's literature. Recently, LCSH celebrated its centenary, and given that the list accounts for the vast majority of controlled English-language subject terms in library catalogues, its future would seem assured. The amount of investment in the standard makes a challenge from a rival difficult to sustain. Alternatives such as PRECIS and COMPASS, developed by the British Library in the 1980s, might have been more theoretically sound, but are now no more (the BL reverting to LCSH in the mid 1990s).

Although LCSH is established as the 'default' vocabulary for general subject indexing (or subject cataloguing), there has recently been serious discussion as to whether it does indeed have a future – at the place that matters most, the Library of Congress. Karen Calhoun's report, *The changing nature of the catalog and its integration with other discovery tools* (2006), commissioned by the Library of Congress, did not have many good things to say about LCSH, and suspicions have already been voiced on cataloguers' e-lists that Library of Congress management might use this in an argument against the standard's application at some point in the not-too-distant future. While LCSH may be a widely implemented controlled vocabulary, the question being asked is whether libraries can afford to continue using *any* controlled vocabulary. It has already been noted that it may not be necessary for the average Google user, a point not lost on library administrators anxious to cut costs.

All controlled vocabularies are expensive to use, and LCSH is particularly expensive given the level of expertise required to use it. In addition, it is very expensive for the Library of Congress (with assistance from other libraries) to maintain it. A thorough application of LCSH actually entails the application of the Subject Cataloging Manual: Subject Headings (SCM), comprising some four loose-leaf volumes. Many cataloguers choose to remain blissfully unaware of these guidelines, and base their heading assignment and construction on the patterns they perceive in their own catalogue, and/or in other databases, such as the Library of Congress Authorities. One suspects that if current trends continue, the SCM might be abandoned at some stage, if only to save the LCSH themselves.

Classification

Classification (or bibliographic classification) is sometimes subsumed under 'subject cataloguing' along with subject indexing. Although it serves a slightly different purpose, some of the processes involved are very similar. Both subject indexing and classification involve *subject analysis*, a rather tricky art that relies on a combination of subject knowledge, careful scrutiny of the resource, and, above all, experience. However, whereas indexing also usually involves the selection of several terms from a thesaurus or list of subject headings that match as far as possible the concepts (subjects) represented by the resource, classification usually involves the selection of just one particular class in a line of classes into which the resource may best fit, relative to other resources. Because the classes form a line in 'subject' order – or, in other words, classified order – it is not so useful to label them with words, which are conventionally ordered by alphabet without regard to subject, so instead a *notation* is used, based on numbers and/or letters (and in some cases other symbols).

Some classification schemes are general, aiming to cover all recorded knowledge, while others specialise in particular discipline and subject areas. Given their notational basis, they can be more easily used across languages, and the most prominent have become established around the world. The most widely used scheme is Dewey Decimal Classification (DDC).Other general schemes used in many libraries are Library of Congress Classification (LCC) and Universal Decimal Classification (UDC). Examples of special schemes include Moys for law and NLM for medicine.

Classification schemes are in fact a form of controlled vocabulary, albeit a rather restrictive one – their classes are supposed to be mutually exclusive, at a conceptual level. They are examples of highly pre-coordinated systems, as it is up to the classifier, and not the searcher, to put each resource in its appropriate place. Of course, resources have a nasty habit of representing multiple topics and complex subjects, in which case more than one class might apply. However, classifiers do not often have the luxury of being able to place multiple copies of an item on different shelves in different classes (or, for that matter, multiple links in an online directory to the same resource – though they may have more scope in that case). Thus classification may be said to be much less exhaustive than indexing – it does not need to take account of *every* topic covered in a resource, only the primary one. To identify the primary topic, however, is not always such a simple task. In any case, when a resource is both indexed and classified, as with most library items, this is often performed by the same person.

Bibliographic classification is mainly used for the purposes of physical shelf arrangement, but even in the online world, classification schemes are useful. They enable catalogue users to browse subjects online in a more *hierarchical* way than do subject headings, in a similar fashion to the physical browsing of shelves – an important method of selection for many users. They also provide the basis for the online directories that were described earlier, even though most directories employ in-house schemes, rather than established ones like DDC. Indeed, many websites, not just those featuring directories, employ one or more taxonomies, even if on a small scale. Information architects (see a section about them below) tend to prefer the term 'taxonomies,' but they are essentially a type of classification scheme, through which links to the various contents of a website are arranged, usually with reference to user needs and language. One of the defining traits of these taxonomies, however, is that they are site-specific, rather like an in-house library classification scheme. Established schemes are rarely used in everyday websites.

What then of the future of the established schemes? Although the digitisation of older printed materials is finally getting under way in earnest (pending the resolution of certain copyright issues), no-one is advocating that the original hard copies be thrown away. Furthermore, the physical publishing industry is showing no signs of an imminent death. It would seem then that some physical collections are here to stay, at least for this half of the twenty-first century. For as long as this is the case, then the established schemes – DDC, LCC, UDC, and so on – will also remain. Whether they will in fact grow by being used to organise the multitude of online resources is still an open question. Certainly, there have been successful demonstrations of how such schemes could be utilised in the online information world, but their adoption by subject gateways and directories has not as yet been very noticeable, compared to the plethora of in-house arrangements. This may change as more libraries and other institutions start 'collecting' online resources on a more general and systematic basis.

Metadata

Metadata have already been mentioned as being key to most information retrieval systems. Librarians have traditionally used the term 'bibliographic data' to refer to *their* kind of metadata (such as the metadata to be found in a catalogue). Nowadays, however, the more generic 'metadata' is gaining popularity among librarians as well as other information professionals. There are two principal reasons for this. First, online publishing has made for a convergence not only of media, but also of collections – the collection of the library is no longer as clear-cut as it once was, increasingly overlapping with those of other information agencies such as archives and museums, and also with the internet as a whole. Thus libraries increasingly find themselves sharing resources with non-library agencies, including those which produced the resources themselves. These agencies may have created metadata for those resources, and even if these metadata do not conform to library-based standards (such as AACR), it might still be worth using – and it is probably economical to do so.

Second, the metadata for online resources is very likely to be online as well, and thus much more accessible than non-library metadata of the past. Indeed, one characteristic of modern metadata is that it is often *embedded* in the resource. Just as the information contained in an online document is marked up so that it can be displayed and structured by an internet browser, so too can the document's metadata be marked up using metatags – tags that define particular information as title, author, date of creation, and so on. Such information may not necessarily be displayed by the browser (that depends on how it is marked up), but it is nevertheless there and can be automatically 'harvested' by a simple computer program.

Thus, libraries may be keen on metadata for reasons of economy and efficiency, and because a broader approach facilitates an expansion of their virtual collections through cross-domain collaborations. However, switching to more generic metadata standards is by no means straightforward, nor does it come without any loss. Libraries have built up huge bibliographic databases according to specific standards, on which most of their online operations are based.

MARC (machine-readable cataloguing)

The most important of these standards from a systems perspective is MARC – machine-readable cataloguing. This is essentially an exchange format used to download and upload bibliographic records (and authority records) into different library management systems. If a computer knows how to read a MARC record, then it can properly index and display the various bibliographic elements it contains. Without the MARC tags and structure to guide it, however, the computer will not be able to identify what element is what – only human cataloguers might be able to do that! Figure 9.1 shows the relationship between the actual resource, in this case a book, its bibliographic data (or metadata) and the MARC record that contains the bibliographic data, plus field and subfield tags, which enable the computer to identify each element of data.

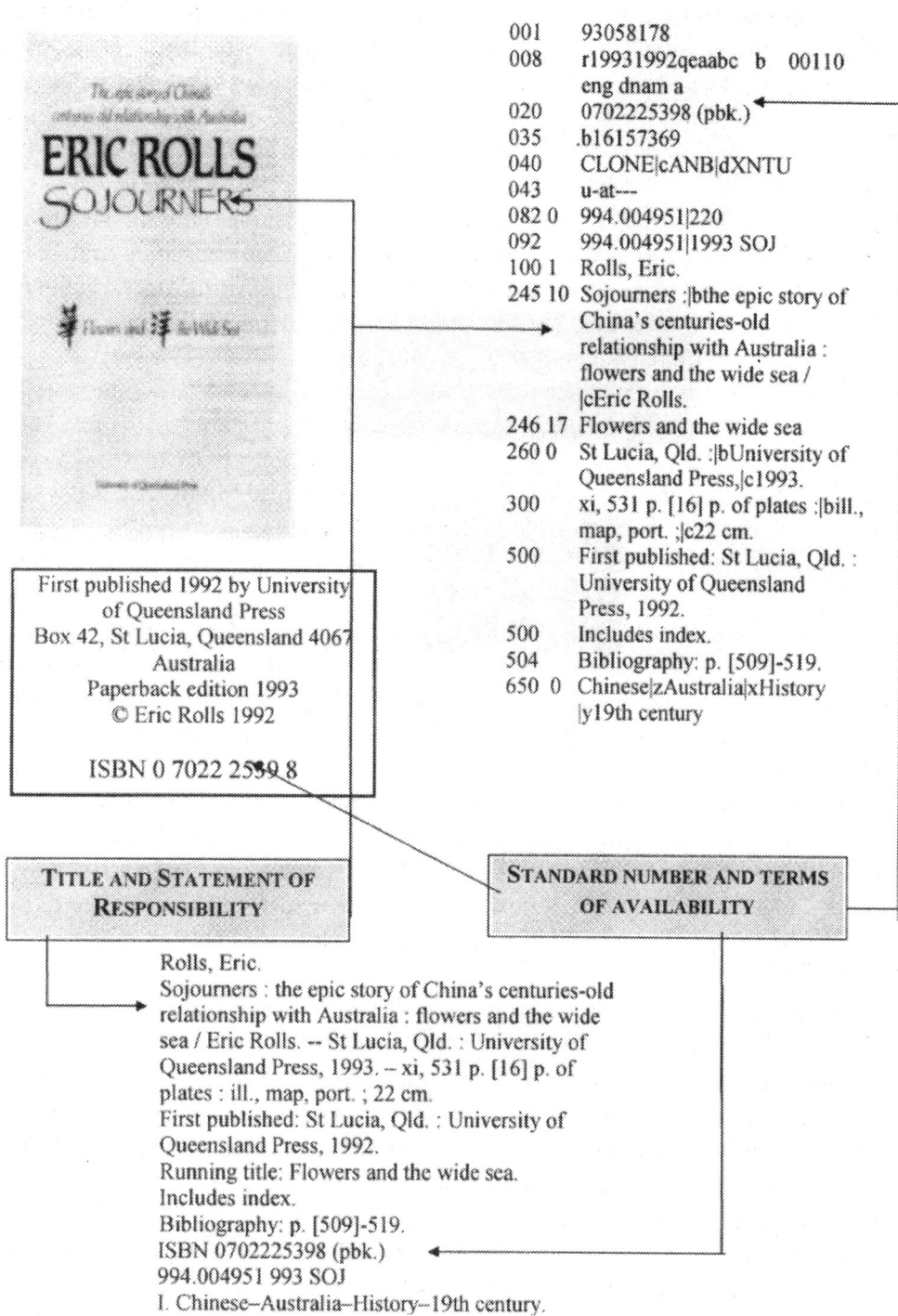

```
001      93058178
008      r19931992qeaabc  b   00110
         eng dnam a
020      0702225398 (pbk.)
035      .b16157369
040      CLONE|cANB|dXNTU
043      u-at---
082 0    994.004951|220
092      994.004951|1993 SOJ
100 1    Rolls, Eric.
245 10   Sojourners :|bthe epic story of
         China's centuries-old
         relationship with Australia :
         flowers and the wide sea /
         |cEric Rolls.
246 17   Flowers and the wide sea
260 0    St Lucia, Qld. :|bUniversity of
         Queensland Press,|c1993.
300      xi, 531 p. [16] p. of plates :|bill.,
         map, port. ;|c22 cm.
500      First published: St Lucia, Qld. :
         University of Queensland
         Press, 1992.
500      Includes index.
504      Bibliography: p. [509]-519.
650 0    Chinese|zAustralia|xHistory
         |y19th century
```

First published 1992 by University
of Queensland Press
Box 42, St Lucia, Queensland 4067
Australia
Paperback edition 1993
© Eric Rolls 1992

ISBN 0 7022 2559 8

TITLE AND STATEMENT OF RESPONSIBILITY

STANDARD NUMBER AND TERMS OF AVAILABILITY

Rolls, Eric.
Sojourners : the epic story of China's centuries-old
relationship with Australia : flowers and the wide
sea / Eric Rolls. -- St Lucia, Qld. : University of
Queensland Press, 1993. -- xi, 531 p. [16] p. of
plates : ill., map, port. ; 22 cm.
First published: St Lucia, Qld. : University of
Queensland Press, 1992.
Running title: Flowers and the wide sea.
Includes index.
Bibliography: p. [509]-519.
ISBN 0702225398 (pbk.)
994.004951 993 SOJ
I. Chinese--Australia--History--19th century.

Figure 9.1 Relationship between a resource and its MARC record. Reproduced from Harvey & Hider 2004, p.214, with permission of the authors

The MARC standard is in fact a family of standards, with slightly different versions of MARC having been developed in various countries. This family grew in membership in the 1970s and 1980s as more and more countries started to automate their libraries, but it has been shrinking over the past decade or so, as the internationalisation of online cataloguing has made national MARC standards more problematic. Most English-speaking countries, including the UK and Australia, are now using MARC21, which is derived from USMARC and CAN/MARC – the North American variants. The official 'lingua franca' is UNIMARC, developed by the International Federation of Library Associations and Institutions (IFLA), but although this is used in several countries, and as an intermediary format when translating from one MARC variant to another, it looks set to become another casualty of North American bibliographic dominance – the fact of the matter is that most MARC records on the 'international market' emanate from the United States.

MARC changed the face of library cataloguing in the second half of the twentieth century, just as the catalogue card standard – three by five inches – had done in the first half. Both standards enabled mass copy cataloguing, the difference being that MARC allowed for mass online copy cataloguing. As long as a library system can read MARC and is hooked up to the internet, it has access, potentially, to millions of bibliographic records. The OCLC database, known as WorldCat, passed the fifty million mark for unique MARC (bibliographic) records a couple of years ago; the RLG database is not too far behind – and recent news of a merger between OCLC and RLG looks set to result in an even more gigantic MARC database. This may not cover all of a library's cataloguing – particularly if the library is a special library – but it is likely to cover most of it. Public libraries in the English-speaking world might expect such databases to cover more than 90 per cent of all their acquisitions, and in many cases more than 95 per cent.

It is not surprising, then, that libraries have systems heavily based on MARC. While the vendors of library management systems are beginning to offer more flexibility, so that they can accommodate metadata in formats other than MARC, many librarians are still reluctant to abandon MARC as their 'base' format. For them it is tried and tested, familiar to staff (or at least cataloguers) and hosts a lot of bibliographic information likely to be lost when translated to a simpler format.

There are librarians, however, who see newer, more generic standards as the way forward. Not only are they not so library-centric, but their structure is more amenable to modern computer programming. Such standards are particularly appealing to those involved in cross-domain projects and the construction of innovative information retrieval interfaces – many in the 'digital library' movement, for instance. Perhaps the most popular generic format standard is Dublin Core, which consists of a mere fifteen elements (see http://dublincore.org/documents/dces), in contrast to MARC's hundreds of fields and subfields. Often, Dublin Core is extended to include some additional elements, according to the nature of the resources for which a format is developed. For instance, the Australian Government Locator Service (AGLS) schema, applied principally by government agencies in Australia, includes the fifteen Dublin Core elements, and adds an extra four (availability, function, audience and mandate).

While both the pro-MARC and anti-MARC camps can produce arguments and examples that support their case, it would appear that MARC and other standards such as Dublin Core will be used concurrently for some time to come. The key, then, will be to support new metadata standards, but at the same time preserve the metadata that use more specific ones. This objective is summed up in another popular term of late – *interoperability*. Information professionals are calling on vendors to make their systems interoperable. Digital libraries aim for maximum interoperability. There are, however, really only two ways to increase interoperability: implement more accurate translations between format and content standards, and/or increase the standardisation of metadata by limiting the scope for competing standards. Both ways necessitate compromise. With format standards continuing to proliferate, it appears that the first way may become more important to the success of information retrieval systems. Vendors who wish to stay competitive will probably need to employ intricate mappings across a range of formats (such mappings are known as crosswalks). These mappings will enable systems to provide federated search facilities, whereby users are offered a one-stop search interface connecting a range of databases and catalogues. The more the metadata and the resources behind the metadata are linked together across databases and systems, the easier it is for users to find what they want. One matching protocol currently being implemented by library system vendors, known as openURL, enables users to find the full text of a resource in a database, based on the metadata found in another.

Information architecture

There is one further area in which 'metadata' has become a new consideration for information professionals moving from physical to digital environments. It has been noted how metadata are often embedded in online documents. In its broadest sense, metadata are in fact embedded in traditional formats, such as the printed book. The information provided on title pages, in chapter headings and even in footnotes ultimately constitutes metadata. It was just not called metadata. Recently, however, a new breed of information organisation professional, the information architect, has started examining the online equivalent of such metadata.

The information architecture (IA) of a website or intranet is now widely recognised as critical to its success. The reason why companies and government agencies are willing to spend large amounts of money to consult with information architects is because websites and intranets can be changed – and hopefully improved – much more readily than can physical information resources. The aim is to provide users with ready access to the information they want – or the information the site owner wishes them to find. This often entails designing information retrieval systems within sites, and as such IA embraces traditional IR and IO. However, IA's focus is on the whole site, rather than specific search systems.

Since the host of the site is the publisher of the information as well as the metadata, everything is up for grabs. This means that the information architect considers not only the development of search systems, but also the presentation and structure of both the data and the metadata, including layout, headings and hyperlinks. The hyperlinking labels that signpost a site's constituent parts represent a new form of metadata, one that is especially associated with the work of information architects. They advise on both the labels themselves (menu choices should be clear, mutually exclusive and so on) and the ways in which they link a site's web pages (its navigation systems). Since the site owner usually has the freedom to publish or not publish, information architects also advise on *what* information should be on a site (and by so doing, overlap with knowledge management, one of the topics of Chapter 13).

The future of information organisation

Conventional library cataloguing is thus being challenged by a broader approach represented by the term, 'metadata.' Whether librarians like it or not (and there are plenty in both camps), metadata are here to stay, while automated approaches to indexing and classification are likely to become more prevalent rather than less. It is not simply that cataloguers are having their job titles changed to 'metadata specialists'. Their job descriptions are being revised as well. The alternative is for their jobs to be deleted or reclassified as paraprofessional work – and this has also been happening in recent times.

When looking at the extent to which cataloguing has been de-professionalised, it is important to distinguish between de-professionalisation due to different priorities and de-professionalisation due to increasing levels of copy cataloguing. Although in the past copy cataloguing would have been part of many professional cataloguers' job, it would usually have represented a lesser part, and it is not altogether unreasonable for this part to have been passed on to paraprofessional staff in a climate of severe budget cutting. Ideally, copy cataloguing should be checked by fully trained original cataloguers – but if the source is reputable then cash-strapped libraries may well be justified in electing to trust that source.

Paraprofessionals have, in some cases, taken over not only copy cataloguing, however, but original cataloguing, and such cases need to be examined very critically. There may not be enough original cataloguing in a library for a full-time professional, but this does not mean that it should not be done by one. One possibility is for it to be outsourced, but then there is a danger of the outsourcing company employing paraprofessionals to cut costs. Another problem is that many professional librarians have not been sufficiently trained to undertake original cataloguing, at least not to the required standard. Again, rather than abandon the assignment, libraries need to look at how this issue might be addressed through short courses and other professional development programs. While many librarians bemoan the lack of cataloguing expertise now available, they have, in part, only themselves to blame. Many libraries are not prepared to devote enough staff time or funds to develop the necessary skills – skills that require as much professionalism as do those for the reference desk or for collection management. If the library is cutting staff across the board, then that is unfortunate, but understandable; if the library is targeting the cataloguing department because other departments are deemed more important or because cataloguing appears to be some kind of 'foreign language', then this is much less so.

While professional cataloguers *should* still be employed, this does not mean that their jobs should remain the same. As already mentioned, many of those cataloguers who remain are having their job descriptions revised – and this is not necessarily a bad thing. Indeed, it is a necessary thing, just as it is for the job descriptions of reference librarians to now include online interaction with users. Cataloguers have no choice but to embrace the future.

So what will cataloguers, or metadata specialists, be doing in this future? Many of them will not only be applying familiar standards such as AACR2 (or RDA) and MARC21, but a wider range of standards across a variety of resource types. Some cataloguers may not be applying the traditional standards at all. They will need to adapt to new and evolving standards in a way that previous generations of cataloguers did not. Moreover, they will be doing more than simply applying particular standards – as metadata professionals they will also be required to manage metadata. This will involve ensuring that metadata are kept up-to-date as resources transform themselves and that new metadata are compatible with existing metadata across databases, through the provision of appropriate crosswalks and user aids. It may also involve a good deal of quality control work and the supervision of paraprofessionals. Metadata specialists may still be relatively 'back-room,' but they will need to take more notice of how users interact with their databases and be less focused on rules.

Although cataloguers will be doing more than creating records in the digital future, it is hoped that they will still find time to do *some*. It has already been noted that many libraries do not need to do much original cataloguing, because of the quantities of MARC records presently available. However, these records do not materialise from thin air: it is only through the cooperation of thousands of libraries and cataloguing departments around the world that these records are created, and to standards that allow them to be shared. If every library merely waited for record copy, it would never come. If they wish to download high-quality copy cataloguing, then in return they must continue to employ professionals sufficiently skilled to contribute original cataloguing to the standards set by bibliographic networks such as OCLC. Libraries cannot look to the Library of Congress to supply all of the world's bibliographic data; indeed, the Library of Congress is currently looking to other libraries to assist *it* through the Program for Cooperative Cataloging.

The alternative is to settle for lower-quality and less detailed metadata, produced by paraprofessionals, publishers and authors. Such metadata may well be better than none, and it may be good enough in certain contexts. It is important for cataloguers committed to their craft to recognise that lower quality does not necessarily mean poor. With the continual squeezing of budgets, compromises are already being reached. Several leading university libraries in the US are reserving professional, detailed cataloguing for only a certain proportion of their acquisitions – those for which it is deemed to add more value. The Library of Congress recently announced that it will cease creating authority records for most series titles (something the British Library abandoned a good while back). The *very* high standards implemented by the Program of Cooperative Cataloging may need to be re-examined. At present, most publications, even most physical publications, are not covered by the program. It may be better, in the broader scheme of things, for it to cover more resources at a slightly less detailed level.

If a more targeted approach to professional metadata creation will prove necessary, then so will a targeted approach to training and education. As metadata specialists need to adapt to different standards and user contexts, then so do trainers and educators. For many years, there has been a debate over the amount of practical application that should be taught in library schools. Those who advocate a more generalised approach, with emphasis on theory and principles, seem to be winning this debate – many university-level courses now only touch on standards such as AACR and DDC, or, at best, offer more in-depth coverage in elective subjects. This situation is not likely to be reversed in the face of more standards and more policy diversity. However, the successful application of sophisticated standards such as DDC and

LCSH does require training, and if they are not covered in the first professional qualification, then they need to be covered (in depth) elsewhere. With increasing numbers of library school graduates ignorant of such standards, training is unlikely to be on hand in many workplaces, outside of the larger libraries. There are some training providers, particularly library networks, currently filling the gap, but more are needed. It seems there are opportunities for library schools to develop professional development offerings to complement the more basic curricula of the entry-level courses.

As with other areas of librarianship, there has been much recent talk of a 'crisis' in cataloguing and indexing. Recent announcements made by the Library of Congress, partly justified through Calhoun's report (2006), will only heighten cataloguers' anxiety. There is much for them to be positive about, however. The likes of Google have heightened users' appreciation for information retrieval to an unprecedented level. They now expect seamless interfaces, plenty of interoperability, accurate metadata, easily navigable websites and intranets. If cataloguers can develop their IO/IR/IA skills in ways that allow users to meet these expectations then their future seems assured. Indeed, their future appears rosy. It has already been suggested that the success of digital libraries depends on metadata, and if there is an area of librarianship on an upward trend, that area is digital librarianship. We are now thoroughly part of the information age – those who provide access to the information are well placed.

References

Anglo-American cataloguing rules 2002, 2nd edn, 2002 revision, Canadian Library Association, Ottawa.

Calhoun, K 2006, *The changing nature of the catalog and its integration with other discovery tool*, http://www.loc.gov/catdir/calhoun-report-final.pdf

Dewey decimal classification 2003, OCLC, Dublin, OH.

Harvey, R & Hider, P 2004, *Organising knowledge in a global society*, Centre for Information Studies, Charles Sturt University, Wagga Wagga, NSW.

ISAD(G): General international standard archival description 2000, 2nd edn, International Council on Archives, Ottawa, Canada.

ISBD (G): General international standard bibliographic description, 2004, 2004 version, Standing Committee of the IFLA Section on Cataloguing, IFLA, The Hague.

Library of Congress 1989 (2002 updates), *Library of Congress rule interpretation*, Library of Congress, Washington, DC.

Library of Congress 1996, *Subject cataloging manual: Subject headings*, 5th edn (2004 cumulation), Library of Congress, Washington, DC.

Library of Congress 2006, *Library of congress subject headings*, 29th edn, Library of Congress., Washington, DC.

Rasmussen, E 2004, 'Information retrieval challenges for digital libraries', *Digital libraries: International collaboration and cross-fertilization: ICADL 2004*, held in Shanghai, China, 13-17 December 2004.

CHAPTER 10
Library and information systems: a work in progress

Tom Denison

As the twenty-first century progresses, there can be no doubt that the nature and form of library automation is undergoing a profound change, as is the role of libraries, their relationships to their parent institutions, their partners and their users. To understand what is happening, the development of library automation needs to be placed in the context of its wider environment, the trends that have affected it, the strategies adopted and the technical changes and world views that have both developed as a result of those strategies and, in turn, contributed to them. The intention of this chapter is to look at those broad trends before considering the current status of the technology and some of the issues that will have an impact on its further development.

Trends in library technology

Clifford Lynch (2000) applied a three-phase process to describe the effects of information technology on organisations and analyse the trends in library automation, starting with the computerisation of traditional library operations in the first phase, moving to the rise of public access in the second and the development of electronic content and the rise of networks in the third. Integral to this progression, he notes, has been 'a rapidly changing environment that includes the publishing and information marketplace, changing modalities of scholarly communication, and evolving capabilities in the user community' (2000, p.60). Similar observations have been made by others, including Ebenezer (2002) and Rosenblatt (1999).

Dorothy Peake (1996) and Cathie Jilovsky (2003) identify the start of library automation in Australia as being the automation of the serials check-in, binding and subscription functions at the State Library of NSW in the 1960s. From there, they both chart developments, including the rise of cataloguing and catalogue production systems in the 1970s, through the production of book and microfiche catalogues and the rise of bibliographic networks (for example OCLC in the USA and ABN in Australia) to the arrival of the turnkey integrated library management system (ILMS; see below), the latter both being underpinned by the establishment of standards for machine-readable cataloguing (MARC), as outlined in the previous chapter. In the process, libraries had automated labour-intensive processes such as acquisition, circulation, serials control and catalogue maintenance, and established online catalogues (the 'OPACs' also discussed in Chapter 9). The development of bibliographic networks, intended to save money, had paved the way for other key changes and cooperative activities, such as cooperative collection development and the provision of online support for interlibrary lending (Peake 1996; Rosenblatt 1999; Jilovsky 2003).

This was the start of Lynch's second stage in which, as a result of automation, services visible to the public began to change. The online catalogue had improved services by potentially providing bibliographic access twenty-four hours a day, first within the library but soon wherever there was access to the network. It was a period of transition, characterised by the development of open network services based on industry standard networking protocols, that laid the groundwork for further change. Online abstracting and indexing services to provide improved access to journals had developed in parallel, although for most users access was possible only through expensive, librarian-mediated sessions. It was also a period of rapidly changing user expectations. Advances came to be taken for granted and demand for even greater access became common since, although the changes had revolutionised public access to the monograph collection and the management of internal processes and resources, there had been little change in the ability to find information in the totality of the collection and many, such as those who rely on serial publications, had gained little benefit (Lynch 2000).

Just as librarians were finally realising their dream of automating the management of their existing collections, however, the world moved on, and libraries were:

> confronted with environmental changes driven by information technology, which quickly moved the focus of attention away from automation towards a series of much more fundamental questions about library roles and missions in the digital age. Libraries were forced to react to developments in information technology (and their cultural and economic consequences) rather than methodically exploiting them. The emergence of the world wide web in the mid-1990s is perhaps the great symbol of this shift (Lynch 2000, p.62).

The explosive growth in the range and type of digital resources available, including abstracting and indexing services, online journals and digital archives, not to mention a vast array of websites and services, confronted libraries with the need to deal with them in ways that were both efficient for libraries but integrated and coherent for their users. The immediate response was to seek a way to turn the OPAC from a comparatively simple listing of a library's collection into a direct gateway to information and services. It soon led to the notion of the digital – and later hybrid – library, with much of the initial work being undertaken not by libraries but by the research community (Lynch 2000). This emphasised the fact that the library was no longer seen as the sole repository of scholarly information. In the new world, that role was seen to be shared (as indeed it always had been) by a loose amalgam that included government, private firms, scholarly societies, university departments and IT services (Rosenblatt 1999). To some extent libraries had once worked in isolation, but in this new environment they would have to adjust to the role of what one hopes would be a key component of a much broader infrastructure, and to achieve that they would need a far more explicit alignment with the strategic goals and targets of their parent institutions (Jilovsky 2003).

Lynch's third and final phase had arrived. In this phase, not only did the problems of access and integration remain but a new set of issues had arisen, formulated by Lynch as: 'how to describe multimedia digital information effectively and affordably; how to archive digital information; how to address questions of authenticity, integrity and provenance; and how to structure services around information that needs to be computationally manipulated rather than merely viewed' (2000, p.66). In this new world, many of the constraints on development were no longer due to technical problems but to the issues of intellectual property (IP) and copyright, and the requirements of licensing agreements.

The subsequent history of library automation has been an attempt to deal with these issues and to again bring order to the management of information resources. It has already led to significant work on digital libraries, and on tools that enable digital information to be more easily found, understood and used: 'extraction and analysis tools for quantitative data, visualisation tools, authoring and editing tools' (Rosenblatt 1999). It has resulted in the development of new expertise and the creation of strategic alliances and collaborative relationships. Ultimately it will lead to new service paradigms.

The digital library is not just information and tools, however. Libraries are becoming more actively involved in facilitating scholarly communication by collaborating with publishers and scholarly societies and by providing more direct assistance to the research process itself. This started with the development of e-presses, for example, Stanford's HighWire Press and RMIT Publishing in Australia, with the goal of providing an alternative to the established scholarly publishing industry and to address some of the problems associated with it, such as pricing, intellectual property issues and long lead times for publication (Treloar & Payne 2006). The establishment of the Scholarly Publishing and Academic Resources Coalition (SPARC), together with the development of software such as DSpace at MIT and FEDORA at the University of Virginia, then contributed to the spread of digital repositories. At first these were primarily e-print repositories, conceived as showcases for an institution's intellectual output. But the range of applications soon grew to collections of learning objects that support the teaching process and to the concept of research repositories to be used not just for the deposit and management of digital objects but as tightly integrated elements of the research process itself. These developments, and the need to maintain an environment of interoperable distributed collections and services, have led to a much closer integration of libraries and other operational units within their parent institutions (Greenstein & Thorin 2002).

Although the situation is fluid, for the most part these changes have been independent of the ILMS (Ebenezer 2002). Indeed, there are those who have argued that many of the new digital library applications are too specific to their institutional context to be appropriate for commercial exploitation (Smith et al. 2003). It is too early to predict the impact of this over the next decade, but if the traditional ILMS is to survive as the centrepiece of library operations, it may need to change radically.

There are also significant implications for the ways in which libraries and their users interact. A number of changes are already evident, for example, many libraries are experimenting with online reference inquiry systems (Fletcher & Hair 2004; Phillips 2004). However, in an environment where round-the-clock access is a given and users prefer online resources regardless of whether they are the most appropriate, 'disintermediation' – with the librarian ceasing to be an intermediary between the client and the various information sources and systems provided – may prove the more common response, with the result that librarians, as John Mills put it in Chapter 6, become 'information phantoms'. Many examples of this can already be seen, with users being able to perform a range of functions, such as renewing loans and requesting materials remotely via the catalogue, and the development of self-service circulation facilities are set to grow even more rapidly with the arrival of RFID (radio frequency identification technology). If there is a benefit for libraries in this, it is that by developing disintermediated services they may be able to reduce the cost of many routine operations and reallocate staff to new roles, resulting in an improved service overall (Rosenblatt 1999).

These changes are now also starting to have an impact on the overall design of library services, with libraries considering ways to reconfigure their physical space in a way that would continue their traditional role while providing a social space to facilitate the exchange of ideas and information. Using technology in a mediating role, they are combining the complementary strengths of the library and IT departments to create an 'information commons', where the technology and information needs of students can be met at one service point (McRobbie 2003).

The integrated library management system (ILMS)

The traditional ILMS – also referred to as integrated library system (ILS) and library management system (LMS) – grew out of the need to manage physical collections. Marshall Breeding (2004a, p.1) describes it as an application based as far as possible on a single shared database that 'automates many library tasks that would otherwise be repetitive, labor intensive, and inefficient'. Cibbarelli (1999) adds that it provides integrated online access to the library catalogue as well as to the functions of cataloguing, circulation, acquisitions and serials management. In general terms, the functionality of these modules can be described as follows.

The *cataloguing* module is central to the traditional ILMS because it facilitates the creation of a quality database that underpins all other modules, protects the investment in the creation of that database by conforming to international standards (MARC/AACR) and so ensures the ability to migrate to future systems. It should include support for original cataloguing, via multiple custom templates to allow for both MARC-based and/or special-purpose cataloguing, the ability to interface with or accept records from bibliographic utilities, and have a Z39.50 copy cataloguing client. It should provide a similar range of functionality for the management of authority records and files and support online authorisation of names and subjects.

In many ways, the catalogue itself is the public face of the ILMS – it is often the module that provides clients with access and the computer peripherals used as referred to as the OPAC or online public access catalogue. Its purpose is to provide a framework for viewing and accessing the institution's collections, specifically the library's holdings and increasingly a vast range of local and remote electronic resources. It should provide a range of search options such as author, title and subject, whether by keywords or controlled terms (the controlled vocabularies discussed in Chapter 9), and support the use of boolean and relational operators, word stemming and truncation. It should have the ability to limit results by criteria such as material type and location and display the loans status of items. It should be able to display cross-references. Extended catalogue functionality should include enriched bibliographic content and display, and self-service features including those that allow users to view and renew loans, initiate recalls and holds, request items, and save or email result sets. It should allow for links to external electronic resources, typically by using the MARC 856 tag to include URLs within the bibliographic database, and provide access to the catalogues of other libraries via a Z39.50 client.

The *circulation* module's main purpose is to control the movement of the physical collection by streamlining the process of issuing loans and all related activities. Loan conditions should be determined using a policy matrix based on class of borrower, type of material and location. It should cover all aspects of dealing with overdues and fines. It should have a holds system, with the ability to transfer items between branches, while sending availability and overdue notices by email. It should be possible to update patron data online or in batch mode. The system should automatically produce circulation activity reports and inventories of all or selected parts of the collection. For academic libraries, it should include an academic reserve desk module, with support for electronic resources and short-term loans.

The *acquisitions* module's primary purpose is to provide internal efficiencies and improved management control over the purchase of materials, particularly monographs. It typically interfaces with the cataloguing module so as to allow single handling of bibliographic data from the time of ordering and the avoidance of duplicate orders. It must maintain an ordering system, including a database of all book and serial vendors, that is capable of generating purchase orders and sending them to vendors, and it must manage funds and budgets related to library materials, in hierarchical relationships, facilitating full accounting procedures and providing a full financial audit trail. It should also support electronic data interchange (EDI) for links to vendors and to external accounting or financial systems.

The *serials control* module allows for the cataloguing and processing of serials subscriptions, and must include accounting data and the ability to manage suppliers and the receipt of serials. It should have a similar functionality to the acquisitions module but also include specific functionality for the management of serials and serial subscriptions, for example, the ongoing receipt of issues, claims, renewals, routing and bindery functions.

An ILMS should be able to handle all of the above within a multi-agency framework, with different rules for each agency or group of agencies so that it can be used by both multi-agency libraries and library networks.

While the first library management systems ran on mainframes and then minicomputers, by the mid 1990s there was a clear trend to client/server architecture, leading to today's multi-tiered systems, in which the user interface resides on a client, the data on a data server, and an application layer, which may comprise several distinct components, is interposed between them. This architecture provides for improved database handling and network performance, and has additional benefits in terms of software maintenance. It also facilitates the connection of a range of clients to the system (Saffady 2000).

Within that framework, Ebenezer (2002) and Breeding (2004a) have suggested several key characteristics of current systems, but the most significant of these are that they:

- use TCP/IP networking protocols;

- have web-based OPACs;

- support UNICODE, hence non-Western characters;

- are built on industry-standard relational database management systems (RDBMS);

- are Z39.50-compliant (client and server);

- support the ILL protocol (ISO10160/61); and

- are EDI-compatible.

In Australia, the more popular large systems currently include INNOPAC Millennium series, Ex Libris ALEPH, Dynix Horizon, Spydus, VTLS Virtua and Endeavour Voyager, while SoftLink, Bibliotech, AMLIB, BookMark, LibCode and Athena are popular with the smaller end of the market – particularly schools – and DB/TextWorks (InMagic) is popular with special libraries. These smaller systems typically have less functionality and scalability than the larger systems but the boundaries are not always clear cut.

As several writers have noted, the ILMS now represents a fairly mature technology with a standard application functionality (Breeding 2004a; Ebenezer 2002), but there have been some recent innovations that will lead to improvements in functionality. Many libraries are providing access to selected services via mobile devices, for example, using products such as Innovative Interfaces AirPAC, which provides a version of the Millennium OPAC tailored for portable devices, and Dynix Horizon Wireless Gateway, which provides a standard wireless infrastructure with features to control the allocation of bandwidth, user authentication and data encryption (Breeding 2004b). Another example is RFID (radio frequency identification), which, despite concerns relating to borrower privacy and data security (Molnar & Wagner 2004), has the potential to provide a platform for simpler self-service loans and the simplification of stocktaking procedures by replacing both barcodes and security tags (Khong & White 2005).

If the ILMS is to serve well in this new environment, then the range of materials managed must include not only the library's physical resources but also all relevant electronic resources. To this end, many system vendors have broadened the scope of their systems by providing powerful metasearching facilities, extended cataloguing functionality (including the ability to use non-MARC metadata schemes such as Dublin Core; discussed in Chapter 9) and are providing additional products, such as customisable library portals, virtual reference services and reference linking systems (Ebenezer 2002). Despite this, they still have some way to go, a fact emphasised by a recent survey of Australian academic libraries, in which many respondents nominated integration and improved access to electronic resources as high priorities for further development (Maquignaz & Miller 2004).

It is yet to be seen how the ILMS will evolve to meet changing circumstances. Breeding (2004a) predicts that one response to this pressure for more sophisticated, and expensive, systems will be a growth in the number of consortia offering centrally managed systems. Indeed, there is some evidence of this within Australia, with successful networks in the Northern Territory (LINNet) and Tasmania (TALIS), interest being shown by public libraries in Victoria via the SWIFT project (Binnion & Cochrane 2004) and at least one vendor, Softlink, offering an ASP (application service provider) service. Another suggestion is that, with the advent of web services – self-contained modular applications that can be invoked across the web as interoperable building-blocks for constructing applications (Gardner 2001) – the ILMS system, or at least its familiar architecture, may cease to exist (Rhyno 2001). While there has been some movement in that direction, for example, with the ALADIN digital library system of the Washington Research Library Consortium (WRLC) and the PYTHEAS open source library system developed at the University of Windsor, Ontario (Rhyno 2002), it is too early to rate this as a significant trend.

Portals

The nature of the public face that libraries present to their users was clearly illustrated by Simon Huggard when he described the results of a user survey conducted at Monash University Library in 2001 (Huggard et al. 2002). Noting that the library at that time provided access to more than 300 databases, representing more than 20,000 titles and employing more than a hundred different interfaces, he found that clients encountered problems even before they delved into those resources, specifically, they had considerable trouble in identifying which resource was relevant to their needs.

The first strategies devised to improve this situation centred on indexing electronic resources via the catalogue. The catalogue can be effective for both physical items within a library and simple websites. However, it is generally inadequate for more sophisticated electronic resources which themselves contain a range of material – assembled by aggregators who in a more limited context are trying to solve much the same problem. The problems in this approach include difficulty in managing licence conditions, such as limitations on the number of simultaneous users, and the number and volatile nature of both individual online resources and aggregated collections, which create an enormous amount of work just in keeping them up to date (Breeding 2004c). Some products are available to assist with the process of updating the local ILMS (for example, Serials Solutions) but these only partially address the problem. As an alternative, many libraries also provide lists of electronic databases and e-journals on their website. These work well as navigational tools for researchers that want a quick way to find such resources but, as with the ILMS solution, they only help in locating the resource at the title level.

In a world dominated by the world wide web, users want to search and access full text. While this is possible in a number of services, such as the aggregated collections presented by EBSCOhost and ProQuest, such products focus on specific subject areas. The real challenge lies in connecting the user with the content of all of a library's electronic resources wherever they are located (Breeding 2004c). To that end, many libraries have expressed interest in dedicated electronic resource management software, either as part of their existing ILMS or as a stand-alone module.

The concept of portals has developed as one response to this problem. Portals are online, typically web-based, services that bring together content from a range of distributed resources in a seamless, integrated way, using technologies such as metasearching and harvesting, so as to collate the results in a form suitable for presentation to the user.

Cox (2003, pp.37-38) lists the core functions of the portal as:

- Browsable (by subject) and searchable database of available resources.

- Cross-searching of multiple resources, regardless of search protocol (usually Z39.50, but also http, ODBC, SQL) and regardless of the format of the metadata … with deduplication and sorting of results, saved searches, also simplification of authentication.

- Use of OpenURL, to carry the user through from hits in bibliographic databases to ways to access the 'appropriate copy' of the full text, or document delivery options.

Portals can provide general access to the resources of specific libraries or of networks of libraries (for example AARLIN, the Australian Academic & Research Library Network), or may be defined by their subject coverage (RDN, the Resource Discovery Network in the UK) or the format of their content (PictureAustralia, MusicAustralia).

Vendors currently market a broad array of products in this area, including not only portal solutions, but also distinct metasearch and linking products. Epixtech Horizon Information Portal, for example, features a consistent search and display interface for the library catalogue and other resources; Endeavor provides a suite of products under the ENCompass banner, with searching across HTTP, XML and Z39.50 enabled resources, and a linking service between journal citations and their related full-text articles; MetaLib, the Ex Libris product, provides for cross-platform searching of multiple resources, using SFX for open linking between local and external resources; and ZPORTAL, from Fretwell Downing, provides for searching of multiple web-based resources, aggregating of search results and content display.

There is a number of continuing issues with library portals, not least of which is that not all electronic resources and services conform to the relevant standards. As Breeding points out, there is also the problem that, from the perspective of maintaining efficiency at an operational level, they represent yet another system. In this context, he comments that 'at a minimum, all the applications that a library employs to manage its electronic resources should draw from the same knowledge base of its electronic holdings. A library should not have to maintain the same information in multiple ways' (2004c, p.33).

Digital repositories

Digital repositories can be thought of as digital collections for which:

- content is deposited, whether by the content creator, owner or third party;

- the repository architecture manages content as well as metadata;

- the repository offers a minimum set of basic services e.g., put, get, search, access control; and

- the repository must be sustainable and trusted, well-supported and well-managed (Heery & Anderson 2005, p.6).

They can take a variety of forms such as e-print repositories, learning object repositories, and institutional repositories and serve a range of purposes such as research, learning, e-science, publishing, records management and preservation. One of the principal drivers of their development has been the perceived need to provide improved access to scholarly communications. SPARC, the US-based alliance established to foster competition in the scholarly communications market, has been particularly active in this regard (Crow, 2002).

According to Heery and Anderson (2005), repositories can be distinguished from collections in that, depending on the purpose of the repository, they provide a number of targeted services, including:

- enhanced access to resources;

- new modes of publication and peer review;

- corporate information management, including records management and content management systems;

- data sharing, including re-use of research data, re-use of learning objects; and

- preservation of digital resources.

Among the more popular repository applications are DSpace and Fedora (flexible extensible digital object and repository architecture). Released in 2002, DSpace is a general-purpose, open source repository application, developed jointly by HP Labs and MIT Libraries, and targeted at multi-disciplinary research organisations. Freely available to other institutions to run in the form in which they find it or to modify and extend, DSpace uses a qualified Dublin Core metadata standard for the description of digital objects, and supports OAI-PMH (open archives initiative protocol for metadata harvesting) (Smith et al. 2003). Fedora, which grew out of work on the Digital Library in the late 1990s (Payette & Staples 2002), takes a different approach. Both an architecture and a software platform, it is an open source, digital object repository system that uses web services to call other services as well as to expose its own. Fedora stores digital content objects either as datastreams contained within the repository or as links to external resources, tying each to a default disseminator, or method of rendering the object.

There are numerous examples of repositories, but the work of the California Digital Library (Greenstein & Thorin 2002) is particularly noteworthy, as are developments at Indiana University, where a number have been implemented, including one that supports the use of visualisation and virtual reality technologies as a medium for artistic creation (McRobbie 2003). In Australia, several universities have established e-print repositories including the Australian National University, Monash University, the University of Melbourne and Queensland University of Technology.

Examining the state of current repository software, Heery and Anderson (2005) identified a lack of functionality that would present problems for all but the largest institutions. They suggested that priority developments should include: 'smart tools' for data extraction and automatic classification; format conversion tools; improvements in the user interface for submissions, including across multiple repositories; and tools to manage the interdisciplinary exploitation of repositories. There are also issues relating to the sustainability of information objects themselves, which, as Bradley (2006) notes, is dependent on a range of technical, social and economic considerations.

To address these issues, there are significant research projects being undertaken by the NDIIP (National Digital Information Infrastructure and Preservation program) in the USA (Friedlander 2002) and the JISC program in the UK (Heery & Anderson 2005). Within Australia, perhaps the most significant project is ARROW (Australian Research Repositories Online to the World), funded in 2003 by the Australian Commonwealth Department of Education, Science and Training (DEST). ARROW supports a number of modules: ePrints, eTheses, ePress, DEST Research Directory and NLA Repository, each with its own content submission forms, workflow and functionality. Using Fedora as its core technology, it is also trialling the Open Journal Systems software. In addition to its web-based interface, resource discovery is supported by a number of strategies, including support for SRU/SRW Z39.50 Next Generation group (ZNG) protocols to allow real-time searching by external systems (Treloar & Payne 2006).

Recalling an earlier comment by Smith et al. (2003), it should be recognised that repositories, and institutional repositories in particular, are just one component of an institution's information infrastructure. Repositories need to be designed in such a way as to interface with other services both within their parent organisations and to external organisations.

So, although some ILMS vendors are now working towards repository functionality as an add-on component for their existing systems, such developments may represent only partial solutions in that broader context.

Open source

One issue that could affect all of these developments is the use of open source software. The Keystone Principles (1999), drafted under the guidance of the Association of Research Libraries and OCLC, clearly intended to promote its use when it stated 'libraries will create interoperability in the systems they develop and create open source software for the access, dissemination and management of information' (Jordan 2004, p.1). While that was a statement of principle, open source projects and software are now beginning to have an impact on some areas of library automation, and there are numerous areas in which open source is used, such as in digital libraries, content linking and in interfacing with the systems of parent organisations (Kochtanek & Matthews 2002). Other examples range from comparatively simple utilities, such as XMLMARC (a utility for converting MARC records to XML), to personalised gateways such as MyLibrary and large-scale projects such as DSpace.

There are also some ILMS projects under development, notably Koha, PYTHEAS and Evergreen. Of these, Koha seems to have made the most headway. Developed in 1999 in New Zealand to address the needs of a small public library, it has a dedicated development community and is now being used by public libraries, not for profit organisations and schools in a number of countries (Eyler 2003). A more recent project, Evergreen, being developed and maintained by the Georgia Public Library Service (GPLS), may have a more promising future. Developed to meet the specific requirements of the PINES consortium of public libraries, a production release of the OPAC was scheduled for July 2006, with the PINES implementation scheduled for September. Work on the cataloguing and circulation functions is also well advanced (GPLS 2006).

Commenting on these, Anctil and Beheshti (2004) note that there is a 'lack of scope in terms of marketing, target audience and international coverage … no corporate outlets for technical support … a general lack of interoperability among the diffuse open source projects, few of which have reached development maturity for testing in pilot libraries'. Such issues would have to be addressed before open source software could make a significant impact in the areas of basic library functionality. Not only that, but vendors would have to change their business models, becoming service organisations that focus on technical support, customisation and value-added products (Kochtanek & Matthews 2002), and libraries would also have to make a greater investment in staff expertise and resources. These changes are possible but unlikely in the short term. It is probable that at least for the foreseeable future library and information systems will continue to be characterised by a mix of proprietary and open source systems.

Conclusion

An underlying theme of this chapter has been the importance of standards capable of underpinning the development of interoperable applications and the presentation of a coherent framework through which users can access information and resources. That there are currently concerns in this area was emphasised by Maquignaz and Miller's survey which reported that most respondents said that the standards of MARC and AACR2 provided such a foundation but noted that others saw the combination of MARC and AACR2 as limiting (2004). XML, an industry-wide format for data and document exchange, and the de facto standard for delivery of web content, may represent the future, in that it has significant potential to facilitate integration between a wide range of systems. At this point in time, particularly with Library of Congress (2006) support for an official specification for representing MARC data in an XML environment, it seems likely that this will happen. As Johnson (2001) notes, however, most bibliographic data are currently held in standard MARC formats, and the change is likely to be both expensive and prolonged.

As in the early 1980s, library systems are once again focused on the integration of services, but unlike the 1980s, the aim is not to develop a single system capable of managing the library's collections. Instead, the aim is to develop a fully interoperable architecture through which the library can provide unified access not only to the library collection, but to the vast array of electronic resources to which it and its partners have access, delivering them to the user's desktop whenever and wherever the user wants. While the long-term consequences of this may involve as yet undetermined changes to the nature of library services, it seems likely that two of the foundations of library automation in the 1980s – MARC and the ILMS – will cease to exist in their current form.

References

Anctil, E & Beheshti, J 2004, *Open source integrated library systems: An overview*, http://www.anctil.org/users/eric/oss4ils.html

Binnion, J & Cochrane, D 2004 'SWIFT – the future library system for Victoria's communities', *VALA 2004: Breaking Boundaries: Integration and Interoperability*, held at Melbourne Convention Centre, 3-5 February, 2004.

Bradley, K 2006, 'Digital sustainability and digital repositories – APSR', *VALA2006: Connecting with users*, held at Crown Towers, Melbourne, 8-10 February 2006.

Breeding, M 2004a, 'Integrated library software: A guide to multiuser, multifunction systems', *Library Technology Reports*, vol.40, no.1, pp.1-87.

Breeding, M 2004b, 'Wireless networks connect libraries to a mobile society', *Computers in Libraries*, vol.24, no.8, pp.29-32.

Breeding, M 2004c, 'The many facets of managing electronic resources', *Computers in Libraries*, vol.24, no.1, pp.25-33.

Cibbarelli, P 1999, 'Library automation: Today's successes and concerns', *Electronic Library*, vol.17, no.3, pp.155-157.

Cox, A 2003, 'Choosing a library portal system', *Vine*, vol.33, no.1, pp.37-41.

Crow, R 2002, *The case for institutional repositories: A SPARC position paper*, SPARC, 2002, http://www.arl.org/sparc/IR/IR_Final_Release_102.pdf

Ebenezer, C 2002, 'Trends in integrated library systems', *Vine*, vol.32, no.4, pp.19-45.

Eyler, P 2003, 'Koha: A gift to libraries from New Zealand', *Linux Journal*, no.106, p.1, http://www.linuxjournal.com/article/6350

Friedlander, A 2002, 'The National Digital Information Infrastructure Preservation program: Expectations, realities, choices and progress to date', *D-Lib Magazine*, vol.8, no.4, http://www.dlib.org/dlib/april02/friedlander/04friedlander.html

Fletcher, J & Hair, P 2004 'Online librarian – real time / real talk: An innovative collaboration between two university libraries', *VALA 2004: Breaking Boundaries: Integration and Interoperability*, held at Melbourne Convention Centre, 3-5 February, 2004.

Gardner, T 2001, 'An introduction to web services', *Ariadne*, no.29, http://www.ariadne.ac.uk/issue29/gardner/intro.html

Georgia Public Library Service (GPLS) 2006, 'PINES (Public Information Network for Electronic Services)', http://www.georgialibraries.org/public/pines.html

Greenstein, D & Thorin, S 2002, *The digital library: A biography*, Council on Library and Information Resources, Washington, DC, http://www.clir.org/pubs/abstract/pub109abst.html

Heery, R & Anderson, A 2005, *Digital repositories review*, http://www.jisc.ac.uk/uploaded_documents/digital-repositories-review-2005.pdf

Huggard, S, Hopley, J, Groenewegen, D, Horne, D, Smith, L & Leighfield, G 2002, 'Monash Library database usage survey', *VALA2002: E-volving Information Futures*, held at Melbourne Convention Centre, 6-8 February 2002.

Jilovsky, C 2003 'Systems librarianship in Australia: A historical perspective' *Library Hi Tech*, vol.21, no.3, pp.297-308.

Johnson, B 2001, 'XML and MARC: Which is right?', *Cataloging and Classification Quarterly*, vol.32, no.1, pp.81-90.

Jordan, J 2004, 'The Keystone Principles and OCLC: Four years later', *Portal: Libraries and the Academy*, vol.4, no.1, pp.1-7.

Khong, G & White, S 2005, 'Moving right along: Using RFID for collection management at the parliamentary library', *Information Online 2005: 12th Exhibition & Conference*, held Sydney Convention & Exhibition Centre, 1-3 Feb. 2005.

Kochtanek, T & Matthews, J 2002, *Library information systems: From library automation to distributed information access solutions*, Libraries Unlimited, Greenwood, CO.

Library of Congress 2006, *MARC 21 XML schema*, http://www.loc.gov/standards/marcxml/

Lynch, C 2000, 'From automation to transformation: Forty years of libraries and information technology in higher education', *Educause Review*, vol.40, no.1, pp.60-68.

McRobbie, MA 2003, 'The library and education: Integrating the information landscapes', http://www.clir.org/PUBS/reports/pub119/mcrobbie.html

Maquignaz, L & Miller, J 2004 'The centrality of the integrated library management system: A strategic view of information management in an e-service environment', *VALA 2004: Breaking Boundaries: Integration and Interoperability*, held at Melbourne Convention Centre, Melbourne, 3-5 February 2004.

Molnar, D & Wagner, D 2004, 'Privacy and security in library RFID – Issues, practices and architectures', *ACM Conference on Computer and Communications Security*, Washington, DC, 25-29 October 2004.

Payette, S & Staples, T 2002, 'The Mellon Fedora project: Digital library architecture meets XML and web services', *Sixth European Conference on Research and Advanced Technology for Digital Libraries*, Lecture Notes in Computer Science, vol.2459, Springer-Verlag, Berlin, pp.406-421.

Peake, D 1996, 'The heroic age of Australian library automation and its immediate aftermath', *Lasie*, vol.27, no.3, pp.4-17.

Phillips, N 2004, 'Electronic and live – online reference two years on', *VALA 2004: Breaking Boundaries: Integration and Interoperability*, held at Melbourne Convention Centre, 3-5 February 2004.

Rhyno, A 2001, 'The end of the ILS', *Inside OLITA*, no.5.

Rhyno, A 2002, *PYTHEAS Introduction*, http://web2.uwindsor.ca/library/leddy/people/art/pytheas/index.html

Rosenblatt, S. 1999, *Information technology investments in research libraries*, http://www.educause.edu/ir/library/erm/erm99/erm9947.html

Saffady, W 2000, 'The status of library automation at 2000', *Library Technology Reports*, vol.36, no.1.

Smith, M, Barton, M, Bass, M, Branschofsky, M, McClellan, G, Stuve, D, Tansley, R & Harford Walker, J 2003, 'Dspace: An open source dynamic digital repository', *D-Lib Magazine* vol.9, no.1, http://www.dlib.org/dlib/january03/smith/01smith.html

Treloar, A & Payne, G 2006, 'The ARROW project after 2 years: Are we hitting our targets?' *VALA2006: Connecting with users*, held at Crown Towers, Melbourne, 8-10 February 2006.

PART 3:

The information environment in the twenty-first century

CHAPTER 11
Beyond the corporate library: information management in organisations

Michael Middleton

This chapter goes beyond the library environment and provides a critical examination of information management principles and applications for a variety of alternative information environments. The library has always been a primary cultural institution for managing information but librarians did not make regular use of the phrase 'information management' until the mid 1970s, after it had achieved currency outside the library environment. A significant factor in the growth of the term was the US government-initiated Commission on Federal Paperwork (1977). The Commission extended its interest beyond the primary focus of paperwork reduction and used the term 'information resource management' as an expression meaning the planning and controlling of information requirements in general.

Some information professionals had at the same time been using 'information management' with approximately the same meaning. This has led to ongoing academic and professional debate about whether 'resource' needs to be part of the phrase. Although 'resource' remains prominent in such professional tags as the Information Resources Management Association (IRMA), 'information management' seems to have become the preferred term in recent years. Even so, its definition remains tenuous.

A difficulty is that both 'information' and 'management' have nuances influenced by context, discipline and application. Information may be understood as intermediate in a continuum between data (symbols arranged for interpretation) and knowledge (information that has been absorbed and comprehended). However many users of the word do not differentiate data, information or knowledge. Management too, is understood in different ways. It may have an operational connotation (organisation of artefacts), a personnel connotation (supervision of people) or a development connotation (strategic planning). Correspondingly, many users of the term management make no distinction between the different applications of management. 'Information management' therefore may be understood as any combination of these interpretations. A more detailed discussion of terminology appears in Wilson (2003) and there is an extended explanation of application in Middleton (2002).

Roberts (1997) saw that there was much to be gained from a pooled view and understanding of the library and information management settings. Further, having proposed a set of conceptual principles for information management, he mapped them against consolidated principles for librarianship. He found that information management had little to offer in terms of a surpassing paradigm. In this respect the analysis that follows (below) respects his approach by itemising elements that are generally well accepted in the library field, but exploring them in a wider context.

Other than IRMA, many professional associations lay claim to information management. Their emphasis depends upon different points of reference. Aslib, for example, which styles itself 'the Association for Information Management', has a foundation in special libraries and information centres (www.aslib.co.uk). It is orientated towards dealing with information as a resource. By way of contrast, the Society for Information Management (SIM) (2005) encourages a membership of academics, consultants, professional leaders and managers in the information systems area.

There are other professional associations that also see information management as being within their purview. They include those whose centre of attention has been records, document or image management. They now cast their net in a wider context. This may well include knowledge management which is sometimes confused with and sometimes differentiated from information management – an issue discussed by Stuart Ferguson and Anne Lloyd in Chapter 13.

If one considers information management within its various interpretations, it can be seen that it involves many elements that are familiar to libraries, but which may be expanded beyond the library environment:

- *Information acquisition*, not only for purchase of and subscription to material coming into repositories, but also for generation of information within organisations through processes such as content management.
- *Information organisation*, not only by cataloguing and classification of materials in a repository, but also by use of digital metadata for information resources that may be records, databases, websites or other digital media.
- *Current awareness*, by reporting not only material that comes into collections, but through provision of environmental scanning, using tools such as database posting, portals and blogs to repackage and re-present information.
- *Resource evaluation*, by determining not just the economic and intellectual worth of material in library collections, but through audit of enterprise-wide information sources.
- *Information quality control*, not simply through standards for cataloguing and maintenance of authority files, but also by means of data dictionaries, data sampling metrics and other means of database validation.
- *Requirements analysis*, not just through determination of sources that meet individual user needs, but through explanation of processes by which they use information so that system interfaces may be created.
- *Preservation*, not only of physical collections, but through development and application of digital preservation and security procedures.
- *Policy*, not confined to such repository matters as collection and use policy, but more broadly applied to corporate information policy.

Each of these information elements is discussed in the following sections of this chapter, with emphasis on their application outside the library domain and their relevance to that domain.

What can be seen from the list is an emphasis on information as distinct from the documents that carry the information. There is also, however, a convergence of information management practices – those within and outside the library environment. As established libraries have moved into the digital environment, librarians have become less concerned with collection, more concerned with provision; less concerned with form, more concerned with content; less concerned with comprehensiveness and more with pertinence and presentation.

Each of these concerns is essentially an extension of what librarians have been doing applied within a broader framework and often without reference to a collection in the traditional sense. This is recognised at the preparatory level in the library profession where many current information studies courses cater for this extended context. (Curriculum issues in education for library and information studies are explored in the final chapter.)

Information acquisition

In their capacity as repositories, libraries have long been in the business of acquiring documents. In recent years, their idea of what constitutes a document has been extended to cover all forms of media including digital media. As digital media have become available, there has been a move from ownership to access. Information management within libraries now includes a significant element of attention to subscriptions and access mechanisms such as consortial arrangements for use of digital aggregations (see Paul Genoni's account of consortia in Chapter 8).

Libraries have generally been concerned with acquisition of, or access to information produced outside their organisation. Usually it is published information, although differentiation between what is published and unpublished is now more blurred than it used to be. It used to be that publishing of physical documents leading to printing was a process accompanied by review, editorial and presentation procedures, each carried out by specialists and meant to refine the content of the original authorship prior to marketing and distribution. This of course still happens and has in numerous cases been transferred to the digital environment. Nevertheless, the advent first of desktop publishing, making use of software within the means of individuals, and then the web, with its straightforward mark-up language, has given a new understanding to publishing. The less stringent meaning of 'to bring to public attention' can be applied in the digital environment. Vanity publishing is given a new lease of life.

Along with personal publishing autonomy, corporate publishing has also become easier to achieve and the distinction between documents internal and external to the organisation has diminished. Information management has promoted the value of the corporate memory embodied in the documents produced by a business, many of which have a life that is principally internal to the organisation. These documents may be in the form of reports, forms and correspondence, aggregated in files, that record fiscal, policy, historical, legal or research aspects of the business. Organisation of these documents for internal use is undertaken using recordkeeping principles (as discussed in the next chapter).

As enterprises convert to digital document production, they have sought ways of associating document management and recordkeeping. They continue to seek ways of balancing the production of internal and public information so that, for instance, fragments of internal documents may readily be incorporated into published documents for marketing purposes. The concept of the content management system (CMS) is a development that supports such acquisition and dissemination of corporate information. The CMS has stemmed from use of intranets to manage corporate information. Software support for a CMS provides a mechanism for producing internal information and making available via the internet anything that an enterprise also wishes to make external – in other words, publish.

As defined by Robertson (2003), a CMS supports the creation, management, distribution, publishing and discovery of corporate information. A successful CMS will be able to support business objectives for information management that include creation and controlled distribution of corporate information, such as information dealing with policy directives, lessons learned, recordkeeping and training. This may be achieved most effectively via interfaces to internal databases, so that information acquisition is database driven.

A CMS is sometimes characterised as having content creation, content assembly and content management components (Asprey & Middleton 2003). Content *creation* is concerned with the authoring process. Software support for it should include:

- Capability of undertaking authoring without reference to underlying mark-up.
- Templates and style sheets that separate content and presentation.
- Metadata creation.
- Interactive help utilities that guide users through complex tasks (wizards).
- Controlling group use of individual documents as they are being developed, using check in/check out facilities.

Content *assembly* is concerned with adjuncts to creation that minimise data duplication and support quality control. Software support includes:

- Integrated authoring environment for utilisation and incorporation of digital data representing image, sound or text from outside sources.
- Inclusion of multiple contributions through devices like bulletin boards.
- Database interfaces that provide for a single source of re-usable content.
- Maintenance of links despite restructuring and presentation in different contexts.
- Authority management so that there are standard lists of names and subjects that may be used within documents.

Content *management* is concerned, like document management systems, with a system that ensures effective process control. Software support includes:

- A repository that locks pages that are in use and provides for utilisation of fragments of documents.
- Versioning that supports sole use of a current version (integrity), along with control for recovery and accountability.
- Security through access levels and audit trails.
- Workflow support through association with other business systems within a framework that is adaptable to change in organisational processes.
- Management reporting of use and performance.

The term digital assets management (DAM) may be used as an alternative to CMS when there is an emphasis on valuing of the information resources that have been created, rather than the creation of them. DAM is therefore particularly associated with the *content assembly* and *content management* points listed above.

Libraries themselves employ content management in conjunction with their portals and many applications have been described (Seadle 2006). From an information management viewpoint, however, CMS have much wider application than the library environment.

Williams et al. (2003) describe CMS deployment at an Australian university in some detail. They discuss its design and implementation at RMIT and give illustrations of downloadable templates, metadata forms and screens from the document authoring and publishing environment. They also undertake initial evaluations of use. An example of the association between recordkeeping and CMS is described by Sprehe (2005), who emphasises the need for recordkeeping to support compliance requirements of legislation. Then he goes on to outline three brief case studies of US government agencies in which electronic recordkeeping has been enhanced through alignment with content management and portal management. Improved support is provided for case file management, electronic publishing, financial management, forms management and executive decision making.

CMS is naturally of interest to organisations that are rich in content such as publishers and broadcast media, which want the 'essence' of their content to be produced and disseminated through multiple outlets. Mauthe and Thomas (2004) provide examples of application in media environments.

Information organisation

Organisation of information continues to be a major preoccupation of information professionals. The library profession showed the way to information organisation through internationally accepted cataloguing standards and a relatively limited number of classification schemes, established to cover the whole field of knowledge (see Chapter 9). Libraries have a legacy of doing this for physical documents. Further, they have adapted their metadata manuals to deal with digital document description – for example cataloguing rules for machine readable formats and web documents. In this way, MARC, the commonly used library metadata format, is able to accommodate descriptions of digital media.

Despite this, the digital environment has encouraged a great number of alternative approaches to information description, particularly for databases. These range from specialised metadata schemes to specialised taxonomies that cover the domains of subject matter. Any database definition for an in-house database is effectively a metadata scheme. It is of interest to information management when the metadata must be shared among different applications. This is almost inevitable as companies try to integrate internal systems through enterprise-wide applications, share with other businesses for e-commerce or establish data warehouses that share the same data, which may be known in different parts of a company by different names.

Standardised approaches to naming and defining data across databases are aimed for in data dictionaries (or what the International Standards Organisation (ISO) calls an information resource dictionary system framework). Use of these provides an information manager with a tool for information quality maintenance and a mechanism for controlling information sharing within an organisation. It also formalises information requirements analysis and specification. Such dictionaries are now also being used among organisations, notably in the health field, to achieve agreed definitions. An example is the data dictionary, published with supplements by the Australian Institute of Health and Welfare (AIHW) (2003).

Between organisations, information sharing is also facilitated by metadata standards. Whereas the library environment essentially has the one scheme, MARC (albeit with variations) for sharing bibliographic data, there are many other schemes used in different environments, for example:

- EDIFACT, an international electronic data interchange standard developed under the auspices of the United Nations for administration, commerce and transport – the scheme and syntax are documented by the ISO (2002).
- A variety of geospatial metadata sets that facilitate organisation and sharing of mapping information, such as those of the US Federal Geographic Data Committee – there is an international standard ISO 19115 of relevance and there are implementations such as that adopted in Australasia (ANZLIC 2001).
- AGLS (Australian Government locator service) (Standards Australia 2002), designed to provided a limited set of metadata for describing government websites, based on an extension of another metadata scheme, Dublin Core (see Chapter 9).

The focus of both data dictionaries and metadata schemes is the description of the different elements of an agent that carries information. A database may be such an agent irrespective of the digital medium on which it is resident. An agent may also be any document in the broad sense of an artefact holding information. If the elements of an agent, such as a compact disk, include its title, creator and playing time, then a data dictionary controls the format of each of these elements. MARC might reasonably be used as a contribution to a data dictionary in a non-library environment.

An extract from the AGLS metadata element set reference description is shown in Figure 11.1. Such a reference set may be used as a standard to form the basis of internal data dictionaries created by different institutions and then used to share data between institutions in a common format. In the example, a single element, in this case DATE, is used.

Dictionaries are also structured to call upon other metadata that describe the subject content of the agents that carry the information. If the compact disk contained a documentary film, then the subject content might draw upon a classification scheme for documentaries. Just as MARC has data elements set aside to accommodate instances from sets of subject headings and classification schemes, schemes such as AGLS provide for use of a range of taxonomies and schemes.

Many classifications, thesauri and comparable controlled vocabularies have been established for description of specialised material. Some examples are:

- COFOG (classification of the functions of government), one of many schemes maintained by the UN, in this case to categorise expenditure according to purpose – part of their international family of economic and social classifications (United Nations 2002).
- ICONCLASS (http://www.iconclass.nl/), an iconographic classification system developed from the work of van de Waal at the University of Leiden – a collection of ready-made definitions of objects, persons, events, situations and abstract ideas that can be the subject of a work of art.
- AGIFT, a three-level hierarchical vocabulary that describes the business functions carried out across federal, state and local governments in Australia (National Archives of Australia 2005).

Element Name:	**Date**
Label:	Date
Definition:	A date of an event in the lifecycle of the resource.
Obligation:	Mandatory
Comment:	Typically, Date will be associated with the creation or availability of the resource. Recommended best practice for encoding the date value is defined in a profile of ISO 8601 [W3CDTF] and follows the YYYY-MM-DD format.
	Qualifiers
Qualifier Name:	**created**
Label:	Created
Qualifier Type:	element refinement
Definition:	Creation date of the resource.
Qualifier Name:	**modified**
Label:	Modified
Qualifier Type:	element refinement
Definition:	Modification date of the resource.
Qualifier Name:	**valid**
Label:	Valid
Qualifier Type:	element refinement
Definition:	A date (often a range) of validity of a resource.
Comment:	Typically, a date the resource becomes valid or ceases to be valid, or the date range for which the resource is valid.
Qualifier Name:	**issued**
Label:	Issued
Qualifier Type:	element refinement
Definition:	A date on which the resource was made formally available in its current form.

Figure 11.1 Extract from *AGLS metadata element set, Part 1: Reference description, version 1.3*, 2002, viewed 8 March 2007, http://www.naa.gov.au/recordkeeping/gov_online/agls/metadata_element_set.html, reproduced with permission of National Archives of Australia

These vocabularies are published for use by anyone. They may be contrasted with the many examples of in-house database definitions and taxonomies that are particular to databases in businesses and research institutions. The in-house vocabularies may, in a way, constitute a map of an organisation's intellectual assets. They represent enterprise knowledge. However, even in such cases there is a growing need to formalise and share description of structures for others to use between businesses or for e-research.

Kremer et al. (2005) undertook an analysis of three in-house examples – the introduction of a glossary for an insurance company, the establishment of a corporate taxonomy at an international professional services firm and the combination of a glossary and taxonomy for document classification and retrieval at an educational institution. From their findings they proposed a procedural model for terminology management that combines glossary and taxonomy use.

The taxonomies referred to above are typically controlled vocabularies, in which objects are described together with relationships such as subsumption (for example 'a plum *is-a* fruit') or meronymy ('a plum skin is *part-of* a plum'). However, they are unlikely to comprise a complete formal ontology where for a domain of interest, knowledge is represented in terms of concepts, their characteristics and all of the relations among them. Thus, a cooking ontology would also need relationship attributes such as *grown-in* to show origin of the plum or *mixed-with* for use in recipes. It is the development of such formal ontologies that will help to underpin the aspirations of the so-called semantic web in which software can be developed better to interrelate search strategies and documents.

Another aspect of information organisation concerns the way that websites are organised. This is called information architecture (Rosenfeld & Morville 2002; see also Chapter 9), although the terminology is also applied more widely to the design and development of many other information products and systems. In the case of the web, it involves design and coordination of interfaces that draw upon databases, metadata, content management and presentation.

Information organisation for the information manager therefore involves a judicious combination of metadata, which require constant attention behind the scenes, and presentation, which *is* the scene.

Current awareness and environmental scanning

Provision of current awareness services by libraries pre-dates libraries' use of computer systems. When the first text-based retrieval systems were developed in the 1960s as a by-product of the publishing process, an initial application was selective dissemination of information (SDI). Librarians acted as intermediaries (and still do) by developing profiles (search term formulations) for their clients. System development has seen an emphasis on clients (often clumsily termed 'end users') setting up their own profiles. Many database services facilitate this self-management through fairly straightforward procedures. However, many end users are not in a position to put the time and understanding into developing their profile. They may therefore profitably turn to information professionals for profile maintenance. The support may come from librarians, consultants or information officers, working independently of any library.

SDI depends upon extraction from databases of new incoming material. It has the advantage of reliability, normally obtained through the controlled description of material that has been through editorial and reviewing processes. However, users may be prepared to reduce reliability in favour of immediacy and subjectivity. For this reason, the blog (short for weblog: web page containing brief, chronologically presented items of information) has become a popular current awareness device.

They are often ephemeral, but when sustained blogs, many of which are maintained by individuals, may be useful combinations of a diary, discussion, current references, news, book reviews, images, and opinion and links on specialist topic areas, thereby achieving 'guru' status for the blog maintainer. Could this be the information manager as guru? As pointed out by Clyde (2004), the best blogs are authoritative sources of current information and opinion related to their topic. They may be created by subject specialists and they may well include contributions from other specialists. Examples of specialist blogs are Freedom of Information and Open Government Blog (http://foia.blogspot.com/), maintained by a UK academic, Steve

Wood, and *Internet Legal Research Weekly's* Inter Alia (http://www.inter-alia.net/). Blogs are also obvious tools for libraries and there are many cases where institutions or individuals are now using them.

The web portal is a more formal approach than the blog. It usually works with the combined resources of an institution and is likely to combine current awareness with access to database and archives. Libraries often play a lead or support role in such endeavours, for example, the Australia Dancing portal (http://www.australiadancing.org/) is hosted by the National Library of Australia.

Environmental scanning is a label that is sometimes applied to current awareness. In some cases, libraries have appropriated it to refer to their SDI services. In an information management sense, however, it is generally more about evaluation and interpretation of the information as well. It is the process by which an organisation extracts information about the general societal, technological, economic and political environment in which it operates and combines this information with business intelligence about its competitors in order to assist its own strategic planning. Disengagement with the material that is scanned (in the sense of a library leaving a patron to do the interpretation of retrieved material) does not apply. There must be analysis and use of the information within the strategic planning framework of the organisation. This may be undertaken by a special unit in an enterprise, or by an organisational strategy that requires sections of a company to undertake environmental scanning as part of their duties.

Choo (2002) has interpreted the framework of environmental scanning to consider organisations as open systems interacting with the environment. He sees these enterprises as 'intelligent'; that is, they are learning organisations that set objectives and improve competitive position, consciously creating, acquiring, organising and using knowledge to support their direction. Thus a learning organisation operates by carrying out appropriate strategies and responses within a continuing cycle of activities that involve sensing the environment, perceiving change and interpreting the significance of the change. The business literature is replete with many characterisations of how environmental scanning may take place, In Choo's case, he opts for four modes: undirected viewing, conditioned viewing, enacting and searching. These represent progressively greater levels of engagement with scanning.

There are many documented case studies of scanning application. An example in which enterprises were analysed to see how scanning influenced strategic decision making was reported by Frishammar (2003). He studied four medium-sized companies listed on the Swedish stock exchange with respect to specific strategic decisions. The companies were in the heavy vehicle, information logistics, environmentally friendly product development and biotechnology sectors. Unsurprisingly, all were found to employ information in strategic decision making. Yet there was varying reliance on 'hard' (numerical, quantitative) and 'soft' (qualitative, discursive, visions, ideas, cognitive structures) information.

The combination of soft and hard information requirement seemed to vary over time in each enterprise. Most respondents to his survey started out with soft information, then moved to hard information as a process continued. The picture provided by respondents was that soft information served as a basis for interpreting which hard information is relevant and which is not. At that stage hard information became more important, leading to the application of analytical methods for studying figures. After this, however, many respondents returned to soft information. A sentiment of many of the respondents was that it was impossible to 'count all the way'. At the time when the actual decision (strategic choice) was taken, intuition and cognitive structures again came into play (Frishammar 2003, p.321).

In each case, companies tended to rely heavily on solicited information. Unsolicited information was less frequently used, although its importance was still recognised. In all companies, information classified as unsolicited was more undirected than directed (that is, the source being intentional or purposeful in information provision). Two of the companies ranked their customers as the most important source of information and the three highest ranked sources in both companies were personal sources. The data show a pattern for three of the four companies, in which internal sources of information were preferred over external ones.

Current awareness is a significant aspect of information management that supports strategic decision making. It involves a combination of obtaining information from a range of structured and unstructured sources, interpreting the information and converting it to corporate knowledge in relation to the business's objectives.

Resource evaluation

Determining the extent and value of library collections is part of the collection management process (as discussed in Chapter 8). Collection assessment has been quantified in the past with such tools as Conspectus, which was structured to provide overviews of strengths, weaknesses and directions of academic collection levels. However, information resource evaluation in an information management context sees a library collection as just one of the information resources for the whole enterprise.

Establishing the extent and effectiveness of an enterprise's information resources is a fundamental aspect of information management, requiring an appreciation of how the information resources support the mission and objectives of the organisation. Simply identifying and categorising the range of information resources can be problematic but the process may be assisted by tools such as the Harvard Information Business Map (Oettinger et al. 1999). This schematic is a two-dimensional representation of information resources that has its horizontal axis plotted from form to substance (with increasing value added) and its vertical axis plotted from product to service. Information resources such as paper, PABXs, financial services or databases are then positioned on the map. Such identification of resources may be extended by determining the extent of information that there is, who uses it, which processes it supports and how well the processes are supported. In the form of an information audit, this should help to identify discrepancies, as well as those of the resources that may be better applied or funded and those that may be unnecessary.

Resource evaluation that distinguishes information resources as sources, systems and services is detailed in the seminal work by Burk and Horton (1988). They used an approach called 'Infomap' and suggested various ways of assessing resources, but ultimately these are grouped under determinations of the importance and the effectiveness of each resource. Infomap also takes into account a third factor – the importance to an organisation of the activities that are supported by each of the information resources. A formula is produced to combine the three elements.

Their method may be criticised for providing an unsubstantiated formulaic approach that leads to ratings that are apparently quantitative, while actually based upon many subjective impressions. It also has the major drawbacks of time and resources required to obtain and reconcile all those impressions about resources. The method does, however, recognise the importance of accounting for policy influences (see the later section on information policy) and, together with a software instrument for capturing data, it caters for managers who like to be able to obtain pictorial overviews of usefulness.

More recently Henczel (2000) describes a seven-stage information audit model that specifically excludes computer systems, on the assumption that a systems audit will follow and complement an information audit. She is at pains to differentiate an audit from an information needs analysis. She sees the former as identifying, not only resources and services, but also how and by whom they are used. Presumably because she is excluding computer systems, she does not make any association between needs analysis and requirements analysis, a term commonly used for helping to design systems (described in the later section on requirements analysis).

Like Burk and Horton, Henczel emphasises the alignment of the audit process with organisational goals and she sees the process as a continuum that continues to modify those goals. In each case, the writers exemplify their procedures with case studies. Burk and Horton provide a detailed analysis of a resources company so they are able to provide many examples of sources such as remote sensing data or correspondence files, services such as couriers or information locating and systems such as drafting/graphics or contracts process control – all assessed within the framework of the activities that they support.

Henczel's case studies are less detailed, but they explain the information gathering methods and purpose. For example, in the case of an Australian government department (2000, p.212), the assessment is described as being within the framework of a broader knowledge management strategy. It addresses issues relating to governance, electronic recordkeeping and document management, information access and retrieval, and information management tools and infrastructure.

As is typical within the management area, there are variations on the auditing process that help to blur just what is being audited (Middleton 2002, p.360). An audit may emphasise either the information flow or the information value. In the case of information flow, it may be called a communication audit and focus on the short interactions of managerial work, many of which are oral (and thus recall the concerns of knowledge management, outlined in Chapter 13). Therefore the ways in which flows are compartmentalised may be addressed along with appropriateness, clarity and efficiency. Information value audits are more concerned with information systems processing activities and the integrity and security of these. A useful definition that encompasses the above variations is given by Robertson (1997) as 'systematic examination of information use, resources and flows, with verification by reference to both people and existing documents in order to establish and monitor the extent to which they are contributing to an organisation's objectives'.

When there is an attempt to ascertain information value as part of an audit, a number of ways have been employed to attempt to quantify value. Two of these are risk analysis and information attribute assessment. Risk analysis tries to quantify information assets in terms of threats and safeguards associated with them. It includes trying to answer the questions of what it might cost an enterprise if some of its information is stolen, lost, insidiously modified or even simply viewed by an uninvited party. What is the likelihood, for example, of a competitor gaining access to research data, leading to a patent application and what financial effect might this have on the corporation? Algorithms have been developed that normalise and sum all such identifiable risks including those pertaining to disasters such as sabotage, in order to establish some insurance value with respect to information.

Alternatively, Oppenheim et al. (2003) adopted a repertory grid technique to ask managers about numerous attributes of nominated information assets. The assets were identified as information about each of the following: business processes, customer, product, organisation, management, personnel, suppliers, accountability and competitors. Examples of information attributes that were assessed included 'changes made to information' (on a scale from slow to quick) and 'level of control of information' (scaled from low to high). By averaging ratings given for these and seventeen other attributes, they developed a metric that gave an indication of corporate information value. Determining information value in a quantitative way is a problematical area, but to the extent that value can be estimated, it forms a useful part of an auditing process.

Quality control

Quality control procedures range from software support for data processing at the technical level through to scrutiny and performance review of management processes. In libraries, the data processing quality control may be through the medium of authority files that support cataloguing processes; the performance review may be of a task such as average time to undertake reference queries.

Each of these procedures has its equivalent in the information management world outside libraries. Many data dictionaries, for instance, provide for data elements to have validation lists – that is, the data instances for a particular data element, such as person's name, may have only certain allowable values. Query answer throughput is a significant aspect of performance review in call centres.

Data dictionaries provide for formalising and controlling the naming of entities, attributes and their relationships within databases, for example by inclusion of:

- Data entities such as elements, tables, rows and keys.
- System entities such as programs and modules.
- External entities such as description of people, documents and devices.
- Identification attributes such as naming along with synonyms or aliases.
- Representation attributes such as data type or number of characters in an element.
- Control attributes such as ownership – who is allowed to change data instances for an element.
- Cardinality relationships – the number of instances in one entity that may be related to instances in a related entity, for example, the number of rows in a table.
- Subtype or subsumption relationships that indicate whether one entity is a part of another (a sedan, for example, is a subtype of car).

When put into effect, data dictionaries support quality control of data as the data are entered. When an operator is required to enter the postcode for an address into a database, for instance, a data dictionary may be used to:

- Validate the operator as a user who is allowed to enter postcodes.
- Have a postcode data element of a limited number of characters.
- Allow postcodes to appear only within the numerical range associated with the country of instance.
- Provide a picklist of allowed postcodes from a scrollable dialogue box for the data element.
- Provide alternative names to be used for the element (for example, zipcode) by operators in different countries.
- Maintain a history of versions of naming and allowed values provided for any picklists.

Although dictionaries help to control data, they have limitations when it comes to fields that are more difficult to validate such as name and address. Data entry operators inevitably make keyboard transcription errors – they may be unable to differentiate forenames from family names or the same customer may have his or her name recorded in different ways in the same organisation (with initials, with full forenames, with slight spelling variations in family name or with family name changing over time). These present problems with identity tracking, or with matching, say, a purchase order and a complaint by the same person.

Standards authorities attempt to provide assistance in this area, for example, Standards Australia has a standard for client interchange information that is presently under revision. Nevertheless, large corporations, even if they heed standards, find it necessary to carry out monitoring of their large data sets. Similarly, smaller organisations responsible for key information used by larger ones must have many data quality checking approaches. An example would be a credit reference agency such as Baycorp Advantage, which sells crucial credit checking information to businesses. The businesses themselves will have supplied much of the information that the agency uses. However, it can maintain data quality using highly structured data and validating data with source bodies (for example, address data with Australia Post) or by using specialist software such as comparators (comparing strings of data for likeness) or soundex (making phonetic matches) in order to identify element occurrences that are effectively the same even if they are recorded differently.

It is worth turning from databases to websites because, since the advent of the web, much has been written about maintaining the quality of web pages. Relevant advice appears in the many style guides that include recommendations about site quality. Corresponding guidance is provided in the checklists that support approaches to website evaluation. Queensland University of Technology's FAVORS (http://www.favors.fit.qut.edu.au/) is one such list, maintained online with examples and references. A summary of the website evaluation criteria that it illustrates is shown in Table 11.1. Information quality is maintained as much as possible at the information acquisition stage for databases, but attention must also be paid to the forms of presentation, typically through websites.

Table 11.1 Website evaluation criteria based upon FAVORS

Criterion	Factors
Functionality	Active links; errors in mark-up; help facilities; layout; search facilities; site maps; alternate text for images.
Authority	Affiliations indicated; Copyright indications; creator responsibility; credentials; editorial oversight; funding source indication; viability.
Validity	Feedback; Ratings and awards; Refereed content; Referring links; Reviews of site; Usage figures.
Obtainability	Cost of access; Format support; Load factors; Metadata; Naming mnemonic; Security protection; Speed.
Relevance	Audience; Balance; Breadth; Controversial content; Currency; Depth.
Substance	Accuracy; Coverage; Detail; Evidence; Explanation; Readability.

Requirements analysis

Librarians are familiar with determining the information requirements of individual clients through the medium of the reference query. They may also be called upon to determine the information-seeking behaviour of groups in order to provide services for a particular set of users. This contributes to information needs analysis. The needs analysis process also occupies systems analysts, who may describe it in terms of requirements analysis. When user needs are being determined as part of a systems analysis process, the analysis is in order to find out the process by which information is sought, more so than the particular sources that might be appropriate. Information managers may have to analyse information-seeking behaviour of a group in order to provide a strategy for providing for the group or they may, at a finer level of granularity, be required to identify information requirements in such a way that the requirements may be used to describe processes for system design.

The broader needs analysis approach usually tries to frame the information seeking approach within a behavioural context. Choo et al. (2000) consider, for example, that information-seeking behaviour is influenced by cognitive, affective and situational factors.

Cognitive factors apply when there is knowledge deficiency and a choice must be made between alternative courses of action in order to make decisions, or because a person needs to make sense of a situation by better understanding of the elements that comprise it. A project manager embarking upon a new project, for example, will be seeking knowledge to address the functional, management and political factors that may have an impact upon the task. There is an expectation that the information that creates this knowledge will be accurate, reliable and pertinent.

Affective factors (discussed in Chapter 6) apply in relation to emotions such as apprehension or anxiety. A person may be motivated because of uncertainty about a frame of reference. It could be a matter of not knowing what is going on with a project stage and therefore seeking understanding to instil self-confidence. At an initial phase of uncertainty, too much unique information can alienate the person from the information subject. Their learning process may then be abandoned in frustration. Instead, if there is persistence and a growing appreciation of information relating to the query, it can be refined, patterns may be recognised, hypotheses may be formed and the accretion of knowledge continues with growing confidence.

Situational factors are influenced by the amount of time and effort necessary to carry out the search, or by whether it will be rewarded within the environment in which it is being undertaken. Beyond the cost and accessibility of material, this may involve the time necessary to learn a retrieval technique for a particular resource or time spent in interpreting information presented in reports that have not been aggregated for ease of use.

Although there are yet to be generally accepted models of information-seeking behaviour, there is a vast body of studies. As might be expected, much of this is undertaken in the area of marketing, in which purveyors of products and services are attempting to anticipate how potential customers seek information. Information management is principally concerned with services and there are many studies where a key factor being considered may be a personal attribute such as youth, gender, age or disability; a discipline such as science or journalism; or a community need such as health or small business. Case (2002) provides a detailed study of research into information needs and illustrates it with case studies that focus upon occupation, social role or demographic group. The procedures for gathering information include:

- *Interviewing* which may be of individuals or focus groups and which may be structured using questionnaires, follow-ups for clarification, explanation of critical incidents or recollections of procedures.
- *Self-reporting* of procedures undertaken.
- *Prototyping* or developing of experimental or mock-up versions of systems and their interfaces, possibly accompanied by usability testing.
- *Observation* of use behaviours, perhaps accompanied by verbalisation, or recorded behaviour such as interface interactions or query logs.

If determination of user needs has a system orientation and understanding of associated processes is to be conveyed to the stage of system design, then the requirements analysis must proceed through a process of data and process modelling in order to make more explicit the level of abstraction that describes information requirements.

There are numerous associated techniques including use of structured English; work process analysis (narrative description of process steps); and more formal graphical approaches, including flowcharting, data flow diagrams; or enterprise modelling. There are also hybrid approaches such as soft system methodology, which combines description and graphic representation, and object modelling, which integrates data and process approaches to systems analysis. An example of software that provides presentation support for a variety of these techniques is SmartDraw (http://www.smartdraw.com/).

Ensuring that the corporate memory is retained and available is a key element of information management. Having in place procedures to achieve this should stem from the information policy level and employ both technical and managerial strategies. The technical strategies should encompass:

- *Media* preservation so that the physical medium holding the information is stored in non-invasive conditions – this may mean pest-free, climate controlled storage for paper; storage sites physically remote from a business; a system of reproducing analogue or digital records; or a means of converting documents in one medium to alternative or additional media.

- *Technology* preservation involving refreshing of data for new technology and migration from outmoded technology – this may mean migrating the software with the data or alternatively providing effective metadata so that new software may continue to process data that had been managed by different software on outmoded technology.
- *Intellectual* preservation, meaning that the integrity and authenticity of information as originally recorded must be addressed to avoid changes that may be accidental or may be intentional (well meant or fraudulent).

If the integrity of ideas is to be maintained then this means keeping the substance of the ideas constant at different levels of abstraction – from data (bits) to text (information). This maintenance must be continued with 'fixity' (Hunter 2000). The information should not be subject to change through technology updates and it is necessary to differentiate update versions, perhaps by digital signature. Other assistance to digital information integrity includes referencing, for example, through persistent URLs (uniform resource locators) that provide a reliable approach to citation; an ability to track provenance through tracing sources using metadata; and continuation of context with respect to the wider environment, such as links to other documents and identification of hardware and software dependencies.

From a managerial viewpoint, decisions about preservation and disposal of documents have long been formalised in the recordkeeping environment, using procedures such as appraisal and tools such as retention and disposal schedules (see Chapter 12). These schedules record metadata about appraised documents that indicate whether they are subject to regulatory constraints such as taxation legislation; how long they should be retained; who has custodianship of them and may make decisions about disposal; whether they should be maintained in different forms (paper, microform, digital); or if they are vital records, never to be destroyed.

Enterprises may use two types of retention schedule: a functional schedule or a departmental schedule. A functional schedule is based upon business functions, such as personnel, sales or travel. These may be repeated in many divisions of the same organisation or within government departments. A functional schedule can be applied across these for consistency of application by the corporation as a whole or by a central organisation such as a state archive body. A departmental schedule is specific to a division or department and uses language particular to its own policy and administration.

Such scheduling information may itself be held in a database and refer to both paper and digital material. It could in fact be integrated with data dictionary information as explored earlier in this chapter, so that at document description level, all the retention information is maintained with other metadata. An initiative that is helping to provide guidance in this area is the *Data dictionary for preservation metadata* (PREMIS Working Group 2005). It has formalised preservation description that is necessary for websites, digital versions of newspaper articles, dissertations and photographs.

The proliferation of digital documents in organisations and the regulatory abuses that have led to litigation and the demise of some large organisations make the development and application of such tools an imperative. Organisations are still coming to terms with what must be done, however. In Singapore a survey of email users was conducted to assess the understanding of email management as official records (Seow et al. 2005). Emails were found to be recognised as important business records and most employees acknowledged their critical importance to work and practice compliance. Yet they were typically left to manage their email on their own. The survey showed that 33 per cent of the respondents saved their emails into personal folders, 25 per cent printed and filed hardcopies in personal files, 19 per cent saved to corporate servers and 18 per cent printed and filed hardcopies in shared files. Many of the respondents expressed increasing difficulty in retrieving their own or colleagues' emails when required.

Although email contains much information of significance to a business, it is unlikely to be considered among the vital organisational records in a recordkeeping sense. Vital records support critical business processes and must be available for business continuity, with backup and re-establishment procedures. A necessary element of a preservation program is a strategy for disaster preparedness that identifies vital records and makes provision for their safety and reconstitution.

Institutions are working in an environment where regulatory efforts concerning information use are intensifying. They must be in a position to respond quickly to legal or corporate requirements for information that may seemingly be moribund. This requires a concerted technical and managerial framework for document preservation.

Information policy

Earlier, information resource analysis was considered holistically within an enterprise. Likewise, information policy is concerned with the planning framework for an enterprise as a whole, rather than being confined to any particular resource within the organisation. As such, it must therefore be informed by public policy and work within the framework of corporate policy.

Public policy that is likely to have an impact upon corporate information policy includes policy that has been enabled within legislation, such as data protection and policy that has been made explicit as directives within government, such as dealing with provision of access to services. It includes policy to do with:

- *Intellectual property*, which has implications for how an organisation makes use of information produced by others and how it protects its own research and development, for example through the patents process.
- *Privacy*, which, for example, will provide a framework spelling out what information about customers may be released to other parties and how and why.
- *Access*, which in the case of government departments will spell out the extent of the publishing obligations, by means of which the public may have access to bureaucratic workings, and data, for example, through websites.
- *Repositories*, which spells out the extent to which private corporate documents and published documents should have copies deposited in state or national repositories.

Jurisdictions typically have an agency that acts as a focus for the development of public policy. An example is the Australian Government Information Management Office (AGIMO) (http://www.agimo.gov.au/).

Table 11.2 Corporate policy constituents, adapted from Middleton (2002, p.442)

Definition	• Define the knowledge that is needed to achieve goals, the information needed to maintain the knowledge, and the ways in which people in the organisation need to use knowledge and information.
Acquisition	• Ensure that appropriate information is acquired externally and generated internally.
Utilisation	• Exploit information fully, to meet all current needs, and to help meet changes in goals and in the operational environment. • Use knowledge and information ethically in all internal and external dealings. • Provide appropriate human and financial resources for managing and developing the use of information and knowledge. • Organise information to facilitate tailored access to individuals and groups and sharing between systems. • Ensure that information reaches all the people who need to use it on time, and in the right format.
Evaluation	• Audit the use of information and knowledge regularly to ensure that what is needed is available, of appropriate quality, and used appropriately and to good effect. • Provide for a coordinated overview of total resources of knowledge and information. • Develop and apply reliable means of assessing the costs and value of information, and the contribution it makes to achieving objectives.
Authority	• Identify the people responsible for managing specific information resources, and those who are 'stakeholders', and ensure that the authority of the managers of information resources matches the responsibility they carry.
Communication	• Promote information interchange between managers of information resources, and between them and stakeholders.
Infrastructure	• Develop and maintain an infrastructure of systems and ICT to support management of information resources and interactions within the organisation and externally.
Access	• Pursue openness of access to information inside the organisation and externally. • Provide for ongoing awareness in disciplinary and managerial specialities. • Provide appropriate security levels. • Safeguard current and historical information resources so that they remain accessible for use at all times.
Preservation	• Ensure preservation of the organisation's 'memory' in the form of its knowledge base. • Provide for business continuity with backup and re-establishment procedures for records supporting critical business processes.
Disposal	• Identify conditions under which information media may be eliminated.
Familiarisation	• Provide appropriate education and training to enable members of staff to meet their responsibilities in using knowledge and information.
Evolution	• Align the definitions as goals evolve and change. • Seek to use knowledge and information to support the management of change initiatives to benefit the organisation, and to create new knowledge. • Use the policy as the basis for information strategies which support business strategy.

Corporate information policy normally will be an element of corporate policy as a whole. It should address aspects of strategic planning in order to provide an agenda for each of the sections that has been looked at in earlier sections. Table 11.2 shows an itemisation of the constituents that policy may include. Orna (1999; 2004) elaborates on these, with examples of strategies that may accompany them and case studies that illustrate policies for public and private sector organisations. Corporate information policy should be framed within an enterprise's mission and objectives and should produce strategies for dealing with each of the information management elements that have been described preceding it.

Conclusion

Information is now generally taken to be a business resource. Its effective management will contribute to business performance. Elements of information management, as itemised above, will contribute to enterprise performance if applied using strategies developed from information policy and undertaken efficiently. Many enterprises are still coming to terms with differentiating information technology management from information management. In some cases they have turned to knowledge management to give more focus to the content rather than the technology for dealing with it. However, information management still seems to be the most appropriate term for describing the recorded information that must be managed by an enterprise. Associated techniques such as information orientation (Marchand et al. 2001) are leading to a measurable way in which to establish the relationship between information use and business performance.

References

ANZLIC 2001, *ANZMETA XML document type definition (DTD) for geospatial metadata in Australasia*, http://www.ga.gov.au/anzmeta/

Asprey, L & Middleton, M 2003, *Integrative document and content management: Strategies for exploiting enterprise knowledge*, Idea Group, Hershey, PA.

Australian Institute of Health and Welfare (AIHW) 2003, *National health data dictionary*, no.12, http://www.aihw.gov.au/publications/index.cfm/title/8964

Burk, CF, jr & Horton, FW, jr 1988, *Infomap: A complete guide to discovering corporate information resources*, Prentice Hall, Englewood Cliffs, NJ.

Case, DO 2002, *Looking for information: A survey of research on information seeking, needs, and behavior*, Academic Press, Amsterdam.

Choo, CW 2002, *Information management for the intelligent organization: The art of scanning the environment*, 3rd edn, Information Today for ASIS, Medford, NJ.

Choo, CW, Detlor, B & Turnbull, D 2000, *Web work: Information seeking and knowledge work on the world wide web*, Kluwer Academic, Dordrecht, Netherlands.

Clyde, LA 2004, 'Weblogs – are you serious?' *The Electronic Library*, vol.22, no.5, pp.390-392.

Frishammar, J 2003, 'Information use in strategic decision making', *Management Decision*, vol.41, no.4, pp.318-326.

Henczel, S 2000, *The information audit: A practical guide*, Saur, Munich.

Hunter, GS 2000, *Preserving digital information: A how-to-do-it manual*, Neal-Schuman, New York.

International Standards Organisation (ISO) 2002, *Electronic data interchange for administration, commerce and transport (EDIFACT)* – Parts 1-8 (No. ISO 9735-1:8).

Kremer, S, Kolbe, LM & Brenner, W 2005, 'Towards a procedure model in terminology management', *Journal of Documentation*, vol.61, no.2, pp.281-295.

Marchand, DA, Kettinger, WJ & Rollins, JD 2001, *Information orientation: The link to business performance*, Oxford University Press, Oxford, UK.

Mauthe, A & Thomas, P 2004, *Professional content management systems: Handling digital media assets*, Wiley, Chichester, UK.

Middleton, M 2002, *Information management: A consolidation of operations, analysis and strategy*, Centre for Information Studies, Wagga Wagga, NSW.

National Archives of Australia 2002, *AGLS metadata element set*, Part 1: Reference description. Version 1.3, http://www.naa.gov.au/recordkeeping/gov_online/agls/AGLS_reference_description_v1-3.doc

National Archives of Australia 2005, *Australian governments' interactive functions thesaurus – AGIFT*, http://www.naa.gov.au/recordkeeping/thesaurus/index.htm

Oettinger, AG, McLaughlin, JF & Birinyi, AE 1999, 'Charting change: The Harvard Information Business Map', *The information resources policy handbook: Research for the information age*, BM Compaine & WH Read (eds), MIT Press, Cambridge, MA, pp.323-246.

Oppenheim, C, Stenson, J & Wilson, RMS 2003, 'Studies on information as an asset II: Repertory grid', *Journal of Information Science*, vol.29, no.5, pp.419-432.

Orna, E 1999, *Practical information policies,* 2nd edn, Gower, Aldershot, UK.

Orna, E 2004, *Information strategy in practice*, Gower, Aldershot, UK.

PREMIS Working Group 2005, *Data dictionary for preservation metadata*, OCLC & RLG, http://www.oclc.org/research/projects/pmwg/premis-final.pdf

Roberts, S 1997, 'The contribution of librarianship to information management', *Introduction to information management*, JM Brittain (ed.), Centre for Information Studies, Wagga Wagga, NSW, pp.23-49.

Robertson, G 1997, 'Information auditing: The information professional as information accountant', *Managing Information*, vol.4, no.4, pp.31-35.

Robertson, J 2003, *So, what is a content management system?*, http://www.steptwo.com.au/ papers/kmc_what/index.html

Rosenfeld, L & Morville, P 2002, *Information architecture for the word wide web,* 2nd edn, O'Reilly, Cambridge, MA.

Seadle, M 2006, 'Content management systems', *Library Hi Tech*, vol.24, no.1, pp.5-7.

Seow, BB, Chennupati, KR & Foo, S 2005, 'Management of e-mails as official records in Singapore: A case study', *Records Management Journal*, vol.15, no.1, pp.43-57.

Society for Information Management (SIM) 2005, *The SIM portfolio*, http://simnet.org/Content/ NavigationMenu/About/Overview/Portfolio/Portfolio_2005.pdf

Sprehe, JT 2005, 'The positive benefits of electronic records management in the context of enterprise content management', *Government Information Quarterly*, vol.22, no.2, pp.297-303.

Standards Australia 2002, *AS 5044.1-2002: AGLS metadata element set - Reference description*, Standards Association of Australia, Sydney, NSW.

United Nations 2002, *List of international family of economic and social classifications*, http://unstats.un.org/unsd/cr/family1.asp

US Commission on Federal Paperwork 1977, *Information resources management*, USGPO, Washington, DC.

Williams, R, Boulton, T & Bartosiewicz, I 2003, 'When one size does not fit all: Distributing content management system and web publishing in a large university', *AusWeb03: Changing the way we work: Proceedings of AusWeb03, the ninth Australian World Wide Web Conference*, A Treloar & A Ellis (eds), Southern Cross University, Lismore, NSW, pp.578-590.

Wilson, TD 2003, 'Information management', *International encyclopedia of information and library science*, 2nd edn, J Feather & RP Sturges (eds), Routledge, London, pp.263-277.

CHAPTER 12
Evidence and memory: records services and archives

Karen Anderson

Records and archives are more than special sources of information – they are the basis of social and corporate memory, kept securely in their context so that they will provide evidence of the transactions they record. This chapter will discuss standards and management strategies that help ensure records remain reliable sources of evidential information, providing organisations and society with corporate, cultural and historical memory, and the tools with which they can see where they have been and learn from the past, in order to make decisions for the future. The chapter aims to provide a broad overview of archives and records – what they are, how they are kept and some of the professional issues in managing them. Although the necessary brevity of the chapter will not do justice to any one of the topics covered, it is hoped that readers will gain an understanding of the important differences between records and publications and between libraries and archives, and that some will be sufficiently interested to read much further.

What are records and archives?

The majority of library collections are made up of published resources, which are usually secondary sources of information compiled by an author. The author will have sifted through other sources of information on a particular topic and compiled a synthesis of that information for readers. Even where a book purports to be a collection of archival materials, such as a series of records or letters about a particular topic, it will have been selected, compiled and edited by someone and then published, providing a number of copies for sale. Although this can be a very useful and valuable thing to do, providing easy access to historical documents in some form and compiled for a particular purpose, much may have been lost in the process. If the records are compiled in a sequence other than their original context, or perhaps mixed with documents from other sources, much valuable information together with their evidentiality will have been lost or at least compromised. Unless the reproductions of the records are published as facsimiles, and care is taken to provide detailed metadata about each document, other intrinsic contextual information will have been lost in the publication process, for example, the size of the document, the handwriting or layout of text and illustrations on the page, ownership marks indicating who has had custody of the item, or annotations on the back or in the margins that may not have been included when compiling and editing the publication.

Records are quite different from published resources. If lost or damaged, a publication can usually be replaced, either through a bookseller or the antiquarian book trade, or another copy obtained on interlibrary loan. But if an original record is lost it has gone forever. Records, therefore, are unique, primary sources, formally defined in the Australian standard AS ISO15489.1 *Records management, part 1: general* (section 3.15) (Standards Australia 2002), as: 'information created, received and maintained as evidence and information by an organisation or person, in pursuance of legal obligations or in the transaction of business'. Records are assets, important to the business or personal lives of their creators and receivers. Some records are vital to proving identity, ownership of property and other assets, the creation of companies and their structure. If disaster strikes and these vital records are lost the consequences are very serious. For example, refugees may become stateless because they cannot prove who they are and where they came from; a business may fail because it has not only lost the legal documents essential to proving its existence and continuing to function, it will have lost its corporate memory too.

Records are by-products of business transactions, an intrinsic part of enacting that transaction, so they provide evidence of who was involved, and when and how the transaction was conducted. They depend on their context for much of their meaning. That is, for a document to be a record, we must know who created it and/or received it, and when and why and what other related transactions preceded and followed it. An understanding of 'why' the record was created is often provided by the records around it, that is, the context of the record. This information about the creator and the record is known as its 'provenance'. Keeping records in the original order in which they were kept when in active use by their creator ensures that vital context is preserved. This order may be a folio and file numbering system in an organisation, metadata designed to be automatically assigned on creation in a digital information system, or a bundle of personal letters in a particular order tied up with a ribbon, kept apart from other letters received by the person concerned. This concept of 'original order' is one that library staff sometimes find difficult to understand and accept. They are trained to treat most information sources as individual items and to impose order through standard subject classification and cataloguing systems used by libraries. Although most records are documents, records can be created in many other formats too. For example, archives may contain photographs, maps, postcards, posters, bound volumes, geological samples, architectural models, audio files, videos, film formats and digital records held in a digital repository. Although it is not always possible to store some formats physically in their original order, because different formats need special storage conditions to ensure their preservation, original order can be maintained through intellectual control methods.

Provenance and original order are key principles in archival theory and management and are explained by Sue McKemmish in 'Introducing archives and archival programs', in which she defines records and archives as follows:

> People and organisations create and use records in the course of conducting business and relating to each other. These records are threads in the social fabric of human interaction. They provide:
>
> • evidence of activities and interrelationships;
> • information about associated people, organisations events and places.
>
> Some records of social and organisational activity are preserved because they are of continuing value to individuals, organisations or society. Records of continuing value are called archives (McKemmish 1993, p.1).

Neither individuals nor businesses need or want to keep everything. Not all records are of continuing value, and those that are not are identified and disposed of in an orderly fashion according to a retention and disposal schedule. Those that are identified as being of enduring value are archival records or archives. Another way of thinking of archives is that they provide a memory, as Anne-Marie Schwirtlich points out:

> The fundamental reason for keeping archives is that they serve as a memory.
>
> Just as individuals dysfunction without a memory so do organisations. Without archival recall they would have no perspective on which to base planning, nothing to prevent them repeating mistakes, no expertise or knowledge except what people remembered, perhaps inaccurately, no way of proving entitlements of ownership or of accounting for their actions. The extra research and energy required to reconstruct missing information can be very expensive, if it can be done at all – that is why we keep archives.
>
> We also keep archives for broader reasons that can be called 'historical' or 'cultural' in addition to financial and administrative reasons. For example, the archives of the Westpac Banking Corporation (formerly the Bank of New South Wales) are vital to the Corporation. But Westpac's archives also form part of the rich memory of the nation as the Bank is our oldest financial institution and has played a very significant role in the development of Australia. All archives share this dual function; they are an essential resource to their creators and provide evidence of their important work over time to the wider community (Schwirtlich 1987, p.6).

Archives as evidence of accountability and appropriate action are essential to the working of democratic government. Yet records taken out of context can be scandalously misleading while being presented as evidence in support of a particular viewpoint. A thought-provoking example of photographic records used in such a way as to mislead the Australian public is the 'Children Overboard' story, in which photographs of a brave rescue of refugees from a sinking vessel on 8 October 2001 were separated from their original captions and used in the press, showing children in the water, allegedly thrown overboard by their parents. McKemmish (2005) gives an account of the events surrounding these photographs and their misuse, while using them to illustrate that the photographs are an archival trace, becoming records in several ways: as records of the HMAS Adelaide; records of the Australian Navy; as well as personal records for the sailors involved. But in their misuse, these photographs were 'an information artefact, presented as evidence that the refugees threw their children overboard, but ultimately proved to be fake' (2005, p.11). The 'Children Overboard' story provides an excellent illustration of the power of records, from which it is easy to see the serious consequences of separating records from their context.

Libraries, records and archives

Libraries and professional librarians meet records and archives in a range of situations. As discussed in Chapter 5, major national and state libraries have a mission to preserve cultural heritage and this entails collecting the papers, along with the publications (if any) of outstanding personalities who have had a significant impact on the community they serve or have made a major contribution to the life, literature or development of the community in some way. Thus, larger libraries have a long tradition of collecting personal archives, sometimes called manuscript collections. These collections often extend to the records of associations and enterprises of importance to the community, including service organisations, unions, churches and businesses. The National Library of Australia is such a collector, for instance, seeking and preserving the personal papers of eminent Australians. The State Library of Western Australia contains the Battye Library which collects not only published material on the history and development of Western Australia, but also collects and manages private (non-government) archives. Similar collections and services in some other states are the Mortlock Library in South Australia, the John Oxley Library in Queensland and the Mitchell Library in New South Wales (as outlined in Chapter 5).

Another point at which libraries and archives frequently meet is in the local studies collections held by many public libraries and universities. As well as published works about the local area, they may take in business records from organisations and companies that have played a significant role in the history and development of the area, and will also collect private archives – personal papers, letters, diaries and photographic collections of people who have contributed to the community over the years. Public libraries may also act as public access points for their parent municipal or city council records. The Charles Sturt University Archives is one that acts as both university archives and regional archives, serving as a repository in the regional network of State Records New South Wales, while also functioning as the records and archives service for the university (Boadle 1995; Charles Sturt University 2006; Doubleday forthcoming).

School libraries sometimes find themselves charged with the custody of the school's archives, although some schools have their own separately established archives and archivist. Private schools lead the field in this area in Australia, and are more likely than government schools to have an archive held separately from the school library and to employ an archivist. School management interest in archives is often triggered by plans to celebrate an impending significant anniversary, such as twenty-five, fifty or one hundred years since the school's foundation. However, a properly established school archives will play an active role in the school's recordkeeping system as well as collecting and preserving memorabilia concerning the school's history and heritage.

In special libraries, particularly in government organisations, libraries and records services may be grouped together under the same organisational umbrella, or integrated into a single information service, serving the entire organisation. In the cases of government records services, the records service must meet all records management standards and requirements for their jurisdiction. These are set by the relevant recordkeeping authority. In Western Australia, for example, the State Records Commission sets and promulgates standards based on advice from the State Records Office of Western Australia, which also provides advice to Western Australian State Government agencies and local government records services. The State Records Office manages the processes leading to approval of recordkeeping plans and retention and disposal schedules, as required under the State Records Act 2000. The National Archives of Australia (NAA) sets standards and provides training and advice for Australian Commonwealth Government agencies under the Archives Act 1983. Every state of Australia has its own recordkeeping authority with a regulatory role under state legislation. These requirements also apply to the records of state-run schools. Records services of state education authorities act as sources of advice and assistance for schools.

An indication of the number and type of archives in Australia and the rich resources in their collections, large and small, can be found by perusing the Directory of Archives in Australia, which is available and updated quarterly on the Australian Society of Archivists (ASA) website (http://www.archivists.org.au/), and the links to archives and archives organisations in Australia on the National Archives of Australia (NAA) website (http://www.naa.gov.au).

Archives and community advocacy

One of the challenges faced by managers of archives is the community misconception that archives are 'old stuff' – dusty volumes lingering in the basement. There is a further, if slightly contradictory belief that anything old will be valuable in some way, and that libraries and archives ought to accept all donations offered to them. This is particularly the case where collecting policies have not been clearly stated and promoted in the community and among the potential donors and users of the archives. These misconceptions die hard. In April 2006, a news item on a British radio station announcing the availability of the 1841 Census on the world wide web referred to the relative ease of access provided by the web, rather than 'having to search through dusty heaps of microfilms'. Although the reporter was aware of some advances in technology, he helped to promulgate the idea that anything archival involved dust and a probable lack of order, simply substituting microfilm for paper in his imagination! Collecting archives in general, if not individual organisations, have a real image problem that has the potential to impede their work and the value placed by society upon their collections. A possible reason for these misconceptions is that most people lack experience of using archival sources. Libraries and museums traditionally have been introduced to children in their primary school years or earlier, but the same is not true of archives. For many, their first contact is prompted by an interest in adulthood in tracing ancestors for family history, or attempting to satisfy curiosity about an aspect of history that intrigues or concerns them. For others, it is engendered by a need to establish their identity and their rights, as in cases of people who need to establish rights to pension benefits or medical services, or the rights of indigenous people who need to reconnect with families, forebears and their traditional lands, either for their own psychological benefit or to establish land rights. Those who were victims of child migration programs have similar needs to overcome disconnection and dislocation that can only be satisfied through records. They often need the services of a professional archivist to help them with their searches.

An outreach project aimed at introducing archival records to school-aged children is the National Archives of Australia's *Vrroom* (virtual reading room). It is aimed at:

> students and teachers throughout Australia and across curriculum areas – from Australian studies and politics to geography, environmental management and technology. *Vrroom* could inform and enrich any kind of learning; and it can help fulfill cross-curricular outcomes related to information literacy (http://vrroom.naa.gov.au).

The website provides a limited selection of records that can be used in a range of ways from whetting interest in historical topics to extending analytical and critical reading, and visual and information literacy skills. Users are introduced to using primary sources and to searching for archival records online.

The online environment will be the natural business and information-seeking environment of the future, although e-government has not yet achieved the full service capabilities envisioned by Barbara Reed's 'Capturing electronic transactional evidence: The future' (2000). In this paper, Reed outlines a quest by an individual for evidence of Australian citizenship and family business experience since arrival in Australia. It leads the reader through the requestor's successful use of an imaginary government portal in which he can:

- make his request;
- gain personal authentication for the purpose of access to the records he needs;
- upload authority from his parents to access their records;
- gain assistance with his search; and
- receive digital copies of the documents which will support his application.

In order to turn the vision into reality, government agencies and archival authorities must capture, manage, preserve indefinitely and provide access to records that are born digital, possibly themselves created through citizen interaction with dynamic e-government web-based services.

Archives contain information of vital public interest to both individuals and entire communities, but some records will contain information about individuals and organisations or businesses that is private, confidential or sensitive. Recordkeeping services must always be aware of protecting individuals' rights to privacy, as well as the needs of governments and businesses to protect security and confidentiality, which must be upheld where it is justified. Responsible recordkeeping services also restrict access to some records in order to ensure the security and preservation of original records, which may be fragile or at risk. Careful procedures are implemented in archives and records management services and in collecting archives to ensure that sensitive personal, business or government information is not inappropriately released; copyright and conditions of deposit agreed with donors are observed; and records in their custody are appropriately protected.

The purpose of keeping archives, however, is to ensure they are available for the benefit of present and future generations. Strategies for providing free and equitable access, where appropriate, are an important part of any recordkeeping regime. Most large archival services not only provide search rooms and reference services but are working towards providing quality digital access to at least the most heavily used records in their care. They must ensure in the course of their service that rights and responsibilities provided through state or federal freedom of information acts or other legislative requirements are met. Government records are withheld from public access for a minimum period stipulated by the relevant act. However, within that period, and within specified limits that vary between jurisdictions, freedom of information legislation allows rights of access to government records provided the applicant can make a case for rights, personal need or public interest under the terms of the act. An example is the rights of applicants to access records about themselves.

Recordkeeping standards

Records managers and archivists have their own body of knowledge, standards and procedures for dealing with records. The recordkeeping profession in Australia adheres to AS ISO 15489-2002 Records Management (2002) as the guiding standard for its work. This standard is the Australian endorsed version of the International Standard ISO 15489, which in turn was inspired by an earlier Australian Standard AS4390-1996, the world's first standard for records management (Stephens & Roberts 1996). The standard is published in two parts: *AS ISO 15489.1 Records management – general* and *AS ISO 15489.2 Records management – implementation guidelines* (Standards Australia 2002). Standards are, by their very nature, confined to definitions and principles. The application of standards in actual recordkeeping programs requires careful strategic planning and a thorough approach to implementation and regular evaluation as the process proceeds. The implementation guidelines in AS ISO 15489.2 provide an eight-step guide to developing and implementing recordkeeping systems (DIRKS), which is soundly based on systems planning and design methodology. A more detailed guide to working through the DIRKS process is available in *The DIRKS manual* (NAA 2001), available on the websites of both the National Archives of Australia (NAA) and the State Records Office New South Wales (SRNSW). *The DIRKS manual* was jointly developed by NAA and SRNSW, and the DIRKS methodology was subsequently incorporated into ISO15489.

If they are to be of any use, guiding standards must be woven into practice. In Australia, each recordkeeping authority has endorsed AS ISO 15489 and developed suites of standards and guidelines specific to its own jurisdiction, providing guidance to practitioners in government agencies. State and national records authorities undertake this advisory role, with most providing introductions to recordkeeping principles, the mandatory standards developed for their jurisdiction and advice on implementing those standards on their websites. State Records New South Wales and the National Archives of Australia both provide comprehensive information for recordkeepers in government agencies in the recordkeeping sections of their websites. The Victorian Electronic Records Strategy (VERS) website is another provider of a comprehensive suite of standards, together with a toolkit and guidelines for their implementation. The VERS suite consists of a standard for Management of Electronic Records, a set of specifications for system requirements, metadata, long-term preservation formats, the electronic record format and export of electronic records. Each specification has an associated advice, providing guidelines for implementation. The VERS Centre of Excellence, developed in 2002, certifies software and supports vendors, monitors compliance with developments in standards and provides advice and training.

Cooperation between Australian recordkeeping authorities

Government archival authorities in Australia work together and pool their expertise. The Council of Australasian Archives and Records Authorities (CAARA) consists of the heads of the government archives authorities of Australia, New Zealand and each of the Australian states and territories. Formerly known as the Council of Federal State and Territory Archives (COFSTA), the name changed in 2004 to reflect the inclusion of New Zealand and the role of its members. CAARA has in turn implemented the Australian Digital Recordkeeping Initiative (ADRI). ADRI aims to pool resources and expertise to find better ways of ensuring that digital records are preserved and made accessible for the future. It currently has an extensive work program – developing generic business cases for digital recordkeeping, best practice manuals, a standard for transfer of digital records between systems, agencies, archives and case studies.

Recordkeeping in a digital world

The major challenge for both the library and the recordkeeping professions is to capture, manage and preserve 'born digital' publications and records and provide access as required by an increasingly computer-literate and mobile public without compromising standards. Reed provides an excellent overview of the wide-ranging problems and issues involved in 'Challenges of managing the digitally born artefact' (2006). The differences between the challenges faced by archives and those faced by libraries are illustrated by differing responsibilities and approaches to selecting or appraising, collecting and preserving web-based publications and records. The Australian Pandora program, in which the national, state and territory libraries of Australia collaborate (see Chapter 5), selects, collects and preserves digital information resources that resemble traditional publications such as electronic journals and informational websites. The latter are mostly static in character – in other words, changes on the websites are relatively infrequent and easily documented, not unlike revisions to a paper-based publication or new issues of a journal. Archives, however, must capture and preserve records generated in dynamic websites that are not only constantly updated but also provide new and different views to each user, depending on the nature of the transaction, the particular user's rights of access and the latest content available in the underlying database. Much depends on the way the system has been designed and set up, thus the ability of professional recordkeepers to work with IT systems staff and advocate recordkeeping standards and strategies is crucial to the future availability of digital archival records.

Many governments and businesses now aim to provide seamless e-services and this brings further challenges. Within organisations, systems and databases have often historically developed in 'silos' or 'stovepipes', with a system for one function unable to communicate with other systems because of software or hardware incompatibility, differing standards or an organisational information architecture that just grew, rather than having been planned and coordinated (Sundberg 2006). This situation is complicated even further when provision of such services involves more than one agency or more than one jurisdiction, and the legislation, communication and compatibility problems that must be solved in order to capture and manage records present even more complex problems for recordkeeping professionals, managers and systems designers. Collecting archives, whose acquisitions policies aim to preserve cultural heritage rather than government or business records, also live in a digital world and increasingly must deal with records that have been created in a wide range of digital software and hardware environments, as well as those on the paper-based formats that traditionally have been the focus of their collections. Whether they are collecting the records of authors, people who are eminent in their target community, sporting or community service associations or individuals' personal and family histories – all are now likely to be created and kept on a computer. The challenge for traditional collecting archives is to move away from a paper worldview, in which even digital objects are versions of static traditional paper formats, and prepare to manage the products of the technological revolution that is transforming the way we think and work and consequently transforming the formats of records we generate.

The digital world also provides advantages and opportunities for more flexible service and more immediate and increased access by the public. All major archives have a web presence that not only provides comprehensive information about their collections and services, but also provides online search facilities and in some cases online access to digitised or born digital records. Some archives have collections that are almost entirely virtual. The John Curtin Prime Ministerial Library (JCPML) at Curtin University in Western Australia was the first prime ministerial library established in Australia and focuses on the life and times of John Curtin, the Australian Prime Minister who held office during World War II, from 1941–1945. JCPML is a leading example of a digital collection, aiming to provide access to 'information relating to John Curtin and his life and times held in the collections of the JCPML and elsewhere'. A considerable part of the resources in its collection consists of digitised copies of documents and photographs and links to digital records held in a range of other institutions such as the National Archives of Australia. Whether in the JCPML collection or elsewhere, access is provided via one seamless interface: the electronic research archive. The JCPML is also exemplary for its outreach programs, providing online resources and travelling programs about archives in general and the JCPML collection for the public and students of all ages, creating both physical and online exhibitions and appointing visiting researchers who are commissioned to publish their research based on the collection. A useful educational resource about archives written by Ann Pederson, *Understanding society through its records* (2001) is available through JCPML's website (http://john.curtin.edu.au/).

The national and state archives of Australia provide their users with online access to their finding aids which are the archival access equivalent of library catalogues and the key to their holdings. However, intellectual control of archives is provided by documenting provenance and context, unlike library collections which are usually arranged and accessed by subject. Australian government archives have adopted the Commonwealth Record Series (CRS), developed by the National Archives of Australia, as the archival control system for managing and describing records. The principal aim of the CRS system has always been to show records in their proper context, providing 'consistent documentation of the administrative context and biographical context out of which the records emerge' (Wagland & Kelly 1994, p.147). Peter Scott (1966, p.502) noted:

> If the record series is adopted as the primary record unit, one avoids all former difficulties in physical arrangement, and one is able to link archives with far greater accuracy to their appropriate context. Provided that one respects the physical integrity of the record series and fully records its administrative context, one is in complete harmony with traditional principles.

Metadata and descriptive standards

Metadata are discussed in Chapter 9, but it is worth bringing up metadata standards in this context because the capture and management of metadata is an essential strategy in managing electronic records for present and future access. The commonly used definition of metadata as 'data about data' is easy to remember but does not provide a very enlightening explanation. A better definition is that used by Anne Gilliland-Swetland – metadata is 'the sum total of what one can say about any *information object* at any level of aggregation'. At a basic level, metadata: 'identifies a resource; provides information about the content and creators of a resource; and places it in context: providing links to other resources by documenting structural relationships' (Gilliland-Swetland 2000).

Most information professionals are familiar with the Dublin Core metadata set of fifteen elements, designed to facilitate resource discovery (Dublin Core Metadata Initiative 2006). The Australian Government Locator System (AGLS) is another resource discovery metadata set designed specifically for web-based resources (NAA 2006). Adrian Cunningham's paper, 'Enabling seamless online access to government', discusses the development of AGLS and outlines its relationship to Dublin Core, which AGLS extends. He then goes on to outline the relationship of the AGLS metadata set to recordkeeping metadata, which necessarily extends the AGLS set (Cunningham 1998). The National Archives of Australia is the leading agency for AGLS development and deployment, because a high proportion of information resources described or required online to support internet-based government services and transactions would be records. Thus AGLS should theoretically be a subset of any standardised metadata set specified for electronic recordkeeping purposes (Cunningham 1998). AGLS has been adopted as an Australian Standard, AS 5044: 2002.

Because records must provide evidence, in other words, conform to standards acceptable as evidence in courts of law, recordkeeping metadata must be able to provide information that demonstrates that a record is the authentic record and has not been altered or tampered with in any way. To ensure this, recordkeeping metadata sets must provide more information than that available in both the Dublin Core set and the AGLS set. A collaborative recordkeeping metadata project set out to provide a comprehensive specification that could be understood within and beyond the recordkeeping metadata community. It focused on records produced and maintained in an electronic networked environment. The project was led by Sue McKemmish at Monash University and included as industry partners the National Archives of Australia, State Records Authority New South Wales and the Australian Council on Archives/Australian Society of Archives Descriptive Standards Committee.

The Recordkeeping Metadata Schema (RKMS) produced by the project did something much more important than provide a set of metadata elements. Rather than treating records as 'passive, document-like information objects', it viewed them through the perspective of the records continuum theoretical model as:

> active participants in business processes and technologies, dynamic objects which need to be associated throughout their life span with ever broader and richer layers of contextual metadata in order to maintain their reliability and authenticity, and to be meaningful and accessible through time and space (McKemmish et al. 1999).

It is worth noting, when using Gilliland-Swetland's definition of metadata given above, which was entirely appropriate for Dublin Core and AGLS metadata, that we are no longer dealing with simple information objects but documenting a complex and continually growing set of *contextual relationships*.

The RKMS is a highly structured schema that groups metadata into subcategories about:

- business, defined in a very broad way to include all kinds of organisational and social activity;
- agents or people conducting or involved in the business;
- records; and
- the relationship of each of the above to business recordkeeping.

It provides a standard for developing other recordkeeping metadata standards and the RKMS framework acts as a metadata mapping tool. It is an overarching standard that can be used to map fields of other metadata standards to the very comprehensive RKMS. Thus it is an aid to translating *between* metadata sets or, in metadata terminology, for providing crosswalks. One of its uses is as a tool when migrating records from one system to another. The results of this research were reported by McKemmish et al. (1999).

A further project, now in progress, is working to solve problems associated with implementing recordkeeping metadata standards. When systems rely on the manual addition of metadata to records, the resulting metadata quality can be variable, or the metadata may not be added at all if the process is avoidable by busy records and website creators. The Clever Recordkeeping Metadata Project (Records Continuum Research Group 2003) aims to:

> develop a proof of concept prototype to demonstrate how standards-compliant metadata
> can be created once in particular application environments, then used many times to
> meet a range of business purposes. The prototype will be implemented in a test-bed site
> to provide a model for best practice.

International archival descriptive standards that have been developed for describing the relationship between archival records include ISAD(G) (General International Standard Archival Description), and their creators: ISAAR(CPF) (International Standard Archival Authority Record for Corporate Bodies, Persons, and Families). These two standards are published by the International Council on Archives (ICA) (1999; 2004). Each provides examples in an appendix, demonstrating the depth and extensive nature of the metadata about the records and their creators that can be documented using these standards. Both ISAD(G) and ISAAR(CPF) have been mapped to the RKMS but 'form a relatively small sub-set of the recordkeeping metadata identified by the RKMS as they are essentially concerned with the retrospective description of Records entities' (McKemmish et al. 1999). Examples of descriptions conforming to both these standards are provided in their appendices. The example in ISAD(G) from Australia is for the papers of Eddie Mabo, deposited in the National Library of Australia (ICA 1999, pp.61-75) and for Mabo as a person in ISAAR(CPF) (ICA 2004, pp.48-53).

Another international descriptive standard for archives is EAD: Encoded Archival Description, now in its second (2002) release. The initial EAD development project, based at the Library of the University of California, Berkeley, and led by Daniel Pitti, was initiated in response to the recognition that that the MARC (exchange format) standard widely used in libraries was inadequate for describing archive and manuscript collections. A brief account of the development of EAD is available at the EAD official website (http://www.loc.gov/ead/). Two special issues of *American Archivist*, devoted entirely to EAD, were published on the release of Version 1.00 of the EAD DTD (Summer and Fall 1997). These were republished as a single monograph, edited by Jackie Dooley (1998). Like ISAD(G), EAD is designed for the retrospective description of static records.

Developing recordkeeping theory

Most of this chapter discusses recordkeeping practice and the environment in which recordkeeping professionals work. However, the practice of any profession is essentially underpinned by theoretical principles. Australians have made important contributions to recordkeeping theory, beginning with the work of Peter Scott and others in the 1960s on the Commonwealth Record Series system, challenging the more traditional 'record group' method of arranging and describing records while maintaining consistency with the principles of provenance and original order. Their work responded to problems in dealing with regular changes in government structures, in which government functions move from agency to agency, as departments are restructured, merge or disappear.

The issues in capturing and managing digital records are also one of the drivers for rethinking traditional approaches to the way records are managed and systems are conceptualised, leading to the development of a new theoretical model. The traditional way of thinking about the relationship between records and archives was expressed in the life cycle model, which concentrated on the management of current records, the final stage of the life cycle being destruction of the record or transfer to an archive. This approach leaves archivists with no opportunity for input into the design of recordkeeping systems, nor the opportunity to appraise records as archival at or before their creation. The life cycle model is most clearly unsustainable in digital environments where it is not feasible to sift through, appraise and dispose of digital records when they are no longer 'active', and are difficult to identify; let alone rescue records rendered inaccessible by their lack of physicality, poor system design and management, and their dependence on software and hardware that is short-lived. Frank Upward traced the history and development of Australian theoretical approaches to archival science and the movement away from the confined, linear view of the life cycle model in 'In search of the continuum: Ian McLean's 'Australian experience' essays on recordkeeping' (1994) and went on to develop a theoretical model first published in *Archives and Manuscripts* (Upward 1996; 1997), compatible with the post-custodial world, in which records exist in a multi-dimensional space–time continuum. The publications page on the Records Continuum Research Group's website is an excellent source for those who would like to read more about the Records Continuum Model and the research it has inspired about the nature of records and archives.

Recordkeeping professionals and professional associations

Recordkeeping professionals work in a wide range of organisations. The largest employers are the national, state and territory recordkeeping authorities – Archives Office of Tasmania, Archives New Zealand, the National Archives of Australia, Northern Territory Archives Service, Queensland State Archives, State Records Authority of New South Wales, State Records Office Western Australia, State Records of South Australia, the Victorian Public Records Office and the Territory Records Office of the Australian Capital Territory. Government agencies of all types have records services that advise on the development and management of systems for business records, working with the appropriate recordkeeping authority to ensure that their retention and disposal schedules and systems are compliant with both archives legislation and the standards adopted and promulgated by the authority. The retention and disposal schedule identifies the record series that are archival, and will therefore be kept indefinitely, and the appropriate retention period for those records that are not archival. These records may need to be kept relatively briefly or for very long periods, and are usually governed by legislation other than archives legislation, such as acts governing the establishment and function of the agency, corporate activity, financial management, workers compensation, privacy, freedom of information and many other matters. It is the responsibility of the professional recordkeepers to identify relevant legislation and ensure that retention and disposal schedules for records across the whole organisation are compliant.

Archivists and records managers find work with a wide range of other types of employer, including private businesses such as the major banks, mining companies and hospitals. As discussed earlier, many private schools employ archivists, with a strong emphasis on collecting archives that capture the tradition and history of the school, but increasingly taking an active role in managing the school's business records. Universities also have archives and records services, some taking an additional collecting role beyond the university's business records, as in the case of the Noel Butlin Archives Centre at the Australian National University, which collects 'the records of companies and firms, trade unions, employer bodies, professional and industry-related organisations and the papers of private individuals whose roles relate to the labour movement, Australian industry and public life' with some collections dating from the 1820s (Australian Society of Archivists 2006). Religious organisations such as dioceses and religious orders frequently have formally organised archives. Public libraries with extensive local history collections are also potential employers of professional archivists. Although there are many historical societies and similar organisations in Australia, these are often run by interested volunteers on limited funding and they are usually unable to afford to hire professionals.

Unlike the situation in libraries, where an appropriate qualification is a requirement for employment in any professional or paraprofessional capacity, a significant number of archivists and records managers in Australia do not hold tertiary professional qualifications. This is gradually changing, driven by requirements of some state regulatory authorities for agencies to conduct regular training needs analyses and skills audits by recordkeeping authorities (Roberts 2004) and increasing awareness of the importance of the role of professional recordkeepers. There is a need for practitioners to have a sound understanding of the body of theory and the principles that underpin practice in order adequately to meet the challenges of capturing and preserving archival records for the future. Nevertheless, neither the Australian Society of Archivists nor the Records Management Association of Australasia requires a university-based qualification in recordkeeping for professional membership. There is no paraprofessional group in the recordkeeping profession that is equivalent to that of the library technician.

The records continuum model and the life cycle model have implications for the way the recordkeeping profession views itself and for the structure of the profession. The life cycle model sees them as distinct, divided into records managers who deal with records in their active phase and archivists who appraise records at the end of their activity and accept into the custody of archival organisations those records deemed to have enduring value. Both the records continuum model and the practicalities of dealing with digital records, discussed in the previous section, demonstrate the artificial nature of this divide. Records managers and archivists who work in business and government environments must work together and should be professionally educated so that they are themselves able to move through and work anywhere in the continuum, whether it be in the continuum dimension principally concerned with creation, capture, organisation or pluralisation of records, illustrated in Frank Upward's diagram of the model (reproduced online, see Upward 1996, Figure 1). Because the records continuum model removes the professional division, it has encouraged the use in Australia of the term 'recordkeeping professionals' to encompass both records managers and archivists. However, Australia still has two separate professional associations, one for records managers and one for archivists.

The recordkeeping community has active professional associations in many countries, as well as international professional organisations. In Australia, the two relevant associations are the Australian Society of Archivists (ASA) and the Records Management Association of Australasia (RMAA). The ASA was formed in 1975 and is administered through a national council. It is active in all states through its branches and through a range of special interest groups open to all members. It aims to:

- promote a professional identity amongst archivists;
- promote the keeping, care and use of archives and encourage research and development in all areas of archival practice;
- establish and maintain standards of archival practice and professional conduct amongst archivists, including standards of archival qualifications and professional training;
- encourage the responsible use of archives including cooperating with other organisations and groups with common interests and concerns;
- encourage communication and cooperation amongst archivists, their institutions and the users of archives; and
- publish and disseminate information relevant to the archival profession (Australian Society of Archivists 2005).

For professional membership, the Australian Society of Archivists is available to those who are employed in a recognised archival institution and either hold a qualification in archives administration and have one year's employment experience, or a degree in any discipline from a university together with two years' employment experience.

The RMAA states its field of interest as follows: 'Records management covers the management of records from their creation to either ultimate destruction or retention as an archive', but cooperates with the ASA in a number of ways. For example, the two associations have a Joint Education Steering Committee which has produced a *Statement of knowledge for recordkeeping professionals* (2006). Both organisations organise conferences and special events for professional development and maintain a close interest in the development and provision of professional education and training. The RMAA provides services to members across Australia and New Zealand, organised into regional branches and sub-chapters, which represent special industry groups. There are three levels of professional membership in the RMAA. In ascending order they are associate, member and fellow. Until 1 July 2007, professional membership status of the RMAA is attainable either through experience alone or through a combination of experience and qualifications. After that date, qualifications are required: a minimum of a vocational diploma for associate status and a minimum of a bachelor degree for member status.

The International Council on Archives (ICA), founded in 1948, is the peak professional association for archivists. Its mission is to 'promote the preservation and use of archives around the world. In pursuing this mission, ICA works for the protection and enhancement of the memory of the world and to improve communication while respecting cultural diversity' (ICA n.d.) The ICA has institutional and individual members in over 190 countries and is:

> a decentralized organisation governed by a General Assembly and administered by an Executive Board. Its branches provide archivists with a regional forum in all parts of the world; its sections bring together archivists and archival institutions interested in particular areas of professional interest; its committees and working groups are engaging the contribution of experts to the solution of specific problems. The ICA Secretariat serves the administrative needs of the organisation and maintains relations between members and cooperation with related bodies and other international organisations. (ICA n.d.)

It maintains close links with international bodies such as UNESCO (United Nations Educational, Scientific and Cultural Organization), ICCROM (The International Centre for the Study of the Preservation and Restoration of Cultural Property) and The International Committee of the Blue Shield which is the cultural equivalent of the Red Cross, working for the protection of the world's cultural heritage.

Conclusion

Archives are kept for their enduring value, that is, for their present and potential usefulness as evidence and memory. The very nature of this evidentiality of records and its relationship to memory is explored in depth in *Archives:Recordkeeping and society* (McKemmish et al. 2005). The book considers current debates and differences of opinion among professional archivists, and aims to generate further discussion, drawing on works of philosophy and theory both within and beyond the bounds of the profession. No-one can predict the way particular records may be used or misused in the future. Archives may be valuable both for their original (primary) purpose and for secondary (informational) purposes. One thing is certain – when separated from their context, records are vulnerable to use as agents of misinformation and manipulation. They only maintain their integrity if they have been kept in their original order, preserved within their context and therefore remain authentic and reliable traces of transactions.

Archives and records management programs are the keys to social memory and responsibility, much more essential than provision of documented facts presented as information. They are crucial to the community and to other information professionals, who should, as part of their own professional information literacy, understand and respect the systems that have been developed to manage them and ensure their integrity, security and survival. Archives provide our cultural memory and are fundamental to democracy, accountability and good governance (ICA n.d.). None of these ideas should be used to bolster professional self-importance and complacency. Changing technologies will continue to provide new opportunities and challenges in an increasingly virtual environment. While endeavouring to meet the challenges, we must continue to explore our professional responsibility and analyse the role played by records in providing evidence and enabling memory.

References

Australian Society of Archivists Inc. (ASA) 2005, 'Objectives', http://www.archivists.org.au/aboutasa.html#objectives

Australian Society of Archivistis, Inc. (ASA) 2006, *Directory of archives in Australia*, http://www.archivists.org.au/directory/asa_dir.htm

Boadle, D 1995,' Origins and development of the New South Wales regional repositories system', *Archives and Manuscripts*, vol.23, no.2, pp.274-288.

Charles Sturt University 2006, *Regional archives*, http://www.csu.edu.au/research/archives/introduction.htm

Cunningham, A 1998, 'Enabling seamless online access to government', National Archives of Australia, http://www.naa.gov.au/recordkeeping/gov_online/agls/Metadata_paper22sept98.html

Dooley, JM (ed.) 1998, *Encoded archival description: Context, theory and case studies*, Society of American Archivists, Chicago, IL.

Doubleday, W forthcoming, 'From system to network? Developments in the State Records Authority of New South Wales regional repositories 1995-2005'.

Dublin Core Metadata Initiative 2006, *Dublin Core metadata element set, version 1.1: Reference description*, http://dublincore.org/documents/dces/

Gilliland-Swetland, AJ 2000, *Setting the stage*, http://www.getty.edu/research/institute/standards/intrometadata/2_articles/index.html

International Council on Archives (ICA) n.d., http://www.ica.org/static.php?ptextid=bref&plangue=eng

International Council on Archives (ICA) 1999, *ISAD(G): General international standard archival description*, 2nd edn, http://www.ica.org/biblio/isad_g_2e.pdf

International Council on Archives (ICA) 2004, *ISAAR(CPF): International standard archival authority record for corporate bodies, persons, and families*, 2nd edn, http://www.ica.org/biblio/ISAAR2EN.pdf

Joint Education Steering Committee of the ASA and RMAA 2006, *Statement of knowledge for recordkeeping professionals*, http://www.rmaa.com.au/docs/profdev/RMAA%20ASA%202006%20Statement%20of%20Knowledge.pdf

McKemmish, S 2005, 'Traces' in S McKemmish et al. (eds) *Archives: Recordkeeping in society*, Centre for Information Studies, Charles Sturt University, Wagga Wagga, NSW, pp.1-20.

McKemmish, S 1993 'Introducing archives and archival programs', in J Ellis (ed.), *Keeping archives*, 2nd edn, Thorpe, Melbourne, Vic, pp.1-24.

McKemmish, S, Acland, G, Ward, N & Reed, B 1999, 'Describing records in context in the Continuum: The Australian recordkeeping metadata schema', *Archivaria,* vol.48, Fall.

McKemmish, S, Piggott, M, Reed, B & Upward, F (eds) 2005, *Archives: Recordkeeping in society*, Centre for Information Studies, Charles Sturt University, Wagga Wagga, NSW.

National Archives of Australia (NAA) 2001, *The DIRKS manual: A strategic approach to managing business information*, http://naa.gov.au/recordkeeping/dirks/dirksman/dirks.html

National Archives of Australia (NAA) 2006, *Australian government locator system (AGLS)*, http://www.naa.gov.au/recordkeeping/gov_online/agls/summary.html

Pederson, A 2001, 'Understanding society through its records', http://john.curtin.edu.au/society/index.html

Records Continuum Research Group 2003, *Clever recordkeeping metadata*, Monash University, http://www.sims.monash.edu.au/research/rcrg/research/crm/

Reed, B 2000, 'Capturing electronic transactional evidence: The future', Keynote address to the Records Management Association of Australia conference, *e-Business transactions: Providing accountability through effective recordkeeping*, held in Canberra, March 2000, http://www.sims.monash.edu/research/rcrg/publications/brermac.html

Reed, B 2006, 'Challenges of managing the digitally born artefact' in *Preservation management in libraries, archives & museums*, GE Gorman & SJ Shep (eds), Facet Publishing, London.

Roberts, D 2004, 'Education and training in a new regime for government recordkeeping: A case study', Paper presented at the *International Congress on Archives,* held in Vienna, 23-29 August, 2004, http://www.wien2004.ica.org/imagesUpload/pres_217_ROBERTS_D_SAE%2004.pdf

Schwirtlich, AM, 1987, 'Introducing archives and the archival progression', in A Pederson (ed.), *Keeping Archives*, Australian Society of Archivists, Sydney, NSW, pp.1-20.

Scott, P 1966, 'The record group concept: A case for abandonment', *American Archivist*, vol.29, no.4.

Standards Australia 2002, *AS ISO15489: Records management*, Standards Association of Australia, Sydney, NSW.

Stephens, D & Roberts, D 1996 'From Australia: The world's first national standard for records management', *ARMA Quarterly*, vol.62, pp.3-7.

Sundberg, H 2006, *Problems in public e-service development*, PhD thesis, Mid Sweden University, Härnösand, Sweden.

Upward, F 1994, 'In search of the continuum: Ian McLean's 'Australian experience' essays on recordkeeping, <*http*://www.sims.monash.edu.au/research/rcrg/publications/fuptrc.html

Upward, F 1996, 'Structuring the records continuum, part one: Postcustodial principles and properties', http://www.sims.monash.edu.au/research/rcrg/publications/recordscontinuum/fupp1.html

Upward, F 1997, 'Structuring the records continuum, part two: Structuration theory and recordkeeping', http://www.sims.monash.edu.au/research/rcrg/publications/recordscontinuum/fupp2.html

Wagland, M & Kelly, R 1994, 'The series system – A revolution in archival control', in *The records continuum*, S McKemmish & M Piggott (eds), Ancora Press, Clayton, Vic., p.147.

CHAPTER 13
Information literacy and the leveraging of corporate knowledge

Stuart Ferguson and Anne Lloyd

Information literacy (IL) has been discussed a number of times in this book. It is a particularly prominent theme in Chapter 2, in which James Herring sees the development of information literate students as the key role of the teacher librarian in today's schools – a priority driven largely by the need to equip students with lifelong learning skills. In Chapter 3, Shirley Oakley and Jennifer Vaughan, also writing from an academic library perspective, refer to the need for IL instruction to prepare students both for academic life and for lifelong learning. This point is reinforced in Chapter 6, where John Mills argues that in academic libraries, including school libraries, the focus is on facilitating independent information seeking and encouraging the development of independent learners.

In its summary of 'core knowledge and skills for library and information professionals' (2003), the Australian Library and Information Association (ALIA) includes 'Information literacy education' and states that this is demonstrated by the ability to: 'understand the need for information skills in the community; and facilitate the development of information literacy and the ability to critically evaluate information'. According to ALIA, one of the key drivers is the need to foster 'lifelong learning, personal fulfilment, improved decision making, knowledge development, innovation, imagination, creativity and cultural continuity' in 'a democratic, progressive, technologically sophisticated and culturally diverse society'. This should be seen in the wider socio-economic and political context (discussed in Chapter 15) with increased commercial competition, as a result of encroaching globalisation, a general roll-back of the power of national states (in the Western countries at least), increased expenditure on information and communication technologies (ICTs) at organisational and national levels, and increased pressure for knowledge generation and innovation in what some call a 'knowledge society'.

Our conception and understanding of what constitutes information literacy (IL) has implications for librarians, educators and teacher librarians who champion IL as a prerequisite for lifelong learning. In each of these contexts IL is conceived in different ways and the way in which it manifests itself is influenced by the concerns of a specific discourse. This chapter explores the concept of IL by considering the nature and manifestation of the phenomenon within two contexts – first in formal education institutions such as schools and universities, where IL takes on a behaviourist perspective and is viewed as the development of skills and attributes; and second in the workplace, where IL takes on a holistic perspective and can be defined as a 'way of knowing' (Lloyd 2003).

The chapter also explores some of the commonalities between IL, especially IL in the workplace, and knowledge management (KM), which is geared to maximising the use of knowledge in organisations and in fostering knowledge sharing – a body of knowledge and practice that is of considerable interest to the library and information science community. In the workplace, it is suggested, understanding how information practice manifests itself can be seen as a critical platform for the development of KM practices. Developing a clear understanding of how information is experienced, accessed, disseminated, made available and in some cases contested, and of the outcomes produced as a result of that interaction, is critical if knowledge managers are to develop systems that will capture the activities related to the construction of knowledge.

Some may question whether there are clear commonalities between information literacy and knowledge management, each of which approaches organisational information needs from widely differing perspectives. However, there is a significant body of literature, especially in the library and information science sector, that sees in the information literacy background of library and information science professionals an opportunity in the knowledge management domain. Indeed, a recent content analysis of the literature included development of corporate information literacy among what it identified as five broad roles for librarians in knowledge management (Van Rooi & Snyman 2006). Some years ago, Standards Australia published a number of 'sample job descriptions', compiled by Karen Bishop and based on her expertise as a recruitment consultant. Included among the six specific key 'knowledge-enabling' tasks performed by the KM positions were 'information literacy' training programs for improved use of information and knowledge resources (2002, p.12). Around the same time, Jan Houghton and Sue Halbwirth, in a paper provocatively entitled 'Knowledge management and information literacy: A new partnership in the workplace?', referred to the need for information professionals to develop additional skills 'if they are to continue their role as a change agent within the information environment of an organisation in the process of moving from information management to knowledge management' (2002, p.76).

The main topics covered in this chapter are: information literacy in the educational sector, including library-based information literacy instruction and recent attempts to embed information literacy in the curriculum of higher education institutions; information literacy in the workplace; and the role of knowledge management in the learning organisation. Before considering information literacy in these different contexts, however, it provides a brief overview of information literacy research and how information literacy is conceived.

Conceiving information literacy: a research perspective

Scholarly and practitioner research over the past twenty years has led to divergent views about what information literacy is and how its practices manifest themselves. This multiplicity of views highlights the importance of understanding the *context* through which IL practice manifests itself and the methodological approaches that influence researchers' exploration, description and interpretation of the phenomenon. When IL is explored in educational contexts it may be conceived as learning about subject matter (Bruce & Candy 2000, p.7) or as an approach to learning (Lupton, 2004, p.89). When workplace contexts are used as the focus of research, the phenomenon can be described as a 'way of knowing' (Lloyd 2003; 2004). When library practitioners research IL, the descriptions of the phenomenon are often confined to the skills and attributes exhibited by the student or client. In the library context, IL is conceived as a measurable phenomenon.

Behavioural approaches, most commonly used by library practitioners and educators, define the skills and attributes of IL and the information literate person separately (Doyle 1992). These approaches analyse and measure observable behaviours, identified most notably in Christina Doyle's (1992) Delphi study of experts' understanding of information literacy. This type of methodological approach is often found in formal educational contexts such as schools or the higher education sector, and has led to skills-based definitions and benchmarks or frameworks for IL, and to calls by academic librarians for IL to be viewed as a 'generic skill'. The most commonly used (and adapted) definition was developed by the American Library Association (ALA) (2000, p.2): 'Information literacy is a set of abilities requiring individuals to recognize when information is needed and have the ability to locate, evaluate and use effectively the needed information.' The behaviouralist approach leads to identifying and assessing those skills and attributes which, it is argued, an information literate student should exhibit in his or her mastery of the formal curriculum and learning context. The *Australian and New Zealand information literacy framework* (Bundy 2004) and ALA's *Information literacy competency standards for higher education* (2000) are two examples of behavioural approaches to information literacy.

In contrast, *relational* approaches to IL focus on people's awareness of it. This approach is drawn from phenomenographic research, which explores experiences of IL in educational contexts (Bruce 1997; Limberg 2000; Lupton 2004). Relational models of IL focus on content and people's experiences of content (Bruce, Edwards & Lupton 2006). Using a relational approach has led to a model that describes 'seven faces of information literacy' (Bruce 1997). More recently, a framework that proposes six frames for IL education has been proposed (Bruce, Edwards & Lupton 2006). The advocates of these approaches argue that IL 'is not a theory of learning, but rather that people's approaches to IL and IL education are informed by the views of teaching, learning and information literacy which they adopt either implicitly or explicitly in different contexts' (Bruce, Edwards & Lupton 2006, p.1).

Constructivist approaches to understanding the phenomenon of IL are still emerging and are found in educational and workplace research domains (Cheuk, 1998; Todd 2000; Lloyd 2004). These approaches examine how individuals use information in the learning process, leading to meaningful constructions (Todd 2000; Lloyd 2004). Ross Todd suggests that becoming information literate is an active process that enables people to construct a sense of their world in a purposeful way. Anne Lloyd's research promotes a clearer understanding of the social, physical and textual information practices and processes that people employ to access, use and contest information in the construction of knowledge (Lloyd 2003; Lloyd 2005). These approaches do not lead to measurements of IL but to frameworks or models that illustrate how IL practice manifests itself and is influenced within a specific context, shaping and being shaped by the outcomes of a developing relationship with information, through the transformation from neophyte user to expert user of information.

The variation in approaches to researching and describing IL was highlighted by Christine Bruce (2000) and has led Lloyd (2005, p.88) to suggest that 'just as there are many faces of information literacy, there are also many ways of understanding, experiencing and conceptualising the phenomenon'. The way we experience IL and the way information practices allow us to know an information environment will differ and will be influenced by the sources of information that are valued by the context (a point developed later in the chapter), our relationships with others within that context, and the practices and processes we use to explore our information environments.

Information literacy in an educational context

In library and higher educational contexts, the term information literacy is used to describe 'functional activities of defining, locating and accessing and evaluating information' (Lloyd 2003, p.89). The ALA definition, which has been adapted by the *Australian & New Zealand information literacy framework* (Bundy 2004), defines an information literate individual as being able to:

- determine the nature and extent of the information needed;

- access needed information effectively and efficiently;

- evaluate information and its sources critically;

- incorporate selected information into their knowledge base;

- use information effectively to accomplish a specific purpose; and

- understand the economic, legal and social issues surrounding the use of information, and use information ethically and legally (ALA 2000, p.3).

In this context, IL is viewed as a generic skill that facilitates individual learning, and is closely aligned to library literacy or computer literacy programs and a way of learning in formal contexts (Lloyd 2005). Given that educational environments value codified forms of knowledge, IL in this context is often tied to information practices and skills that facilitate access to written forms of knowledge (codified knowledge) that underpin learning through formal curricula. The emphasis of IL in an educational context therefore is to develop skills and competencies that will enable the individual to 'access and evaluate information, to think about information and to demonstrate and document the process of that thinking' (Lloyd 2005, p.83).

Information literacy instruction in libraries

In recent years, the library and information sector has tended to use the term 'information literacy instruction' (ILI) in place of older ones such as 'bibliographic instruction', 'user education' and 'library orientation', although the last two are still heard. The term bibliographic instruction often refers to the more mechanistic process of instructing library clients on how to locate and use print-based bibliographic material that is physically held by the library, and instruction in general use of library materials, reference books, indexing and abstracting services. The more 'modern' focus on user education encompasses all activities that relate to teaching library clients how to make the best possible use of the library. Such programs are considered part of a library's range of information services, especially in the educational sector – a point made in Chapter 6. Other areas of library and information service, most notably public libraries, take interest in ILI but the emphasis there tends to be computer literacy or specific areas of information and communications technologies (ICTs) use, such as internet searching. The focus of ILI in the educational sector is on assisting resource discovery by teaching students and other clients how to find information resources for themselves using specific information retrieval tools, beginning with the library catalogue. In other words, the approach is very much the skills-based one outlined earlier.

The role of the information librarian has been covered elsewhere. John Mills (Chapter 6) and Tom Denison (Chapter 10) have already referred to the decline in the role of the librarian as information intermediary. Here it is enough to note that the role of information intermediary – a critical role in the 1970s with the rapid growth of remote online databases (typically expensive and difficult to search) – has to some extent declined with the growth of the world wide web, the development of more intuitive human-computer interfaces (HCIs) and the attempt by many libraries, especially in the higher education sector, to deliver information resources and services directly to their clients' computer desktops (Ferguson & Ferguson 2005, p.44).

As this has happened, the role of the librarian has tended to shift from that of information gatekeeper to one that encompasses a far greater responsibility for the empowerment of the client through one-on-one instruction (increasingly using asynchronous and synchronous forms of electronic communication), formal user education classes or computer-assisted instruction. This has been encouraged by many universities, which increasingly identify information literacy and lifelong learning skills in their graduate attributes. The emphasis, as Maurice Line put it a few years ago, 'is gradually but relentlessly shifting from teaching to independent learning', which has 'implications for the structure and nature of higher education' that, Line felt, were 'yet to be fully grasped' (2000, p.67).

Clearly one-on-one instruction on resource discovery for library clients is a very time-consuming and labour-intensive approach to ILI. In the past, the main means of cutting down on one-on-one instruction has been the provision of user education classes. Class-based instruction has benefits in terms of the sheer efficiencies of one-to-many delivery but there are problems in that the instruction is not generally provided at the point of need – when the students need help finding material for assignments. Typically, introductory classes are conducted at the beginning of the academic session, with follow-up classes near assignment time – if students are lucky. Examples may be generic and ILI is not usually an integral part of student learning.

Moreover, classes entail a considerable commitment of staff time and with universities increasingly turning to distance education they are not always feasible. One common solution has been the development of instructional material that students can access in their own time. In the 1980s, many libraries developed high-quality videotapes, which allowed for a degree of user orientation and could be used by individuals, groups or classes. The development of computer-assisted instruction (CAI), using optical disks for instance, introduced a level of interactivity that meant students could try out skills learnt and even obtain feedback on how well they had absorbed the new knowledge. CAI packages offer several advantages over face-to-face instruction, for instance:

- savings in terms of staff time (which may offset development costs);

- availability of packages when staff are not available;

- standardisation of instruction;

- accessibility of packages from different workstations; and

- ability of clients to go at their own pace.

The development of web-based ILI packages is a natural progression from the earlier library-based CAI programs, as libraries try to take their virtual library services to clients' desktops. With access to such electronic tutorials, students have an element of interactivity that was previously difficult and certainly time-consuming to reproduce. Moreover, the tutorials put students in control of their own learning. As Margaret Appleton and Debbie Orr put it (2000, pp.17-18), such programs 'are ideal for learners who enjoy working through a course at their own pace and provide the opportunity for learners to be in control of the sequence of the learning program'.

It is worth noting that these packages should – and typically do – go beyond the teaching of mere information searching skills. An examination of the better packages demonstrates the application of sound pedagogical principles, such as those enunciated several years ago by Nancy Dewald, when she argued, for instance, for a high degree of interactivity, the use of feedback and a determined focus on learner centred education (1999). Moreover, given the tendency for students from school, college and university sectors to 'google' their information enquiries, most libraries in the higher education sector include resource discovery tools beyond those provided by the library, including search engines and subject directories, as well as introducing some basic ideas on web resource evaluation.

While one of the main drivers for the development of web-based ILI packages in the tertiary education sector has been the push into distance education, it is worth noting that on-campus students also benefit from their availability. They reach staff and students who never set foot in a library and, more important, they are available when the library client needs to use them – part of what Anne Lipow described as 'point of need access' (1999). Moreover, with point-of-need access to such programs, there is also a motivational factor – as Nancy Fjällbrant puts it, 'Students, who have a real need for information, for example in connection with projects, have much higher motivation than those who simply attend a course' (2000, p.27).

There are those who argue that online tutorials are less effective in terms of learning than face-to-face instruction. Martin Churkovich and Christine Oughtred (2002), for example, found that students who received face-to-face instruction performed better in a post-test than those who had completed a tutorial, and felt more confident about their library skills than the latter group. They claim also that students' learning experience is best when a mixture of face-to-face and online instruction is provided (p.33). This does not address the needs of off-campus students, however, and even for on-campus students it assumes that university libraries – already stretched in terms of human and financial resources – can continue providing instruction in both modes.

Information literacy instruction in the curriculum

Regardless of their possible benefits, web-based instructional packages are far from perfect. If the software is to provide feedback to students, examples need to be generic, and as such they cannot be linked by students to their work. A few years ago, ILI tutorials came in for significant criticism from several commentators:

'for being tedious and text-heavy' … 'presented as stand-alone lessons, disconnected from course or assignments' … 'lacking sufficient interactivity to create adequate active learning experiences' … and 'communicating an academic research process that is not relevant to students' expectations' (Kasowitz-Scheer & Pasqualoni 2002).

Such comments suggest that there is a need for libraries' ILI programs to be more closely aligned with students' coursework.

Philippa Levy (2000, pp.47-8), drawing on a constructivist notion that 'knowledge is constructed through, and builds upon, experience', suggests that 'skills are most effectively learned when related to learning needs arising directly from academic work'. A growing body of opinion suggests that ILI tutorials should be integrated into academic programs (Stubley 2003) – a point made by James Herring (Chapter 2) in his study of the school sector. Where ILI 'remains an add-on, or extra-curricular, learners generally tend to forget these skills very soon' (Karelse 2000, p. 44) and, as a European survey put it, 'Information literacy is not a "library thing" – and it is not concerned only with database searching and boolean logic; information searching is a part of the learning process and should be taught as such embedded in the curriculum' (Skov & Skærbak 2003, p.332).

Developments such as the ILI tutorials discussed above are small steps, but they represent important stages in the establishment of a new educational paradigm (new at least for the higher education sector, if not schools). In this paradigm, librarians, like their academic colleagues, attempt to guide and support the student's learning experience – preferably in collaboration with academic staff and others whose expertise lies in the area of educational design. A team approach is necessary because teaching, learning and information resources cannot be compartmentalised. Britain's INSPIRAL case studies provide a useful summary of the key issues in the integration of information resource provision and online learning, which include factors such as 'strong central learning support services (including the library and the teaching and learning support unit)', 'close collaboration between learning support units, and with academics' and a 'commitment to teaching and learning, not just to technical developments' (Currier 2003). Online ILI programs, it is suggested here, are not an optional extra among the information services offered by libraries. Librarians in the tertiary education sector are increasingly seeing the need to embrace new educational paradigms and work with others in the sector to support the needs of the independent learner.

Information literacy as a measurable phenomenon

Despite the growing link between ILI and the curriculum in the tertiary sector – mirroring what has evolved naturally in the school sector – it remains the case that the focus is on codified forms of knowledge (in this instance, published information products) and that ILI is largely geared to the development of skills and competencies. It has been suggested that the majority of IL definitions that derive from an educational context share common elements, such as information seeking, informed choice of information sources, evaluation and selection (Webber & Johnston 2000). This view of IL as a product or outcome has led to claims that IL is a generic set of skills which once learnt are easily transferable across other contexts (Lloyd 2005) and that IL, as an outcome-based product, is a prerequisite for lifelong learning (Grassian & Kaplowitz 2001). Whether it is enough to create lifelong learners, however, is another matter.

In the education sector, evidence of a student's achievement of information literacy is often described in terms of tangible and measurable sets of information practices and development of a set of attributes (Bundy 2004; Doyle 1992). As indicated earlier, this conception of IL as a measurable phenomenon is illustrated by the development of standards and guidelines for the higher education sectors (ALA 2000), according to which the facilitation of IL in students is closely connected to the research process and linked to library orientation sessions, library skills sessions, computer literacy and referencing sessions.

Lloyd (2003; 2005) has argued, however, that definitions of IL as a skills-based outcome narrows the conception by focusing on skills and processes. This reductionist approach to IL, it is suggested, does not explain or express what it means to be information literate or to function as information literate outside the educational context. This is demonstrated by turning to the other context or 'landscape' for IL considered in this chapter – the workplace.

Workplace conceptions of information literacy

Research into workplace IL has begun to illustrate the depth and complexity of IL as a *process*, by seeking to uncover and describe the relationships and structures that influence and even contest (oppose) an individual's entry into a information environment (such as an educational or a workplace setting). Workplace IL research also seeks to uncover the factors that influence a new worker's developing relationship with information, which will act as a catalyst for learning about the requirements of work. In this view of IL, experience of social, physical and textual sources of information (or 'modalities'), and the interconnection between them, occupies a central place in understanding IL as a phenomenon. This has led Lloyd, who draws from constructionist/ecological perspectives, to advocate a more holistic approach to exploring and describing the phenomenon of IL (2003, 2004, 2005). She has described IL as a meta-competency and information literate people as being embodied within context – as knowing expert users of information who have a deep connection and fluency with the sites of knowledge within a specific information landscape (Lloyd 2003; Lloyd 2005, p.84).

Information literacy as a process leads to knowing the world by means of access to information, in all its manifestations, and information use. In order to know the information environment, the individual must also develop a critical approach to thinking about the veracity of information and the textual, social and physical relationships and practices that facilitate access and transfer of knowledge. Information literacy is inextricably linked to learning because it acts as a catalyst, preparing the learner to connect and interact with sources of information and sites of knowledge, and to think about the information and the processes related to that connection (Lloyd 2006a, p.183). The knowledge that results is influenced by the sources of information available within the information environment. Information literacy is a way of knowing, of being in the world and interacting with it through engagement and interaction with signs, symbols, artefacts and people, from which information relevant to the context, and thus meaning, can be drawn.

Firefighter study

Research conducted by Lloyd (2004; 2005) extends the concept of information literacy and illustrates both the complexity of the phenomenon and the role that social and physical sources of information play in the process of coming to know about an information environment. For Lloyd, the current definitions of IL used in educational contexts are problematic because workplaces and workplace problems are often messy and open-ended, requiring novel and non-linear approaches to problem solving that are often intangible and may not be measurable. IL is not solely related to accessing information through text but requires engagement with other sources of information that constitute an information environment. This leads to Lloyd's definition of IL as a 'way of knowing' and information literate people as having 'a deep awareness, connection and fluency with the information environment'. 'Information literate people', she goes on, 'are engaged, enabled, enriched and embodied by social, procedural and physical information that constitutes an information universe. Information literacy is a way of knowing that universe' Lloyd 2006b, p.578).

In her study of the information literacy practices of firefighters, Lloyd highlighted IL as a holistic and interrelated practice, in which the newcomer to the environment develops practices that facilitate access to information and construction of knowledge. At the same time, the newcomer is also subject to information 'affordance' (what is offered in the environment) and mediation by experienced practitioners, who see their role in ensuring that newcomers develop an understanding of actual practices of the workplace through their access to sites of information that reflect what is valued by the community of practice. The role of social information, disseminated through other workers and within a social space, is recognised by Lloyd as having a significant influence on the development of IL practices relevant to gaining access to relevant and authentic workplace information. The social space affords opportunities for existing tacit knowledge about practice and profession to be transferred to newcomers (see below for a discussion of tacit knowledge), facilitating the development of collective understanding about the workplace and its practices.

The firefighter study introduced a range of information modalities that have not been explored in library-based IL research. These modalities are described as social and physical sources of information. Lloyd argued it was not until firefighters accessed the complex embodied information of a community of practice and the bodily information related to real world experience, that they became firefighters with a full knowledge and understanding of firefighting practice (Lloyd & Somerville 2005). For this to occur, firefighters needed to couple together codified forms of knowledge (explicit knowledge accessed through text) with social sources (accessed through the community of practice) and physical sources (accessed through the body). In order to do this, a range of information practices – which are silenced in the educational context – are given a 'voice' and developed as part of coming to know the 'narrative' that underpins the discourse of practice. The following section briefly explores these modalities.

Textual information

Codified forms of knowledge are manifested through print and electronic print media. These sites are recognised by librarians and are accounted for in the development of IL standards and guidelines. This formal site of knowledge facilitates 'knowing about' or 'knowing that' (Blackler 1995) and can be described as predictable information that cannot be fully understood until experienced. Initially, access to textual information helps the newcomer shape his or her understanding of the larger organisation and its practices, and their place in it. In the firefighter study, codified knowledge represents the formal requirement of work and is represented in administrative and procedural manuals, and in the formal curriculum of initial training. At the emergent level, there is a high acceptance of codified form of knowledge, and information access and use remains uncritical.

Social forms of information

Social forms of information relate to information about the core values, beliefs and attitudes related to practice and profession. This type of information is tacit and its meaning is difficult to articulate in written form. It is made available to newcomers through narration and storytelling. Through these practices, workplace knowledge is deconstructed and information is disseminated in a way that facilitates the development of shared understanding about practice and profession, which introduces and eventually binds newcomers to the community of practice, and through which experienced practitioners can mediate and influence interpretations about practice. Social information is highly contestable and can be afforded *or denied* to the newcomer by the community of practice.

Physical forms of information

Physical information is accessed through bodily experience and is observed through the bodies of other practitioners. The body 'reflects the consciousness of our engagement with information. It is at once the collector of sensory information, a site of knowledge and a disseminator of information to others' (Lloyd 2005, p.86). In the workplace, the body becomes the intersection between codified forms of knowledge and information drawn from the actuality of practice. Observation of practice allows others to draw information about performance that can be compared to their own. Observing bodily practices of novices in a workplace environment affords embodied expert workers opportunities to 'fill in the information gaps' by signalling what is missing from novice learning. Rehearsal allows the subject body to connect codified information with actual practice.

For instance, in their early stages of training, firefighters access codified knowledge by developing textual practices. This enables them to engage with formal requirements of work and facilitates learning the rules and regulations of work in safe and predictable ways – in effect they learn to act as a firefighters. It is not until they actually enter the workplace, however, that they begin the process of engaging with the community of practice and with bodily information, and that they begin to develop a deep understanding of practice and profession, thus *becoming* firefighters. In the firefighter study, the outcomes of becoming information literate were identified as the transition from subjective positions – which occurs when information practices focus on codified sources of knowledge – to intersubjective positions that occur when IL practices extend to include social and physical sources of information.

Issues and themes in workplace information literacy

The workplace definition of IL provides a much broader definition of information literate people and of information literacy, which raises issues that must be explored by librarians if they are to realise fully their claim of being IL champions and facilitators of lifelong learning. Candy (2006) has noted that learning through formal institutions (such as schools, TAFE colleges and universities) is only a minor part of 'people's learning through their lives'(2006, p.54). Candy notes that many structural changes demand continued learning throughout life, including:

- the emergence of new occupations and careers – a continuous change towards the information society;

- the explosion of knowledge;

- increased globalisation;

- changes in the nature of work, families and communities through changing lifestyles; and

- changes in information and communication technology (ICT) (adapted from Candy 2006, p.54).

The workplace definition above attempts to recast information literacy as a phenomenon more deeply connected with people's formal and informal meaning-making activities in all contexts than has been previously articulated. It also recognises that information is accessed, disseminated, used and transferred within a social space or context. It suggests that IL should not be defined according to its skills-based characteristics, nor as a series of decontextualised skills, because reducing the phenomenon to this level limits our conception of the phenomenon and our understanding of what being information literate means. Instead, IL should be defined as the ability to know *what there is* in a landscape and to draw meaning from this through engagement and experience with information. This ability arises from complex contextualised practice, processes and interactions that enable access to social, physical and textual sites of knowledge.

The concept of IL as a generic set of skills and attributes contributes to those grand narratives of Western pedagogic practice that value 'mentalistic' ways of learning and codified knowledge above all other forms and ways of knowing, although the latter are just as critical to ensuring the development of the 'whole person'. This can lead to a reductionist position for IL education and facilitate the continued development of front-end models (Beckett & Hager 2002) where, as noted already, IL education is treated as separate from curriculum and often treated as a 'one-off class' early on in a student's educational career.

The role of the workplace community in facilitating IL practice also becomes a central focus when determining how IL manifests itself, and this has implications for librarians who undertake the championing of IL. Developing an understanding of the complex ways in which information is 'afforded' to novices by experts can lead to new ways of understanding how IL education can be delivered by librarians in ways that reflect the mentoring, scaffolding and guiding practices undertaken by experts who afford opportunities for newcomers to engage with information that is relevant to practice. As suggested earlier, this may be done best in collaboration with experts such as educators.

The firefighter study suggested that information can be a highly contested commodity that may be denied when interests and values do not reflect those of the individual or the community. The concept of information contestation (where information is withheld or denied or meets barriers) has implications for knowledge management which often views the capture of 'tacit' knowledge as an unproblematic process, removed from the internal competitive concerns of individuals who compete for both emotional and financial rewards within an organisation.

Knowledge management and the learning organisation

Understanding information literacy and how it manifests itself is generally regarded in the library and information science (LIS) community, at least, as central to knowledge management (KM), which focuses on capturing and managing the tacit dimensions of information dissemination and transfer of knowledge within an organisational context. One of the key premises underlying this chapter is the thought that there are important commonalities between IL, the subject of considerable academic research, and KM, which is a largely business-driven management paradigm, drawing heavily on information management practice (as discussed in Chapter 11) and theories of the learning organisation.

In a much quoted paper in *Australian Library Journal*, Marianne Broadbent, one of the most influential Australian commentators on KM in the LIS sector, suggests that in order to implement KM it is necessary to understand an 'organisation's information flows' and to implement 'organisational learning practices which make explicit key aspects of its knowledge base'. KM, according to Broadbent, 'is about enhancing the use of organisational knowledge through sound practices of information management and organisational learning' (1997, pp.8-9). For an account of the use of information management tools and techniques by learning organisations, see Chapter 11 by Michael Middleton. Here it is suggested that if KM initiatives are to be effective they need to be based on a sound understanding of workplace IL.

First, what is meant by the term knowledge management? Herein lies a major problem because there are many definitions of KM – people from a LIS background tend to focus on codified, textual forms of knowledge, whereas in the field of information systems the focus is the underlying systems and technologies, and in the human resources sector it is people. It is worth noting that a 2002 review by Hlupik et al. identified eighteen distinct definitions of KM (Bouthillier & Shearer 2002). The following definition, however, taken from the Australian KM standard, provides a reasonably good starting point:

> A trans-disciplinary approach to improving organisational outcomes and learning, through maximising the use of knowledge. It involves the design, implementation and review of social and technological activities and processes to improve the creating, sharing, and applying or using of knowledge.
> Knowledge management is concerned with innovation and sharing behaviours, managing complexity and ambiguity through knowledge networks and connections, exploring smart processes, and deploying people-centric technologies (Standards Australia 2005, p.2).

A glance at the long list of KM 'enablers' in the standard – some thirty-four 'tools, techniques and activities' used to implement knowledge initiatives in organisations – helps to put some flesh and bones on the definition, and reinforces the widespread view that KM does indeed involve a trans-disciplinary approach. Many of the enablers are drawn from information management in its various guises and from information systems and technology. More than half, however, are management tools, techniques and activities, most focusing on human resources, which is hardly surprising, given KM's emphasis on 'leveraging' (or providing value to) an organisation's intellectual assets, fostering innovation and change throughout the organisation, and developing the required organisational culture (Ferguson & Hider 2006).

Equally unsurprising is the fact that several enablers relate to the social sources of information discussed earlier, such as after action reviews (AARs), communities of practice

(CoP), communities of interest (broader in scope than CoPs), meetings and 'share fairs', mentoring and coaching, narrative management, physical environment, play theory, reflection, social network analysis, storytelling and strategic conversations (Standards Australia 2005, pp.35-49). Moreover, some of the technologies listed are specifically geared to inter-personal communication and knowledge sharing (examples include email, chatrooms, wikis and blogs). Curiously, the standard does not list information literacy as an enabler, instead presenting an alternative term, 'knowledge literacy', and contrasting it with IL, which it defines narrowly as 'the ability to find and use information'. It is beyond the scope of this chapter to explore the distinction (see Ferguson 2006).

A common distinction between information management and knowledge management is that the former is concerned primarily with the management of 'explicit' forms of knowledge, such as policy documents, the contents of databases or corporate records (in other words, what the LIS community would call information), whereas KM represents an attempt to manage all the intellectual assets in an organisation, including the knowledge locked away in people's heads, a significant portion of which is what could be termed 'know-how'. Leaving aside the fact that many of the early proponents of information management were just as interested in leveraging people's knowledge and skills – and also leaving aside the philosophical problem some have with the notion that people's knowledge can be 'managed' – it is true to say that, if someone were to be asked whether an organisation had any KM problems, the first example that would probably spring to mind is the issue of people leaving the organisation with heaps of 'know-how' that is thus lost to the organisation. If asked about information management problems, however, most would probably think of IT.

In order to establish the scope of KM, it might help to consider a few key studies. Thomas Davenport and Laurence Prusak capture the scope best in their description of organisational management as 'a fluid mix of framed experience, values, contextual information and expert insight' that is typically 'embedded not only in documents or repositories but also in organisational routines, processes, practices and norms' (2000, p.5). Karl Wiig (1993, p.156), one of the most influential and most often cited writers on KM in the business sector, includes in his account of corporate knowledge assets: skills and habits (clearly tacit knowledge), procedural knowledge, historic records of past decisions, 'lessons-learned' reports, computer programs (a form of procedural knowledge), memory of a particular 'case' (anecdotal knowledge) and organisational structures, systems and procedures (embedded knowledge). In an empirical study of twelve organisations from the private and public sectors, France Bouthillier and Kathleen Shearer (2002) identified what they saw as KM methodologies: focus on communication (for instance, communities of practice), focus on storage and retrieval (such as knowledge mapping), focus on selected dissemination and focus on action or virtual collaboration. Again, it is worth noting the strong focus on social sources of information.

Underlying many accounts of KM implementation lies the well-known distinction between *tacit knowledge* (mentioned earlier) or, in other words, the knowledge locked up in people's heads – a highly valuable commodity, especially in knowledge-intensive industries such as law and high finance – and *explicit knowledge*, or the codified forms of knowledge that most in the LIS community would call information (and seen earlier in this chapter as the focus of IL in the higher education sector). From this distinction, Ikujiro Nonaka and his colleagues developed a much-cited model of organisational knowledge creation. In this model, tacit knowledge interacts with explicit knowledge in a spiralling process in which individuals learn from others and from the shared knowledge of the organisation, thus creating new knowledge which in turn becomes part of corporate knowledge and part of a new spiral of knowledge creation. The model demonstrates four types of interaction, represented by the acronym, SECI, and illustrated here through reference to corresponding types of information system and technology:

- Socialisation involves individuals in the sharing of tacit knowledge, using, for instance, groupware such as Lotus Notes.

- Externalisation involves expressing tacit knowledge in a form that can be understood by others. Knowledge-based systems such as expert system allow a specific area of personal expertise to be encoded in a knowledge base for later interrogation by another person.

- Combination entails the collection of explicit knowledge, from sources inside and outside the organisation, and its combination, editing, processing and distribution (what LIS professionals might call information consolidation). There are many examples of combination, in which knowledge (if that is indeed the correct word) starts and finishes in explicit form – for instance, an electronic document management system.

- Internalisation involves converting newly created knowledge, which is in explicit form, into the organisation's tacit knowledge, through training and individual learning, using, for example, corporate learning software (adapted from Nonaka & Konno 1998).

The process of socialisation presents a parallel with the earlier account of workplace information literacy, mentoring and the transition from subjective to intersubjective positions. This particular version of socialisation includes the proposition that tacit knowledge can be transferred between or among individuals without recourse to explicit knowledge or information. Here it is suggested, however, that just as it is information that is transferred in an online chat session (text on a computer screen), so too in a face-to-face meeting. One speaker transmits a piece of information, which a listener hears, interprets and, perhaps, assimilates into his or her body of knowledge. This is a new piece of knowledge, however – it is a construct of the *listener* and not something that has been transferred seamlessly from one person to another. Knowledge management may provide a useful focus on human aspects of organisational culture that some believe information management undervalued, but it tends to conceal one of the basic facts about corporate health, namely that information is the life-blood of an organisation.

Rather than talking about the knowledge being shared or knowledge 'flow' as some commentators have it (Nissen 2006), it might be more helpful to say that the information that is transferred in the process of socialisation can result in the framing of group experiences, which may in turn lead to *negotiated* ways of understanding. This is not to say that knowledge is shared, but that information is shared along with information about how it might be shared, framed and understood. Thus, it might be better to consider a meeting, for instance, in terms of the information that is exchanged rather than as a transfer of tacit knowledge. This information may be assimilated into the knowledge systems of the meeting's participants, but in most cases the only record of a meeting is a set of minutes that conveys only basic facts such as decisions made – a very 'thin' form of information. Much of the context is lost. In some cases, however, context is important, hence the references earlier to 'narrative', 'story-telling' and anecdotal knowledge. One of the meeting participants may report on, say, a trip to an overseas branch of the company or on a particular project, and that 'narrative' – which might be termed 'thick' information – may be of use at another time or elsewhere in the organisation. How is that narrative captured and is it worth taking the time and effort to capture it?

Knowledge management has its share of information disasters, such as the large consumer products company that attempted to create a knowledge depository, only to create an 'information junkyard' that failed to capture the varied nature of people's work (McDermott 1999). For knowledge management to be effective, it is suggested, it is important for managers to understand issues such as:

- the information that is valued by the organisation's communities of practice;

- the modalities of information – textual, social and even physical – that influence knowledge development;

- practices that influence the transfer of information among individuals or groups within an organisation, which ultimately reside as sites of knowledge that can be mined; and

- an understanding of the outcomes of IL practices in relation to organisational development and corporate leveraging of knowledge.

These are all areas in which the qualified and proactive information professional can contribute to his or her learning organisation.

Conclusion

Information literacy is a contextual practice that is influenced by the discourse, discursive practices and sources of information that are valued and legitimised by a specific organisation. As this book has demonstrated again and again, the influence of context has to be taken into account when examining the theory and practice of information science. Information literacy practice will manifest itself in different ways, depending on the context, because the focus of what information is valued will influence how it is accessed and used. Lloyd (2003, p.88) has argued that 'effective information or knowledge management systems depend on workforces able to operationalize the cognitive, affective and embodied skills of information literacy, to solve workplace problems independently and to develop new strategic knowledge'. In this respect, IL is seen as a catalyst for learning about workplace practice. In this chapter it is suggested that IL – as developed by workplace IL research – pursues the same goal as KM, which is to develop and nurture the knowledge sharing practices and information literate workforce that are necessary if organisations are to be adaptive, innovative and robust.

In the information driven economies of the twenty-first century, employees who are able to develop information pathways and to create new corporate knowledge will provide the strategic difference between a highly successful business that is able to leverage its corporate knowledge for competitive gain and those that cannot (Lloyd 2003, p.88). Library and information professionals have their part to play, but this necessitates understanding information literacy as a holistic practice that draws on sites of knowledge that may not be epistemic or codified but which nonetheless are central to learning about workplace practice. As a key group of IL champions, they need to be aware of a broader meaning for IL than the narrow one implied by their focus hitherto on the transfer of information searching skills. The idea of lifelong learning has for a long time been reduced to educational contexts and an individual's movement in and out of formal study as career paths change. The research into workplace IL demonstrates the way in which people engage not only with formal (explicit) educational curricula but with informal curricula – which may be tacit and embodied – and are driven through learning to work collectively.

In highlighting the commonalities between workplace IL and KM, however, one should not lose sight of their differences. If definitions of IL are shaped largely by context, so also are these two distinct bodies of theory and practice. Whereas IL, for instance, focuses on the professional (subjective and intersubjective) development of people within organisations, from novice to expert, and the ability to work collectively, KM takes a broader approach, in the sense that personal development is only one of many objectives in the sharing of corporate knowledge. In particular, KM focuses on the generation of new knowledge and innovation, as distinct from the transmission of the existing stores of corporate knowledge and understanding that characterises workplace IL. The focus of IL, therefore, is largely the transformation of the individual from novice to expert, the inculcation of organisational values and training, while for KM it is largely that which is shared (knowledge), the development of informed decision making and strategic issues.

The emphasis here on the commonalities between the two fields of study is driven by two concerns. First, library and information science professionals have demonstrated considerable interest for several years in KM and how they can contribute to KM initiatives in their organisations. Their interest and expertise in IL, while limited by an over-emphasis on formal educational contexts, makes them appropriate players in the multi-disciplinary KM domain. Second, library and information science professionals sometimes lose sight of the fact that libraries often constitute substantial organisations in their own right (a point taken up in Chapter 17). Library managers need to understand the issues associated with information transfer and knowledge generation among their own workforce if they are to continue thriving as change managers and to develop thriving information agencies in the twenty-first century. In highlighting the commonalities between IL and KM, it is intended not to pay lip-service to the popular notion that librarians make good knowledge managers but to map out areas of enquiry for researchers and practitioners who are eager to contribute to corporate information and knowledge management.

References

American Library Association (ALA) 2000, *Information literacy competency standards for higher education*, http://www.ala.org/acrl/ilstandardlo.html

Australian Library and Information Association (ALIA) 2003, *The library and information sector: Core knowledge, skills and attributes: Core knowledge statement*, http://www.alia.org.au/policies/core.knowledge.html

Appleton, M & Orr, D 2000, 'Meeting the needs of distance education students,' *Information literacy around the world: Advances in programs and research*, C Bruce & P Candy (eds), Centre for Information Studies, Charles Sturt University, Wagga Wagga, NSW, pp.11-24.

Beckett, D & Hager, P 2002, *Life, work and learning: Practice in postmodernity*, Routledge International Studies in the Philosophy of Education 14, Routledge, London & New York.

Bishop, K 2002, *New roles, skills and capabilities for the knowledge-focused organisation*, Business Excellence Australia, Sydney, NSW.

Blackler, F 1995, 'Knowledge, knowledge work and organizations: An overview and interpretation, *Organization Studies*, vol.16, no.6, pp.1021-1046.

Bouthillier, F & Shearer, K 2002, 'Understanding knowledge management and information management: The need for an empirical perspective,' *Information Research*, vol.8, no.1, http://InformationR.net/ir/8-1/paper141.html

Broadbent, M 1997, 'The emerging phenomenon of knowledge management', *Australian Library Journal*, vol.41, no.1, pp.6-24.

Bruce, C 1997, *Seven faces of information literacy*, Auslib Press, Adelaide, SA.

Bruce, C 2000, 'Information literacy research: Dimensions of the emerging collective consciousness', *Australian Academic and Research Libraries*, vol.31, no.2, pp.91-109.

Bruce, C & Candy, P (eds) 2000, *Information literacy around the world, Advances in programs and research*, Occasional Publications, no.1, Centre for Information Studies, Charles Sturt University, Wagga Wagga, NSW.

Bruce, C, Edwards, S & Lupton, M 2006, *Six frames for information literacy education*, http://www.ics.heacademy.ac.uk/italics/vol5iss1.htm

Bundy, A 2004, *Australian and New Zealand information literacy framework: Principles, standards and practice*, Australian and New Zealand Institute for Information Literacy and Council of Australian University Librarians, Adelaide, SA.

Candy, P 2006, 'Health and human services and information literacy', SD Garner (ed.), *High-level Colloquim on Information Literacy and Lifelong Learning*, held at Bibliotheca alexandrina, Egypt, November 6-9 2005, sponsored by UNESCO, NFIL, IFLA, http://unesdoc.unesco.org/images/0014/001448/144820e.pdf

Cheuk, B 1998, 'An information seeking and using process model in the workplace: A constructivist approach', *Asian Libraries*, vol.7, pp.372-390.

Churkovich, M & Oughtred, C 2002, 'Can an online tutorial pass the test for library instruction? An evaluation and comparison of library skills instruction methods for first year students at Deakin University', *AARL*, vol.3, pp.29-33.

Currier, S 2003, *INSPIRAL case study 4: Edge Hill College of Higher Education: Post-Graduate Certificate in Teaching & Learning in Clinical Practice* (Introductory Module), http://inspiral.cdlr.strath.ac.uk/documents/INSPcasestudy4EH.doc

Davenport, T & Prusak, L 2000, *Working knowledge: How organizations manage what they know*, 2nd edn, Harvard Business School Press, Cambridge, MA.

Dewald, NH 1999, 'Web-based library instruction: What is good pedagogy?' *Information Technology and Libraries*, vol.18, no.1, pp.26-31.

Doyle, CS 1992, 'Outcome measures for information literacy within the national education goals of 1990', *Final report to the National Forum on Information Literacy: Summary of findings*, ERIC Clearinghouse on Information Resources, ED372763, Syracuse, NY.

Ferguson, S 2006, 'AS 5037-2005: Knowledge management blueprint for Australian organisations?', *Australian Library Journal*, vol.55, no.3, pp.196-209.

Ferguson, S & Ferguson, A 2005, 'The remote library and point-of-need user education: An Australian library perspective', *Journal of Interlibrary Loan, Document Delivery & Electronic Reserve*, vol.15, no.3, pp.43-60.

Ferguson, S & Hider, P 2006, 'Knowledge management education in Australia', *Education for library and information services: A festschrift to celebrate thirty years of library education at Charles Sturt University*, Occasional Publications, no.2, Centre for Information Studies, Charles Sturt University, Wagga Wagga, NSW.

Fjällbrant, N 2000, 'The development of web-based programs to support information literacy courses', *Information literacy around the world: Advances in programs and research*, C Bruce & P Candy (eds), Centre for Information Studies, Charles Sturt University, Wagga Wagga, NSW, pp.25-36.

Grassian, ES & Kaplowitz, JR 2001, *Information literacy instruction: Theory and practice*, Neal-Schuman, New York.

Houghton, JM & Halbwirth, S 2002 'Knowledge management and information literacy: A new partnership in the workplace?', in P Ward (ed.), *Continuing professional education for the information society, Proceedings of the Fifth World conference on Continuing Professional Education for the Library and Information Science Professions*, pp.70-79, Saur, Munich.

Karelse, C 2000 'INFOLIT: A South African experience of promoting quality education', *Information literacy around the world: Advances in programs and research*, C Bruce & P Candy (eds), Centre for Information Studies, Charles Sturt University, Wagga Wagga, NSW, pp.37-60.

Kasowitz-Scheer, A & Pasqualoni, M 2002, 'Information literacy instruction in higher education,' *Trends and Issues*, ERIC Digest, June 2002.

Levy, P 2000, 'Information specialists supporting learning in the networked environment: A review of trends and issues in higher education', *The New Review of Libraries and Lifelong Learning*, vol.1, p.45.

Limberg, L 2000, 'Is there a relationship between information seeking and learning outcomes?' *Information literacy around the world: Advances in programs and research*, C Bruce & P Candy (eds), Centre for Information Studies, Charles Sturt University, Wagga Wagga, NSW, pp.193-207.

Line, MB 2000, 'The lifelong learner and the future library,' *The New Review of Libraries and Lifelong Learning*, vol.1, pp.65-80.

Lipow, A 1999, 'Serving the remote user: Reference service in the digital environment', *Information online and on disc: Strategies for the next millenium: Proceedings of the Ninth Australasian Information Online On Disc Conference and Exhibition*, held at the Sydney Convention and Exhibition Centre, 19-21 January 1999, Information Science Section, ALIA, http://www.csu.cdu.au/special/online99/proceedings99/200.htm

Lloyd, A 2003, 'Information literacy: The meta-competency of the knowledge economy?' *Journal of Librarianship and Information Science*, vol.35, no.2, pp.87-92.

Lloyd, A 2004, *Working information: Developing a grounded theory of information literacy in the workplace*, PhD thesis, University of New England, NSW.

Lloyd, A 2005, 'Information literacy: Different concepts, different contexts, different truths?' *Journal of Library and Information Science*, vol.37, no. , pp.82-88.

Lloyd, A 2006a, 'Drawing from others: Ways of knowing about information literacy performance', in D Orr, F Nouwens, C Macpherson, RE Harreveld & PA Danaher (eds), *Proceedings 4th International Lifelong Learning Conference: Partnerships, Pathways and Pedagogies*, held at Rydges Capricorn Resort, Yeppoon, Qld, pp.182-192.

Lloyd, A 2006b, ' Information literacy landscapes: An emerging picture' *Journal of Documentation*, vol.62, no.5,pp.570-583.

Lloyd, A & Somerville, M 2005, ' Working Information', *Journal of Workplace Learning*, vol.18, no.3, pp.186-198.

Lupton, M 2004, *The learning connection*, Auslib Press, Adelaide. Cited in Lupton, M, Glanville, C, McDonald, P & Selzer, D 2004, *Information literacy toolkit*, Griffith University, Brisbane, http://www.gu.edu.au/centre/gihe/griffith_graduate/toolkit/infoLit/InfoLitToolkit.pdf

McDermott, R 1999, 'Why information technology inspired but cannot deliver knowledge management', *California Management Review*, vol.41, no.4, pp.103-117, ABI/Inform, Ovid.

Nissen, ME 2006, *Harnessing knowledge dynamics: Principled organizational knowing and learning*, IRM Press, Hershey, PA.

Nonaka, I & Konno, N 1998, 'The concept of "Ba": Building a foundation for knowledge creation', *California Management Review*, vol.40, no.3, pp.40-54.

Skov, A & Skærbak, H 2003, 'Fighting an uphill battle: Teaching information literacy in Danish institutions of higher education', *Library Review*, vol.52, no.7, pp.326-332.

Standards Australia 2005, *Knowledge management – a guide, AS 5037-2005*, 2nd edn, Standards Australia, Sydney.

Stubley, P 2003, 'Skills move to VLEs', *Update*, vol.1, no.7, p.35, viewed 18 August 2003, http://www.cilip.org.uk/update/issues/oct02/article4oct.html

Todd, R 2000, 'A theory of information literacy: In-formation and outward looking', *Information literacy around the world: Advances in programs and research*, ed. C Bruce & P Candy, Centre for Information Studies, Charles Sturt University, Wagga Wagga, NSW, pp.163-175.

Van Rooi, H & Snyman R 2006, 'A content analysis of literature regarding knowledge management opportunities for librarians', *Aslib Proceedings*, vol.58, no.3, pp.261-271.

Webber, S & Johnston, B 2000, 'Conceptions of information literacy: New perspectives and implications', *Journal of Information Science*, vol. 26, no. 6, pp. 381-397.

Wiig, KM 1993, *Knowledge foundations*, Schema Press, Arlington, TX.

CHAPTER 14
The historical perspective: where we've come from

Ross Harvey

This chapter cannot hope, and does not intend, to emulate the achievement of Peter Biskup's definitive overview of the history of libraries and librarianship in Australia (Biskup 1994). It is not a potted history of Australian libraries and librarianship. Nor does it attempt to provide the level of detail about aspects of Australian library history that is found in journal articles on the topic or in the papers presented at the seven Australian Library History Forums that have been held from 1985 to 1997. Instead, it aims to provide a framework within which library and information management professionals at the beginning of the twenty-first century can reflect on the history of their profession, its actions and its structures, and in doing so appreciate how awareness of the past can be helpful in being more effective in present and future professional practice. It is inevitably a personal and probably an idiosyncratic view: as is stated later in this chapter, 'history is a slippery beast with few, if any, universal truths to impart' which is shaped by the set of beliefs held by the historian.

Why study Australian library history?

David Seaman notes about today's libraries and their users that

> Ours is a world in flux, where books and manuscripts, recordings and films, are
> migrating out from our shelves and reading rooms into the digital world. Where once
> one went to a library building full of printed objects, now those holdings travel to our
> desks, offices, classrooms, phones, iPods and PDAs (Seaman 2005, p.55).

These are radical departures from previous practice. How can the study of library history help us to best manage these massive changes? Why should information professionals devote some of the limited amounts of time they have available to dwelling on the past? There are many ways of answering these questions and some of them are examined here.

The most commonly-expressed reason is noted in the introduction to this book, where Stuart Ferguson suggests that 'by exploring the relationship between library history and wider socio-economic developments … [librarians] may develop a more sound critical understanding of the current processes of change'. That is to say, study of the past is of direct assistance in managing the present. This theme was colourfully expressed by Australian historian Manning Clark in 1975: 'the point of knowing the past is to force our ghosts to keep their distance, and give us some liberty' (Clark 1975, p.13). Clark was referring to the study of Australia's often turbulent and unsavoury history of European settlement, but his point is valid also for its library history, although this has fewer ghosts than, say, the early days of convict settlement in Tasmania or in

New South Wales. Similarly, American library historian Wayne Weigand refers to identifying 'tunnel vision and blind spots' through the study of library history so that they can be avoided as we plan for the future:

> Like society in general, every generation of library and information professionals must apply to the past it has inherited a set of questions unique to its time and circumstances in order to better understand its present, so that it can prudently plan its future. Our own generation is no different. Our alternative – to craft a set of tunnel-visioned plans and strategies for the future that carry with them many of the systemic gendered, class, age, occupational, ethnic, and homophobic blind spots marking so much of our past – is, in my opinion, unacceptable (Weigand 1999, p.26).

Another set of reasons for studying library history revolves around the idea of professional behaviour and professional ways of thinking and skill levels. British librarian WA Munford suggested that 'The maturity of a profession may be judged – although there are of course other tests – by its pride in its own past' (quoted in Ollé 1967, p.7). Raymond Irwin is another British author who has written extensively on the rationale for studying library history. One reason he suggests is that the knowledge and understanding it can provide has the potential to elevate the librarian above that of a mere technician. Irwin writes (using the convention of his period that the masculine encompasses the feminine): 'If all that interests the young librarian is a bread and butter wage as a technician, then there is little in history that he need bother about ... He can carry out his duties competently enough' (Irwin 1958, p.512). Such study provides 'a sense of proportion' that helps us to avoid the 'contemporary habit to worship the present moment as though it were the one critical point in our history'. Those who do so 'forget that every today was once a tomorrow' (Irwin 1958, p.511).

More recently on this theme, Jean Preer has suggested that knowing library history has a significant role in librarianship's continued existence and strength as a profession. 'Lacking historical perspective', she suggests, 'we may not understand what is unique and important about the work of libraries and librarians and may be poorly equipped to distinguish librarians from other, more newly minted, information professionals' (Preer 2006, p.77). Preer uses examples from US library history during the 1930s, such as the introduction of new technologies in libraries and the stand of the American Library Association (ALA) against racial discrimination by deciding not to hold its conferences in cities where discriminatory laws would be imposed, to illustrate these points in the contemporary US context. For example, she notes public surprise at 'the current stand of US librarians against the USA PATRIOT Act' but points out that 'no-one who has studied the development of the professional voice of librarians should be surprised. This is our history' (Preer 2006, p.83).

Irwin and Munford are British, and Weigand and Preer are American. Australian authors have also addressed these questions, using a theme of understanding our place in the world. Boyd Rayward commented in 1988 that 'the larger historical, cultural, political, and social environments ... help shape the development of library collections, functions and services' (Rayward 1988a). John Levett argued at greater length for the study of library history as an essential part of the curriculum to which librarians are educated. 'If we do not know our history', he contends, 'we cannot possibly understand our present culture, nor comprehend its place in the constructed universe' (Levett 1993, p.3).

History is to us as anatomy is to the surgeon: we need to understand the structure, the skeleton, the musculature, the organs of our past, in order to come to terms with the present and constructively to address the future. Although the past may be another country, the people who lived there are directly related to us. We build on their achievements, and attempt to come to terms with their mistakes. There is an unbroken and inevitable link between what they did, what we do, and what will be done by our successors. To step into the present without understanding and appreciating its antecedents, is as to move into a foreign land with no notion of its language, culture or mores (Levett 1993, p.1).

How do we structure history?

The previous section posed questions about why studying library history is important, and provided some responses. The next questions to ask are about how history should be presented. How do we structure or 'arrange the history when the facts have been discovered? Which shall take precedence – place, period or type of history?' (Ollé 1967, p.13).

These seemingly innocuous questions are difficult to answer, and the responses to them change depending on the period in which attempts are made to answer them. History is a slippery beast with few, if any, universal truths to impart. It relies on ascertaining facts (which may in themselves require re-interpretation and revision as new facts are discovered or verified) and presenting them according to a whole set of beliefs held by the historian and by the readership for whom the historian is writing. How history should be written, for whom and with what agenda is energetically argued in Australia, with the 'History Wars' debate engaging even the country's Prime Minister, John Howard, in its criticism of the overly negative 'black armband' views of mainstream historians (McKenna 1997). Although this kind of debate about revisionist history and its use towards overtly political ends has not yet been obviously manifested in Australian library history, aspects of it have been seen in publications about library history elsewhere. One could, for instance, explain the recent interest in lost and destroyed libraries, seen in the books *Lost libraries* (Raven 2004) and *Libricide* (Knuth 2003), in this way, as examples of a gloomier cast given to library history, and *Libricide* as a polemic for capitalist ideologies.

Another illustration of the ways in which history is constantly being revised is found in the example of the destruction of the famed Library of Alexandria, founded about 300 BC. If we were asked about this library and its end, most of us would answer that it was destroyed by a major earthquake and the ensuing fire that engulfed Alexandria in the year 48 BC, or words to that effect. That is, its destruction can be pinned down to a specific point in time and to a specific cause. However, research published recently has shown that this was definitely not the case, that its demise took place over at least 300 years, and that there were many causes. Lionel Casson puts its end in about AD 270 (Casson 2001, p.7) and Matthew Battle suggests that there may have been more than one library and more than one major fire, but that the final demise came in perhaps the fourth century AD (Battle 2004, p.24). A recent account pays particular attention to how the demise of the Alexandrian Library has been mythologised, frequently reformulated and used for political and polemical purposes (Raven 2004, pp.11-21 and elsewhere).The myth is an enduring one, still being harnessed for political purposes, as its current reincarnation in the digital age as the Bibliotheca Alexandrina, the 'New Library of

Alexandria ... dedicated to recapture the spirit of the original' (http://www.bibalex.org/), indicates.

The key text for Australia's library history is Biskup's definitive overview of the history of libraries in Australia (Biskup 1994). This is arranged on the basis of types of libraries, with chapters about the history of state, public, national, school and special libraries, libraries in tertiary institutions, and archival and manuscripts repositories; additional chapters provide an overview and examine associations of librarians, cooperation and networking, and issues (which Biskup labels 'debates and arguments'). The principal emphasis of Biskup's book is on library history as presented through the history of its institutions, with a secondary emphasis on some of the mechanisms that shaped Australian libraries (such as cooperation) and with relatively little emphasis on the people who shaped these libraries or the technologies that supported them and forced changes.

Biskup's intention was, of course, to examine the history of libraries, not the history of Australian librarians or library technologies, as indeed its introduction makes clear, and his book is an essential starting point for the serious historian. But the fact remains that its emphasis on institutions, rather than people, technologies, networking, or the many other focuses that history can have, and its relative lack of reference to broader social movements that shape libraries and the societies in which they reside and to which they respond, provide us with a particular bias. All history is inevitably biased – and readers must recognise the biases and respond to them as they read library history.

What library history has been published?

The previous section asked how history should be presented, how it could be structured to make it meaningful to its intended audience, rather than merely a recitation of facts. This section looks at the same questions from a different point of view. It considers the kinds of publications in which library history has been published and looks at how these have changed over time.

Until recently, history, as someone famously once said, was the story of dead white males (or, even more pejoratively, of dead white European males). This term refers to a tradition of history which stressed the contribution of males, usually European, and downplayed or even ignored the contributions of other groups such as women and non-Europeans. (Similarly, there is the 'Great Man' view of history.) Much history, and this includes library history, has been biographical, and – not surprisingly – dead white males have featured heavily. Library history has also concentrated heavily on the history of institutions, as seen in the example of Biskup's book about Australian library history (Biskup 1994). Relatively little attention has been paid until recent years on placing libraries within the broader social contexts from which they arise, in which they exist and to which they respond.

The Dead Germans Project is an example of the biographical approach, although one with an unusual genesis and which is developed in a novel way. The Dead Germans Project website encourages students at one US library school, and others who are interested, to contribute short biographies of 'significant individuals ... [who] provide the theoretical and practical base of the information sciences'. It is based on the contention that the library and information professions lacked coherence and were fragmented because they lacked 'a set of significant theoreticians that provided the intellectual foundations of the field': in other fields, such as sociology, the theoretical foundations were developed by key theoreticians such as Marx, Weber and Durkheim – that is, dead Germans. For librarianship, at least as represented by the contributions to the Dead Germans Project website, the range is considerably wider than just dead Germans. The obvious contenders are present (Gutenberg, Naudé, Cutter, Dewey, Asheim, Vannevar Bush, Shera, Carnegie, Ranganathan – although this list includes a Frenchman and an Indian) as well as some who are not, at least on the surface, as obvious (Alexander the Great, Berlioz, J Edgar Hoover, Mao Zedong, Adelaide Hasse, Miranda Lee Pao). Many biographies of librarians have been published, as a check of any large library's catalogue will indicate.

Examples of the history of institutions are also heavily represented in the published literature. The major libraries have, as ought to be expected, their history (or sometimes histories) – examples from Australia's neighbour, New Zealand, include histories of the Turnbull Library, Wellington (Barrowman 1995) and the Auckland Public Library (Barr 1950, Colgan 1980). Histories of related organisations that have played key roles in library development are also well represented. As just one example, and a very incomplete example at that, publications about the activities of the Carnegie Corporation include books about the Carnegie libraries established with funding from the Corporation (Bobinski 1969, Jones 1997), about the influence of the Carnegie Corporation on New Zealand librarianship (Rochester 1990) and about the development of American college libraries (Radford 1984).

Until recently, relatively little attention was paid to placing libraries within the broader social contexts from which they arise, in which they exist and to which they respond. This is, however, changing. New ways of thinking about history and about how history is written are also influencing the historians of libraries. Over the last decade, library historians, while not ignoring the traditional ways of enquiry and presentation of their results such as biographies and institutional histories, have become more focused on the roles of libraries and librarians as part of larger social issues. Four examples of this 'new' library history, which often challenges conventional thinking, illustrate this different approach. *Lost libraries* (Raven 2004) is a stimulating, at times confronting, collection of papers that focus on the destruction, loss and cultural genocide of significant past and recent libraries, ranging from their accidental (such as the 1966 Florence floods) to the deliberate, which has a very long history indeed. The subtitle of Rebecca Knuth's *Libricide* (2003) – 'the regime-sponsored destruction of books and libraries in the twentieth century' – indicates its concerns. Battle's *Library: An unquiet history* (2004) reminds us that, contrary to popular wisdom, libraries and reading have been the setting over centuries, if not millennia, of many vigorous and sometimes disastrous and destructive ideological battles. Nicholas Basbanes' *A splendor of letters* (2003) is one of many examples of a wider examination of the role and place of reading, writing and books in our current society, much of which places strong emphasis on the changes caused, or that will be caused, by the increasingly digital environments in which information is constructed, promulgated, received and used.

Australian library history has been no different in its publication patterns, broadly speaking. As with library history published elsewhere, it has in the past seen strong emphasis on biographical publications. These include Festschriften (collections of essays published to honour a person, usually around the date of their retirements). Two Australian examples are *Innovation no stranger* (Burn & Palmer 1982) in honour of Ira Raymond and *An enthusiasm for libraries* (Whyte & Radford 1988) in honour of Harrison Bryan. Festschriften, like all collections, can be mixed bags but usually contain useful and sometimes significant contributions to the history of Australian librarians and librarianship, albeit reflecting the concerns of the period in which they were published. Australian library history publications also include biographical material, such as the autobiographies by Axel Lodewycks (1982) and Harrison Bryan (1994). Publications about Australia's library history also include (not surprisingly) journal articles on a wide range of historical topics, published in no small number and not the minority interest that is frequently assumed. Boadle (2006, p.70) notes a 1996 study by Maxine Rochester that reported, '"library history" comprised the largest single category of research articles ... published during the period 1985-94 in *ALJ* [the *Australian Library Journal*]'. Theses submitted as requirements for research degrees contain important historical material that has not always been published. Indicative examples include Michael Talbot's doctoral thesis on the history of the Library Association of Australasia, a precursor to ALIA, from 1896 to 1902 (Talbot 1985) and David Jones' doctoral thesis on William Herbert Ifould and his role in the development of library services in New South Wales from 1912 to 1942 (Jones 1993).

Many documents written with audiences other than today's students of history in mind now provide key material for historians of Australian libraries, although this was not their primary purpose when they were written. Several influential surveys and reports are essential reading for the student of Australian library history. CW Holgate was the first of a long line of experts, British and later American, to visit Australia, and his descriptions were published as *Account of the chief libraries of Australia and Tasmania* (Holgate 1886). Other key reports include the Munn-Pitt report (1935) and the McColvin report (1947), both of which were key to the establishment of effective public library services, and the Tauber report (Tauber 1962) which focused specifically on academic and research libraries and their collections. These reported the observations of foreign experts, from the US in the case of Tauber and Munn (the latter funded by the Carnegie Corporation, whose influence on Australian librarianship has been significant) and for Holgate and McColvin from the UK. The Munn-Pitt, McColvin and Tauber reports were instrumental in generating debate by librarians and their political masters and funding bodies, leading in some cases to action that established new library services or improved existing ones. Other reports are more home grown; an example is the Horton report on public libraries in Australia (1976). Biskup's summary of the key reports to the mid 1990s (1994, Chapter 1) is highly recommended for the reader who would like an overview.

Papers presented at conferences are another source of writings about library history worth investigating. For Australia, general conferences such as the biennial Australian Library and Information Association (until 1988 the Library Association of Australia) occasionally contain papers that are historical in nature. A recent example is Peter Thompson's paper about aspects of practice at the Sandhurst Mechanics Institute and Free Library, Bendigo, presented at the 2006 VALA conference (Thompson 2006). However, the most significant are the publications arising out of the seven Australian Library History Forums held between 1984 and 1996 (Morrison & Talbot 1985, Biskup & Rochester 1985, Rayward 1988b, Upward and Whyte 1991, Rayward 1993, McMullin 1996, McMullin 1997). The papers presented at these meetings have been analysed by Boadle. Demographically speaking, fifty-five presenters, twenty-six of whom were librarians, sixteen library educators and six archivists, delivered seventy-nine papers (Boadle 2006, p.72). Although Boadle is principally interested in the role of archivist in writing and publishing Australian library and archives history, his analysis of the Australian Library History Forums also provides details of the topics covered for library history. One interesting conclusion he makes is 'the importance of the completion of a sustained piece of research for a RHD [research higher degree]' as 'much more significant drivers of library history production ... than ... the celebration of anniversaries. Anniversaries ... have given rise mainly to reminiscence and reflection' (Boadle 2006, p.79).

It is possible to discern some key issues to have engaged Australian library and information professionals during the last century and which are engaging the historians of Australian libraries in recent years. One is a lack of public support for libraries, including the need for free public library services in the decades up to the 1930s (Cunningham 1961 is an example). Another theme is the relevance of professional associations, with histories of associations of librarians being written (for example, Talbot 1985). Education for librarianship in Australia is attracting attention from a historical perspective (one example is Carroll & Harvey 2006).

The evolution of libraries

Where did libraries come from? Why is this important to know? Although these are sweeping questions, some general observations may be helpful to our understanding of Australian library history, in particular of why the current structures of libraries developed and the way they are evolving in a digital environment. (This section is based on the ideas expressed in Knuth 2003, Chapter 2 'The evolution and functions of libraries').

Knuth notes the crux of the matter:

> As societies grow in complexity, they increasingly depend on systems of knowledge that serve to connect various types of behavior, apply lessons from the past to future enterprises, and organize the indispensable activities of modern living. Written language fosters memory and makes these memories retrievable in a body of literature whose value has partly to do with the advantage it gives each generation over the last. ... As long as a civilization exists, the preservation of experience, of social intelligence or 'knowledge', is a derived necessity (Knuth 2003, p.19).

Libraries have their origins in the need for records which preserved and communicated knowledge, first in pictures and symbols which became increasingly abstract, then later as alphabets (Fischer 2003). One of the key drivers of this was the need to record commercial transactions. Different media were used over millennia to record information and were superseded by new media: clay tablets, papyrus scrolls, vellum codices and paper books in earlier periods. This cycle of replacement of one media type with another that stores more information is continuing today with CDs being replaced by DVDs, with terabyte storage now affordable for the home computer, and with petabyte storage being developed for the storage of science datasets. As the number of media items grew, so too did the mechanisms and institutions whose purpose was to store and produce the appropriate record on request.

The earliest known libraries, Knuth suggests, were Egyptian, dating from about 3000 BC (Knuth 2003, p.21). We are on firmer ground with the Sumerian civilisation, which it is known developed 'archives of governmental, legal and business records and preserved texts and treatises of religion, astrology, medicine, mathematics, literature' (Knuth 2003, p.21). Later still, Assyrian libraries were large and they had catalogues. These archives and libraries initially served the ruling elites – government officials, religious elites and rulers – and this continued for many centuries. (Some maintain that it is still the case today.) Knuth comments that 'Throughout history, texts and libraries have played an important role in preserving religious and dynastic records and in supporting the activities involved in running an empire' (Knuth 2003, p.21), that is, in legitimising those elites currently in power. Greek and Roman libraries have been thoroughly researched and described (Casson 2001 is an accessible and readable short history of them). By these periods the patterns of library development were changing, and some wealthy individuals were able to afford private libraries. Large collections aiming to be comprehensive and inclusive of all knowledge were developed, the library at Alexandria being the best-known example.

The Roman Empire was for many centuries the dominant world government, but, as it declined, so too did its libraries, although many libraries of wealthy individuals survived. As Knuth succinctly puts it, 'the fall of Rome marked the beginning of a period of hard times for Western culture and its written expression' (Knuth 2003, p.23). During the Middle Ages, learning was kept alive by religious institutions such as mosques (much classical knowledge was kept alive in Islamic, not Christian, institutions) and monasteries, 'where the preservation and copying of ancient texts became a part of religious practice' (Knuth 2003, p.23). The Renaissance witnessed the building up of large private collections by wealthy noblemen with the revival of classical literature and learning, and later the rise of humanism. The modern university began to evolve and required large collections of manuscripts to support learning.

The introduction of printing in the middle of the fifteenth century 'brought a secularisation of knowledge that laid the social and cultural foundations for modernity' (Knuth 2003, p.24). Texts became more accessible and affordable, Latin became less dominant in favour of vernacular languages and literacy levels rose. Libraries, formerly the province of elitist institutions such as churches and universities or of wealthy individuals, became more accessible to others, resulting in major social reforms such as the Protestant Reformation. In Knuth's words, 'the possibility of a new relationship between man and God based on direct access to scripture revolutionized ideas about the abilities and rights of the individual ... and eventually played a part in revolutionary activity and the evolution of democracy' (Knuth 2003, p.24). Influences such as these led over four centuries to the industrial society of the nineteenth century and to a burgeoning middle class which promoted libraries for the masses.

This extremely condensed account of 5,000 years of the evolution of libraries in the Western world can be interpreted in many ways. One theme that seems to help one understand the roles that libraries play now, and perhaps also the future roles in an increasingly digital environment, is that described by eminent French book historian Roger Chartier. Chartier views the earliest libraries as attempts to bring together:

> the entire written patrimony of humanity in one place [which, as time progressed] proves an impossible task, though. When print produced a proliferation of titles and editions, it ruined all hopes for an exhaustive collection. Even for those who held that a library must be encyclopedic, selection was an absolute necessity (Chartier 1994, p.63).

To understand the reasons why this task was impossible it is necessary to be aware of many other factors, such as the increasing availability of this written patrimony as printing techniques were developed and became more widespread, the increasing literacy in many countries, the rise of the middle classes who placed value on and were economically able to support learning, and much more.

By the end of the nineteenth century, the library, Knuth comments, had lived through more than three thousand years of 'experimentation and adaptation', evolving into the library as we know it today:

> an institution that met critical social needs. Among its many responsibilities were preserving the information that forms the basis of government, the economy, property rights and national and ethnic identity; rationalizing and supporting social, political, and religious systems, creeds, world views, and ideologies; disseminating information and underpinning education, intellectual development, and social progress; and supporting advanced or 'high' culture (Knuth 2003, p.27).

Knuth posits four functions or responsibilities of the modern library: preserving collective memory, maintaining belief systems, supporting nationalism and national identity and societal development. Not all libraries carry out all of these roles, and not all take on all of these responsibilities. Armed with only a cursory knowledge of how libraries evolved, such as in the brief overview provided above, it is readily apparent where these functions came from.

It can confidently be expected that libraries will continue to evolve, as will the functions they perform and the responsibilities they shoulder. It may even be possible, with a detailed knowledge of the history of libraries, to envisage with some degree of accuracy what these new functions might be.

The evolution of libraries in Australia: the case of public libraries

Libraries in Australia share many of the characteristics of libraries elsewhere, but not all. Why have these differences arisen? This section uses the example of public libraries to illustrate some of the historical factors that have shaped their evolution in Australia. Public libraries throughout the world can, depending on their size and the country in which they are located, be active in all of the roles of the modern library: preserving collective memory, maintaining belief systems, supporting nationalism and national identity and societal development. The history of public libraries in Australia is in part the story of the tensions between some of these responsibilities.

Visitors to Australia might wonder why the Australian public library system does not compare favourably with those in other similarly developed countries with which they are familiar. Part of the answer lies in the dominance in the past in Australia of Mechanics' Institutes (also Schools of Arts in New South Wales and Queensland, and Institutes in South Australia) and more recently of circulating libraries (also known as subscription libraries or commercial lending libraries) which arguably retarded the development of a strong public library system by comparison with some of its overseas contemporaries. Other parts of the answer lie in the roles of the state libraries in providing public library services and in the relationship between state governments and local government, but they are not noted here.

The libraries in the Mechanics' Institutes were among the first to be established in Australia. One of them, a Mechanics' Institute founded in Melbourne in 1839, is still operating as the

Melbourne Athenaeum (Arnold 1987, p.77). The Mechanics' Institutes also housed lecture rooms and, sometimes, museums. Their background lies in the British working-class self-improvement movements, transplanted to Australia in the mid nineteenth century. With only a couple of exceptions, one being the Melbourne Athenaeum already noted, they did not thrive. Their original aim, to educate workers, was quickly supplanted by the need to generate income in order to survive. Anette Bremer and Martin Lyons see their history from the 1890s as a 'constant struggle to stay solvent': they operated in an environment of tension between the authorities – principally local and state governments – who provided subsidies and 'still envisaged them as aids to working-class self-improvement' but 'their readers turned to them increasingly as suppliers of popular fiction' (Bremer & Lyons 2001, p.210). Unlike the modern public library, which has managed more successfully to balance the dual roles of serving an educational mission and catering to 'the readers' voracious demands for purely recreational reading' (Bremer & Lyons 2001, p.210), the Mechanics' Institutes usually failed to resolve this dilemma. They declined in number and importance as the twentieth century progressed.

The influence of the circulating libraries (known also as subscription libraries or commercial lending libraries) comes at a later date, their heyday being in the decades of the 1930s to the 1960s. They differ from the libraries of the Mechanics' Institutes in that they were operated as commercial profit-making concerns, with no educational role intended. Members of these libraries paid a fee, usually quarterly, half-yearly or annual, which entitled them to borrow a set number of items. Like the Mechanics' Institutes with their British origins, the circulating libraries were akin to similar operations in both the UK and the US where, by the 1930s, a large number operated. By comparison with their American equivalents which had average collection sizes of about 150, Australian circulating libraries were larger operations with average numbers of books in their collections averaging in the low thousands, and some operated as members of chains (Arnold 2001, pp.191-192).

The earliest circulating library in Australia was the Australian Subscription Library, Sydney, a forerunner of what is now the State Library of New South Wales, established in 1826. Their number remained small in Australia in the nineteenth century and the start of the twentieth century. From about 1930, as John Arnold puts it, 'their growth can only be described as spectacular'. He provides statistics for Melbourne to illustrate this – 89 in 1930, 408 by 1940, then declining but still over 300 in 1955, down to about 87 in 1974 (Arnold 1987, pp.77-78 and Appendix 2). Arnold considers that the influence of these circulating libraries on book distribution and on reading was considerable and that 'there can be no doubt that, for a time, the commercial library had a detrimental effect on the municipal library'. He suggests that over time their success positively, although indirectly, influenced the development of municipal public libraries by forcing local councils and librarians to 'reassess the role of public libraries and to build up their stock and make their libraries more open and appealing' (Arnold 1987, p.90).

At the same time as the circulating libraries were reaching their peak of popularity, concerned Australians were looking to outside assistance in their quest to improve public library services, and the Free Library Movement was developing – surely no coincidence. KS Cunningham describes the role of ACER (the Australian Council for Educational Research) from 1930 to 1947 in improving library services in Australia and in promoting free public library services (Cunningham 1961). One example is ACER's relationship with the Carnegie Corporation from about 1930. Before this date the Carnegie Corporation had very little input into Australia, with only four Carnegie libraries established compared with seventeen in New Zealand in the period 1890–1917 (Cunningham 1961, p.7). ACER's interest led to Carnegie money funding the visit to Australia of Pittsburgh librarian Ralph Munn and the Munn-Pitt report (Munn & Pitt 1935), to the establishment of ACER's library group with the intention of promoting library services in Australia, to funding from the Carnegie Corporation to be used for 'the purpose of taking appropriate action to educate public opinion in the various Australian States upon the place of free libraries in the community' (Cunningham 1961, p.19), to the establishment of the Free Library Movement (1935 in New South Wales and in other states in following years), and to the arranging of British librarian Lionel McColvin's visit in 1946–1947 and the publication of the McColvin report (McColvin 1947).

A highly recommended short history for a key period in the development of public libraries in Australia, 1890 to 1945, has been written by Jones (2001).

Coda: the past and the future

Chartier, whose view of the evolution of libraries as one of necessarily doomed attempts to construct encyclopaedic collections was noted earlier in this chapter, provides a view of the role of the library in the digital present and future:

> The library of the future seems indeed to be in a sense a library without walls ... the library of the future is inscribed where all texts can be summoned, assembled, and read on a screen. In the universe of remote communications made possible by computerized texts and electronic diffusion, texts are no longer prisoners of their original physical, material existence ... there is no longer a necessary connection between where they are conserved and where they are read. The opposition long held to be insurmountable between the closed world of any finite collection, no matter what its size, and the infinite universe of all texts ever written is thus theoretically annihilated: now the catalogue of all catalogues ideally listing the totality of written production can be realized in a universal access to texts available for consultation at the reader's location (Chartier 1994, pp.89-90).

Although Chartier does not specifically refer to Australia, there is no doubt that his view is as applicable in this country as it is elsewhere: Australian libraries are part of the global networks made possible through networked computing. Over the last twenty-five years we have seen the development of national infrastructure to support libraries such as the Australian Bibliographic Network (later Kinetica and now Libraries Australia), large-scale projects to make Australian content available in digital form such as the Australasian Digital Theses Program (http://adt.caul.edu.au) and Australian Periodical Publications 1840–1845 (http://www.nla.gov.au/ferg/index.html), plans to establish a national site licence for online databases and many other initiatives, the aims of which are to provide online access to digital content, both Australian and from anywhere in the world, for all Australians – although we are not there yet. The local public library now provides online access to a wide range of online databases, and increasingly library transactions are possible without visiting the library.

The concept of 'library as place' is, on the one hand, disappearing as these activities happen and, on the other hand, is becoming stronger as a focus for social activities. The ever-prescient

Chartier has also commented on this, his observations being an example of how an understanding of the past informs the future of libraries. As already noted, he sees the history of libraries as in part tensions between 'the dream of a universal library' and the reality that 'all collections, however rich they may be, can only render a partial image of the desired totality'. The results have been manifested as 'the fear of losing or of missing something' which lead to building complete collections, copying of books, printing of manuscripts, building of great libraries, catalogues of all printed knowledge and other attempts at comprehensiveness. But 'overabundance' got in the way. In the print world there was simply too much material to allow completeness. Chartier comments:

> Faced with this dual concern of loss and excess, tomorrow's library (or today's) can play a decisive role ... Long-distance communication of electronic texts makes thinkable, if it is not already here, the universal availability of written heritage, although no longer consecrating the library as the place of conservation and communication of this patrimony. Any reader, from wherever he or she may be reading, is capable of receiving any of the texts that make up this library without walls and even without place where ideally one may find, in digitalized format, all of the books of humanity (Chartier 2005, pp.9-10).

Shades of Google Scholar! Chartier argues, using examples from the history of the book and of libraries, that tomorrow's libraries have roles to play in the preservation of written heritage, teaching new readers, and as a place for social interaction. First, original books and manuscripts which have been digitised must not be destroyed, because this means we 'could lose our ability to understand a textual culture identified with the objects that have transmitted it ... more than ever ... one of the central tasks of libraries is to collect, protect, inventory and make available the objects of the past' (Chartier 2005, p.9). Second, 'libraries should also be tools where new readers can find their way into the digital world ... the library is well equipped to play a central role in the apprenticeship of the tools and techniques capable of giving to even the least expert reader a mastery over the new formats of the written word' (Chartier 2005, p.9). Third, a goal for tomorrow's library:

> should be to recreate around the book forms of sociability that have been lost. The long history of reading teaches us that over the centuries reading has become a silent and solitary endeavour, thus breaking even more sharply with the practices of sharing the written word that always lastingly strengthened family ties, friendships, scholarly work, or militant commitments ... libraries should increase the number of opportunities and ways for discussion of this written heritage and its intellectual and aesthetic creativity. In doing so, they can contribute to the construction of a public sphere that extends to all humanity (Chartier 2005, p.9).

There are definitely lessons to be learned from the study of the history of libraries, lessons that can be put to good use in the continual search by librarians for improvement of the services they offer. However, the Australian library profession currently lacks interest in its history. Where can new entrants to the profession of librarianship in Australia find out about its history? The occasional historical article appears in Australia's two key librarianship journals, the *Australian Library Journal* and *Australian Academic & Research Libraries*, and are scattered among other journals, and a small number of conference papers presented at professional library conferences are concerned with this history. Subjects on library history are currently offered only at one university-level librarianship program and at one TAFE-level program. Such poor coverage in our professional education programs undermines the profession's confidence in its future.

References

Arnold, J 1987, 'Choose your author as you would choose a friend': Circulating libraries in Melbourne, 1930–1960, *La Trobe Library Journal*, vol.10, no.40, pp.190-199.

Arnold, J 2001, 'The circulating library phenomenon', in *A history of the book in Australia 1891–1945: A national culture in a colonised market*, M Lyons & J Arnold (eds), University of Queensland Press, St Lucia, Qld.

Barr, J 1950, *Auckland public libraries 1880-1950: A brief historical description*, Library Committee of the Auckland City Council, Auckland.

Barrowman, R 1995, *The Turnbull: A library and its world*, Auckland University Press, Auckland.

Basbanes, NA 2003, *A splendor of letters: The permanence of books in an impermanent world*, HarperCollins, New York.

Battle, M 2004, *Library: An unquiet history*, Vintage, London.

Biskup, P with Goodman, D 1994, *Libraries in Australia*, Centre for Information Studies, Wagga Wagga, NSW.

Biskup, P & Rochester, M (eds) 1985, *Australian library history. Papers from the second Australian Library History Forum*, Canberra, 19-20 July 1985, Canberra College of Advanced Education, Canberra, ACT.

Boadle, D 2006, 'Using history: Historical research and publication by Australian librarians and archivists', in *Research Applications in Information and Library Studies Seminar (RAILS 2): Proceedings of the 2nd Research Applications in Information and Library Studies Seminar*, National Library of Australia, Canberra, 16-17 September 2005, A Lloyd & B Pymm (eds), Centre for Information Studies, Wagga Wagga, NSW, pp.69-79.

Bobinski, GS 1969, *Carnegie libraries: Their history and impact on American public library development*, American Library Association, Chicago, IL.

Bremer, A & Lyons, M 2001, 'Mechanics' Institute libraries: The readers demand fiction', in *A history of the book in Australia 1891-1945: A national culture in a colonised market*, M Lyons & J Arnold (eds), University of Queensland Press, St Lucia, Qld, pp.209-225.

Bryan, H 1994, *No gray profession: Reminiscences of a career in Australian libraries*, Auslib Press, Adelaide, SA.

Burn, M & Palmer (eds), C 1982, *Innovation no stranger: essays in Australian librarianship in honour of Ira Raymond*, Investigator Press for the Barr Smith Library, Adelaide, SA.

Carroll, M & Harvey, R 2006, 'A hybrid form: Undergraduate qualifications for librarianship in Australia', in *Education for library and information services: A festschrift to celebrate thirty years of library education at Charles Sturt University*, P Hider & R Pymm (eds), Centre for Information Studies, Wagga Wagga, NSW.

Casson, L 2001, *Libraries in the ancient world*, Yale University Press, New Haven, CT.

Chartier, R 1994, *The order of books: Readers, authors, and libraries in Europe between the fourteenth and eighteenth centuries*, Polity Press, Cambridge, UK.

Chartier, R 2005, 'Death or transfiguration of the reader', in *Migrations in society, culture, and the library: WESS European Conference*, Paris, France, March 22, 2004, T Kilton & C Birkhead (eds), Association of College and Research Libraries, Chicago, IL, pp.3-13.

Clark, M 1975, 'Not even for the Lord's Prayer', in *Melbourne studies in education 1975*, S Murray-Smith (ed.), Melbourne University Press, Carlton, Vic., pp.1-13.

Colgan, W 1980, *The Governor's gift: The Auckland Public Library, 1880-1980*, Richards and Auckland City Council, Auckland.

Cunningham, KS 1961, *The Australian Council for Educational Research and library services in Australia,* ACER, Melbourne, Vic.

Fischer, SR 2003, *A history of writing*, Reaktion, London.

Holgate, CW 1886, *Account of the chief libraries of Australia and Tasmania,* Whittingham, London.

Horton, AR (chairman) 1976, *Public libraries in Australia*: *Report of the Committee of Inquiry into Public Libraries,* Government Printer, Canberra, ACT.

Irwin, R 1958, Does library history matter?, *Library Review,* no.128, pp.510-513.

Jones, DJ 1993, 'William Herbert Ifould and the development of library services in New South Wales, 1912–1942', PhD thesis, University of New South Wales, Sydney, NSW.

Jones, DJ 2001, 'Public libraries: Institutions of the highest educational value', in *A history of the book in Australia 1891-1945: A national culture in a colonised market*, M Lyons & J Arnold (eds), University of Queensland Press, St Lucia, Qld, pp.157-175.

Jones, T 1997, *Carnegie libraries across America: A public legacy*, Wiley, New York.

Knuth, R 2003, *Libricide: The regime-sponsored destruction of books and libraries in the twentieth century,* Praeger, Westport, CT.

Levett, J 1993, 'Introduction', in *Libraries and life in a changing world: The Metcalfe years, 1920-1970. Papers from the fifth Australian Library History Forum*, University of New South Wales, 6-7 November 1992, WB Rayward (ed.), University of NSW, School of Information, Library and Archive Studies, Sydney, NSW, pp.1-3.

Lodewycks, KA 1982, *The funding of wisdom: Revelations of a library's quarter century,* Spectrum, Melbourne, Vic.

McColvin, LR 1947, *Public libraries in Australia: Present conditions and future possibilities,* Melbourne University Press for the Australian Council for Educational Research, Melbourne, Vic.

McKenna, M 1997, *Different perspectives on black armband history*, Australian Parliamentary Library Research Paper 5 1997–98, http://www.aph.gov.au/ LIBRARY/Pubs/rp/1997-98/98rp05.htm

McMullin, BJ (ed.) 1996, *Instruction and amusement. Papers from the sixth Australian Library History Forum*, Monash University, 1 November 1995, Ancora Press, Melbourne, Vic.

McMullin, BJ (ed.) 1997, *Coming together. Papers from the seventh Australian Library History Forum*, Royal Melbourne Institute of Technology, 12 October 1996, Ancora Press, Melbourne, Vic.

Morrison, E & Talbot, M (eds) 1985, *Books, libraries & readers in colonial Australia. Papers from Australian Colonial Library History Forum*, Monash University, 1-2 June 1984, Monash University Graduate School of Librarianship, Clayton, Vic.

Munn, R & Pitt, ER 1935, *Australian libraries: A survey of conditions and suggestions for their improvement,* Australian Council for Educational Research, Melbourne, Vic; reprinted 1967, Libraries Board of South Australia, Adelaide, SA.

Ollé, J 1967, *Library history: An examination guidebook,* Cheshire, Melbourne, Vic.

Preer, J 2006, 'Louder please: How library history can help us claim our future', in *Research Applications in Information and Library Studies Seminar (RAILS 2): Proceedings of the 2nd Research Applications in Information and Library Studies Seminar*, National Library of Australia, Canberra, 16-17 September 2005, A Lloyd & B Pymm (eds), Centre for Information Studies, Wagga Wagga, NSW, pp.77-83.

Radford, NA 1984, *The Carnegie Corporation and the development of American college libraries, 1928–1941,* American Library Association, Chicago, IL.

Raven, J (ed.) 2004, *Lost libraries: The destruction of great book collections since antiquity,* Palgrave Macmillan, London.

Rayward, WB 1988a, 'Preface', in *Australian library history in context. Papers from the third Australian Library History Forum*, University of New South Wales, 17–18 July 1987, WB Rayward (ed.), University of NSW, School of Librarianship, Sydney, NSW.

Rayward, WB (ed.) 1988b, *Australian library history in context. Papers from the third Australian Library History Forum*, University of New South Wales, 17–18 July 1987, University of NSW, School of Librarianship, Sydney, NSW.

Rayward, WB (ed.) 1993, *Libraries and life in a changing world: The Metcalfe years, 1920-1970. Papers from the fifth Australian Library History Forum*, University of New South Wales, 6-7 November 1992, University of NSW, School of Information, Library and Archive Studies, Sydney, NSW.

Rochester, MK 1990, *The revolution in New Zealand librarianship: American influence as facilitated by the Carnegie Corporation of New York in the 1930s*, Vine Press, London.

Seaman, D 2005, 'The migrated library: Distributed, malleable, enmeshed, immediate', in *Migrations in society, culture, and the library: WESS European Conference*, Paris, France, 22 March 2004, T Kilton & C Birkhead (eds), Association of College and Research Libraries, Chicago, IL, pp.55-64.

Talbot, M 1985, 'The Library Association of Australasia, 1896–1902', PhD thesis, Monash University, Melbourne, Vic.

Tauber, MF 1962, *Resources of Australian libraries*, Australian Advisory Council on Bibliographical Services (AACOBS), Canberra, ACT.

Thompson, P 2006, '"Does it matter if the users are actually dead?": A database to reconnect with the borrowers and collection of a hundred year old library', *VALA 2006: Connecting with Users: 13th Biennial Conference and Exhibition*, 8-10 February 2006, Melbourne, http://www.valaconf.org/vala2006/papers2006/38_Thompson_Final.pdf

Upward, F & Whyte, JP (eds) 1991, *Peopling a profession. Papers from the fourth Australian Library History Forum*, Monash University, 25–26 September 1989, Ancora Press, Melbourne, Vic.

Weigand, W 1999, 'Tunnel vision and blind spots: What the past tells us about the present: reflections on the twentieth-century history of American librarianship', *Library Quarterly*, vol.69 no.1, pp.1-32.

Whyte, JP & Radford, NA (eds) 1988, *An enthusiasm for libraries: Essays in honour of Harrison Bryan*, Ancora Press, Melbourne, Vic.

CHAPTER 15
The social, political and cultural context of libraries in the twenty-first century: an overview

Jake Wallis

What is the role of libraries in the networked society, in the knowledge economy and within the culture of the virtual? Previous chapters have provided valuable discussion of the continuing relevance of libraries to society. How can we conceptualise the cultural environment within which libraries operate? Libraries have always been situated within a broad social and political context. The latter half of the twentieth century was a period of intense social change, with the pace seemingly increasing as we hurtled towards the end of the century – although Ross Harvey's study in the previous chapter suggests that this may have been a short-sightedly subjective perspective. What is the impact of this period of change on the role of the library within society in the twenty-first century? What factors are significant in re-envisaging the place of the library in an evolving social and political context? This chapter will address these questions. The discussion will draw upon a number of themes including the role of knowledge, learning and technology in society; changes in lifestyle, in work and entertainment; competition; and service culture.

In the late nineteenth century the steel tycoon Andrew Carnegie began investing the fortune he had amassed over a lifetime of commerce. He was no longer investing in the railroads or the steel industry, rather he poured his wealth into the construction of public libraries throughout his adopted home, the United States of America, the country from which his riches had grown, as well as across Scotland, the homeland he had left in debt as a boy. The Carnegie libraries are a significant legacy in the history and tradition of the public library. Carnegie was a man formed by his own working-class background in Scotland and the new life, the land of opportunity, that he had found in America. He recognised the value of opportunity, of betterment. He knew from his own experience that people want – and need – the chance to develop, strive and achieve. Carnegie saw the wealth (in every sense) that education could provide. In an age of low levels of literacy, a time when the cost of books and of education was prohibitive for many of the population in both the old world and the new, Carnegie aimed to make them available to working-class people, to people like the man he himself had once been.

Carnegie lived at a time when education was part of an elite culture, available to only those whose families could afford to have them at study rather than at work. The world has changed significantly since Carnegie's lifetime. Education and knowledge are widely recognised as powerful factors in enabling social mobility and economic success. Access to education as a fundamental human right is enshrined in Article 26 of the *Universal declaration of human rights* (United Nations 1948).

From post-industrial to knowledge societies

Research into the changing nature of the US economy in the postwar period identified an increase in knowledge work – those occupations which deal explicitly with the production, processing or manipulation of information (Machlup 1962). This shift in the economic activity of many advanced nations has been described as 'the coming of post-industrial society' (Bell 1973). Bell's assertion was that this change was a significant transformation in the nature of society, that the raw driving force of the post-industrial society was no longer energy, as it had been during the industrial period, but information.

The work of researchers such as Machlup and Bell has provided the foundations for the theory of the Information Society; the idea that we have moved into a new form of social organisation which is based around the production, processing and manipulation of information as central activities. The proliferation and ubiquity of networked information and communication technologies are significant factors in conceptualising the Information Society. Manuel Castells, a prominent proponent of the theory, prefers the term 'the network society' (Castells 1996). While there is significant debate in academic circles as to the validity of various conceptualisations of the Information Society (Webster 1995; Robins and Webster 1999), the notion that information, knowledge and the tools to enable their possession, manipulation and communication are of heightened significance has permeated modern thought and policy. For anyone living and working in one of the modern world's advanced nations it would be hard to deny the significance of information and technology in one's daily life, although their ubiquity may conceal their very presence and impact.

The terminology has changed over the past three decades; from post-industrial or information society to networked or knowledge society, with similar descriptions of the economy – knowledge, new and even the weightless economy. What are the features of this networked, information intensive society? With her conception of the 'informated organisation' Soshana Zuboff describes the impact of this social and economic environment on business corporations, yet her comments might be applied across all organisations:

> The informated organisation is a learning institution, and one of its principal purposes is the expansion of knowledge – not knowledge for its own sake (as in academic pursuit), but knowledge that comes to reside at the core of what it means to be productive. [...]
> To put it simply, learning is the new form of labor (1988, p.395).

In the post-industrial society that Bell and others describe, education, skills and professional accreditation are important determinants of social success. Castells emphasises changes in our perceptions of time and space, the globalising of our outlook that is encouraged by the speed at which flows of information collapse geographical distance. John Urry (2000) tries to encapsulate this complex global flow by talking about 'mobilities' – of people, commercial products, information, images and technologies. What is common to these accounts is the idea of change that is rapid, constant and intense.

Cultural diversity in a networked world

The opportunities and threats of this globally interconnected world have been recognised at both international and national levels. Current disparities in wealth, well-being and opportunity may be reinforced by a digital divide between those with access to information technologies, global communications networks and the skills to utilise and capitalise upon their capacities, and those without any of these advantages. This inequality at an international level may be reproduced within global regions or within nations themselves. One of the United Nations Educational, Scientific Cultural Organization's (UNESCO) major fields of action is its communication and information programme. The specific aims of the programme are to:

- Promote the free flow of ideas and universal access to information.

- Promote the expression of pluralism and cultural diversity in the media and world information networks.

- Promote access for all to information and communication technologies (UNESCO 2006).

In this mission, UNESCO is striving to preserve the relevance of fundamental principles on access to information and freedom of expression, within the evolving context of globalisation and the development of the networked society, such as Article 19 of the *Universal declaration of human rights*: 'Everyone has the right to freedom of opinion and expression; this right includes freedom to hold opinions without interference and to seek, receive and impart information and ideas through any media and regardless of frontiers' (United Nations 1948).

UNESCO uses the term 'knowledge societies' to describe the technologically enabled yet culturally diverse communities that its programs aspire to develop (UNESCO 2005). The emphasis is primarily on encouraging the free flow of ideas and cultural expression within global information networks. This will, of course, be dependent upon infrastructure development (telecommunications networks, diffusion of technologies within societies). Through another of its subsidiary organisations, the International Telecommunication Union (ITU), the United Nations is attempting to encourage and stimulate the development of global connectivity by bringing together stakeholders from government, industry, international and civil society organisations (ITU 2006).

Australia as an information economy

Advanced nations are, by definition, ahead of the rest in terms of infrastructure development. Nevertheless, the social impacts of technology and global communications networks remain significant. The Australian government has recognised that the cycle of change will be an ongoing challenge for long-term economic and social development, and has identified what it sees as the shared features of successful information societies:

- A growing dependence on sharing knowledge and information between individuals, communities and organisations to coordinate economic and social relationships.

- The institutionalisation of continuous innovation, productivity improvement, and education and skills formation.

- An openness to the global economy through trade, investment and exchanges of information, knowledge and skills (Department of Communications, Information Technology and the Arts 2004).

The emphasis is on knowledge, education and global interconnection. It is the effective use of knowledge that is a key feature of the Australian government's strategy; as a foundation for effective social interactions and for innovation and productivity. In its policy statement, *Australia's strategic framework for the information economy 2004-2006*, the Department of Communications, Information Technology and the Arts (DCITA) describes four objectives for Australia as an information economy:

- To promote social cohesion by ensuring that particular sectors, groups of Australians and regions are not left behind.

- To secure Australia's information economy against external and internal threats and to promote Australia's interests in the emerging global information economy.

- To remove barriers to information economy development.

- To make government an exemplar in the use of ICT to improve citizen engagement, efficiency and effectiveness of service delivery.

The government as champion and exemplar in the delivery of online services is explicitly stated and represents an evolution in its role, from accountable authority to transparent service provider. The policy of modernising government or, more specifically, modernising the way that citizens interact or transact with their government is, similarly, a key plank in the United Kingdom government's strategy for the use of information and communication technologies (UK Government Cabinet Office 2004; Wallis 2005a). Efficiently administered government is vital for aspiring knowledge economies, where governance must support and encourage both information flow and innovation.

The citizen of the information society

What of the citizen? What demands does the evolution of the knowledge economy place on us as individuals? As with governments, citizens must adapt themselves into effective participants in this process of ongoing transformation. The proportion of our social interactions that take place online will continue to grow as we use networked technologies to undertake a range of daily activities – to learn and work, communicate with others, interact with government, shop and entertain ourselves.

Marginalisation within the information society may result not simply from a digital divide but from a divide between those with the range of literacies required in digital environments to navigate through encounters (communications, transactions, information seeking, informal and formal education) and those without the literacies (Bundy 2004; Martin 2005). The key skills for successful interaction within networked societies will be generic abilities; lifelong learning and information literacy (as Stuart Ferguson and Anne Lloyd suggest in Chapter 13). The importance of lifelong learning in producing the highly skilled workforce required by the knowledge economy, as well as in alleviating social exclusion, is stressed by the Australian government (Department of Education, Science and Training 2003).

The Australian Library and Information Association (ALIA) sees the development of information literacy among the population as vital not just for the economy but for democracy itself. ALIA views information literacy as crucial in that it overarches a number of social, economic and democratic goals:

- Participative citizenship.
- Social inclusion.
- The acquisition of skills.
- Innovation and enterprise.
- The creation of new knowledge.
- Personal, vocational, corporate and organisational empowerment.
- Learning for life (ALIA 2003).

These global and national environmental trends signify an emphasis on access to education for all, based on both democratic and economic imperatives. Learning is presented as the primary driver in the development of social capital. Andrew Carnegie's view of the significance of education for all members of society is today a key strand of government policy in those developed nations which aspire to compete in a global knowledge economy.

Libraries in every sector are crucial to such aspirations. The emphasis on the creative use of knowledge, a continuous cycle of innovation, career flexibility, upskilling, retraining and lifelong learning – all features of social policy in the information society – necessitates access to information resources of quality for work, education and leisure. In Australia, this policy is clearly iterated; 'participation in learning should be universal' (Department of Education, Science and Training 2003). Libraries play an integral and essential part in learning at all levels, as many of the preceding chapters have demonstrated. The universality of this process reinforces the importance of the role that libraries play in ensuring that their clients and communities have access to the resources that they require in order to participate in the information society.

Knowledge and the culture of global information

People's understanding of knowledge has changed significantly, however, since Carnegie's time, and libraries are changing in the way that they deliver their services to reflect this. As the world has become ever more interdependent and interconnected, libraries have evolved from repositories of knowledge (that is, the explicit knowledge discussed in Chapter 13) into gateways to a vast range of networked resources. From a public library in Australia, a client may access a local history collection or explore the treasures of the Smithsonian Institution in Washington DC, USA.

Modern tastes and sensibilities blur the boundaries between elite and popular knowledge and culture. The public library may stock Shakespeare and Grand Theft Auto. The growth of flexible, student-centred, often electronically mediated, learning raises questions as to what constitutes a learning experience. A traditionally homogenous view of culture is less appropriate to an interconnected world of satellite television, global travel and migration, websites and networked communications, the mobilities that Urry (2000) describes. Modern societies are awash with diverse cultural values, difference and plurality. One need simply turn on the television to glimpse the global flow of cultural values as it washes by. The predominance of American cultural content on television networks is readily apparent. The imbalance in transborder data flows (the movement of informational content across national boundaries), from developed to the developing countries, has long been an issue of debate at international level (Brown-Syed 1999).

The role that UNESCO plays in encouraging cultural and linguistic diversity in the digital information environment has already been noted. UNESCO's aim in this context is to facilitate the development of culturally diverse information societies where local knowledge, culture and traditions take their place within global communications networks in order that they may be strong enough to withstand a flood of non-indigenous cultural and linguistic content and values. Standardised global consumer brands and services – the operations of which use international networks of people and technology – represent a 'McWorld' (Barber's term (1996), quoted in Urry 2000), a unified global culture and economy. UNESCO's projects are a response to the threat that this process of globalisation poses to existing indigenous forms of culture and social organisation. Popular grassroots responses come from within the developed world in the form of anti-globalisation protests which have been vocal and at times violent, at international meetings of the World Trade Organisation and the G8 group of governments (Canada, France, Germany, Japan, Italy, Russian Federation, United Kingdom, USA). Similar protest and dissent is reflected in the developing world in the activities of indigenous movements on local issues.

The intersection between the local and the global is underlined by such conflicts. A prominent example of this can be seen in the activities of the Zapatista movement. A political and paramilitary organisation located in the Chiapas region of Mexico, the Zapatista Army of National Liberation (to give the group its official title) draws its support from the indigenous population of the region, and campaigns against the Mexican government on issues of local sovereignty. Through its subversive (and ironic) appropriation of the internet as a medium of communication, the Zapatista movement has been able to bypass the traditional media to communicate with wider Mexico and the world at large. The movement has used this communications strategy, and the words of its eloquent and enigmatic leader Subcomandante Marcos, to highlight the local impact of globalisation in developing countries while linking into an international network of anti-globalisation protest.

The postmodern information environment

The range of information channels currently available to individual citizens in advanced societies is diverse (books, newspapers and other publications, satellite and digital broadcasting, the web, mobile phone, text message, e-mail), and almost so numerous and constantly engaging as to threaten our capacity to process the information that we receive. Information comes in disaggregated chunks, decontextualised, appropriated and commodified. An increasingly visual culture (of brands and logos, websites, advertisements and video clips) presents a constant array of images, the meaning of which, without depth and context, is consumed without time to process or reflect, thus becoming fleeting, artificial and insubstantial.

What is the impact of this culture of the visual, which is of fleeting informational significance, on debate and understanding within democratic society? Here it is worth drawing on the concept of a public sphere, an idea closely associated with the German social theorist Jürgen Habermas. The public sphere is an arena within civil society within which lies the essence of democracy; discussion, debate, the formation of opinion and consensus (Habermas 1974). The globalisation and commodification of information and communication, the superficiality of a visual culture, the power of the market, the decline of public service culture and the growth of consumerism – all these factors may be seen as threats to the quality of the information that informs the public sphere and, in turn, to the democratic process itself. As Urry puts it:

> Debate is concerned as much with image, meaning and emotion, as it is with written texts, cognition and science. The global economy of signs, of globally circulating information and images, is transforming the public sphere into an increasingly denationalized, visual and emotional public stage (2000, p.201).

A global public sphere and collective intelligence

An alternative perspective might be to suggest that this trend constitutes a broadening of the frame of debate and the growth of a global public sphere, in which individuals are free to select the individual information sources that they believe define, shape and reflect their own experience. It has been suggested already that the global networking of communications technology facilitates this individual selection of information channel, be it an online newspaper, celebrity gossip website or the latest communiqué from the leader of an obscure indigenous rebel group in Mexico.

Alternative social and protest movements are able to use the global connectivity of the internet to promote their interests and link with similar groups worldwide. This connectivity is comparatively cheap and allows these groups to compete for attention with more established interests within society (such as governments or corporations) whose communications hierarchies may not be as responsive to interaction with the prevailing social mood. Pippa Norris (2001) notes the potential of this connectivity for protest groups (such as environmentalists, human rights, anti-war or anti-globalisation movements) in challenging authority, and encouraging pluralism and engagement within civic society. Yet this potential is also available to groups whose interests do not align with the values of pluralism and democracy such as the far right, extreme nationalist organisations, fundamentalist religious groups and terrorist organisations. Non-democratic groups can use the medium to great effect using visual imagery and multimedia to deliver powerful emotional impact (Wallis 2005b). In Iraq, for instance, insurgent groups have distributed video in digital format of hostages being beheaded.

Established cultural authority is diluted as the information environment broadens and fragments. Trust in collective intelligence, branding and ease of access become preferred criteria in the selection of information channels, surpassing traditional notions of what constitutes objective and authoritative sources (Morville 2005). One need only think of developments in the online environment as illustrations; take, for example, the growing usage of the collaboratively created online encyclopedia Wikipedia (http://en.wikipedia.org/wiki/Main_Page); end-user and community tagging of self-published digital content, for instance, photographs on sites such as flickr (http://www.flickr.com/) and collections of favourite links on de.licio.us (http://del.icio.us/); or the range of alternative media sources such as the international Independent Media Centre network (http://www.indymedia.org/).

The library as postmodern institution

Libraries operate within this postmodern cultural context and, like many institutions, must evolve to retain their relevance. The American media commentator and academic Herbert Schiller (1996) describes the overarching and fundamental impact on society of the changing environment in which information is produced, disseminated and consumed: 'The spectacularly improved means of producing, organising and disseminating information has transformed industrial, political and cultural practices and processes' (Schiller 1996, p.46). Yet many facets of the social and cultural context in which libraries sit, themselves underline the continuing importance of the role of the library for society at large. Given the growing fragmentation of the media and information environment, it may be all the more important for civil society to have institutions that stand for learning about that which is unknown to us from our own experience, about accepting difference as enriching, about plurality and cultural diversity. Libraries serve this function and in this sense provide for society overarching, unifying values of tolerance, of the acceptance of alternative points of view and of the willingness to engage with differences of perspective.

Libraries are evolving from warehouses of books into publishers and disseminators of digital information. They play a role in the preservation and promotion of cultural heritage through an increasing number of initiatives to digitise significant local collections. Preservation activity is evolving to respond to the challenge presented by the 'born digital' resources which now form a significant component of our cultural heritage. The National Library of Australia has been archiving Australian digital content from the web since 1996 through the Pandora project. (Chapter 5 provides a detailed description of the national strategy to collaboratively collect and preserve Australia's digital heritage.) Through its Community Heritage Grants Scheme, the National Library is taking steps to preserve and provide access to local heritage collections of national significance.

The empowerment of direct access to online information has stimulated a process of disintermediation across a number of industries. Travel is a notable example. (See also the discussion of disintermediation in Chapters 6 and 10.) Direct access to information can be sought using networked technologies, and arrangements and transactions can be carried out online. Mediating agents can effectively be bypassed. This process still requires access points to the information environment, and advice on the use of technology to connect to, navigate through and make effective use of the digital information available. The competition that libraries face with book and coffee shops, video rental stores and home entertainment has intensified (as discussed by Chris Jones in Chapter 1), yet Carnegie's vision and legacy of the library as an empowering force within the community remains relevant.

As people spend ever greater amounts of their time in virtual environments, the library as place, as community space, takes on renewed significance. Castells (2004) notes the major challenge faced by the Information Society in fostering social inclusion and shared cultural values: 'A society of individualism is a society which is extraordinarily dynamic, but at the same time a society of potential isolation in terms of the cultural meaning that could be shared by society' (Castells 2004, p.163). Public libraries can combat urban alienation and technological isolation by standing as space (both physical and virtual) in which all are welcome to enter, where one can become part of a community.

In more tangible terms, the networking of the public library system and the provision of community access – not just to computers and networks, but also to the skills with which to make effective and creative use of communications technology and digital information – are essential components of policies to combat the digital divide, facilitate lifelong learning and, ultimately, encourage social inclusion. Libraries across all sectors are valuable in purely economic terms because of their skills in managing the raw material of the knowledge economy, information. They are environments in which creativity, learning and the expression of ideas are stimulated. The public library in the networked society will be multifaceted, driving economic growth through the facilitation of learning while fulfilling essential social policy functions. Generating social capital through inclusion, access and sense of community, public libraries also embody the cultural values of openness and diversity necessary for civil society.

References

Australian Library and Information Association (ALIA) 2003, *Statement on information literacy for all Australians*, http://www.alia.org.au/policies/information.literacy.html

Bell, D 1973, *The coming of post-industrial society*, Penguin, Harmondsworth, UK.

Brown-Syed, C 1999, 'The new world order and the geopolitics of information', web edn, http://valinor.ca/csyed_libres3.html; originally published in *LIBRES: Library and Information Science Research*, January 1993.

Bundy, A 2004, 'One essential direction: Information literacy, information technology fluency', *Journal of eLiteracy* vol.1, no.1 http://www.jelit.org/6/

Castells, M 1996, *The rise of the network society*, Blackwell, Oxford, UK.

Castells, M 2004, 'The information city, the new economy, and the network society' in *The information society reader*, F Webster (ed.), Routledge, London, pp.150-164.

Department of Communications, Information Technology and the Arts (DCITA) 2004, *Australia's strategic framework for the information economy 2004-2006*, http://www.dcita.gov.au/ie/publications/2004

Department of Education Science and Training (DEST) 2003 *Lifelong learning in Australia*, http://www.dest.gov.au/sectors/higher_education/publications_resources/other_publications/lifelong_learning_in_australia.htm

Habermas, J 1974, 'The public sphere', *New German Critique*, no.3, Autumn, pp.49-55, http://www.jstor.org/journals/0094033X.html

International Telecommunications Union (ITU) 2006, http://www.itu.int/home/index.html

Machlup, F 1962, *The production and distribution of knowledge in the United States*, Princeton University Press, Princeton, NJ.

Martin, A 2005 'DigEuLit – a European framework for digital literacy: A progress report', *Journal of eLiteracy,* vol.2, no.2, http://www.jelit.org/65/

Morville, P 2005, *Authority*, http://semanticstudios.com/publications/semantics/000057.php

Norris, P 2001, *Digital divide: Civic engagement, information poverty, and the internet worldwide*, Cambridge University Press, New York.

Robins, K & Webster, F 1999, *Times of technoculture*, Routledge, London.

Schiller, H 1996, *Information inequality*, Routledge, New York.

UK Government Cabinet Office 2004, *Autumn performance report 2004,* http://www.cabinetoffice. gov.uk/publications/reports/psa/autumn_delivery/apr2004.pdf

United Nations 1948, *Universal declaration of human rights*, http://www.un.org/Overview/rights.html

United Nations Educational, Scientific Cultural Organisation (UNESCO) 2005, *Towards knowledge societies*, UNESCO Publishing, Paris.

United Nations Educational, Scientific Cultural Organisation (UNESCO) 2006, *Communication and information sector*, http://portal.unesco.org/ci/en/ev.php-URL_ID=1657&URL_DO=DO_TOPIC&URL_SECTION=201.html

Urry, J 2000, 'Mobile sociology', *British Journal of Sociology*, vol.51, no.1, pp.185-203.

Wallis, J 2005a, 'The web, accessibility and inclusion: Networked democracy in the United Kingdom', *Library Review*, vol.54, no. 8.

Wallis, J 2005b, 'Cyberspace, information literacy and the information society', *Library Review*, vol.54, no.4.

Webster, F 1995, *Theories of the information society*, Routledge, London.

Zuboff, S 1988, *In the age of smart machines*, Basic Books, New York.

CHAPTER 16
Ethics and law for information practice

Jan Houghton and Jennifer Berryman

The foundation of ethical practice in librarianship has been a commitment to a set of values based on the right of every individual to access information and to enjoy intellectual freedom and freedom of expression. This commitment has long been reflected in the statements of national professional associations, including the Australian Library and Information Association (ALIA) and international bodies such as the International Federation of Library and Information Associations (IFLA). Over the long history of librarianship, it has never been easy to maintain these values in the face of political and cultural pressures that have sought primarily to control access to information and limit individual freedoms, albeit in the name of the greater public good. In the literature of librarianship, much has been written about the role of ethics and the conflict of professional and legal obligations, but increasingly practitioners today, in both librarianship and other newer and emerging fields of information work, are finding there are new challenges in practice.

In Australia, as in many countries, these ethical challenges are coming on a number of fronts; political and legal, technological, economic and social, as well as from within the different areas of library and information work. There is a wave of new legislative responses to developments in technology, concerns over national security and a range of other factors arising from political and social change. Democratic governments everywhere are seeking greater control over access to information and a greater right to know who is seeking and using information and for what purpose. There have always been ethical challenges from developments in the technology for accessing and controlling access to information and in the twenty-first century the internet is the focus. It was recognised very early in the development of the internet that new rules, global rules, would be needed for cyberspace where the old (geographic) boundaries no longer existed (Johnston & Post 1996).

Global challenges to traditional values are coming from other directions too, particularly in relation to global equality in information access. This is known as the global digital divide, although what this means and how it is measured is subject to much debate (see, for example, Selwyn 2004, Warschauer 2002). We do know that the development of information and communications infrastructure has been very uneven around the world and that governments have made different decisions about access priorities. The World Summit on the Information Society (WSIS), held between 2003 and 2005, demonstrated the importance of global issues being addressed by those in practice as well as by governments and big business. Professionals need to be both aware of these issues and willing to make a contribution to the directions taken – professional objectivity versus social activism is a key ethical issue.

Challenges are also coming from the changing nature of library and information work itself and an increasingly diversified field of practice. Practitioners are now dealing with a broad range of organisational contexts from traditional libraries to businesses large and small, from government agencies to not-for-profit organisations, and they are using a range of technologies and information systems to manage and provide information products and services. This complexity is giving rise to conflicts of professional ethics not only in complying with legal requirements but with business concerns such as the need to protect corporate and proprietary information. The compatibility of business ethics with information ethics is another area of ethical concern. Practitioners in these different areas often appear to have different values or at least different priorities. They may have been educated in other disciplines and trained within other professions that have their own ethical traditions. There are cultural differences also among practitioners in different countries, where social and political pressures vary. In Australia there are particular ethical issues related to access and use of indigenous knowledge. Within the library and information professions, some practitioners are beginning to question the usefulness and appropriateness of the core values and asking whether they continue to be relevant in these times of increasing insecurity and rapid social and technological change. Others are choosing to become more proactive in order to prevent what they see as the erosion of these values.

In this chapter, the nature of ethical practice in library and information work in Australia today is examined against these various challenges, with a focus on the growing list of laws and regulations seeking to control access to information and in the process threatening to undermine core professional values. There is an outline of current Australian law, both federal and state, in a range of areas relevant to library and information work, including intellectual property, privacy, censorship, freedom of information and national security. The term 'information ethics' is used to refer to the study of ethics and values in library and information work and how these intersect with the prevailing social, legal and political climate. Key questions to be explored include: Do ethics matter? Are the traditional values still relevant? How do practitioners reconcile ethical conflicts? Is it possible to be both ethical and legal?

Ethics and ethical practice

There are different theoretical approaches to the study of ethics, although a detailed exploration of these is beyond the scope of this chapter. There are useful introductions in basic philosophy texts or in online resources such as the *Internet encyclopedia of philosophy* (http://www.iep. utm.edu/) or the *Stanford encyclopedia of philosophy* (http://plato.stanford.edu/). Weckert and Adeney (1997) provide an overview of the main ethical theories and the philosophical ideas from which they derive. In brief, there are three main levels of ethical thinking: meta-ethics, which is concerned with how ethics are developed and how we make moral judgements; normative ethics, which is concerned with stances that might be taken on what is right and wrong; and applied ethics, which is concerned with the ethical positions that might be taken on specific issues such as censorship (this is sometimes called micro-ethics). The focus in this chapter will be on the understanding of ethics at the third level, that is, the ethical positions that practitioners might take on the range of issues that arise in practice and how these judgements are influenced by normative ethics, that is, the norms or ethical standards set by the profession. The terms ethics, morals and values tend to be used interchangeably although they do have distinct meanings. In the literature of information ethics it is most common for values to be seen as a subset of morals while ethics represents how these values are applied – to put it simply, 'ethics are about the way we behave and the values we hold' (Iacovino 2002, p.57). Understanding that behaviour and the values on which it is based is the key to understanding ethical practice in any profession.

Livia Iacovino (2002, p.63) defines professional ethics as 'ethics which concern professional behaviour, judgement and choices'; the choices are about moral questions. Should we do something that is morally right even if we know the consequences might be harmful or, alternatively, should we do something apparently wrong if the consequences may be desirable? (McGarry 1993, p.168). The notion of making choices, of exercising judgement based on the values of the profession, is an important characteristic distinguishing professional practice from other forms of work (see for example Bayles 1989, Freidson 1983, Froehlich 1997, McDonald 1995) but there is always the potential for conflict with organisational or business values and legal obligations. Also, because we come with our own set of personal values developed from our social and cultural environment, there is another area of potential conflict for the individual. At the meta-ethical level, Iacovino argues that our professional behaviour depends on whether we see ethics as rules or norms imposed by the professional community or as a 'system of personal choice of conduct' or both (2002, p.59). This becomes an important distinction for us if the professional community tries to enforce its norms, for example, through peer pressure or written codes of ethical behaviour. The use of codes to articulate values and guide behaviour has been a characteristic of the library and information professions but a contentious one as will be seen a little later in this chapter.

The relationship between law and ethics is one often referred to in the literature of information ethics. Iacovino argues that law cannot substitute for ethics in relation to human behaviour, rather it is complementary. She distinguishes between ethical obligations and legal obligations. Individual privacy, for example, is legally protected but it is also a professional ethic that should be adhered to without need of legal sanction. She argues that the relationship is one based on 'mutual trust and respect rather than through legal pressures or sanctions' and that 'concepts of trust are central to professionalism' (Iacovino 2002, p.63). Others have also argued that it is not enough for professionals to act legally. While the law might provide a structure for ethical decision making, its rules are based on authority rather than morality; that is, the law does not necessarily tell us what is good or bad, only what is legal or not based on prevailing social or economic need norms (Buchanan 2004, p.5). In other words, we also need an ethical framework and, for practitioners, this is something that can be provided by their profession. Iacovino (2002, p.59) points out that unethical behaviour can lead to illegal behaviour; for example, the failure of duty of care has the potential to lead to a company facing an action for negligence. There is another side to this in that practitioners must respect and conform to the law regardless of personal or professional ethics and this can sometimes lead to ethical dilemmas in practice. This has been seen in relation to censorship particularly, and more recently the legal requirements of national security legislation. This will be discussed later in the chapter.

Robert Hauptman also sees ethics as primarily about choice. He describes much of the discussion about ethics in the library and information field as 'pedantic quibbling' and 'esoteric complexifying' and argues that understanding ethics comes down to understanding that ethical behaviour is about two possibilities; either 'one holds that something is good or evil and acts upon this belief or one considers the potential results of one's actions and acts accordingly' (2002, p.6). In other words, all the theorising is merely commentary and it is what we do or choose not to do that matters. He argues, for example, that we either support core values such as intellectual freedom and provide access or we don't and apply censorship – there is no middle ground. Hauptman's book, *Ethics and librarianship*, is worth reading in more detail because his very black and white view of ethics in library and information work is provocative and a good starting point for thinking about the role of ethics in practice.

Do ethics matter? Capurro argues that information ethics is not a 'peripheral social discourse but a hot topic at the networked intersection of cultures and political regimes' (2000, p.2). Ethics are important, and addressing ethical issues is at the heart of professional practice. Certainly, the volume of literature on this topic generated by both practitioners and scholars suggests that there is a high level of awareness of and concern for ethical issues. However, Hauptman argues that ethics matters 'but apparently not very much to librarians' (2002, p.132) and that we treat values as 'theoretical constructs' only, discussing them in the literature but failing to respect them enough to implement them in practice (2002, p.133). There are other views on this of course, but if Hauptman is just a little bit right then there is a demonstrable gap between what is claimed for the profession and what is practised and therefore we have to be careful about trying to claim the moral high ground from politics and business.

History of information ethics

As already mentioned, there is a long history of writing about ethics and values in this field. Everard (2001) points out that ethical concerns about the impact of information technology on society were being voiced by Plato in about 410 BC. Plato raised questions about privacy, access, ownership, security, use and the right to know that we are still grappling with today. Moving on to the last decades of the twentieth century and continuing today, we find these questions being constantly discussed (see for example Mason et al. 1995, Montague Smith 1997, Severson 1997, Stichler & Hauptman 1998, Woodward 1990). Three key contributors in the field of information ethics have been Thomas Froehlich, Rafael Capurro and Robert Hauptman.

Froehlich reviewed the literature of theoreticians and practitioners and suggested a framework for the discussion of ethical issues. He concluded that, while theoreticians were concerned with broader issues of social responsibility, practitioners were more concerned with current ethical problems and conflicts in their particular field of practice, for example, privacy and confidentiality and with conflicts between professional and organisational demands (1992, p.316). In 1997, Froehlich conducted a major survey of ethical and legal issues in library and information services for UNESCO and identified the issues practitioners perceived to be of importance and concern (Froehlich 1997). Capurro, the director of the International Centre for Information Ethics (ICIE) sees information ethics as a broad multidisciplinary multicultural field developing from a Western tradition with a basis in Athenian democracy, from which comes the focus on freedom of expression and freedom of access (ICIE 2001). The ICIE website (http://icie.zkm.de) and its journal, the *International Review of Information Ethics*, are both useful resources. Writing about twenty-first century ethical challenges, Capurro (2000) argued that technology, and the web in particular, created both dangers and opportunities ahead for the 'core freedoms'.

Hauptman's focus is much more on applied ethics or the ethics of practice and what decisions or choices professionals make when faced with conflicts arising from the organisational context or from legal obligations. His two books (1988, 2002) are key readings. As suggested earlier, he takes a more critical view and is concerned that librarians are trained simply to provide information regardless of the consequences because when they do consider consequences, problems are raised that have to be dealt with; he calls this 'unthinking information provision' (2002, p.2). He concludes his more recent book with a discussion of why ethics matters and why professionals need to do more than pay lip service to values.

Professional values in library and information work

What is the set of values that underpins library and information work? There are various views on this in the literature. Michael Gorman (2000) analyses the concept of values and defines them in a way that equates values with beliefs. He describes values in librarianship as 'enduring' in that they have maintained their relevance over a long time and as concerning both the means and the ends, that is what we do and the outcomes of what we do. Gorman identified eight core values: stewardship, including preserving the human record; service to individuals, community and society; intellectual freedom; rationalism, by which he means good management of processes and programs; literacy and learning; equity of access to recorded knowledge and information; privacy, including confidentiality of library records of use; and democracy, that is, maintaining democratic values and ensuring an educated citizenry (2000, p.27). Koehler (2006) found a similar list of shared values when he examined key writings in the literature.

Gorman's list of core values, based in traditional librarianship, is often referred to by others, although their applicability in all information work environments, including libraries as they operate today, is sometimes questioned. Computing professionals, for example, or web designers working with information may well have different priorities in relation to information access and control from librarians, archivists or records managers (Iacovino 2002, p.66). However, as they also have many common interests in practice, these differences are usually manageable within the specific work context and, in any case, different priorities do not necessarily mean different values. An examination of the literature on business ethics shows considerable commonality with information ethics; for example, the idea that the corporate world has a responsibility not just to its stakeholders but to the broader society equates to the concern that information professionals have with raising standards of literacy in the community to ensure equity of access. Carroll (1991) describes this responsibility as embodying standards, norms or expectations that reflect a concern for what is fair, just or in keeping with the respect or protection of stakeholders' moral rights, where stakeholders include consumers, employees, shareholders and the community (1991, p.41). Pearlson and Saunders (2005) discuss the ethical treatment of information within business, particularly in relation to the management of information systems and the use of the internet; they found that the four aspects raising most ethical issues are privacy, accuracy, property (or ownership) and accessibility. There is no evidence to suggest that information professionals in a corporate environment are any better or worse than those in traditional library environments in recognising and addressing ethical concerns.

A survey of librarians from a number of countries asked what they considered to be the most important ethical values in their profession. It was found that where differences in values occur among library and information professionals they are usually a function of different roles and responsibilities (Dole et al. 2000). Archivists, for example, value preservation of the record very highly whereas law librarians are more concerned with copyright issues (2000, p.288). The researchers concluded that these differences did not necessarily reflect different values but different priorities. This study also found that some differences in values occurred among professionals from different countries, particularly along the digital divide, reflecting local political, economic and cultural concerns. Not unexpectedly, developing countries place greater emphasis on literacy and information literacy; Australia, New Zealand and the United States place preservation of the record fairly high on their list (2000, p.294). The three values rated highly by professionals in all types of work and in all countries were client service, equity of access and intellectual freedom (2000, p.294). This was a preliminary study and had some methodological limitations, as the authors acknowledge, but it provides a good indication that, while there are differences, the core values appear universal and enduring, to use Gorman's term. This finding is supported by a comparative analysis of codes of ethics from different countries which found the principle of intellectual freedom was emphasised strongly (Trushina 2004). Koehler (2006) has found considerable agreement about values among writers on ethics, studies of practitioners and codes of ethics of professional associations (see also Koehler & Pemberton 2000).

For IFLA, ethics has been a key issue and as an organisation it has been concerned to extend the ethical framework of professional library and information work to include wide social considerations and the fundamental human right to know (Byrne 2004a) In 1997, IFLA established the Committee on Free Access to Information and Freedom of Expression (FAIFE) to 'advocate and defend intellectual freedom' in library and information services and in so doing provided an 'ethical core' for the profession globally (Byrne 2004a). In 2002, IFLA published the *Glasgow declaration on libraries, information services and intellectual freedom*, reinforcing the commitment to intellectual freedom (IFLA 2002). ALIA has also moved to a broader understanding and promulgates a list of seven core values expressed not as single concepts but more as statements of ethical standards (ALIA 2002a). They incorporate the values articulated by Gorman and others in relation to service, excellence and so on, but, most important, they include two values that reflect the notion of social commitment: the promotion of the free flow of information and ideas, and respect for the diversity and individuality of all people. The implications arising from these for professionals, particularly in relation to information and access and control, will be discussed later in the chapter.

Codes of ethics of professional associations also act as expressions of shared values because they are the recognised and accepted values supported and promoted by the professional association (Koehler 2006). The nature of these codes and what purpose they serve is the next question to be explored.

Codes of practice

In general terms, professional codes of ethics have a range of purposes including socialising members into the values of the professional group, providing the broader community with an indication of what the profession represents and raising awareness of ethical issues. Codes may be enforced through legal or punitive means, as in the medical and health area, for example, but normally it is peer pressure and recognition of approved behaviour that is used to promote the code and the desired behaviour. For library and information professionals, the codes of behaviour provided by the many professional associations range from those which are judicial in nature, that is, more concerned with obligations and consequences to those which are aspirational, that is, intended to express ideals of behaviour rather than rules (Koehler 2006). The ALIA code falls into the latter category as do many of the codes emanating from professional associations which have their basis in librarianship (see, for example, the codes of the American Library Association (ALA) and the Chartered Institute of Library and Information Professionals (CILIP). Codes from around the world are available through the IFLA website). In the study by Koehler (2006) referred to earlier, a wide variation in types of codes was found around the world due primarily to the code's intended function but also in part to different political and cultural contexts.

Trushina (2004) suggests that ethics are particularly important in the library and information professions because of the focus on service to people, and the use of codes for regulation is now very common. The earliest one is that developed by ALA in 1938, although most have been produced in the 1980s and 1990s (Trushina 2004, p.417). However, their use has always been contentious and some consider they serve little purpose if they are not legally enforceable because practitioners pay them little attention and they are too general to be workable in every context. Wengert (2001, p.506), for example, argues that libraries play crucial roles in lives in their communities and should contribute in broad ways through social improvements, not with a narrow view of ethics that is presented in codes; he sees the library as teacher rather than merely provider. Others argue in favour of broad ethical codes which act as a guide to thinking about ethical issues, provide support to practitioners in their decision making and reflect the commonality of values among practitioners worldwide but can allow for flexibility in application (Sturges et. al 2003, Hill 1998).

Juznic et al. (2001) argue that the extensive use of technology in information work today requires 'a serious rethinking of codes which were devised in an age dominated by print' and that the need to keep up with technology has worked against the systematic examination of ethical issues (2001, p.76). Hauptman has a different perspective believing that modern ethical dilemmas raised by current law and technology can still be solved within the 'ethical structures that have served us for more than two millennia' and we do not need a new ethical perspective just because the technology has changed (2002, p.5). The question of the continuing relevance of traditional values, as exemplified in professional codes, will be dealt with later, after an overview of the legal and regulatory environment for library and information management work.

Australian law

The main areas of law are described briefly here and their impact and operation further discussed in the final section where the intersection of legal obligations and information ethics is discussed in more detail. Appendix 2 shows these laws by federal and/or state jurisdiction and includes useful Australian and global sources of information on their introduction and their operation. Actual legislation can be accessed via Austlii (http://www.austlii.edu.au/) or Comlaw (http://www.comlaw.gov.au/). The Australian Law Reform Commission (ALRC) (http://www.alrc.gov.au), and corresponding state law reform commissions, are good general resources on Australian law, as are the Attorney-Generals' Departments at federal (http://www.ag.gov.au) and state levels. The federal Parliamentary Library (http://www.aph.gov.au/library/) regularly publishes briefs on current policy and legal issues and there is a range of independent groups also monitoring and commenting on relevant issues and policy developments (see Appendix 2). ALIA monitors and reports on legal issues and developments of interest to library and information professionals. While a detailed understanding of this legislation is not necessary for most practitioners, a certain level of awareness about existing law and proposed legal developments is important. For practitioners in some areas of library and information work, a greater depth of understanding of particular laws will be needed: for example, in libraries providing internet access to children. There is also a range of international laws and agreements that affect professional practice in Australia. Where relevant they are referred to here and further discussed in the next section.

Intellectual property

There are three broad areas of law related to intellectual property, all of which are the responsibility of the federal government, namely copyright, patents law and trade marks. It is the first which is of primary concern to professionals who manage information, provide access to information and disseminate information, although those in more specialised fields, for example, law librarians, will also be concerned with patents and trade marks. The Commonwealth Copyright Act 1968 (and its amendments) is the principal legislation covering all states and territories. Copyright is a complex area of law protecting the rights of people who express ideas or information in a variety of media including text, visual, sound and broadcasting; copyright protects the expression of the ideas or information not the idea or information itself. Copyright can be infringed in a number of ways if the material is used without the permission of the copyright owner. The Australian Copyright Council provides good explanations of current law and what it covers or does not cover and is the key source for maintaining awareness of new developments in copyright. Important recent amendments relate to digital material (Copyright Amendment (Digital Agenda) Act 2000), changes to copyright resulting from the Australia-US Free Trade Agreement (AUSFTA) and the Copyright Amendment Act 2006 which amended copyright in a number of areas including non-commercial activites of libraries and enforcement. This is an area where international treaties are also important; in particular, those administered by the World Intellectual Property Organisation (WIPO) to which Australia is a signatory; for example, the Berne Convention, first established in 1886 and the more recent TRIPS agreement of 1994. The WIPO Copyright Treaty of 1996, which seeks to extend intellectual property laws to databases, is not yet in force since it is awaiting ratification (Nayyer 2002).

Censorship

In Australia, censorship by governments relates primarily to the regulation of offensive content in the various forms of media but can also apply to content deemed seditious. This is discussed separately below. Constitutionally, there is no general right to freedom of expression although Australia is a signatory to the International Covenant on Human Rights. The federal government has responsibility for two main areas of legislation – broadcasting content, including the internet, and imported material, including film and video, games and publications. In relation to the latter, the main legislation is the Classification (Publications, Films and Computer Games) Act 1995 (Cth). State governments have responsibility for locally produced material, although they have agreed on a National Classification Scheme and have enacted complementary legislation. The Office of Film and Literature Classification (OFLC) is responsible for classifying material using the National Classification Code, which is based on four key principles: adults should be able to read, hear and see what they want; minors should be protected from material likely to harm or disturb them; everyone should be protected from exposure to unsolicited material that they find offensive; and the need to take account of community concerns about depictions of violence (including sexual violence) and the portrayal of persons in a demeaning manner (see Appendix 2).

The primary legislation governing broadcasting is the Broadcasting Services Act 1992 (Cth) and the Broadcasting Services Amendment (Online Services) Act 1999 (Cth), and the Australian Communications and Media Authority (ACMA) has responsibility for monitoring the implementation of both. Of main interest to library and information professionals are the provisions relating to content regulation. These are explained on the ACMA website (http://www.acma.gov.au/). The Online Services Act in particular was introduced in response to concerns about offensive and illegal material on the internet and the exposure of children to this material. The ACMA also approves codes of practice developed by commercial broadcasters and monitors those of the public broadcasters, ABC and SBS.

Privacy

The purpose of privacy legislation is to protect the privacy of individuals in their dealings with government and private sector organisations. There is no constitutional right to privacy. The principal legislation is that first enacted by the Commonwealth in 1988 to apply to the federal public sector and later extended in 2000 to cover the private sector. The legislation is intended to ensure Australia meets its international obligations in accordance with the United Nations International Covenant on Civil and Political Rights and the privacy guidelines of the Organisation for Economic Cooperation and Development (OECD) (ALRC 2006). It is based on a number of key principles relating to the collection, use, access and dissemination of personal information, and its operation is monitored by the Office of the Federal Privacy Commissioner (see Appendix 2). There is a range of complementary legislation in some states and territories, although only New South Wales, Victoria, Tasmania and the Northern Territory have specific privacy legislation. The complementary legislation covers such matters as health information, the use of surveillance devices and the interception of telecommunications.

Currently, Western Australia, South Australia and Queensland do not have privacy legislation although the latter two states have set administrative guidelines for privacy standards and all have indicated an intention to introduce legislation in the future. Also, the ALRC is currently inquiring into the extent to which existing laws are effective in the protection of privacy in Australia and is expected to report in 2008 after extensive consultation. The Office of the Federal Privacy Commissioner and the Australian Privacy Foundation provide up-to-date information on the range of privacy legislation across Australia. In addition to the protection of information about individuals, practitioners also need to maintain awareness of federal and state laws relating to data security and electronic communications. These are not detailed here but information is available from the sources referred to at the beginning of this section.

Freedom of Information

Freedom of Information (FOI) legislation is intended to provide individuals and groups with access to information held by federal and state ministers, departments and other government agencies including public libraries and archives. This information may be general material held by the agency relating to its work or specific material about decisions which have been made including how those decisions were made. Individuals may also apply for access to information held about them. Access to some material held by government agencies is made exempt from the legislation. These are usually documents that have been deemed confidential to protect public or private interests. There are a number of appeal procedures. There is FOI legislation enacted in each state and territory as well as for the commonwealth government, which was first enacted in 1982. State legislation is generally modelled on the Commonwealth Act but there are some differences. Practitioners need to be aware of the potential of FOI requests for information held by their agency and the procedures for dealing with it, which are detailed in the relevant federal or state legislation. Freedom of information laws have attracted much criticism because of the cost and difficulty of using them to obtain information from government agencies and a recent review by the commonwealth ombudsman suggested the establishment of a FOI commissioner to monitor the operation of the legislation at the federal level (Banisar 2006, p.43).

National security

Increasing concerns over national security at the beginning of the twenty-first century have led to the introduction of a broad range of anti-terrorism legislation, which has a direct impact on the work of library and information professionals since much of it relates to access and use of information. The national security page on the website of the federal Attorney-General's Department lists the main pieces of legislation found either in anti-terrorism acts or in other laws. It is a long list. Each state and territory also has a range of complementary law. The Parliamentary Library has a comprehensive list of resources on this area and details key legislation amended or introduced since 2001. There are too many separate laws and regulations to discuss individually. Some legislation containing specific provisions related to access and use of information is listed in Appendix 2. Practitioners should ensure they maintain an awareness of the full range of federal and state laws and regulations related to terrorism, particularly because these are continuing to be introduced. These cover a range of legal areas including those outlined above; privacy (for example, surveillance, telecommunications, personal information) and censorship of publications and internet content. One area that has generated much controversy and concern over human rights including freedom of expression has been the use of sedition offences; the ALRC has been conducting an inquiry into this (see Appendix 2).

Information ethics and legal obligations

The framework for the discussion of ethical issues and legal obligations is an extension of that developed by Capurro (ICIE 2001) who identified four categories of ethical issues: human rights and responsibility as described in Articles contained in the Universal Declaration of Human Rights; information production for which issues related to intellectual property are at the forefront; information collection and classification including issues related to censorship and control; and information access and dissemination where the main issues relate to societal and individual access and the right to communicate and the right to privacy. A fifth category is added here, covering professional responsibility for the quality of practice including issues of legal liability for information provision. Inevitably, there is some overlap among these areas but it provides a useful way of exploring the complex range of issues and laws. More technical issues to do with the reliability of systems, technical standards, network security, computer fraud will not be dealt with in this chapter since they would seem to have more to do with competency and criminality.

For each category, the major challenges facing the library and information professional are summarised, examples of available legal and professional supports are highlighted and the implications for professional practice considered. The interplay between legal and ethical issues has been discussed earlier in this chapter. It is important to note here, however, that legislation in all its forms often follows after society's need is identified (Oppenheim & Smith 2004, quoting Malley 1990). Given this tendency, considered reflection on the codes of practice and their own ethical position provides significant support for information professionals as they manage their way through complex and conflicting issues. If there is one theme that runs through the following overview, it is the need for balance – balance between personal and professional values, the diverse values of communities served and the societal values expressed in legislation.

Human rights and responsibility

This section focuses on the role of the library as a social institution in promoting democratic ways, and the associated implications for individual information professionals. Although the library's significance to different elements of society has been recognised since the days of the Alexandrian Library, it is only since the nineteenth century that libraries have been 'recognised as necessary to society' as a whole (Byrne 2003, p.116). The emphasis on the role of the library in supporting democratic values has been more recent, both in established Western democratic societies and in the societies of the developing world (Byrne 2003, Hamilton & Ole Pors 2003). Part of this shift in focus has seen the library expand its role from being an institution providing access to self-education to becoming an important advocate for freedom of access to information. Access to information and freedom of expression – two sides of the same coin – are seen as basic elements of an informed and educated citizenry, which is itself a cornerstone of the democratic way of life. Further, as well-patronised public spaces, libraries provide a forum for public engagement with ideas and knowledge (Byrne 2003). The bedrock of the library's position in society is the United Nations Universal Declaration of Human Rights (1948), in particular Article 19 (the right to freedom of opinion, the right to seek, receive and impart information with freedom) and Article 27 (the right to participate in the cultural life of the community and to enjoy the benefits of scientific advancement). As discussed earlier, these rights find more concrete form in a range of professional codes of conduct, at both national and international levels.

The ideals encapsulated in these declarations and codes are admirable. However, translating them into professional practice and creating and managing library and information services that fulfil these ambitions is not easy, either at a societal, organisational or an individual level. An added dimension to this challenge is the continuing digital divide, both within single societies (see, for example, Lloyd & Bill 2004) and globally (United Nations, International Telecommunication Union 2004). Byrne observes the 'considerable evidence that libraries may be considered as instruments for the reproduction of social class and maintaining the dominance of the literate and educated' (Byrne 2003, p.122). Carney (2003) also questions whether libraries have equitably served all people in society, a position supported by UK research into the social impact of libraries that found highly variable quality in services across the country (Muddiman et al. 2000). Despite this variety in practice, library and information services do continue to act as agents for change, involved in creating national identity through preserving documentary heritage, supporting universal education as the people's university and supporting skills acquisition and development in reading and accessing information. However, in making decisions about the composition of the community they serve, what priorities they have and where they will allocate resources, consciously or unconsciously, those decisions continue to disadvantage some groups in society. This situation highlights the status of declarations of rights and codes of practice as aspirational ideals (Hamilton & Ole Pors 2003), which must be translated into action by individual information professionals.

The role of the information professional as activist has a long history. Samek (2004) documents the history of 'progressive librarianship' from the 1930s in the United States and argues it is 'inextricably linked' to the concepts of intellectual freedom and human rights (2004, p.4). Samek and also Carney (2003, p.49) see the more recent origins in the 'social responsibilities movement' of the 1960s and the formation of ALA's Round Table on Social Responsibilities. Carney also reminds us, however, that setting out on this path put the information professional at odds with a basic tenet of the profession – the role of the information professional in 'providing neutral and unbiased service and information' (2003, p.49). Intervention programs such as literacy programs are already a first stop along the way to a more activist approach, suggesting it is less a question of taking or not taking an activist role. Rather, the issue can be seen on a continuum with individual information professionals taking a personal stance on the degree to which they actively engage in societal change. There is substantial evidence from practitioner reporting of professional activities that many individuals already take the step beyond Hauptman's 'unthinking information provision', referred to earlier in the chapter.

Winston and Quinn (2005) describe instances of activism by library and information professionals in times of crises (for example, attempts to prevent the looting and destruction of cultural institutions in Iraq in 2003) and times of political and social change (for example, the role of the ALA in lobbying against aspects of the US Patriot Act which threaten individual privacy and suppression of materials that might be controversial). Beyond the question of an active professional role as a change agent, there are other personal matters to be considered. Byrne (2004b), for example, argues that if librarians and information professionals accept and abide by the UN's Universal Declaration and the professional codes of practice, they must do so at a very personal level as well as at an organisational level; for example, in the management practices adopted, in the ethical stance taken towards colleagues and staff, in negotiating contracts with database vendors, in professional practices such as collection development, and in ensuring the privacy of users is not violated.

Information production

Major ethical and legal concerns relating to the production of information include issues such as ownership of information and the impact of new media on both the production and dissemination of information. While intellectual property includes copyright, patents and trademarks, library and information services are most concerned with copyright matters. Article 27 of the UN Universal Declaration provides 'guarantees of protection of both *moral* and *material* interests of authors' (Byrne 2002, p.278), principles enshrined in copyright laws which strive for a balance between allowing the individual to benefit materially from their creative output and ensuring that society as a whole benefits from the generation of new knowledge. More recently Anglo-American copyright regimes have been extended to include the concept of moral rights, intended to protect the creator's rights of attribution and integrity (Byrne 2002). Worthy of particular note in this discussion of the ownership of information is indigenous knowledge. Indigenous knowledge encompasses a wide range of material, including both artefacts created by indigenous people and artefacts created about them, such as the 'cultural documentation' (Moorcroft & Byrne 1996, p.88) held in books, films and government records; material created by and now owned by non-indigenous people.

While the evolution of the digital environment has provided opportunities for increased access to information, the related commercialisation and commoditisation of information have created a number of challenges for those concerned with protecting the 'diffusion of knowledge through society' (Maxwell 2004). In this new context, 'intellectual property rights present [information professionals] with challenges at all stages of the information management cycle' (Muir 2006, p.5), with the balance at present tipping towards the rights of the individual creator (Byrne 2002). As an example, the Australia-United States Free Trade Agreement 2004, among other matters, extended copyright protection to the life of the author, plus seventy years. This change was an extension of twenty years, an outcome considered detrimental for libraries, students and researchers (Rimmer 2006). As mentioned earlier, there is considerable activity at the international level to further regulate intellectual property and there is evidence that there is now increasing similarity or 'harmonisation' among the laws of individual countries in the direction of greater protection (Nayyer 2002).

New ways of producing information in the digital environment may also restrict access to information. These include the move from library and information services purchasing information in the form of hard copy books and journals to entering into licensing agreements to use information for specified periods of time. Library and information services are finding 'access to electronic content in journals is becoming more restricted', for example, through licence agreements that limit the number of 'single instances of access' with access 'curtailed' when the limit is reached (Withers 2006).

Another example of restricted use is the prohibition of any copying, even for fair dealing purposes. Information professionals also need to be aware of the existence and impact of database protections in some jurisdictions and anti-circumvention provisions, such as encryption software, which may have a significant impact on the ability to store and preserve information. Even if, for example, a library and information service 'has legitimate rights to manipulate the information [...] digital rights management (DRM) may provide a legally insurmountable obstacle' (Muir 2006, p.6). Finally, with the globalisation of both the production, dissemination and use of information, across all of these issues lies the matter of which jurisdiction prevails.

The tightness of legislative control in the area of intellectual property ownership means the challenges facing information professionals are less likely to be ethical ones. However, there are calls for information professionals to play a more active role in asserting societal rather than individual rights. Statements from associations such as ALIA (2001a), for example, clearly identify the profession's interests and positions in relation to matters such as contractually based restrictions that appear to override copyright legislation. As a response to these 'new forms of enclosure' (Kranich 2004), library and information professionals along with other public interest advocates, are seeking ways to counter restrictions such as digital rights management. Information commons are digital resources and virtual spaces for 'producing and sharing information, creative works and democratic discussion' (Kranich 2004, p.1). Examples include licensing initiatives such as Creative Commons (www.creativecommons.org), open access journals and institutional commons. The concept of the information commons with its emphasis on 'ensur[ing] open access to ideas and the opportunity to use them' (Kranich 2003) echoes the traditional role of library and information services. The continuing health of the commons relies on support and advocacy, and library and information professionals are called upon to take an active role in providing this support and advocacy (Besser 2002, Kranich 2004). This path is not without challenges for the information professional, such as those resulting from 'value conflicts over the role of the market' (Bradley 2004).

Information collection and classification

The most significant and longstanding ethical issue presenting itself in this category relates to censorship in a range of less or more obvious guises such as selection versus censorship or the non-neutrality of classification schemes. Concern over censorship is closely tied to the fundamental freedoms discussed earlier, the free access to information and the freedom to express opinions, and has been an issue for information professionals for as long as the profession has existed. Again the information professional will find both legal and professional support, and again the application of either law or code of practice is where the real challenge surfaces (Oppenheim & Smith 2004), as individuals find themselves engaged in balancing personal and professional positions, legal obligations and ethical responses. Information content most likely to trigger censorship challenges includes political, social, sexual or religious material, and while often laws will define what is or is not permissible, as noted earlier, legal solutions 'do not always keep pace with society and its new standards' (Oppenheim & Smith 2004, p.163).

Issues around censorship surface most obviously in the decisions made about what to include in the information made available by the library and information service, whatever the format. These questions must be answered in respect both of traditional print-based collections and, for instance, information available via internet links created by library and information professionals. Those professionals in charge of collection development continually make judgements about what to include and what not to acquire. Once again a tension may be found, in this instance between personal values, organisational values and espoused professional values. First, the decision not to select for the collection is in itself not necessarily a form of censorship. Asheim's distinction (Asheim 1954, cited in Moody 2005) continues to provide solid guidance, differentiating between selecting being about finding reasons to include an item in a collection and censorship seeking to find reasons to exclude an item. Despite the clear-cut nature of this advice, however, it sometimes remains difficult to differentiate between censoring material and making a professional judgement (Wengert 2001), with some research suggesting the information professionals themselves are more likely than others to act as censors (Moody 2004). This type of self-censorship is revealed when information professionals use arguments such as little literary quality, no demand or limited resources to justify decisions not to add material to collections. Information professionals need also to be aware of other more hidden ways in which material may be subjected to censorship (Byrne 2004c). Further ways in which acquisitions and cataloguing processes may inadvertently or intentionally restrict access to material include outsourcing acquisition decisions to mainstream vendors, labelling of material to designate genre or warnings (Moody 2004) or search engine algorithms (Hinman 2005).

A second tension may surface between the obligations of the information professional towards his or her local community and the profession. Tasked with serving the entire community equitably, how does the information professional respond to demands from individuals or groups within that community to restrict access to some information, knowing that such an action contravenes the professional code of ethics? On a broader societal scale, a similar ethical dilemma has been thrown up by the destruction of the World Trade Center in 2001 and the subsequently tighter legislative control on both access to information and freedom of expression. The legislative nature of the controls and sanctions makes the consequences of taking a professional stance to protect both these freedoms potentially more hazardous for the individual information professional, with custodial sentences possible. Oppenheim and Smith (2004) caution that the danger of not acquiring material 'because of the problems it might cause' is still censorship, although a more generous view suggests that 'suppression of one text is not necessarily censorship' (Oppenheim & Smith 2004, p.164), identifying censorship as more to do with the systematic and widespread curtailment of access to types of information.

Under the topic of censorship, indigenous knowledge and access to it is again worthy of note. Protocols such as the Aboriginal and Torres Strait Islander Protocols for Libraries, Archives and Information Services (ALIA 1995) alert information professionals to the need to consider the confidential or sensitive nature of some indigenous material, and to acknowledge this in their work practices by identifying and implementing required restrictions of access, in negotiation with Aboriginal and Torres Strait Islander people in the community served. Restricting access to this kind of information is not however considered censorship within the profession.

Information access and dissemination

A major ethical challenge facing information professionals at the beginning of the twenty-first century has less to do with the information resources they collect and make available but rather with the information they gather about the people who access those resources and how they use them. The right to privacy is another recognised in the UN Declaration of Human Rights and, unlike some other legal and ethical issues considered in this section, is 'well embedded in law' (Levett 2005). In western democracies, most jurisdictions have legislated to protect individual privacy and the data collected about individuals, although not all national legislation deals with privacy in the same way (Bellman et al. 2004). The basic principle of privacy receives further support from international and national associations such as IFLA and ALIA.

For information professionals, legislation relating to privacy protections deals with two different sets of data. First, there is the personal information – names and addresses, demographic details – collected about users as part of the 'authorisation' of their use of the library or information service. Information professionals have a long and robust tradition of protecting this information, enshrined in professional codes such as ALIA's Statement on Professional Conduct (2001b). Indeed, other business and public sector organisations are now catching up, as governments legislate to ensure privacy of personal data in the networked environment. Second, there is the record of what people do with the information resources provided by information professionals, such as records of online databases searches, email and web searches. Again, libraries have a long tradition of protecting any circulation data collected about use of resources, a tradition reflected in low levels of concern about privacy relating to library use (Sturges et al. 2003). However, in the networked environment it is more difficult to provide protection. In the first instance, people's use of the resources is much more visible, with the 'parameters of privacy in this new environment' (Sturges et al. 2003, p.45) still being established. An example of the challenges confronting information professionals, as information is increasingly recorded and disseminated in electronic form, is the US Freedom to Read Protection Act, re-introduced into the US Congress in 2005. Munoz (2004) in her legal analysis of the argument for supporting the Act, highlighted the complexity of developing a legal regime for a networked environment based on what has gone before. Munoz concluded that since the internet is recognised legally as a public place, much of the activity that takes place there is public communication. Unlike public communications in the physical world, however, there are records of these internet-based communications and Munoz, at least, suggested that existing privacy legislation cannot be assumed to provide protection.

The operating environment of information professionals has changed in another way and, in a 'post-9/11 world', continuing high concern about national security issues also presents challenges for information professionals. A tension exists between protecting the rights of the individual and contributing to the protection from terrorist activity of both individuals and communities. Levett (2005) argues that as professionals our first duty is to our users, as users, suggesting privacy of both personal detail and transactional records has primacy for information professionals, even though our legal obligation may be to hand over the information. Further complicating this situation is ambiguity and possible conflict about the different laws: for example, national security, privacy and freedom of information legislation all have the potential to conflict (Sturges et al. 2003). Ultimately, professional practice in this changing environment calls for watchful and considered judgement and, some argue, a more active engagement in creating the laws and ethical codes that will govern behaviour. Munoz (2004, p.73), for example, calls for information professionals to exercise their professional role in contributing to the resolution of issues such as protection of records of transactions in the 'new and strange' world of the internet. Similarly in Canada, Caidi and Ross (2005, p.90) call for more active engagement on the broader front, arguing that now information professionals have been 'thrust into a politically charged environment', they should be both 'more vocal and visible' in fulfilling their professional obligations to their users.

A second major challenge to freedom of access to information are continuing calls to regulate or filter online content, and for library and information services to filter online content. Access to 'undesirable' internet sites can be regulated in different ways, including industry self-censorship and government legislation. Codes of practice, such as the ALIA code (2002b), make clear the profession's position on regulation of online content, asserting that the basis for making information available and accessible is a professional one, rather than a political, religious or moral one. If the information is legally available, library and information professionals have a professional responsibility to provide it, or at least not to prohibit access to it. The arguments are similar to those in the censorship debate and information professionals may find themselves facing a similar challenge, that is, being called upon to take a professional stance that may be personally morally repugnant, for example, making pro-anorexia websites available, or may be at odds with the values of the community they serve. Where jurisdictions have legislated to mandate filtering, for example in the US with the Children's Internet Protection Act 2004, library and information professionals must grapple with how to ensure they are compliant with the legislative demand (Minow 2004).

Professional responsibility

By claiming special status in society, members of a profession have 'special responsibilities to be careful, competent and honest in their work' (Ferguson & Weckert 1998, p.379). The concept of professional practice, and the evolution of the digital environment and the related commercialisation of information, themes discussed throughout this chapter, come together in the area of professional accountability. Stuart Hannabuss (2000) puts the case that the changing working environment 'has placed information liability centre stage in professional practice' in a detailed analysis of the issues confronting the information professional, issues that include liability and professional negligence, which in turn rely on standards of reasonable care and duty. Duty of care, a legal concept, requires that professionals of all kinds exercise reasonable care in fulfilling their responsibilities.

Two main areas of concern relate to 'fees for service and repackaging information' (Ferguson & Weckert 1998, p.380). While charging for services is indicative of entering into a contractual arrangement, Ferguson and Weckert conclude that, at least for those information professionals working in the public sector, this is less of a concern. However, repackaging of information clearly results in a new product, a product for which the information professional can be held accountable. Some areas of professional practice may be more exposed than others, such as health information services (Muir & Oppenheim 1995) or private information consultants (Vickers 1992). However, professional liability issues may surface in any area of professional practice, including in public libraries (Kanter 2000) and indexing services (Browne

1996). Some professional bodies, taking this risk seriously, are offering professional liability insurance (Smith 2005) and other professional responses to this increased level of accountability have included extensive use of exclusion clauses and disclaimers, which, while offering protection in some instances, may not be relied upon in all cases (Ferguson & Weckert 1998).

Their changing role, from collector of information resources to a more proactive role in creating, analysing and consolidating information, places information professionals in a more exposed position, although Ferguson and Weckert (1998) observe that fears of large scale litigation have proved unfounded. More important for the profession perhaps, is the broader issue of exactly what responsibility an information professional is prepared to assume (Ferguson & Weckert 1998). On the one hand, codes of practice claim professional status for the information professional, a major part of which is command of a specialised body of knowledge. On the other hand, reliance on disclaimers to offer protection against legal action explicitly sends the message that the professional does not stand by the quality of the service they provide.

Conclusion

This chapter has explored the nature of ethical information practice in an increasingly complex domestic and global environment, in which the range of laws affecting the work of library and information professionals presents new challenges to traditional values and notions of ethical behaviour. Do ethics still matter? The overwhelming evidence is that the basis of practice remains underpinned by the traditional values that have served the profession for so long. This is not to say that all professionals share an equal understanding of or commitment to these values and certainly they are given different priorities in practice. There appears, however, to be a general understanding within all areas of the profession that ethics matter and that traditional values are still relevant. Is it possible to be both ethical and legal? This is the harder question. Professionals accept that it is their responsibility to adhere to the law and endeavour to reconcile ethical conflicts in the best interests of their clients and employers. As part of this, keeping up to date with developments in law is a key factor. For many, however, professional activism is also an important responsibility and through this they aim to contribute to the development of ethical laws for access and provision of information.

References

Australian Law Reform Commission (ALRC) 2006, *ALRC issues paper 31: Review of privacy*, Australian Government, Canberra, ACT.

Australian Library and Information Association (ALIA) 1995, *Aboriginal and Torres Strait Islander protocols for libraries, archives and information services*, www.alia.org.au/policies/atsi.protocols.html

Australian Library and Information Association (ALIA) 2001a, *Statement on copyright and intellectual property*, www.alia.org.au/policies/copyright.intellectual.html

Australian Library and Information Association (ALIA) 2001b, *Statement on professional conduct*, www.alia.org.au/policies/professional.conduct.html

Australian Library and Information Association (ALIA) 2002a, *ALIA core values statement*, www.alia.org.au/policies/core.values.html

Australian Library and Information Association (ALIA) 2002b, *ALIA Statement on online content regulation*, www.alia.org.au/policies/content.regulation.html

Banisar, D 2006, *Freedom of information around the world 2006: A global survey of access to government information laws*, http://www.privacyinternational.org

Bayles, MD 1989, *Professional ethics,* Wadsworth Publishing, Belmont, CA.

Bellman, S, Johnson, EJ, Kobrin, SJ & Lohse, GL 2004, 'International differences in information privacy concerns: A global survey of consumers', *The Information Society,* vol.20, no.5, pp.313-324.

Besser, H 2002, *Commodification of culture harms creators*, http://www.ala.org/ala/washoff/contactwo/oitp/infocommons0204/besser.htm

Bradley, F 2004, 'Enabling the information commons', *ALIA 2004 Biennial Conference: Challenging Ideas*, Gold Coast, QLD.

Browne, G 1996, 'Professional liability of indexers', *Indexer,* vol.20, no.2, pp.70-73.

Buchanan, EA 2004, 'Introduction', *Journal of Information Ethics,* vol.13, no.2, pp.5-7.

Byrne, A 2002, 'The sounds of silence: Copyright and human rights', *Australian Academic and Research Libraries,* vol.33, no.4, pp.275-283.

Byrne, A 2003, 'Necromancy or life support? Libraries, democracy and the concerned intellectual', *Library Management,* vol.24, no.2, pp.116-125.

Byrne, A 2004a, 'IFLA and professional ethics', *The Australian Library Journal*, vol.53, no.1, http://www.alia.org.au/publishing/alj/53.1/full.text/byrne.html

Byrne, A 2004b, 'Libraries and democracy: Management implications', *Library Management,* vol.25, no.1/2, pp.11-16.

Byrne, A 2004c, 'The end of history: Censorship and libraries', *Australian Library Journal,* vol.53, no.2, pp.133-151.

Caidi, N & Ross, A 2005, 'To serve and protect? Privacy and libraries in the post-9/11 information environment', *Feliciter,* vol.51, no.2, pp.89-91.

Capurro, R 2000, 'Ethical challenges of the information society in the 21st century', *International Information & Library Review,* vol.32, no.3/4, pp.257-276.

Carney, SM 2003, 'Democratic communication and the library workplace', *Journal of Information Ethics*, vol.12, no.2, pp.43-59.

Carroll, AB 1991, 'The pyramid of corporate responsibility: Toward the moral management of organizational stakeholders', *Business Horizons,* vol.42, pp.39-48.

Dole, WV, Hurych, JM & Koehler, W 2000, 'Values for librarians in the information age: An expanded examination', *Library Management,* vol.21, no.6, pp.285-297.

Everard, J 2001, 'We are Plato's children', *Library Management,* vol.22, no.6/7, pp.297-302.

Ferguson, S & Weckert, J 1998, 'The librarian's duty of care: Emerging professionalism or can of worms?' *Library Quarterly,* vol.68, no.4, pp.365-389.

Freidson, E 1983, 'The theory of professions: State of the art' in *The sociology of the professions: Lawyers, doctors and others*, R Dingwell & P Lewis (eds), Macmillan, London.

Froehlich, TJ 1992, 'Ethical considerations of information professionals' in *Annual Review of Information Science and Technology (ARIST)*, vol.27 ME Williams (ed.) Learned Information, Medford, NJ, pp.291-324.

Froehlich, TJ 1997, *Survey and analysis of the major ethical and legal issues facing library and information services,* IFLA Publications 78, KG Saur, Munich, Germany.

Gorman, M 2000, *Our enduring values: Librarianship in the 21st century,* American Library Association, Chicago, IL.

Hamilton, S & Ole Pors, N 2003, 'Freedom of access to information and freedom of expression: The internet as a tool for global social inclusion', *Library Management,* vol.24, no.8/9, pp.407-416.

Hannabuss, S 2000, 'Being negligent and liable: A challenge for information professionals', *Library Management*, vol.21, no.6, pp.316-329.

Hauptman, R 1988, *Ethical challenges in librarianship,* Oryx, Phoenix, AZ.

Hauptman, R 2002, *Ethics and librarianship,* McFarland & Co, Jefferson, NC.

Hill, M 1998, 'Facing up to dilemmas: Conflicting ethics and the modern information professional', *ASLIB Proceedings*, vol.50, no.4, pp.71-78.

Hinman, LM 2005, 'Esse est indicato in Google: Ethical and political issues in search engines', *International Review of Information Ethics*, vol.3, pp.19-25.

Iacovino, L 2002, 'Ethical principles and information professionals: Theory, practice and education', *Australian Academic & Research Libraries,* vol.33, no.2, pp.57-74.

International Center for Information Ethics (ICIE) 2001, *The field*, 2006, http://icie.zkm.de/research

International Federation of Library Associations (IFLA) 2002, *The Glasgow declaration on libraries, information services and intellectual freedom*, http://www.ifla.org/faife/policy/iflastat/gldeclar-e.html

Johnston, DR & Post, D 1996, 'Law and borders: The rise of law in cyberspace' *First Monday*, vol.1, no.1, http://www.firstmonday.org/issues/issue1/law/index.html

Juznic, P, Urbanija, J, Grabrijan, E, Miklavc, S, Oslaj, D & Svoljsak, S 2001, 'Excuse me, how do I commit suicide? Access to ethically disputed items of information in public libraries' *Library Management,* vol.22, no.1/2, pp.75-79.

Kanter, R 2000, 'Legal issues resulting from internet use in public libraries', *Feliciter,* vol.46, no.1, pp.18-19.

Koehler, W 2006, 'National library associations as reflected in their codes of ethics: Four codes examined', *Library Management,* vol.27, no.1/2, pp.83 100.

Koehler, W & Pemberton, JM 2000 'A search for core values: Towards a model code of ethics for information professionals', *Journal of Information Ethics*, vol.9, no.1, pp.26-54.

Kranich, N 2003, *Libraries and the Information Commons: A discussion paper, prepared for the ALA Office of Information Technology Policy,* http://www.ala.org/Template.cfm?Section=oitp&Template=/ContentManagement/ContentDisplay.cfm&ContentID=50942

Kranich, N 2004, *The Information Commons: A public policy report*, http://www.fepproject.org/policyreports/InformationCommons.pdf

Levett, J 2005, 'From vigilance to vigilante', *Australian Library Journal,* vol.54, no.1, pp.3-5.

Lloyd, R & Bill, A 2004, *Australia online: How Australians are using computers and the internet 2001*, Australian Census Analytic Program, Australian Bureau of Statistics, Canberra. ACT.

Mason, RO, Mason, FM & Culnan, MJ 1995, *Ethics of information management,* Sage, Thousand Oaks, CA.

Maxwell, TA 2004, 'Is copyright necessary?' *First Monday*, vol.9, no.9, http://firstmonday.org/issues/issue9_9/maxwell/index.html

McDonald, K 1995, *The sociology of the professions,* Sage, London.

McGarry, K 1993, *The changing context of information : An introductory analysis,* Library Association Publishing, London.

Minow, M 2004, 'Lawfully surfing the net: Disabling public library internet filters to avoid more lawsuits in the United States', *First Monday*, vol.9, no.14, http://firstmonday.org/issues/issue9_4/minow/index.html

Montague Smith, M 1997, 'Information ethics', *Annual Review of Information Science and Technology*, vol.32, pp.339-365.

Moody, K 2004, 'Opinions and experiences of Queensland-based public librarians with regard to censorship of materials in public library collections: An exploratory analysis', *ALIA 2004 Biennial Conference: Challenging Ideas,* Gold Coast, QLD.

Moody, K 2005, 'Covert censorship in libraries: A discussion paper', *Australian Library Journal,* vol.54, no.2, pp.138-145.

Moorcroft, H & Byrne, A 1996, 'Intellectual property and indigenous peoples' information', *Australian Academic and Research Libraries,* vol.27, no.2, pp.87-94.

Muddiman, D, Durrani, S, Dutch, M, Linley, R, Pateman, J & Vincent, J 2000, *Open for all? The public library and social exclusion. Volume one: Overview and conclusions*, http://eprints.rclis.org/archive/00003775/01/lic084.pdf

Muir, A 2006, *Preservation, access and intellectual property rights challenges for libraries in the digital environment*, http://www.ippr.org.uk/publicationsandreports/publication.asp?id=464

Muir, A & Oppenheim, C 1995, 'The legal responsibilities of the health-care librarian', *Health Libraries Review*, vol.12, no.2, pp.91-99.

Munoz, RE 2004, 'A legal analysis of the ALA's support of the Freedom to Read Protection Act', *Journal of Information Ethics,* vol.13, no.2, pp.58-77.

Nayyer, K 2002, 'Globalization of information: Intellectual property law implications', *First Monday*, vol.7, no.1, http://www.firstmonday.org/issues/issue7_1/nayyer/

Oppenheim, C & Smith, V 2004, 'Censorship in libraries', *Information Services and Use,* vol.24, no.4, pp.159-170.

Pearlson, KE & Saunders, CS 2005, 'Using information systems ethically' in *Managing and using information systems*, Wiley, New York, pp.192-213.

Rimmer, M 2006, 'Robbery under arms: Copyright law and the Australia-United States Free Trade Agreement', *First Monday*, vol.11, no.3, http://firstmonday.org/issues/issue11_3/rimmer/index.html

Samek, T 2004, 'Internet and interaction: An infrastructure for progressive librarianship', *International Journal of Information Ethics (IJIE)*, vol.2, no.11.

Selwyn, N 2004, 'Reconsidering political and popular understandings of the digital divide', *New Media & Society,* vol.6, no.3, pp.341-362.

Severson, RJ 1997, *The principles of information ethics,* ME Sharpe, New York.

Smith, PH 2005, 'An ounce of prevention is worth a pound of cure: Professional liability insurance', *Texas Library Journal,* vol.81, no.1, pp.22-23.

Stichler, RN & Hauptman, R (eds) 1998, *Ethics, information and technology readings*, McFarland & Co, Jefferson, NC.

Sturges, P, Davies, E, Dearnley, J, Iliffe, U, Oppenheim, C & Hardy, R 2003, 'User privacy in the digital library environment: An investigation of policies and preparedness', *Library Management,* vol.24, no.1/2, pp.44-50.

Trushina, I 2004, 'Freedom of access: Ethical dilemmas for internet librarians', *The Electronic Library,* vol.22, no.5, pp.416-421.

United Nations 1948, *Universal declaration of human rights*, http://www.un.org/Overview/rights.html

United Nations, International Telecommunication Union 2004, *Why a summit on the information society*, http://www.itu.int/wsis/basic/why.html

Vickers, P 1992, 'Information consultancy in the UK', *Journal of Information Science,* vol.18, no.4, pp.259-267.

Warschauer, M 2002, 'Reconceptualizing the digital divide', *First Monday*, vol.7, no.7, http://firstmonday.org/issues/issue7_7/warschauer/index.html

Weckert, J & Adeney, D 1997, 'The meaning of ethics' in *Computer and information ethics*, Greenwood Press, Westport, CT, pp.1-14.

Wengert, R 2001, 'Some ethical issues of being an information professional', *Library Trends,* vol.49, no.3, pp.486-509.

Winston, MD & Quinn, S 2005, 'Library leadership in times of crisis and change', *New Library World,* vol.106, no.1216/1217, pp.395-415.

Withers, K 2006, 'Intellectual property for all', *Prospect*, vol.25 August, http://www.ippr.org.uk/articles/index.asp?id=2294

Woodward, D 1990, 'A framework for deciding issues in ethics', *Library Trends,* vol.39, pp.8-17.

CHAPTER 17
Library managers today: the challenges

Damian Lodge and Bob Pymm

As they move along their career path, librarians, like many professionals, are likely to take on higher levels of responsibility for staff, collections and the budget, while at the same time having less opportunity to exercise their traditional technical skills and knowledge. This can bring challenges, with newly appointed managers having to acquire new areas of expertise while doing less of the professional tasks with which they may feel more comfortable. However, the importance of the manager's role in planning and directing the future growth of the library cannot be overestimated and in the rapidly evolving world of the twenty-first century library and information environment, well-developed management skills are essential to the continuing success of the organisation.

Depending upon the organisation, the level and responsibilities of the manager will vary enormously. However, for virtually all library and information managers, their position will exist within a broader organisational environment and while senior managers may be responsible for an entire library service or significant part thereof, it is likely that in the context of the organisation as a whole, they will be part of a larger middle-management cohort working towards the organisation's overarching goals.

The nature of this relationship varies depending upon the type of library, but a common approach is for library managers to be accountable to library management committees or boards. Thus public library managers often report to council boards, university librarians may report to the university council, and the law librarian may report to a senior grouping of partners in the firm. Library managers may also report to an individual manager such as the Head of Public Services for a local council or a Pro-Vice Chancellor of Academic Services in an academic setting. Evans et al. (2000, p.9) clarify the nature of this relationship by noting the difference between accountability and responsibility: 'Responsibility is what one must do, whereas accountability is the being answerable for an action. Thus, accountability is important in the process of enforcing responsibility.' Here one sees library managers being accountable to a board, committee or senior manager, with the responsibility of successfully managing the library's budget, staffing, adherence to occupational health and safety guidelines and so on.

No organisation has ever existed in a vacuum and increasingly the library and information professions are having to respond to a growing level of external factors over which they have little or no control. These, together with challenging issues within the organisation, over which management have greater but by no means complete control, create an environment in which active and responsive management is crucial to the success of the enterprise. Such a management style requires flexibility, a proactive rather than reactive approach to problem solving, good, hard data to inform decision making and assist in the planning process, and the ability to bring staff along with the seemingly never ending cycle of change.

In order to properly understand today's operating environment, and help in predicting and thus planning for tomorrow's, managers need specific quantitative and qualitative data regarding local conditions and the external environment. Without this, success in managers' traditional activities of planning, organising, leading and controlling will be less assured. In an environment of rapid change, tightly controlled budgets, increasing user expectations and competition provided by online information providers, library managers need to make significant decisions which will have long-term consequences. These decisions relate to prioritising competing activities and targeting limited resources appropriately. Information to assist in this process is essential. Thus setting up the practices and processes to acquire and interpret the data gathered, and then exploit its potential to build and develop the organisation, is fundamental to the management role in twenty-first century libraries. Figure 17.1 illustrates how the information gathered from across the operating environment feeds into the long-term strategic direction of the organisation.

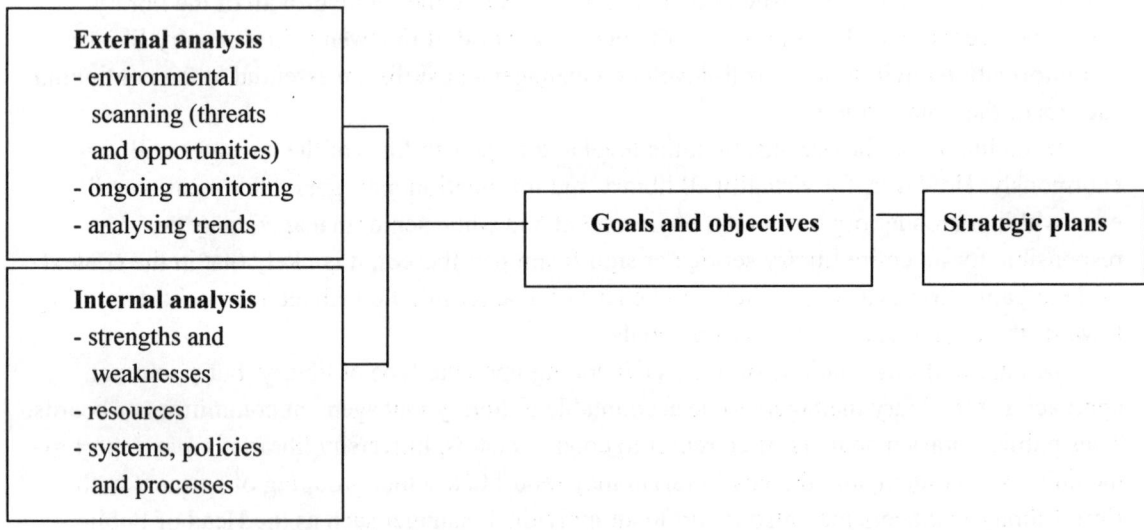

Figure 17.1 Information and strategic direction (adapted from Morrison 1992, p.86)

External and internal analysis

Analysis of the external environment is a major task that needs to be undertaken regularly in a disciplined and ordered manner. The 'big picture' information gathered through such a process helps provide sufficient information to supply a context or parameters within which the more detailed information gained through internal analysis can be applied. External factors range across a wide spectrum of issues, including the social perceptions of libraries and their role; advances in technology; the changing nature of information products; client expectations; the explosion of information access provided by the internet; and the role of publicly funded institutions in an increasingly 'small' government world. Internal factors include budgets;

collections; staff expertise; facilities; and relations within the broader organisational structure. Essentially these and related factors can be consolidated into a number of major categories that managers need to address in planning for the longer term future of their organisations. These comprise performance measurement; costs and budgetary issues; changing nature of collections and their delivery – from traditional to digital; convergence between libraries, archives, records management and some areas of information technology (IT) – and competition; user needs and expectations, and those of non-users; marketing and image; structures and flexibility; and staffing.

It is useful to use some form of scanning tool on a regular basis. One well-known example is a SWOT analysis (Strengths, Weaknesses, Opportunities and Threats) to evaluate both the external and internal environments in order to build a clearer picture of the world in which the organisation operates. Strengths and weaknesses refers to the internal environment, the library itself, and things over which it has some control, such as the shape of the collection or the level of staff expertise, while opportunities and threats exist in the external world, outside the control of the library, and have to be either avoided or exploited in some way.

A number of studies have shown that organisations that invest significant effort in some form of environmental scanning do benefit through improved planning and decision making (Choo 2001, p.8). Choo also reported that one of the major benefits derived through the scanning process was the way in which it required staff to participate in face-to-face discussions on planning issues (2001, p.8). Enabling staff involvement in the long-term planning process has been proven to offer considerable benefits to the organisation as a whole. Cole (2005, p.600) notes how properly functioning teams provide a range of input to the decision-making process that enhances the outcomes (more brains produces better outcomes). While some decisions are best handled by management alone, few if any of the longer term strategic directions can be set in place without considerable consultation with staff and stakeholders external to the organisation. This requires substantially more time to be devoted to the decision-making process, but the trade-off should be staff who understand and are committed to the direction taken and stakeholders who feel they have at the very least had their concerns addressed and been kept informed. This process builds trust and greater understanding and is worth the additional effort required.

As part of the information-gathering and disseminating process, managers need to adopt a number of approaches that include at least some of the following techniques:

- Talking to colleagues and reviewing the professional literature in order to see what others are reporting or doing.

- Looking more broadly at the environment within which the library functions: for a university library, for instance, it is the higher education sector generally; for a public library it is the local council district it serves.

- Undertaking surveys and questionnaires of users and, ideally, non-users.

- Brainstorming with all staff.

- Conducting focus groups with targeted sets of clients or open forums to encourage more wide-ranging input.

- Collating relevant statistical data.

Traditionally, longer term planning has relied on historical data gathered with the understanding that the future can be predicted, based upon past results. This provides one platform upon which to build an understanding of how well the organisation is travelling but it is also important that any environmental scanning process goes more widely than a simple reliance on statistics and trend data.

The work involved is significant, but the results should play a major role in directing the future activities of the organisation. A recent 'big picture' scan was undertaken by OCLC (Online Computer Library Center) (2003), aimed at identifying the significant issues and trends affecting the world's largest library consortium. Another, highly detailed, report of a London public library system, including a SWOT analysis and in-depth examination of the costs involved in providing various services, illustrates the level of attention that is now being placed on the role and position of library systems in the twenty-first century in an effort to ensure their relevance and cost effectiveness (Lewisham Library and Information Service, 2005).

Performance measurement

One of the initial tasks faced by managers in gathering the relevant data is to try to assess the current situation – how well is the organisation meeting its current goals and objectives? And how relevant are these goals and objectives to the broader goals of the organisation as a whole? The necessary statistics and other evidence that best represent how the library is progressing are often referred to as performance indicators. Basic performance indicators are ratios that commonly compare a statistic over time, such as loans per year, short reference enquiries for March or items catalogued for the period June to December. Performance indicators can also be quite complex such as the number of inter-library loans that were supplied to the department of human resources in PDF format over the last year. Performance indicators generally show more than a single statistic can, and they are particularly useful for comparative purposes (for instance, across time – year by year, or geographically – comparing one library to a similar one fifty kilometres away).

Comparing figures with other public libraries in the same region/council/shire is common practice, as is comparing certain statistics from one academic library to another. This comparison is called benchmarking as it enables library managers to see how their libraries are performing against the same key indicators from other libraries. When benchmarking indicators such as number of loans, number of professional library staff or new serial titles, it is important to note that these comparisons can only be valid if one is comparing like with like. This is also true for the type of library – in other words, comparing a public library's staffing establishment, number of loans or new serial titles with those of an academic library will not provide a relevant comparison. An example of benchmarking can be found at the Council of Australian University Librarians (CAUL) website (www.caul.edu.au/stats). Here there is a number of indicators such as library expenditure, user population, serial titles and document delivery statistics supplied by each academic library in Australia, providing a valuable data bank of information over a considerable period of time.

When measuring the performance of the library's services or collections, it is common practice to use inputs, outputs and outcomes. Inputs cover areas such as the budget, buildings, staff and the integrated library management system (ILMS) (see Chapter 10). The CAUL statistics mentioned above mostly cover inputs. Outputs include measures such as the number of loans for the year, reference queries answered, items catalogued or number of new borrowers added to the system. It is important to note here that outputs are able to show a certain amount of information about a given service or collection but outputs generally fail to show service or collection quality. Outcomes are able to show how well the library's web catalogue is meeting the needs of the client group or how effective the information literacy/library training sessions are. These outcomes are assessed through the use of quantitative and qualitative measures.

Quantitative and qualitative methods of measurement have been used in tandem for many years to gain a deeper understanding of an activity or process. Quantitative data are usually numeric data whereas qualitative data is descriptive, usually in the form of words. Quantitative data are very helpful as they can provide concrete information on, say, the number of short reference queries answered or how many librarians attended in-service training sessions for the preceding year. Most library systems are set up to provide quantitative data in the form of the reports they generate, such as the number of loans for each branch library broken down into months or the number of electronic reserve titles accessed for a given period. However, quantitative data are unable to show the quality of the services provided, the skill of the librarians on the reference desk, client satisfaction or the quality of the online reference collection.

Matthews (2003) provides an excellent listing of quantitative measures in his book *Measuring for results*. He lists a number of input and process measures, most of which are easily obtained from the ILMS, such as active registered clients and usage statistics or the routine statistics that most libraries compile from sources such as door counters and reference counters.

Quantitative data can hint at the full picture by comparing, for example, the current year's usage figures for a service with the previous three years. Finding say that the figures have dropped by 15 per cent each year for the last three years would indicate that the service may not be being used optimally, a database may no longer meet the clients' needs or the service had not been marketed as effectively as it had in the first year.

Qualitative measures will help in analysing this quantitative information and may be able to explain better why this database has had a drop off in users over the last few years. To obtain information using qualitative methods, librarians undertake interviews, focus group or descriptive surveys with their users or client groups. By undertaking these types of qualitative measurement methods, which are often more expensive and more time consuming than quantitative methods, library managers are able to obtain primary information from their clients. Depending upon the type of measurement undertaken, clients are able to say how they feel about a certain service, what they like about it, what they dislike about it and may even be able to provide some ideas for change. Qualitative methods also allow managers to find out the reasons why people use a service and why they do not, whereas quantitative methods will only tell how many clients were active compared against the total possible client community (for instance, number of local residents or number of staff and students).

Often, experienced library managers will have a gut feeling as to why a certain service is not working as well as expected, or they may have overheard comments from clients in the library. These feelings or overheard comments should not be ignored and should provide the catalyst to undertake a more methodical look at the problem area.

By having a group of measures that are directly related to the library's goals and objectives run over a period of time, the organisation should be able to gain a good understanding of how it is performing. By combining these measures with benchmarking from other, comparable libraries, a clear picture will emerge on how successful the library is in meeting client expectations relative to its peers. A library manager going into a board meeting with hard evidence on how the library is performing is able to provide a clear, readily understandable case for any requests for increases in resources.

For larger organisations, standardised software packages tailored directly to the library market exist to assist managers in measuring the quality of the services they provide. LibQUAL+ is one example where the developers state that they provide:

> a suite of services that libraries can use to solicit, track, understand and act upon users' opinions of service quality … The program's centrepiece is a rigorously tested web-based survey bundled with training that helps libraries assess and improve library services, change organizational culture, and market the library (LibQUAL+ 2006).

Similar packages exist throughout the world, with the Ambit Insights survey (2006) (previously known as Rodski) being another suite of questions and analysis software used in Australia by academic libraries to measure service quality and levels of staff and client satisfaction.

Not all the information obtained from such surveys, questionnaires or other information gathering exercises in the library is going to be positive. If this is the case, the library manager must be able to work through the information gathered to assess its impact and work out, with staff, a strategy to implement change that may see the negative turn into a positive for the library. When surveys provide positive feedback, library managers should exploit this information through marketing and promotion and celebrate these results with staff.

Costs and budgetary issues

With the majority of libraries and information centres reliant on public financing for the bulk of their funding, maintaining costs and managing within budget have always been demanding tasks. This is especially true today with increasing costs, decreasing budgets and high levels of accountability a reality for many organisations. Close attention needs to be given to the major budgetary components which for virtually all information providers will be staffing and the collection – whether physical or digital.

Staffing, which typically takes 50 per cent or more of any library's budget, is an area where a manager usually has limited flexibility. Reducing costs by reducing staff numbers over a short period of time is rarely a realistic option. Like many other areas, libraries have seen in recent years a trend towards casualisation of the work force, with many staff employed under temporary contracts. This provides greater flexibility for managers but also creates problems of staff recruitment, training and development, management, commitment levels and retention. With staff comprising such a major proportion of the budget, it is essential for any manager to take a close interest in staff recruitment, performance appraisal and on-going professional development. It is vital to get this 'right' in order to get the best value for money from the staffing dollars.

In an attempt to control costs, there has been an ongoing move for many years to outsource certain activities. This entails contracting with a commercial vendor to provide services which the library will no longer undertake. Traditionally this has included the conversion of card catalogues, cataloguing of special collections and serials acquisitions. This has grown, however, and today entire library services have been outsourced with a view to reducing costs through greater efficiencies. An example of a less radical and more commonly adopted approach was that undertaken by the Brisbane City Library Service in outsourcing acquisitions and technical services. This has been seen as a very positive step with successful outcomes for the libraries and their users (Robertson 2005).

Outsourcing does provide increased flexibility, can be cost effective and removes the routine tasks, leaving library staff to focus on the more strategic, value-added services. However, there are also disadvantages in the loss of control and expertise that may arise with the movement of core activities out of the organisation. Whether the cost benefits remain long term is still unclear, with further longitudinal research studies required. A significant literature has grown up over the benefits or otherwise of outsourcing with little doubt that this is an approach to library provision that will continue to attract a high level of interest into the future. Estes suggests that outsourcing is likely to be the largest growth area for librarianship over the next five to ten years (quoted in Ebbinghouse 2002), and for any manager facing pressures to do more with less, it is an option that cannot be ignored.

Another issue that is likely to become more pressing in the coming decade is that of charging for services traditionally seen as free. The move towards 'user pays' across a wide range of activities and institutions is a general one that is unlikely to recede, and while core activities may continue to be exempt it is likely that there will be pressure to raise funds through charging for non-core or what are seen as purely recreational services. There has been considerable discussion of the impact of any changes to the concept of an essentially free public service, including the ethical issues involved. Having an understanding of these issues will help managers when faced with difficult decisions to balance budget cuts with user charges. An older paper (Hudson 1995) provides a good overview of the discussions at the Victoria and Albert Museum in the UK regarding charging for a range of services, and Abelsnes (1998) looks at the broader public policy implications of introducing charging.

Costs relating to building and maintaining the collection (see Chapter 8) represent another area in which close attention is required. Vagaries of the exchange rate, growing demands on budgets for non-collection purposes, escalating costs, the move to digital formats and the continually increasing volume of traditional materials available have made it very difficult for most libraries even to maintain their collections at levels previously realised. Comprehensive, long-term statistics are necessary to fully understand the impact of these and related issues. In the UK, Loughborough University has attempted this in recent years and provides detailed reports on a wide range of issues affecting the UK library and information profession (LISU 2005, Section 5). It reports:

- The number of serial titles published in the UK/US has grown from 71,000 print titles in 1987 to 186,000 in 2004 plus another 40,000 online journals in 2004 that did not exist in 1987.

- UK/US book publishing has risen from 154,000 titles in 1987 to 301,000 in 2003.

- In the period 1994–2004, inflation was 29%. Academic book prices rose at around the same rate. Serial subscription prices rose by 108%.

Figures such as these illustrate clearly the resourcing issues faced by any library manager with the daunting task of providing the best possible collection for their users.

The changing nature of collections

The continuing growth in traditional print-based publishing and the take-off in online only publications present a serious challenge for library managers with static or slow growing budgets. More than ever, selection and acquisition choices need to be focused on user requirements and considerable efforts have to be made to understand those needs. Different user populations will demand different things. It is unlikely that the public library will see its fiction collections moving away from print in the foreseeable future. Yet for most academic libraries, there has been, and will no doubt continue to be, a significant shift towards the acquisition of online resources at the expense of print acquisitions (see Chapter 3). Many academic and special libraries are looking closely at usage and finding similar trends – clients prefer the ease of access of online materials. In a lengthy but fascinating article looking at law library collections from a US perspective, Chiorazzi (2003) highlights the move from traditional print materials to online resources, citing examples such as Drexel University's Law Library which, by 2001, subscribed to only 300 print journals compared to over 6,000 electronic ones. He concludes with the view that there has been a fundamental shift in the 'use, organization and content' of academic law libraries, posing real challenges to their role and position over the coming years.

This growth in the development of online collections has meant there are less resources available to purchase traditional materials which, as was noted above, are still being published in ever increasing numbers. This, together with the well-known Pareto Principle which indicates that 80 per cent of use comes from 20 per cent of the collection, makes the traditional acquisition process less appropriate in the twenty-first century library. In academic libraries in particular, management needs to consider the just-in-time approach to acquisitions where print-based materials are concerned. In this scenario, the majority of print titles are only acquired when requested. Given the speed with which most commercial suppliers can deliver copies it is an approach that could be a cost-effective alternative to the usual method of more general selection and acquisition against subject profiles. It would almost certainly result in fewer print titles being acquired, with a corresponding decrease in the costs to purchase, process and store these items, leaving more resources available to handle the increasing level of online publications for which the demand is greater.

Decisions such as these once again emphasise the need for managers to be well informed. Gathering data on client needs, use of the collections and demand for services has to be undertaken and interpreted within a context provided through assessment of the external environment. In addition, managers need to examine closely all of their activities in order to try to understand the real costs involved for the benefit or value provided. Doing this can be a relatively straightforward process using a standard pro forma and costings in order to understand the overall expenditure associated with an activity or service. Nelson et al. (2000, p.99) provide a number of basic costing worksheets that can be tailored by individual organisations to suit their needs. From such worksheets, a standardised set of results can be produced and compared to the perceived value or benefit of the activity or service to the organisation and its users. As noted earlier, obtaining qualitative measurements such as the perceived value of a service is often harder than working out the costs involved, given that value is a nebulous concept, difficult to quantify and often subjective in nature. Basic statistical information drawn from the library management system regarding usage may provide a foundation for understanding value, but further input from staff and users as to their rating of the quality, usefulness and worth of a particular activity is also necessary in order to gain a clearer appreciation of the overall benefits related to that activity and thus its true worth.

With the growth in electronic resources, libraries are faced with management issues related to accessing these materials. The traditional approach of purchasing an item which the library then owns 'for ever' is less likely to be relevant to digital items, for which the usual approach is to license access to the materials through a third-party vendor. Issues arise concerning negotiating license and ongoing fees, the bundling of resources which may or may not suit the users of a particular library and longer term concerns over continuing access to earlier, archived material. While these resources have proven popular with most users, the Pareto Principle comes into play again, with a small number of databases meeting the vast majority of user needs. Yet frequently, as Paul Genoni points out (Chapter 8), libraries cannot just subscribe to this subset of material but must take the package on offer, containing a number of resources likely to be very little used by the library's clients (Chiorazzi notes that in one study of law library online use, over 90 per cent of queries accessed less than 10 per cent of the databases available.) Given the costs involved, and for many electronic resources, the very low level of usage, one tactic managers may pursue is to look towards sharing subscription costs with like organisations.

With libraries having a long record of cooperation across a wide range of activities, resource sharing is not a new concept and can provide significant benefits to its individual members. Establishing consortia or local networks is not a straightforward task and requires a considerable level of negotiation, but if successful the longer term benefits in cost sharing and increased negotiating power may well make this approach worth the effort. In addition, working closely with similar organisations can provide a forum for information and idea sharing, as well as being invaluable in offering a sympathetic sounding board for the airing of difficulties and challenges in a mutually supportive environment. Networking has always been an important part of the manager's role and will continue to offer substantial benefits for those actively involved.

In the foreseeable future, most libraries and other information centres will continue to hold hybrid collections of both print and digital resources. However, the move towards greater use of electronic resources means that managers will have to focus more on the most effective ways of making these resources available to their users and the issues associated with less control of a collection that is no longer owned but leased. In a very real sense, management will be involved with more technical issues, needing to relate closely to their IT colleagues as well as their traditional suppliers. In addition, the existing boundaries between libraries, archives and records management may well become blurred while at the same time the links with IT and computing generally will become stronger in order to deal with the growing online collections and conversion of existing analogue (non-digital) collections.

Convergence and competition

One of the impacts that growing numbers of digital resources have had is to build and strengthen bonds across traditionally separate areas of information management. Digital files share similar characteristics, regardless of their content. They are stored in the same way and accessed in a similar manner. As growing numbers of digital files are created in-house and stored for long term availability on local computer networks, the distinction between the roles of records management and archiving becomes blurred. Essentially, it becomes a continuum from the time of record creation to its preservation for the long term. Similar skills and understanding are required, and decisions made at the time of a record's creation affect its long-term storage and accessibility. This also applies to libraries that may be creating large numbers of files through programs to digitise physical collections such as newspapers, photographs, sound recordings or even moving images. Again, decisions made at the point of capture will affect access and preservation over the long term and the traditional approach of lending out copies becomes irrelevant when users have access to a digital file containing the data they need.

All of these activities require active cooperation with IT departments in order to ensure that the process of managing large scale digitisation programs, acquisition of suites of databases, licensing arrangements and the provision of access to this wide range of materials proceeds as smoothly as possible. Library managers will need to have a good understanding of the principles and standards behind networking, digital formats, file distribution and longer term archiving and preservation so that they can properly represent their interests in dealings with IT professionals, database vendors and others.

Given the increased role of information technology in the delivery of information products, in particular online resources freely available via the internet, there has been considerable debate over the continuing role of the physical library and its relevance. Lang (1999), at the time Director of the British Library, noted the changing relationship between the library building and its collection. Depending on the type of library, it may be that the building is becoming less necessary to hold the collection. But the building can and should have relevance to users seeking intellectual or social encounters, with the staff who work within the building able to provide added value for those accessing the collection – wherever it is located. It is essential for library managers to focus on the amenity of their physical building, its infrastructure and the role it plays within their target group, and promote that role as fully as possible. With well-trained, client focused staff, a physical space that provides an inviting and supportive environment for users, a collection – both physical and online – that meets user needs in a timely and convenient fashion, and services tailored to provide quality and value that match user needs, the library should continue to thrive, despite the competition from online services claiming that it is no longer relevant, or from students working at home, who think that Google supplies all the answers. In addition, as Chris Jones (Chapter 1) and Jake Wallis (Chapter 15) have pointed out, libraries are generally seen as an important public space, part of the social capital, offering a safe and comfortable environment from the sometimes challenging outside world (see, for instance, State Library of NSW 2000). Promoting this image, rethinking services, targeting user groups and broadening its role will all help to position the library into the twenty-first century.

Usherwood et al. (2005, p.90) refer to libraries, museums and archives as 'repositories of public knowledge' (RPKs) with a commonality of purpose that has seen intellectual and administrative support for their common role as sources of public knowledge. With administrators and bureaucrats looking at ways of reducing costs it is likely there may be a move towards some rationalisation in roles and activities across these traditionally separate institutions. Managers will need to work closely with their colleagues across the range of RPKs to see where cooperative activities may be possible and closer links forged. This would result in a stronger presence and less ambiguity for the users who currently may have difficulty in differentiating the most appropriate source to answer their information need. The work undertaken by Usherwood et al. (2005, p.97) in the UK indicates that RPKs have a high level of public support, with most people currently believing 'that it is important for society to maintain and sustain the established repositories of public knowledge'. However, they also note that RPKs are valued and trusted more than they are actually used. This paradox is an issue that RPK managers need to address in order to ensure their continued support at a political level. Better understanding of user needs and expectations is one area in which increased efforts can be made to try to ensure that this perception of value and trust is transformed into activity directly related to the RPK.

Client needs and expectations – library users and non-users

Correctly identifying user wants and needs and tailoring services appropriately has become increasingly important in the modern library with its rapidly changing environment. Marketing activities are based upon the information gathered through needs analysis, use studies and information audits. Managers therefore need to set in place ongoing programs to assess the information and recreational needs of users, and preferred modes of delivery. They should also try to identify special or niche requirements for local populations or targeted groups.

Undertaking such work is time consuming and labour intensive yet somehow it has to be done. There are commercial organisations or consultants who undertake this kind of work on a regular basis and it may be that using an established expert in the field, while costing more up front, will pay dividends in the long run with a better result delivered in a timely manner. Relying on regular staff who have to be taken off their normal day-to-day activities in order to take on the gathering and synthesis of a wide range of data may well be problematic for most busy workplaces. However, staff involvement in the overall process can help provide insights into their user community that they would otherwise not gain and Evans and Ward (2004, p.241) suggest that the best result is obtained through employing a mix of staff and outside expertise to undertake any assessment project.

The range of data to be gathered will depend upon the aims of the process, the user community and the availability of resources. Focusing on specific user groups or targeting particular activities helps to narrow down and make more manageable an assessment process that otherwise may appear to be too daunting. Evans and Ward (2004, Chapter 8) discuss various data gathering methods which, as mentioned in the introduction to this section, need to cover a range of alternatives from targeting individuals, running focus groups and collating statistics to mail surveys and observation studies. Whichever approach or approaches are adopted, interpreting the data requires considerable thought and discussion. It is important not to jump to conclusions. Staff and colleagues elsewhere should be asked for their input to the process and care should be taken to ensure that the data are fed into the planning program within the broader context supplied by an environmental scan (as discussed in Chapter 11) and associated information. Together these data provide a powerful tool in the shaping of future services and their delivery.

Identifying non-users of the library and trying to engage with them is also a necessary part of the library manager's role. Like virtually all businesses, libraries find it easier to retain existing clients rather than to go out and find new ones, and this is obviously an important factor to keep in mind when developing new services or looking at discontinuing old ones. However, growth is a natural aim for any organisation and an expanding client base is an important indication of a healthy institution. Achieving this depends upon a number of variables which, again, can be clarified through an information-gathering process that identifies non-users and attempts to find out why they are non-users. Evans and Ward (2004, p.255) note a range of reasons for non-use including not knowing about the product or service, its not being available when they need it, not needing it, a bad experience in the past and preference for an alternative. If one reason stands out then it is easier for the organisation to address the issue through some form of new or improved service design and targeted marketing exercise. Growing and diversifying the client base is a key factor in building the organisation's strength and ensuring its ongoing viability, making a strategic marketing plan essential for virtually any library.

Marketing and image

Kotler (2003, p.9), one of the key writers in this area, defines marketing as a societal process in which 'individuals and groups obtain what they need and want through creating, offering and freely exchanging products and services of value with others'. Kotler goes on to quote Peter Drucker, another well-known writer in the area of strategic management, who states that marketing's main aim is to 'know and understand the client so well that the product or service fits him and sells itself. Ideally, marketing should result in a client who is ready to buy. All that should be needed then is to make the product or service available' (Drucker 1973, in Kotler 2003, p.9).

Librarians for many years had a strong competitive advantage in the information market. Before the internet age, access to a wide array of information was limited to the major libraries with little competition in the collecting or provision of such information. The links among the client, the librarian and the service provided by the librarian were very clear, and many users had few alternatives. The introduction of the internet signalled the introduction of competition in the provision of information and has radically changed the availability of information resources in our society. As noted earlier, many users prefer to access online materials and in many cases, libraries also regularly find their information via the internet rather than through the more traditional means.

The emergence of competition is not limited to information services and increasingly appears in the areas of entertainment and leisure. Welch notes that competition for libraries can come from:

> other libraries; other information services; organisational records services; other departments or services in our own organisation; bookshops; other ways for our clients

to spend their time; the various information services we offer within our library; and other people and colleagues (2006, p.17).

Competition in the information marketplace has seen library managers try a number of different strategies to bring clients into the library to use the services. Youth services librarians have targeted 12-18 year olds with programs such as 'Libraries are Loud' which aims to encourage young adults into the library by running social and educational activities such as performances by local bands and speakers on how to get an after-school job. At the other end of the age spectrum, many public libraries run programs targeted at the over-sixties to introduce them to the internet, often using volunteers to provide one-on-one support to take some of the stress out of their first encounters with the new media. For any such programs, careful evaluation of their success or otherwise is essential in order to establish their value and priority in taking up scarce resources.

New public libraries are being built with other cultural services such as art galleries and museums within the same building or else in close proximity, forming a cultural precinct. Often such facilities are close to or integrated with a shopping centre, so that visiting the library or gallery becomes a regular part of the normal shopping trip. This approach has proven successful both in Australia and elsewhere, with public libraries showing increases in patronage when located with shopping complexes (Johnstone 1998, section 4).

Competition in the shape of the large retail book giants such as Borders has created a revolution with its stores having huge book stock levels, DVDs and CDs, with clients able to browse, sit and read in a comfortable environment, have coffee and cake, listen to music and see an author or musician perform all in the one place. Commercial retailers such as Borders have built their shops into destinations, and public library managers need to match these services by building or redeveloping library facilities and staff attitudes to ensure libraries can compete with such retailers on equal terms. Long dead is the idea that libraries are places where noise, food and books cannot comfortably coexist.

Creating a positive public image of a library can be one of the most challenging and most vital jobs that managers and their management team will face. Each type of library will have to address this issue differently but the bottom line, common to all, relates to knowing their users and their wants. Understanding these is the key to marketing success and one important approach in gaining this understanding is to break down the client base into homogenous groups based upon similar characteristics. In a public library this break-down may be done based upon age, whereas in an academic library it may be by degree level (say, undergraduate, postgraduate and research).

Breaking down users into groups is called segmentation, and doing this allows library managers to create targeted products or services tailored specifically for a particular client group. Examples may be story time for pre-schoolers, DVDs for primary-school age children, junior fiction, magazines and the internet for youths/young adults, and large print fiction, books on CD and newspapers for older adults. This detailed focusing makes the marketing effort easier and generally more successful, with the 'right' product or service aimed at the group likely to want it the most.

Public libraries have a very difficult task when building their public image compared to other types of libraries, due to the large number of potential market segments they serve. This compares to, say, law library users who may be limited to a couple of target groups – such as lawyers and paralegals asking for specific legal information. The law library can thus build its image within the law firm by marketing its services and its skill base directly to these relatively small and tightly focused groups. Public library managers have the challenge of reaching a multi-faceted user community that comprises a wide range of interests and potential groupings.

To build a strong public image successfully, library managers must understand the role of marketing and promotion in the 'selling' of quality library services. Many people associate marketing and promotion with selling a product or service for a fee, however, the principles and strategies involved are just as applicable to not-for-profit service organisations such as libraries which provide most of their services for no charge.

The marketing plan

One approach most larger libraries will adopt is a marketing plan which can help concentrate the marketing effort over a set timeframe. A marketing plan needs to have a direct relationship with the library's strategic plan, indicating the major goals and objectives of the organisation. If the marketing plan has little relevance to the strategic directions or mission of the library then the outcomes from the marketing exercise will not help the library achieve its broader objectives and outcomes.

The use of a SWOT analysis has already been discussed in relation to environmental scanning for strategic planning. It can also be used in a more focused fashion to help management develop its marketing strategy. By completing a SWOT analysis from a marketing perspective the library manager is able to obtain information about the strengths of its services and the skills of its staff, and identify why people are not utilising certain services (weaknesses). Library managers will need to examine what opportunities currently exist to provide new or improved services in a cost effective manner and consider threats, such as competition, that will affect the size and nature of their market.

Another important aspect of developing a library's marketing plan is to consider the marketing mix, comprising the four 'Ps': product, price, promotion and place. Kotler (2003, p.15) states that the marketing mix 'is a set of marketing tools the firm uses to pursue its marketing objectives in the target market'. The make-up of the tools can be varied enormously to suit a service, collection or program being offered by a library. This flexibility assists in developing marketing programs that are targeted at the different client groups. It is worth considering each of the components that comprise the marketing mix.

Product

This consists of looking at and analysing existing library services and establishing what is being done, whether it is being used and whether it is cost effective.

Pricing

It is also necessary to understand the full cost of providing a particular service. While most library services are delivered free to their users, there is a cost in delivering them that is carried by the organisation. It is important to relate this cost to the service – is it worth spending money to deliver one particular service while another misses out due to a lack of resources? Understanding the costs involved and the possibility of pricing certain services while retaining others as free services is an important judgement to be made in any marketing proposal.

Promotion

This component examines areas such as advertising, publicity and public relations in order to raise awareness at the broad and specific levels. Thus library managers will want to promote the library as a destination, the library as a brand and specific services through any means possible. A wide range of strategies is available including doing 'infomercials' on local radio, getting guest speakers/visitors to generate local publicity, conducting regular columns or guest spots in newspapers and radio, and the development of pamphlets and fliers promoting specific services.

Place

Place includes the library location, coverage and transport as well as the time and place of service delivery. Public libraries benefit greatly from locations that provide easy parking and access, are on a route into the shopping centre or are positioned otherwise in a way that encourages casual drop-in. For multi-campus libraries in the higher education sector, common in universities, issues arise relating to location of specific subject materials (who holds what) and with how efficiently the material/collection is moved between the various library buildings to meet client needs across the academic institution.

Goal of the marketing plan

The goal of the marketing plan is to ensure that the limited resource base of any library is focused on meeting the 'real' needs of their diverse user base in the most effective manner. These needs will change over time and thus the marketing plan too will need to be a 'live' document, evolving as the library moves to anticipate and respond to ever-changing user needs. For some users, the library may be a quiet place to catch up with the daily newspaper or attend a community meeting, while others may spend days there researching a topic in depth, working with the widest possible range of resources. Alternatively, a growing trend is to use the library's online resources from home, not actually visiting the physical space at all. This range of potential users and their requirements calls for considerable flexibility and responsiveness on behalf of the library in delivering its services to meet this diversity of needs. No static marketing plan can ever hope to address all of these requirements, but with a clear development and review cycle, and a concentration on key result areas, a carefully thought through plan will materially assist in meeting and predicting user needs. If it couples this with an appropriately structured organisation – responsive and flexible enough to meet this evolving world – the organisation will find itself strongly placed to meet the challenges of the new millennium.

Structures and flexibility

Organisational structures serve to indicate lines of authority, specialist activities and relationships across an organisation. They illustrate how different work activities or areas relate to each other, where responsibilities lie and how communication flows within the organisation. By their very nature, they indicate a hierarchy and areas of specialisation that suit a specific environment, and the larger and more complex that environment is, the more complicated and rigid the structure becomes. Once that environment changes – which is happening with increasing rapidity today – this complex structure may no longer be as useful in helping achieve the organisation's goals. Yet, modifying the structure can be a difficult and long-term process requiring considerable skill and perseverance for success.

Radical change to the organisational structure, particularly of large organisations, rarely happens and a quick look at most libraries' organisational charts will show a familiar set of relationships. However, there has been a growing trend to build a level of flexibility into the formal structure and also into the staffing itself. It is no longer possible (if it ever was) for someone to be certain about the nature and shape of their job and responsibilities over the longer term. It is inevitable that it will change and staff, together with the organisation itself, have to be responsive to those changes.

With new products and services being defined, user expectations growing, and increasing concerns over ethical standards and openness, managers will find it more difficult to maintain a tight control over all aspects of the work of an organisation. Delegation has become ever more important – together with the associated need for proper training for subordinates. The establishment of activity-based teams with a clear focus and objectives will see the role of senior management move to one of coordination rather than supervision. With smaller, focused teams there is the potential for greater flexibility and increased staff commitment to the activity itself rather than the less tangible concept of the broader organisation. Thus, maintaining the overriding presence of the organisation's mission is another of the challenges to be handled by senior management.

In such an environment, with more day-to-day decision making made further down the authority chain, the resultant freeing up of time allows senior management to concentrate on the strategic issues. These will relate to the identification of opportunities and threats in the environment and the rapid response of the organisation to those challenges. In order to meet these challenges, senior management has to have fostered in staff a sense of achievement and confidence that they can cope with sudden change and that the organisation will support them in dealing with this new endeavour. If flexibility and responsiveness are seen as imposing stress and instability into the workplace, with staff feeling overwhelmed and lacking confidence in management and its aims, then the benefits to the organisation are completely lost. The task for management is to establish strong communication systems, encourage staff input into decision making, enable staff training and development and build enthusiasm and commitment to the future direction of their organisation. This underlines the key role that good, informed and committed employees play in the success of the organisation. Selecting, recruiting and developing such staff is an important part of any manager's role in the twenty-first century library.

Staffing

As noted earlier, the most significant budget item in the majority of libraries is the cost of staffing, usually comprising 50 per cent or more of total budgets. This, together with the complexity involved in building, developing and keeping a skilled workforce in the face of a wide range of internal and external pressures, makes a focus on staffing essential for any library manager. These pressures typically include the problems of casualisation, ageing of staff, succession planning, credential creep, outsourcing, merging of departments, greater demand for training and professional development and implementation of performance management systems.

Casualisation of staffing

Casualisation of the workforce is not a library-specific issue but exists across all fields of employment. The use of casual staff in public and academic libraries to assist permanent staff in the provision of services during busy periods (for instance, weekends or during academic semesters) or for special projects is a common practice. Many unions fight over the level of casualisation of the workforce (percentage of staff that are employed on a casual basis), whereas many library managers, library boards, and TAFE and university directors have argued that casualisation of the workforce allows for greater flexibility of the staffing profile and a reduction in ongoing staff-related costs (such as provisions for long service leave). It seems inevitable that in today's rapidly changing environment, the flexibility offered by the use of casual staff who can be hired or terminated relatively easily is attractive to many library managers. In addition to providing flexibility, using casual staff also provides an opportunity to examine the 'fit' of the new staff member within a library team and the skills they possess. If they do not work out successfully, their contract can be terminated or not renewed and if they do work out well, they are in a good position to apply for any permanent positions that may become available. In fact, this is a common method by which newer staff, with limited experience, obtain permanent positions.

As noted by Canterbury City Library (NZ) in its strategic planning document (1997), there are benefits and drawbacks to the use of a casual workforce: 'Increasing casualisation of the workforce has implications on demands for training, the necessity of thorough internal communication of policy and procedure and the opportunity to benefit from changing (more flexible) patterns of working hours.'

Ageing of the workforce

Ageing of the library workforce is an ongoing issue as the current baby boomer generation reaches retirement age, with a consequent impact of large numbers of experienced, often senior staff leaving within a relatively short period of time. The impact of this is not only a loss of expertise and knowledge (one of the KM issues discussed in Chapter 13) but it also makes the identification and development and training of suitable replacement staff a high priority. Teece (2006) states 'right now there is a surge of apprehension about the ageing library workforce which the profession's statistical profile suggests may be valid'. Once again, a good manager will be aware of this and have in place some form of human resource management plan to cope with this eventuality.

Succession planning

Succession planning is one mechanism that assists the workplace to cope with senior staff retiring. When implemented successfully this planning mechanism ensures staff in middle management have been properly trained to take on their manager's position when they leave (Singer et al, 2004). This has a number of benefits to both the individual and the organisation as it enables the person moving into the new position to be effective from the beginning. Succession planning can be implemented at any level and involves on-the-job training with staff spending time with their manager learning the job and acting in the position when the manager is away. This approach, together with more formal training and development, will help the organisation avoid some of the difficulties and potential disruption caused by the departure of a long-serving member of staff.

'Credential creep'

'Credential creep' is a popular term used to describe the increasing tendency to ask for higher qualifications in order to be considered for a particular position. Increasingly, staff are undertaking further studies – from diploma to degree and from undergraduate awards to postgraduate qualifications. While providing staff with higher levels of base knowledge, this can also cause challenges for employers who find it difficult to provide appropriate work for those with higher level qualifications. For employees it can result in a level of frustration when it is felt that the work available to them does not sufficiently exploit their knowledge and skills. Once again, managing this potential conflict is an integral part of the manager's role in ensuring that the best use is made of the skill base available.

Outsourcing

Outsourcing of traditional library tasks has already been noted in discussions of budgets and cost effectiveness issues. In relation to staffing it can be a useful tool but needs to be carefully managed. As for the use of casual staff employed by the library, the outsourcing of a particular task or tasks to an external body that undertakes to do the work provides flexibility for the library and a clearer understanding of the costs involved in undertaking a job. Often, however, the task that is outsourced is undertaken within the library itself by staff contracted to another organisation (the supplier of the outsourcing service). The relationship between these contract staff and the usual library employees will have to be carefully managed to avoid any potential for conflict or confusion over roles. A simple example, such as whether the contract staff should answer telephones, illustrates the sort of issues that need to be worked out with the agency before contract staff are brought on site.

Merging departments

Merging organisational departments is a growing problem as the tightening of budgets and the restructuring of departments has led to the merging of library and information technology departments in universities, schools and special libraries. One of the outcomes of such a merger may be that the manager of the new area may not be a librarian but rather the person previously responsible for the IT department. This can cause difficulties in having a senior manager in overall charge of library functions who has little or no direct experience of the library environment. Benedetti (2003, p.31) states this could be an advantage as the manager may rely on the senior librarian's experience to make decisions, but this will not always be the case. Thus it is essential for any library manager to maintain a positive and energetic profile within the broader organisation, including building strong relationships with management in related areas in order that they can have a voice in any reorganisation and merger discussions.

Performance appraisal/management

Libraries are under increasing pressure to show that they are meeting set goals and objectives. This is also true for individual library staff, with performance management and feedback becoming more common and increasingly formalised within the workplace. Performance management of staff is usually an annual event, where the staff member sits down with his or her direct manager to discuss achievements and goals set over the period since the last performance management review. This provides an opportunity for both manager and staff member to provide feedback on each other's performance – it should not be a one-way street. During an appraisal, managers will identify any areas of concern and seek to set in place changes to overcome these while at the same time providing positive feedback for a job well done. This is also an opportunity for staff to discuss training and related needs and to negotiate an ongoing development plan to build their skill base and promotion prospects. Undertaking such appraisals is a time-consuming and frequently stressful process for both staff and employers. It has to be handled carefully and in a sensitive manner if it is to have the positive outcomes that such a process should provide for both the library and the staff member involved.

Professional development

Professional development and training are the responsibility of both the manager and of the employee. Training opportunities exist both formally and informally throughout libraries, library associations, consultants and education providers. Library staff training programs can be developed in-house, usually taking the form of on-the-job training opportunities or exploiting the knowledge of staff members to undertake a formal or informal training session on a particular aspect of their work. External training providers can be contracted to supply training on a specific subject such as using a new software package, or staff can be sent to regular courses offered by a number of companies specialising in training for library staff. In addition to training for specific tasks or jobs, the broader issue of professional development – building the knowledge and abilities to further one's career within the profession – should also be a joint concern for staff members and their managers. Indeed, ALIA requires members to undertake a certain level of continuing professional development in order to remain current with the rapid changes taking place within the profession.

Staff recruitment

Staff recruitment is a vital process for any library manager. Managers will look to advertise vacancies in newspapers, trade publications or library association websites. For most positions, managers will develop a set of selection criteria based on what they feel describes the key skills and experience necessary for the applicant to be considered for a position. These criteria will usually cover specific skills or knowledge, such as cataloguing rules or experience with a particular software package, as well as broader, more general attributes, such as team skills and the ability to prioritise in a busy working environment. For a manager, the challenge lies in evaluating candidates against such criteria. For specific skills this may be quite straightforward – someone can be asked, for instance, to actually catalogue one or two items before the interview – but for the more generic attributes such as working under stress or being a good team player, it is far more difficult to assess candidates. Thus more effort and greater care must be taken in designing questions to elicit reliable responses against such criteria (often the use of a 'made up' scenario is helpful) and to use other avenues, such as depth of experience and referees' comments as indicators. It is important to try to identify those with these attributes as they are harder to acquire via training and development than the more technical skills which are relatively easily taught and learnt.

Increasingly, applicants for library positions are coming from a wide range of backgrounds. The traditional liberal arts graduate attracted to the profession is now competing against those from less traditional areas such as business or IT. Also, many applicants may have had one or more careers and are looking to take on new challenges in the LIS field. This broader range of potential candidates for a position brings real possibilities for a manager looking to enrich the staffing balance of his or her library by bringing in new ideas, attitudes and experience which, one hopes, may provide an impetus for change and innovation.

Once new employees have accepted a position and started work they should be given an induction into the workplace by their immediate supervisors. This induction process can be as long as six months or as little as a week and usually involves introducing the workplace to the new employee by explaining work practices, functions of the position, reporting relationships, occupational health and safety principles and administrative basics such as sick leave and flex time. The Thames Valley Health Libraries Network Professional Development Group published its induction program, describing its main functions as:

- A systematic introduction to the people and services in the library and the organisation

- To enable the new member of staff to become part of the team

- To introduce new staff to the ethos and standards of the library

- To encourage a sense of commitment on the part of new staff members as well as reinforce it in existing staff (Thames Valley Health Libraries Network 2004)

Managers and supervisors must ensure a successful induction of new staff members, as this has a big impact on how well they will fit in with the organisation's culture and will also affect their ability to reach satisfactorily the probation requirements written into their employment contract.

Conclusion

In conclusion, managers are facing many challenges in staff recruitment and development to ensure the ongoing success of their libraries. The casualisation of the workforce and the ageing of many library staffing profiles may lead to staff shortages in the near future and will certainly change the culture and outlook of many organisations. The coming decade will see a greater emphasis on staff flexibility, participative management practices, a rapid evolution in the nature of the work performed and an increasing emphasis on working smarter and delivering more for less. At its heart, however, there will still be a focus on meeting client needs and providing a service that only trained, confident staff, working in an environment where their skills and knowledge are fully utilised and their opinions valued, can deliver.

This chapter has considered a broad range of managerial functions and challenges that library and information workers will face in the coming years. This is no different from any other profession. As long as there is a focus on gathering real data to inform managerial decision-making, increasing knowledge of our users and their needs, building networks and responding quickly and flexibly to the changing environment, then the coming years will be years of success and achievement. Couple this with an increasingly knowledgeable and well-trained workforce and the future for the profession looks bright indeed.

References

Abelsnes, K 1998, *Social responsibilities discussion group: Fees for library services*, IFLA, http://www.ifla.org/VII/dg/srdg/srdg1.htm

Ambit Insights 2006, *Why conduct a library survey?*, http://www.ambitinsights.com/Products/?product=LibrarySurveys

Benedetti, J 2003, 'Managing the small art museum library', *Journal of Library Administration*, vol.39 no.1.

Canterbury City Library (NZ) 1997, *Analyses and background information to the strategic directions for the Canterbury Public Library 1997–2007*, http://library.christchurch.org.nz/Policy/StrategicPlan/Background/

Chiorazzi, M 2003, *Books, bytes, bricks and bodies: Thinking about collection use in academic law libraries*, http://www.law.arizona.edu/Library/internet/publications/library/documents/paretoarticle.htm

Choo, CW 2001, 'Environmental scanning as information seeking and organizational learning', *Information Research,* vol.7 no.1, http://informationr.net/ir/7-1/paper112.html

Cole, K 2005, *Management: Theory and practice,* 3rd edn, Pearson Education, Sydney.

Drucker, P 1973, *Management: Tasks, responsibilities, practices*, Harper and Row, New York.

Ebbinghouse, C 2002,'Library outsourcing: A new look, *Searcher,* vol.10, no.4,http://www.infotoday.com/searcher/apr02/ebbinghouse.htm

Evans, GE, Ward, PL & Rugass, B 2000, *Management basics for information professionals*, Neal-Schuman, New York.

Evans, GE & Ward, PL 2004, *Beyond the basics: The management guide for library and information professionals*, Neal-Schuman, New York.

Hudson, C 1995, *Charging for information services in UK museums and libraries*, Acta, Antwerp, pp.113-115, http://www.sibmas.org/congresses/sibmas94/antw_34.html

Johnstone, L 1998, *Public libraries and shopping centres*, http://www.slq.qld.gov.au/serv/publib/build/seminars/shop

Kotler, P 2003 *Marketing management*, 11th edn, Prentice-Hall,Upper Saddle River, NJ.

Lang, B 1999, 'Library buildings for the new millennium', *IFLA's 11th International Seminar: Library building in a changing environment*, August 15-19 1999, Shanghai, http://www2.db.dk/pe/china/ifla-11.htm

Lewisham Library and Information Service 2005, *Best value review 2003/4*, http://www2.lewisham.gov.uk/lbl/CouncilMeetings/Committees_post0502/OAndSBusinessPanel/documents/Dec2004/ovr_scr_bus_pan_LibrariesBVR_20dec04.pdf

LibQUAL+ 2006, 'LibQUAL+: Charting library service quality', http://www.libqual.org/

LISU (Library and Information Statistics Unit) 2005, *LISU annual library statistics 2005*, http://www.lboro.ac.uk/departments/ls/lisu/downloads/als05-s1-p1-8.pdf

Matthews, JR 2003 *Measuring for results: The dimensions of public library effectiveness*, Libraries Unlimited, Westport, CT.

Morrison, JL 1992, 'Environmental scanning', in *A primer for new institutional researchers*, MA Whitely, JD Porter & RH Fenske (eds), The Association for Institutional Research, Tallahassee, FL, pp.86-99, http://horizon.unc.edu/courses/papers/enviroscan/

Nelson, S, Altman, E & Mayo, D 2000, *Managing for results: Effective resource allocation for public libraries*, American Library Association, Chicago. IL.

OCLC (Online Computer Library Centre) 2003, *Environmental scan: A report to OCLC membership*, http://www.oclc.org/reports/escan/introduction/default.htm

Robertson, S 2005, *Successful outsourcing of acquisitions and technical services*, http://e-prints.alia.org.au/archive/00000064/

Singer, P, Goodrich, J & Goldberg, L 2004, 'Your library's future', *Libraryjournal.com*, Reed Elsevier, http://www.libraryjournal.com/article/CA470985.html

State Library of New South Wales 2000, *A safe place to go: Libraries and social capital*, http://www.sl.nsw.gov.au/pls/publications/pdf/safe_place.pdf

Teece, P 2006, 'Workwatch: Librarians in the job market: A strange dichotomy', *inCite,* http://alia.org.au/publishing/incite/2005/12/workwatch.html

Thames Valley Health Libraries Network Professional Development Group 2004, *Induction: Guidelines for good practice*, Thames Valley Strategic Health Authority, http://www.tvsha.nhs.uk/libraries/doc/Induction_guide.pdf

Usherwood, B, Wilson, K & Bryson, J 2005, 'Relevant repositories of public knowledge? Libraries, museums and archives in 'the information age', *Journal of Librarianship and Information Science*, vol.37, no.2.

Welch, L 2006, *The other 51 weeks: A marketing handbook for librarians*, rev. edn, Centre for Information Studies, Wagga Wagga, NSW, 2650.

CHAPTER 18
Education for library and information service

Gillian Hallam

There is much discussion in the literature about the challenges facing education for workers in the library and information science (LIS) sector. Michael Gorman, president of the American Library Association (ALA) in 2005–2006, has gone so far as to declare that there is a 'crisis in LIS education' (Gorman 2004; Berry 2004; Seavey 2005; Mulvaney & O'Connor 2006; Dillon & Norris 2005; Stoffle & Leeder 2005), although Gorman later modified the statement to indicate that there were perhaps 'critical issues', rather than a crisis per se (Gorman 2006). The critical issues he referred to were multidimensional, and indeed interlinked, encompassing the perceived lack of a core curriculum for the discipline, the apparent gulf between LIS education and LIS practice, and the pressing need for career-long learning and development. Here in Australia, Ross Harvey asserted that 'something's amiss with university-based education for librarianship in Australia' (2001, p.15). Levett lamented in his editorial to the *Australian Library Journal* that Harvey's article had met, disappointingly, with 'resounding silence' (Levett 2001, p. 1). The topic of LIS education appears to attract plenty of criticism, but very few constructive ideas to respond positively to the challenges presented.

One of the fundamental issues that appears repeatedly in the literature is the vexing question about the positioning of the profession. Is LIS a graduate profession of highly skilled individuals valued for their expertise and professionalism or is it a profession of anyone who works in a library, regardless of their qualifications (Library and Information Association of New Zealand 2005)? While the concept of a profession has a number of intrinsic characteristics that encompass the social relevance of the field, the autonomy of the practitioner and the existence of a code of ethics, it is important to consider some of the key attributes of a profession within the context of LIS education. These attributes may include:

- The existence of a body of theoretical knowledge serving as the foundation for professional practice.

- The need for extensive education and training.

- The existence of a formal professional association.

- The development of specific standards of professional competency deemed appropriate for entry into the profession (Bramley 1969, p.7).

Rochester argues that the cognitive base is central to the ethos of a profession:

> The main path for advancement of any profession is the development of the unique and identifiable knowledge and skills that it professes. This gives social recognition and prestige to the profession; it leads to material rewards, relatively secure and well paid and interesting work, with the hope of a career path. It also means the relative freedom

of the professional in their day-to-day work. This advancement has been the pursuit of
librarians in Australia (Rochester 1997, p.1).

Across all disciplines, there is considerable debate about the current challenges facing those
involved in professional education, whether at the institutional level of university, college or
faculty, or at the personal level of educator. Within the LIS profession, these are indeed
challenging times for educators who are directly responsible for the development of the new
information professional – while concurrently contending with the multiple demands of
students, employers, professional associations, university management and governments. While
'seismic changes' (Feather 2003) have made themselves felt in the field through the application
of information and communications technologies, new approaches to information provision and
access, reforms across higher education and indeed changes across society as a whole, many of
the issues and concerns have been consistently discussed for decades. Much of the argument has
hinged on the disparate viewpoints that exist between LIS educators and LIS professionals, and
the vociferous debate continues today, peppered with ideas such as 'mistrust',
'misunderstandings', 'tensions' and 'the need for consensus'. There are exhortations to engage
in 'genuine dialog' (Moran 2001, p.52) or to 're-engineer the relationship between LIS
departments and the profession' (Feather 2003). This chapter does not seek to resolve the
arguments, but rather to invite readers to engage with the range of issues that confront LIS
education in Australia and to consider the role that they might play in the future to help change
these long-standing problems and concerns.

The Australian context is introduced by a review of the historical perspectives of education
for the LIS sector in this country, moving from the apprenticeship model to that of formal
education. The chapter also explores the need for standards of professional education, achieved
in Australia through the course recognition process undertaken by the professional association.
As each educational institution submits an annual course return (discussed below), an analysis
of the data on the student cohort and the staffing situation is presented, framed by the changing
environment of education in Australia. The predominant, recurrent issues are discussed – the
scope of the curriculum, the perceived gulf between research and practice, and the need for
career-long learning. The chapter concludes by reinforcing the idea that the future of effective
and relevant LIS education is a matter for all people involved in the profession to work together
to ensure that the profession does have a real future.

Historical perspectives of LIS education

Bramley (1969) provides a valuable overview of the development of professional education,
outlining the evolution of education for the library profession in both the United Kingdom and
the United States of America. One key factor in the history of professional education was the
introduction – and acceptance – of formal examinations by specific professional associations,
with an associated syllabus that represented the core body of knowledge of the given profession.
Following the establishment of the Library Association in the United Kingdom in 1877, the
council of the association focused on the need for formal training of library assistants, with
much discussion about the relative merits of the apprenticeship approach as opposed to
professional examinations. Examinations were indeed introduced, with the first one being held
in 1885 with three candidates. Initial topics encompassed English literature, an understanding of

another European language, principles of classification of the sciences, elements of bibliography, including cataloguing, library administration and management, and general literary history.

Bramley argues, however, that at that time, not only was there no significant body of theoretical knowledge to be mastered, as 'library administration, classification and cataloguing were virtually unexplored subjects' (1969, p. 13), but also, inevitably, there were no courses of instruction on offer to potential students. It is also important to remember that most library assistants at that time would not have had any schooling beyond the age of fourteen, so their formal education would have been limited to a basic level of reading, writing and arithmetic. The meagre level of the financial rewards of librarianship meant that the majority of those who did work in libraries 'were badly educated and limited in their ambitions' (Bramley 1969, p.14). Modifications and adjustments were made to the syllabus and the examination over the ensuing years, but the lack of candidates remained a significant problem. In the early twentieth century, the main focus of library training was technical proficiency and administrative competence. Practical skills strongly outweighed any interest in scholarly or intellectual achievement.

In 1909, the Library Association agreed to establish a register of members. Those people wishing to become a qualified librarian, therefore, were required to become a member of the Library Association and pass the examination to be awarded a diploma. University College London introduced its own diploma qualification in 1919. The library school council of University College comprised six members appointed by the university and six by the Library Association. There were ninety-eight students in the initial intake. With qualifications offered by both the university and the association, the end result was a glut of professional librarians, chasing all too few jobs, with the inevitable consequence of people accepting positions with depressed salaries.

The next significant stage in the development of library education resulted from discussions held between the Library Association, the Carnegie United Kingdom Trust, the Ministry of Education and the principals of a number of colleges of further education. Soon after the end of World War II, seven new schools of librarianship opened, offering a one-year program with a new syllabus covering cataloguing, classification, bibliography, assistance to readers, library organisation and the history of English literature. There were undoubtedly tensions between the teaching staff who sought to develop the students' understanding of concepts and principles, and the Library Association examiners who seemed preoccupied by the detail of technical skills. The schools actively sought to conduct their own internal examinations. By the early 1960s, a further group of library schools was established by technical colleges or colleges of commerce. In 1964, the Library Association introduced a new syllabus that was designed for a two-year course that encompassed the theory, skills and techniques of librarianship. A radical move was made with the Library Association ceasing to play its role as the examining body, to allow the schools to examine their own students. The Library Association moved into the role of standards body, responding to the need to determine and maintain the standards of education for librarians.

In the United States, professional education and vocational training have long been part of the university scene. This made it far easier for a school of librarianship to be established at a university, so that in 1887 Melville Dewey founded the inaugural School of Library Economics at Columbia College, where he was librarian. Bramley notes that:

> it was not Dewey's intention to devote overmuch time to the theoretical principles of librarianship ... the course was essentially empirical in character. In addition to accession methods, and classification and cataloguing, other skills taught at the school included library handwriting and the use of the typewriter (1969, pp.78-79).

Historical discussion indicates that there was considerable resistance to the idea of the library school on the part of members of ALA (founded in 1876) who believed that the apprenticeship approach to training within the library setting was more appropriate. It has been reported that the establishment of the first library school at a university was probably 'more a happy accident than part of some grand design by Dewey' (Bramley 1969, p.80). Nevertheless, this accident proved to be an inspiring precedent for other universities. By the early twentieth century, library schools required college graduation as a prerequisite for entry into a library course. (Note: the philanthropist Andrew Carnegie spent millions of dollars to establish libraries across the United States and beyond. This huge investment necessarily raised significant questions about the staffing of these institutions, resulting in considerable funding programs for library schools and scholarship opportunities for students.) However, while education in the United States emphasised the actual course of instruction rather than an examination, it was found that the quality of instruction varied widely across the different institutions. This led to the introduction of a system of accrediting courses to ensure specific standards of education could be met. As the professional body, ALA was keen to adopt the accreditation role. Then, as now, the Masters programs tended to be the ones that were accredited, while the Bachelor courses were not.

History of LIS education in Australia

While there was a close nexus between developments in library education and the professional association in countries like the United States and the United Kingdom, there were specific challenges in Australia. Bramley argues that:

> The establishment of a professional association is an essential step in the crystallisation of professional ideals and aims, and it was the inability of librarians in Australia to found a permanent professional organisation which for a long time retarded the development of a system of education for Australian librarians (1969, p.109).

The challenges to the establishment of a professional association included the geographical and political realities of Australia, with its federated system of states and territories covering an extensive land mass, as well as the difficulties in realising the true professional status of librarianship. Early attempts at tuition for library staff were introduced at the Public Library of New South Wales by the librarian HCL Anderson. Having attended the Second International Library Conference in London in 1897, Anderson aspired to see a process like the one introduced in the United Kingdom, with library training and an examination leading to the qualification of a diploma. He introduced classes at the Public Library, initially for staff of the Library, but later for other interested students. Anderson also pioneered the use of the Dewey Decimal Classification scheme and published a guide to the cataloguing rules.

The Munn-Pitt report (1935) presented the findings of a survey which aimed to examine the library situation in Australia. The report highlighted the pressing need for a single professional body that could encourage and support library education in Australia. The Carnegie Corporation, which had funded the study, provided further funding to John Metcalfe, then deputy principal librarian with the New South Wales Public Library, for an international study tour to discuss issues with key members of the UK Library Association and ALA. Metcalfe's subsequent report contained the proposal to establish a professional body that could play a significant role in improving the standards of library training.

The Australian Institute of Librarians (AIL) was founded in 1937, with the express goals of establishing professional unity to raise the standards and status of librarianship in Australia. Membership of the Institute was restricted to 'professional librarians'. The theme of the first conference held in 1938 was standards of librarianship and library training, culminating in the establishment of the Committee on Standards and Training to develop policies on education and training. The Board of Examination and Certification was convened in 1941, later becoming the Board of Education. Through a series of summer schools and semester programs, tuition was initially provided by three key employers, the Commonwealth National Library and the public libraries of New South Wales and Victoria 'to prepare librarians to organise and provide access to the increasing volume and complexity of materials in government libraries' (Rochester 1997, p.17). Reforms in the education sector led to the need for school libraries, with the Library School at the Public Library of New South Wales offering a teacher librarians' course. Rochester (1997) examines the debate between educators and practitioners about the need for a generalist or a specialist education for different library sectors, such as teacher librarians, children's librarians, special librarians and archivists, with the AIL strongly resisting challenges to its policy of a generalist curriculum.

Initial steps to formalise the education and training of librarians in Australia were delayed by the Second World War, but ultimately took place in 1944 when the AIL introduced a 'qualifying examination'. In 1949, the Australian Institute of Librarians (AIL) became the Library Association of Australia (LAA), open to a broader spectrum of members, and with the acceptance of elective specialist papers in the examination. The examination was renamed the 'registration examination' and formed the main career pathway for librarians until 1980. The registration exam comprised nine papers, with three foundation topics, four core subjects and two elective subjects (Bramley 1969). The library schools within the three major libraries continued to prepare students for the exam.

At the same time, the LAA actively encouraged the development of independent library courses. Rochester has argued that 'formalized education in universities and colleges meant the increasing professionalization of librarianship' (1997, p.57). The first academic qualification was introduced by the University of New South Wales in 1960 as a Graduate Diploma of Librarianship, with the university both teaching and examining its students. The award was deemed equivalent to the association's registration exam. In 1963, the General Council of the LAA adopted the formal position that librarians should hold a postgraduate qualification. However, in 1965, the government introduced colleges of advanced education and institutes of technology as a new area of tertiary education. Library education fitted into this domain, with a number of courses emerging at the undergraduate level. Since 1968, the professional association has accepted both undergraduate and graduate qualifications as first award courses.

In 1970, in response to the changing dynamics of the workforce and a shortage of professional librarians, the first library technician course was introduced by Whitehorse Technical College in Box Hill, a suburb of Melbourne, with a curriculum that focused on vocational, practical skills as opposed to theoretical knowledge. The course covered 'library procedures, display techniques, audiovisual techniques, business procedures, together with subjects such as sociology and staff supervision' (Rochester 1997, p.52). The LAA moved to accept the course recognition criteria for library technician courses in 1977, subsequently introducing a new category of membership for library technicians in 1978.

Course recognition issues

In 2000, the International Federation of Library Associations and Institutions (IFLA) developed its *Guidelines for professional library/information educational programs – 2000* (IFLA 2000). These international guidelines were developed to address the quality of graduate and professional level LIS programs primarily, and are therefore very general in their scope, given their potential application across such a broad spectrum of jurisdictions. The *Guidelines* encompass the broader framework (such as context, mission, goals and objectives), curriculum, faculty and staff, students, administration and financial support, and instructional resources and facilities. In their study of standards of LIS education across the world, Dalton and Levinson (2000) identified three models that aim to establish and maintain the standards for LIS education: governmental monitoring; formalised LIS accreditation/approval processes; individual course/departmental standards. The processes in place in the United Kingdom, through the Chartered Institute of Library and Information Professionals (CILIP), in the United States, through the American Library Association (ALA), and in Australia, through the Australian Library and Information Association (ALIA), all represent the second model, that of formalised LIS accreditation/ approval purposes, although each is distinctive (Hallam et al. 2004).

At the local Australian level, ALIA acts as the standards body for the library and information profession. ALIA holds responsibility for the recognition of the university and TAFE courses that provide a library and information studies qualification. As noted, the course recognition process is directly linked to the categories of membership of the Association, specifically in terms of the associate membership which requires members to hold an ALIA-recognised LIS qualification at undergraduate or graduate levels, and the library technician membership, with members holding an ALIA-recognised library technician qualification. Other categories of ALIA membership include general member, student, associate fellow and fellow, as well as institutional member.

Under the education standards process, ALIA currently recognises eighteen courses leading to library technician qualifications (ALIA 2006a), the majority at the level of the Diploma in Library and Information Services. One university offers the qualification as an Associate Degree in Science (Library Technology) and another as a Bachelor of Science (Library Technology). At the professional level, ten universities offer ALIA-recognised LIS courses at undergraduate and graduate levels (ALIA 2006b). This compares with sixteen library schools in

1990. Five of the ten institutions offer courses at both undergraduate and postgraduate levels; one university limits its offering to an undergraduate program. Four universities offer only postgraduate programs (Graduate Diploma or Masters). One university offers only a Masters course, either as a general professional program (Master of Information Management or teacher librarianship (Master of Learning Innovation). Harvey has noted that 'librarianship has perhaps always had an identity crisis in that it can be argued that it encompasses every field of endeavour' (2001). The multidisciplinary nature of librarianship today requires knowledge and skills that cut across information technology, management, psychology, education, communications, law and human services. A response to this situation can be found in the diverse intellectual emphases in different institutions in terms of faculty or discipline affiliation for the LIS school – courses can be found in schools or faculties of information technology, business, management, humanities and social sciences, media and information, law, business and the arts, and education.

It has been noted that, when international comparisons are made, there is an apparent imbalance between the total population and the number of institutions offering LIS courses in Australia. Current figures are presented in Table 18.1.

Table 18.1 Comparative data for LIS schools (2005)

Country	LIS schools	Population	Ratio – LIS schools: population
Australia	10	20 million	1:2 million
Canada	7	33 million	1:4.7 million
United Kingdom	14	60 million	1:4.3 million
United States	50	295 million	1:5.9 million

This imbalance means that not only are the Australian LIS schools competing for graduate enrolments within their own institutions, to encourage students to study towards the Graduate Diploma in Library and Information Studies rather than, say, a Graduate Diploma in Justice Studies, but also there are arguably too many institutions competing for the small number of students nationally who do in fact wish to pursue an LIS career. In contrast to the United States (usnews.com 2006), no formal data are published in Australia to assist students assess the quality of LIS schools and their staff.

The relatively small numbers of LIS students at individual universities increases the vulnerability of the courses themselves. It is immensely challenging for an academic unit with perhaps four academic staff and less than a hundred students to be influential and respected when there are programs with thousands of students and hundreds of faculty staff in the overall pool of tens of thousands of students enrolled at a university. In 2001, Schauder estimated that it took 31.43 full-fee paying Australian students to cover the employment costs of one academic staff member. If the course requirements are eight academic subjects for a Graduate Diploma, with the worst case scenario of two academics running four units each, the minimum enrolment just to cover salaries is 62.86 full-time students. Harvey (2001) and Bundy (2001) have proposed that Australian LIS courses should have a minimum of six academic staff dedicated to the LIS discipline. They have calculated that this model would require an annual full-time graduate student enrolment of 188.57 students which, given the multiplicity of library schools in

Australia, is unsustainable. What are the implications of students having, for example, only two teaching staff for the whole course? Surely it is critical to have a balance of staff with diverse professional experience to provide the opportunity for a range of views to be presented?

The ongoing process of reform in higher education in Australia has specific implications for LIS education. As universities strive to achieve greater efficiencies, the principles of economic rationalism inevitably apply. The bulk of the available funding will go towards the bigger and stronger (and more influential) disciplines where high numbers of students are guaranteed, such as medicine, law and business. Smaller niche disciplines like library and information science have found their autonomy and their identity threatened. Independent 'library schools' have progressively been subsumed into LIS departments, to ultimately become nothing more than a discipline stream, or even just a single course, within a school within a faculty. In many cases this means that the LIS schools 'have been forced into alliances with other disciplines, and it is unlikely that any school now teaches courses over which they have full control' (Genoni 2005a). This in turn has implications within the framework of course recognition by ALIA as local conditions in individual universities may make it increasingly difficult to compare 'apples with apples' in terms of the content of the curriculum.

In recognising courses at the professional level and the library technician level, ALIA draws on its core education policies: *ALIA's role in education of library and information professionals* (ALIA 2005a), *Courses in library and information management* (ALIA 2005b) and *Library and information sector: Core knowledge, skills and attributes* (ALIA 2005c). Seven key criteria are taken into consideration: course design, curriculum content, student assessment, staffing, resourcing, quality assurance mechanisms and infrastructure. As courses may be offered, of course, in diverse ways – for instance, face to face, online or as a hybrid of both – ALIA seeks to ensure that learning outcomes will be consistent across the various delivery modes (ALIA 2006c). Institutions planning to offer an LIS course are required to submit documentation to respond to the seven criteria and to be open to scrutiny through a site visit by a panel of LIS educators and industry practitioners. The courses are monitored through the submission of an annual course return (ACR).

It is acknowledged that course recognition is a valid alternative to the onerous task of assessing individual qualifications in determining eligibility for membership of the Association. The process of course recognition further serves to reassure potential employers about the range and level of skills and knowledge of graduates entering the workforce (Nicholson & Tattersall 2001). Concerns have been expressed about the 'mediocrity of the course recognition process', with ALIA 'preferring to recognise almost every course for the maximum period rather than use its teeth to effect real change and improvement' (Harvey 2001), although at a later juncture Harvey (2004) has acknowledged that ALIA does indeed regularly scrutinise the courses for currency and relevance. This is achieved through the ACR submitted by each university. In 2005, the ALIA Education Reference Group reviewed and revised the ACR process with the goal of gathering data that would be comparable across the different education institutions and would help develop a more cohesive picture of LIS education in Australia.

It could be argued that the two principal stakeholders in the immediate education process are the students and the academic staff. For ALIA-recognised courses, the ACR is a mechanism to capture information at the micro-level about the individual courses and at the macro-level about general trends in LIS education, from the dual perspectives of the student cohorts and staffing levels.

LIS student issues

It has been noted that to become a librarian, students may enrol in either undergraduate or graduate studies. While the postgraduate courses, such as a Graduate Diploma in Library Studies or a Master of Information Management, will have a clearly defined, discrete cohort of students, the undergraduate programs may have a common qualification such as a Bachelor of Arts or Bachelor of Information Technology, with students distributed across a number of different streams, only one of which may be the LIS stream. In some faculties, the enrolment in one specific subject, such as LIS Professional Practice, may be the only way to discretely identify the LIS student cohort. Unfortunately, this situation makes it very difficult to rely on any definitive statistics for student enrolments.

The data collected in the 2005 ALIA ACRs indicate that there are currently about 1,550 students enrolled in the graduate programs and about 950 students enrolled in undergraduate courses. Figure 18.1 presents the enrolment trends over the ten-year period 1996–2005. Numbers of students enrolled in graduate courses peaked in 1997 (1,917 students), then dropped noticeably over the period 1997–1999, with a low of 1,373, which reflects the timeframe when full-fee paying courses were introduced for graduate courses in Australia. The 1997 spike highlights the students 'getting in fast' before the graduate fees were introduced. As many students study part-time, the corresponding drop in graduating full-time students occurs in 2000 and in part-time students in 2002. However, the past few years indicate greater stability in numbers of students and graduates.

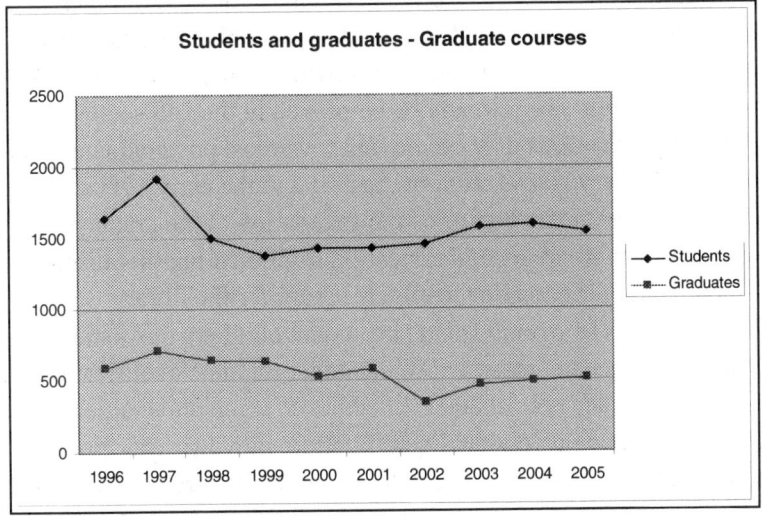

Figure 18.1 Number of students and graduates – LIS graduate courses, 1996–2005

The figures for undergraduate students (Figure 18.2) show a drop of almost 54 per cent from the 1997 high of 1,745 students to the 2005 figure of 811. A number of undergraduate courses have closed over the past few years, which can be directly attributed to the impact of the higher education reforms which are discussed later in this chapter. In contrast, the number of graduates completing the undergraduate courses has remained stable, highlighting the trend for a significant number of undergraduate students to drop out of courses before graduation, an issue that was raised in the Australian Government's Higher Education Review (Department of Education, Science and Training 2005).

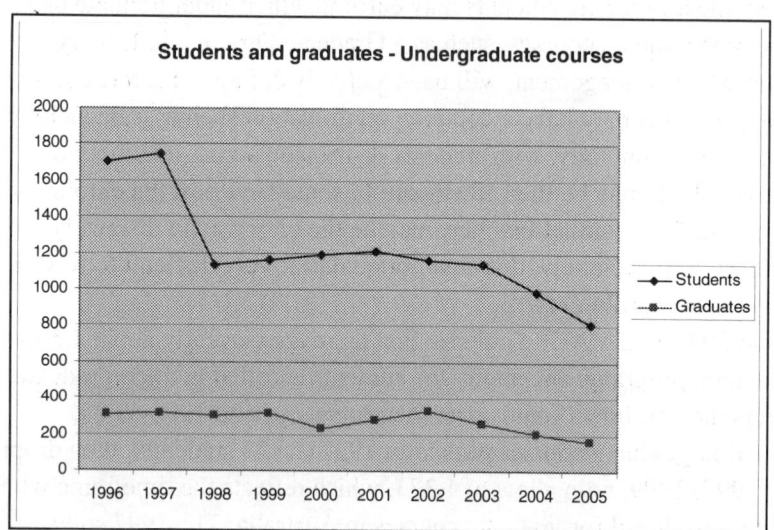

Figure 18.2 Number of students and graduates – LIS undergraduate courses, 1996-2005

The data collected in the ACRs indicate that, on average, about 30 per cent of graduate students complete their course in any year, compared with about 20 per cent of undergraduate students. While these figures naturally reflect the respective duration of the courses, there is also a higher drop-out rate for undergraduate courses, resulting in a lower number of graduates overall in this category. On average, around 700 new graduates theoretically enter the workforce each year, although a significant proportion may already be employed in the LIS sector.

Ironically, the market for LIS qualifications may be moving towards a postgraduate entry model, as was first proposed by the Library Association of Australia in the early 1960s. IFLA has stressed the importance of an undergraduate degree as the foundation to the graduate qualification: 'Students should acquire a broad general education (topics from other disciplines) as a significant preparatory component of the total education program for the library/ information professional' (IFLA 2000). The overall trends in student numbers in Australia indicate that proportionally fewer students are interested in the undergraduate qualification, dropping from 47 per cent in 1997 to 34 per cent in 2005. In addition, some universities now offer a coursework Masters as the standard professional qualification, moving away from the Graduate Diploma as the entry-level qualification, referred to as 'credential creep' (Macauley 2004), a phenomenon discussed by Bob Pymm and Damian Lodge in Chapter 17. Paul Genoni indicates that this may be the beginning of a trend towards both students and employers expecting a Masters degree as the standard entry level: 'There are sound pedagogic reasons for this being the case. There have long been questions as to how well a 12-month course prepares graduates for the workplace. This issue is becoming more critical as the expansion of required skills and knowledge demands constant additions to the curriculum' (Genoni 2005a).

Sue Myburgh (2003) has commented on the problems of offering LIS programs at the undergraduate level, with falling enrolments and the perceived poor quality of students resulting in a number of institutions closing down their bachelor courses. In the United States, masters courses are the only accredited programs. The graduate diploma as we know it survives only in Australia and South Africa, with an ever increasing number of universities, internationally, offering masters courses. Myburgh highlights the underlying pedagogic reasons:

> A post-bachelor master's degree should become the basic pre-professional training. The graduate diploma is not enough. It is not possible to meet the needs of the profession within this framework. We don't need more superficialists, who train within a one-year time frame, and have a smattering of bits and pieces of knowledge across a discipline area that is too wide to capture within one year (2003).

Ross Harvey and Susan Higgins, however, highlight the problems of industry recognition of the higher degree:

> Professionally-recognised bachelor's qualifications … are accorded the same professional status as graduate diplomas or masters degrees. Holding a masters qualification in Australia is not usually linked to higher levels of pay; pay scales are theoretically the same for all first professional qualifications. There is, therefore, no financial incentive to pay the extra costs incurred in studying at the masters level (2003, p.151).

Student fees are a critical issue in the context of Australian university education, where funding, rather than pedagogic principles, tends to drive many of the educational decisions. In 2005, Dr Brendan Nelson, the Minister of Education, Science and Training responsible for recent higher education reforms, stated that 75 per cent of undergraduate study costs are funded by government, with the student responsible for 25 per cent of the costs, either payable up-front or deferred as a student loan (Nelson 2005). Graduate programs, however, are full-fee paying, with no government subsidy and with fees ranging for graduate diploma programs from about $7500 to $12,000, depending on the institution. Masters programs range from $12,000 to $24,000. Student loan schemes are available for graduate students.

This financial situation notwithstanding, many LIS students enter the graduate course as part of their strategies for career change. The student cohort in LIS programs is an interesting one, with a wide diversity in academic background, employment history, personal interests and life experiences, all of which adds richness to the profession they join. Myburgh stresses that, in her experience:

> Undergraduates (if they have come directly from school) typically do not have the life experience which is necessary to understand this complex and sophisticated blend of art and science that forms the backbone of the profession. It is only after more experience of human nature, individually and within organisations, that some appreciation of the role of information and knowledge (not reading or documents) can be fully understood.

IFLA recommends that 'students should acquire a broad general education (topics from other disciplines) as a significant preparatory component of the total education program for the library/information professional' (2000), thereby encouraging the postgraduate avenue for LIS education. This is particularly important for academic libraries. Dalton and Levinson (2000) make reference to anecdotal evidence to indicate that 'for work in the academic [library] sector, employers prefer to recruit LIS professionals with a master's level qualification in a separate subject, in addition to the professional LIS qualification'. It can also be argued, however, that the undergraduate degrees provide a career pathway for aspiring library technicians who wish to upgrade from a vocational diploma to a professional qualification (Harvey & Higgins 2003).

While the universities are required to ask students to complete a graduate destination survey, the number of returns is disappointing, resulting in unreliable data. Anecdotally, it appears that graduates often obtain part-time work in the first instance – either while still studying, or after completing the course – and secure full-time work within six to twelve months. In recent months, however, students in South East Queensland have reported that most jobs on offer are in fact for full-time work, and they would actually prefer part-time employment. Graduates who are working in an LIS environment while studying are generally offered promotion upon completion of their course, or they are successful in applying for a higher level position with another employer.

Within the vocational education and training (VET) sector, the data collected in the ALIA ACRs indicate that the number of students enrolling in library technician courses has also dropped significantly over the past decade, from 3171 in 1996 to 2,028 in 2005, down around 36 per cent. There has been a 26 per cent reduction in the number of qualified diplomats, from 536 to 397 (Figure 18.3).

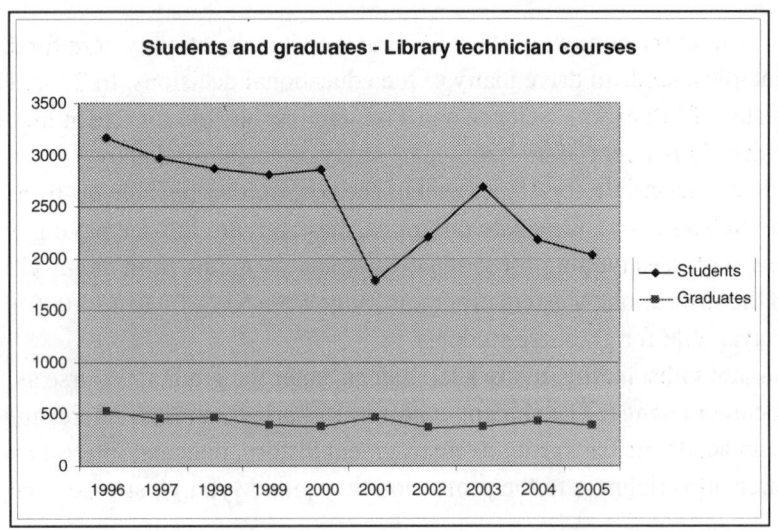

Figure 18.3 Number of students and graduates – library technician courses, 1996–2005

Significant changes were made in the area of education for library technicians and library assistants in 1999 with the development of the new national training package, the Museums and Library/Information Services Training Package. Because of this overarching cultural focus, specific VET sector statistical information covers student numbers enrolled in the complete training package, indicating around three thousand library and information services students each year (National Centre for Vocational Education Research 2005, p.22). The agency responsible for the formulation of the Museums and Library/Information Services package was CREATE (Cultural Research Education and Training Enterprises Australia), with considerable industry consultation. In 2004, advice on training for the cultural sector was transferred to

Innovation and Business Skills Australia (IBSA) as the relevant industry skills council. The training package currently comprises three specific components: the Competency Standards, which are units of competency that reflect discrete workplace outcomes; the Assessment Guidelines, which describe the industry requirements for assessment; and the Qualifications Framework, which details how the units of competency are packaged into nationally recognised qualifications (IBSA 2005). The Australian Qualifications Framework (AQF) qualifications for the cultural sector include Certificates II–IV, Diploma and Advanced Diploma. There is currently some discussion in the VET sector about the feasibility of some TAFE institutions introducing a Vocational Graduate Diploma in Library and Information Services. These days, some library technicians choose to progress their careers by undertaking a university course in LIS studies, while, on the other hand, it has been noted that Library Technician courses also attract a number of students who already have tertiary qualifications (Carroll 2005), reflecting the complexity of the qualifications within the LIS sector.

The original goals of education for library technicians was to offer a complementary, but distinct, career path to that of librarians. It was not envisaged to be a pre-professional program. Carroll (2002) has noted, however, that the structure of the national qualifications framework and the competency standards now sees the educational outcomes at the higher levels of vocational education dovetailing with university learning outcomes. This situation presents employers with specific challenges when recruiting. It appears that not all employers acknowledge the professional status of new graduates, meaning that too many new librarians find themselves 'functioning in that grey area inhabited by both the professional and para-professional' (Carroll 2002). Employers do need to consider how to best accommodate this convergence of qualifications so that the profession continues to attract people with strong analytical, evaluative and critical thinking skills and the potential to become future leaders.

It will be important to watch future student enrolment patterns. The Australian employment market is predicted to decline significantly in the next decade, with large numbers of 'Baby Boomer' workers exiting from the workforce, and fewer young people entering paid employment. It is anticipated that there will be immense competition for capable and talented workers: will the LIS sector be in a position to attract the brightest and best candidates to join its professional ranks, and what strategies can be used to ensure a positive future for the profession?

LIS educator issues

It has been frequently stated that practitioners and educators inhabit two different worlds, with insufficient interplay and interaction between them. 'Many librarians have little firsthand experience with library education after they graduate. They don't go back to the schools for alumni functions, and often their knowledge of what is happening in the schools comes to them second- or third-hand' (Moran 2001, p.54). Library educators may equally well be totally out of touch with current industry practice. The gulf between LIS education and LIS practice is specifically highlighted in courses in the United States, which fall into the discipline area of information science, known as i-schools, where the focus is often 'information-oriented to the exclusion of libraries' (Seavey 2005, p.54), as well as in situations where significant tensions exist between the demands on academic staff, on the one hand to secure funded research projects, and on the other hand to provide education for the profession.

There are concerns that the influx of lecturers from disciplines other than library science, who may have never worked in a library, is having a negative impact on the quality of teaching within the LIS discipline and, by extension, on the quality of the graduates. Anxious comments suggest that, with the current cohort of doctoral students coming through the i-schools, there will be no new generation of LIS educators who have the required knowledge and skills to develop library professionals. Seavey notes that 'considering a fairly simple demand model, the situation turns pretty grim: potential faculty members who actually understand the institution of the library are fairly few and far between' (2005, p.55). Dillon and Norris counter these views by presenting data that 'cast serious doubts on the claim that there is a lack of research being conducted in LIS library schools' (2005, p.285), with the next generation of LIS faculty clearly recognising that library-related research topics are central to their professional expertise. Nevertheless, in Australia there is clear evidence that there has been a progressive decline in numbers of academic staff members in the LIS discipline (Figure 18.4). Over the period 1996–2005, the number of staff decreased literally by 50 per cent, from 130 to 64. Over the same period, the VET sector has experienced a similar decline in staff, dropping 43 per cent from 79.2 FTE to 45 (Figure 18.5).

Not only are the numbers dropping, but the educators themselves are 'greying'. 'Library education in Australia expanded rapidly in the late 1970s and 1980s, and a number of those who joined the teaching departments in their early period of growth still remain' (Genoni 2005b). This situation raises serious issues in terms of the currency and relevance of the curriculum in such a dynamic field as LIS. It is essential that the curriculum itself is dynamic, providing graduates with the knowledge and skills they will need as soon as they join the workforce. Libraries and information centres are very different places in 2006, compared with twenty or even ten years ago. Staff development for existing academic staff is therefore crucial.

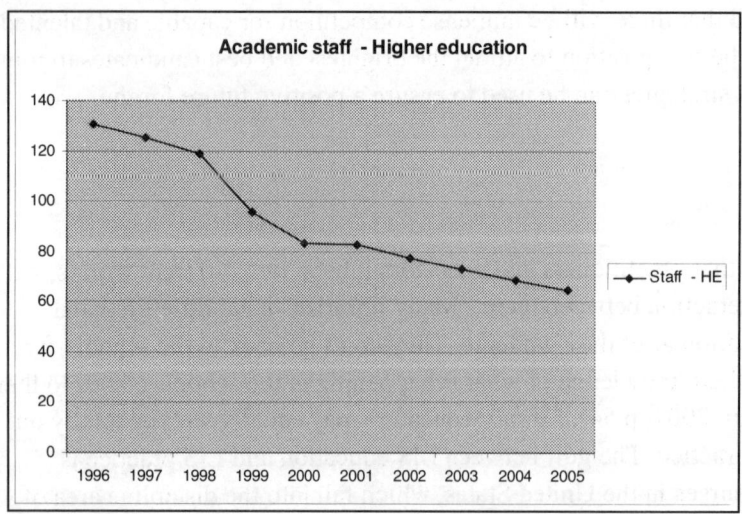

Figure 18.4 Number of academic staff – LIS higher education, 1996–2005

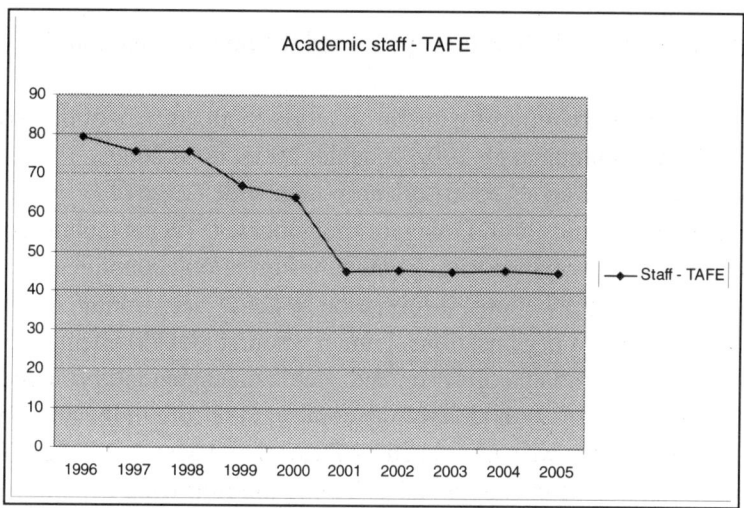

Figure 18.5 Number of academic staff – TAFE, 1995–2005

At this point in time it would appear that there are few incentives to become an educator. It is rare for library and information professionals to be willing to invest several years of their life to obtain a higher degree when the remuneration they will be finally offered as a lecturer, with little or no teaching experience, is going to be substantially less than the remuneration they would receive by remaining in the workforce and potentially winning promotion to the senior ranks as an industry practitioner (Genoni 2005b). Within the academic institutions, the funding to employ casual academic staff in order to help individuals gain experience in the classroom is also becoming harder to acquire. Inevitably, without effective succession planning, LIS departments become increasingly vulnerable.

The push for educators to 'publish or perish' further adds to the inherent tensions, especially when the high impact academic journals are not the regular reading material for practitioners. Equally well, however, there has been some degree of criticism about the lack of professional reading undertaken by practitioners – or at least that 'researchers and practitioners do not read each others' literature' (Haddow & Klobas 2004). This means that 'as academics relentlessly push the profession towards theory and abstraction, practitioners pull with equal might toward day-to-day relevance' (Mulvaney & O'Connor 2006, p.38). The tensions between research and practice are discussed in more detail later in the chapter, following an exploration of the curriculum issues, where, nonetheless, specific tensions between educators and practitioners are apparent.

Curriculum issues

In the United States, Michael Gorman has made education for librarianship one of the central themes of his presidency of the ALA for 2005–2006, with considerable professional discussion about the lack of a core curriculum for the discipline as offered by the various library schools and a lack of consensus and consistency about the breadth and depth of LIS syllabi (Mulvaney & O'Connor 2006). As LIS educators, Brine and Feather have noted that: 'so far as the academic curriculum is concerned, there is probably general agreement about the broad scope of knowledge and understanding which the new entrant to the profession needs to acquire. There is rather less clarity and consensus about the skills which are needed if s/he is to function effectively' (2002, p.253).

This view is supported by the literature reporting on the situation in all corners of the world (Middleton 2003; Myburgh 2003; ur Rehman et al. 2002; Koehler 2003; Raju 2003; Maceviciute 2002; Irwin 2002; Tedd 2003). LIS educators propose a wide range of competencies, skills, knowledge areas, topics or modules for their courses. Terms include social informatics, knowledge management, information management, information economics, information resources development, IT applications, information systems, networking, internet, virtual library, management of information organisations, human resource development, information organisation, information retrieval, collection and access management, professional ethics and so on. The role of skills in information technology comes to the fore in the analysis.

The taxonomy of discipline knowledge was articulated by Dressel and Marcus (1982). In this taxonomy, discipline knowledge can be characterised as having the following components:

- Substantive knowledge: the concepts, facts, and types of problems dealt with by a discipline.

- Language and symbols: the terms and representation systems (linguistic, mathematical or symbolic) used to communicate in the discipline.

- Structure: the organisation of knowledge within a discipline, including methods of thinking and problem solving; methods of collecting, analysing and interpreting information; and conventional methods of communicating.

- Values: the beliefs that guide our decisions about which problems to solve, the methods to choose and how evidence is evaluated.

- Relationships to other disciplines: the principles that determine how a discipline is related to other disciplines, largely determined by the other five components.

In discussing the curriculum developments in Dutch LIS schools, Roggema-van Heusden (2004, p.99) refers to 'specific expertise' which is defined as the 'necessary knowledge and experience and insight relevant to the invariable aspects of the problem'. Many synonyms can be used to refer to this core set of skills. Such synonyms include 'subject-specific knowledge', 'content knowledge' or 'subject matter expertise'.

Beyond this discipline-specific knowledge, however, there has been a growing interest within the higher education sector in strategies that will help students develop life skills that can allow them to 'function across different cognitive domains or subject areas and across a variety of social and, in particular, employment situations' (Bridges 1993, p.45). Skills such as problem solving, critical thinking, effective communication, teamwork and ethical thinking are all examples of the life skills in question. Together these life skills form the core set of workplace skills and abilities desirable in graduating students and new employees. They complement the discipline specific skills and professional knowledge acquired by students through their university study. Within the literature many synonyms have been used to refer to this core set of skills. Such synonyms include 'transferable skills' (Atlay & Harris 2000), 'key competences' (Mayer 1992) 'generic skills' (Oliver & McLoughlin 2001) and 'graduate attributes' (Down et al. 1999).

Extrapolating from the work by Watson and Crick, Partridge and Hallam (2004) draw on the metaphor of DNA to describe the two aspects of generic capabilities and discipline knowledge. Like the strands within the genetic concept of the double helix, the two ribbons of professional knowledge and personal attributes are intertwined and complementary. Together the two ribbons symbolise the 'unique patterns of DNA' (Watson 1981) that determine the specific characteristics and qualities of the library and information professional.

The diverse approaches to LIS education standards have been mentioned. In terms of curriculum in the United States, ALA accredits LIS courses using the *Standards for accreditation of master's programs in library and information studies 1992*. In these standards, the criteria for the curriculum are highly generalised, but encompass the 'evolving body of knowledge that reflects the findings of basic and applied research from relevant fields' (ALA 1992). This is a specific concern to Gorman (2004), but critics of Gorman's views argue that to define a core curriculum for the purposes of the accreditation of courses would be both prescriptive and stifling, especially in such a dynamic field as library and information science.

In the United Kingdom, the merger of the Library Association (LA) with the Institute of Information Scientists (IIS) to form the Chartered Institute of Library and Information Professionals (CILIP) in 2002 prompted the development of a common view of the body of professional knowledge (BPK) for the new association.

> [The BPK] establishes the unique knowledge, which distinguishes library and information professionals from professionals within other domains ... and sets out the broad framework of areas of knowledge and practice that characterise information and library work. It is designed to be flexible and adaptable, as the areas will evolve and develop over time to accommodate changing needs (CILIP 2005, p.1).

CILIP emphasises that the BPK is not presented as a core curriculum, nor does it seek to indicate the level of knowledge or skill that should be achieved by individual practitioners seeking recognition and/or qualifications.

ALIA has also adopted a more conceptual approach in terms of articulating the core knowledge, skills and attributes (2005c). The key characteristics of the LIS workforce are presented as:

- Promoting and defending the core values of the profession.

- Understanding and responding to people's information and learning needs.

- Managing the storage, organisation, access, retrieval, dissemination, preservation and use of information.

- Developing, delivering and evaluating information facilities, services, sources and products.

- Envisioning and planning future directions for the library and information sector.

- Advancing library and information science and its application to information services (ALIA 2005c).

The core knowledge and skills encompass the knowledge of the broad context of the information environment, an understanding of information seeking, information infrastructure, information organisation, information access, information services, sources and products, information literacy education and the generation of knowledge, to foster a culture of research and evidence-based practice (ALIA 2005c). In addition, value is placed on the generic skills and attributes that are an essential dimension of an effective profession: communication skills, ethical standards and social responsibility, critical, reflective and creative thinking, problem-solving, skills in the areas of ICT application, project management and business acumen, team relationship skills and self-management. The ALIA statement notes the spread of conceptual and evaluative thinking required by librarians and the practical skills demonstrated by library technicians, as well as acknowledging that the level to which individuals have requisite knowledge, skills and attributes will depend on their formal qualifications, work experience, professional development and the role/s they perform. ALIA concludes that 'as all areas of library and information practice will continue to evolve and develop over time, the overall framework of knowledge, skills and attributes needs to be able to encompass the changing nature of the discipline to ensure a flexible, adaptable and innovative profession' (ALIA 2005c). This provides a descriptive, rather than prescriptive framework for the curriculum.

Wagner has indicated that the future direction of LIS education will be determined by examining 'what skills will be required by library information professionals to enable them to adapt to new and changing demands in society' (2000, p.128). While this appears a simple statement, one major issue associated with the curriculum of LIS courses undoubtedly hinges on the vexing question of what the 'information profession' is all about. One new graduate has commented that it is difficult to get an understanding of the profession until you are actually working in the field (O'Connor 2001, p.1). There is plenty of inconclusive debate about job titles and work descriptions and about what distinguishes workers in the LIS sector from other areas of practices in the information environment (Nicholson & Tattersall 2001, p.2). This challenges us to ask how can we actually develop a relevant curriculum if we don't know what needs to be included in the course? Specifically, how can we develop a relevant curriculum for both traditional and emerging employment paths?

Part of the problem results from the enormous diversity of employment opportunities across a wide range of information environments, from the broad levels of academic libraries, public libraries, state and national libraries, to the narrower levels of special libraries and information centres, such as law libraries, music libraries and health and medical information centres. Opportunities also exist beyond this more traditional library context, with career avenues within fields such as knowledge management and internet and intranet development. Each area of specialisation would ideally like its own tailored education program for potential employees. Tenopir (2002) discusses the inherent challenges:

> Schools of library and information science are working on keeping up with technology, planning recruitment, and revising curricula, but I wonder how LIS programs can continue to be all things for all people. How can programs provide sufficient courses and educational opportunities for those who want to become competitive intelligence specialists, children's librarians, electronic publishers, and academic reference librarians? In particular, how can they do all this while maintaining or growing doctoral and undergraduate programs and bringing in new recruits for master's degrees programs?

Stoffle and Leeder (2005, pp.316-7) present a valid argument when they state that:

> While the needs of the profession should play a role in determining the curriculum, allowing dissatisfied practitioners to dictate the requirements of LIS programs will undoubtedly lead to disaster. The goal of today's LIS programs is not to provide specialized training to prepare students for specific positions, but to give students a

broad education in the field that will serve as a foundation for any related career path they may choose.

In discussing the issue of a broad-based course of study for students who wish to become law librarians, Middleton and Hallam (2001, p.183) indicate that:

> LIS educators, needing to maintain meaningful and relevant curricula for an uncertain future, have avoided provision of training for precise vocational skills. Instead they aim for flexibility and adaptability so that students develop a thorough understanding of the principles that may apply in a variety of situations, many of which are unanticipated.

Beyond this, it is important to understand how the curriculum can be utilised as a vehicle for students to acquire 'the conceptual structures and thinking processes of a particular discipline' (Toohey 1999, p.55). Core qualities of effective information professionals include the ability to naturally focus on the user as an integral element of information transfer and use, and the ability to critically evaluate information products and services. A further facet to consider is the underlying premise that the LIS profession is a caring and sharing field of endeavour, with a high level of personal and professional interaction based on networking and collaborative activities. Ideally, the curriculum needs to also include these philosophical, and possibly affective, concepts to achieve the desired professional mindset. In addition, it should be noted that some elements in the course reflect the socially critical approach to curriculum. Librarianship, particularly the area of public librarianship, strongly espouses the values of social justice, equity of access to information and intellectual freedom (points discussed in Chapters 15 and 16). LIS courses need to address these issues to consider what knowledge and skills are particularly valuable in the role of library and information professionals within society as a whole.

LIS research and LIS practice issues

Building on the discussion of curriculum issues for the professional domain, there are inevitable tensions between the dimensions of theory and practice in the academic arena, and indeed Grogan (1983) raised this as a persistent issue in the education of librarians. While in principle research and practice should enjoy a mutually beneficial relationship to create 'a strong theoretical framework within which a practitioner community can develop' (Haddow & Klobas 2004), it has been argued that practitioners have long felt that educators were out of touch with practice. This concern has resounded in the field ever since the first qualifications were discussed (Steig 1992, cited in Dillon & Norris 2005, p.291). Rothstein's 'Anthology of abuse' (1985) documents 'the criticism LIS programs endured over the course of ninety-four years between 1887 and 1981 (Stoffle & Leeder 2005, p.313). Today, with LIS studies increasingly offered as a postgraduate qualification, there are clear expectations that students should acquire a high level of theoretical knowledge, yet there is also an overt demand for practical skills which can be applied on Day 1 in the workplace. For practitioners, cataloguing and online searching are two areas where these tensions consistently emerge: 'I cannot understand how so many (information profession graduates) have so little practical knowledge of how to search for information in an online world. They may have some theoretical knowledge but, in my experience, they frequently don't know how to implement it' (Swan 2000, p.4).

The dichotomy between mental and manual, theoretical and practical, mind and body has long been a central concept in western thinking, reflecting the philosophies of Aristotle and Plato through to Descartes. Gibbons et al. (1994) describe two modes of knowledge. Traditional discipline knowledge 'as taught in ivory towers' is referred to as Mode 1 knowledge, while Mode 2 encapsulates socially distributed knowledge, 'as produced and applied in the workplace'. The problem facing educators teaching professional courses is how to achieve the desired balance between the two modes of knowledge, particularly to develop the potential to explore and create Mode 2 knowledge, without the educational levels dropping to the level of competency-based training, which offers the practical dimension of training for library technicians and library assistants.

Theoretical knowledge encompasses beliefs, facts and ideas, which can then be applied by the practitioner to solve professional problems. The value of conceptual education was recognised by White (1989, p.4): 'The emphasis must be on education, the understanding of issues and concepts and the development of skills and tools with which to deal with specific problems that arise in libraries and that nobody can fully predict and anticipate.' At the same time, it is acknowledged that in the workplace, graduates will indeed need to gain practical skills to perform the operational tasks that are part and parcel of the positions they hold. The issue of professional learning and how a professional evolves has been considered by Boshuizen et al. (2004). Their work provides an interesting insight into the broader areas of professional development and preparation. They propose that a professional, regardless of discipline, progresses from the status of novice to that of expert by 'a process of continually transforming the repertoire of knowledge and skills that make up expertise'. In short, they suggest that lifelong learning is the key to professionals becoming experts in their own fields. According to Boshuizen et al., a professional must develop both academic knowledge and professional knowledge, with academic knowledge imparted via formal education in a university and subsequently transformed into professional knowledge by learning in the workplace.

Garrod and Sidgreaves note that LIS schools 'remain challenged in initial professional training by the need to prepare graduates for a wide variety of information service outlets' (1998). It must be stressed that entry-level qualifications are the starting point, not the end point – 'A first professional course should be acknowledged to be simply an important first step in the career, supplemented by continuing education as an essential ongoing process to gain the knowledge and skills needed to support a successful career' (Middleton & Hallam 2001, p.193). While the universities can adopt a proactive stance to incorporate new areas of knowledge and skills into the LIS curriculum, new developments in practice require existing staff to grow and develop. It has become imperative for practitioners to keep their skills and knowledge current and relevant. In Australia, ALIA launched its professional development (PD) program in 2000 to encourage members to face the challenges of the future:

> The dynamic environment of the library and information sector dictates the need for
> library and information professionals to remain flexible and adaptable to change...
> Lifelong learning extends and develops the knowledge, skills and competencies of
> practitioners. It also enables them to prepare for their work more effectively, to broaden
> their careers and to undertake new tasks' (ALIA 2001).

Significantly, the distinction is made in the PD program between the necessity of developing both LIS specific areas (for instance, information resources, resources acquisition and management) and generic areas (teamwork, effective communication, critical and evaluative thinking).

Elaine Jennerich describes the importance of career-long learning using the metaphor of caring for fine timber: 'The relationship between LIS education and staff development is akin to the care of fine woods. A graduate comes to us with one coat of high quality varnish. It takes years of development, training and personal motivation to add the layers that create a luster of excellence' (Jennerich 2006).

Conclusion

Undeniably, as it has done since its introduction, LIS education continues to face immense challenges. Perhaps some of the grounds for concern and anxiety reside in the inconstant environment in which we now live and work, with the 'dynamic of perpetual change' (Ray 2001, p.250). It has been argued that the exponential growth of digital information is causing an existential dilemma for many library and information professionals: 'If books and libraries embody modernist values such as linearity, order, hierarchy and structure, the web page and the internet reflect postmodern values: nonlinearity, equality of value and randomness'(Ray 2001, p.251). If this is the case, then LIS educators face the challenge of determining, in the educational context, how best to accommodate these new values without forfeiting the profession's traditional core values. The discipline is in transition, among sweeping cultural, social, economic and technological changes. Metaphors of seismic activity abound – 'The digital earthquake [has] changed the information landscape' (Durrance 2003, p.9), while waves of blogs and wikis warn that we will drown in the 'tsunami of information' (see also Bruck 2002). A key strategy for the future will be to work collaboratively to make the most of the opportunities that do emerge.

> While it is still possible that the internet revolution will swamp LIS/IS education, it appears to me that recent efforts by thought leaders from a variety disciplines, including LIS, are likely to succeed in bringing an interdisciplinary convergence that will result in forging a new discipline that will more effectively develop and harness technologies, systems and practices with the aim of bringing the benefits of convergence to society (Durrance 2003, p.10).

In the twenty-first century, libraries and information agencies require staff with innovative ideas and vision to create and sustain valued, effective services to users, and to contribute to the success of the parent organisation. Career-long learning is therefore integral to professional success and individual professional development needs to be supported through a combination of education, personal achievement and work-based opportunities. The process of developing these innovative, visionary and successful library and information professionals is not the sole responsibility of the LIS educator, but must be viewed as a career-long learning process that involves the individual, universities, training providers, employers and professional associations: 'Library schools don't operate in a vacuum … LIS education needs a healthy infrastructure involving faculty, students, alumni and practitioners' (Ling 2005, p.3). In Australia, ALIA seeks to foster the collaboration of the diverse stakeholders by working with the universities and TAFE colleges to ensure the quality of the LIS programs recognised by the association (ALIA 2005a; 2005b; 2005c; 2006c), by encouraging and supporting practitioners to participate in the professional development scheme (ALIA 2005d) and by encouraging employers to work with the library educators in the provision of formal LIS programs and to support professional development and workplace learning for their staff (ALIA 2006d). LIS education is a critical issue for the professional association, but beyond this it is also a critical issue for the profession in its entirety. It requires concern, cooperation and collaboration – today, tomorrow and into the future.

References

American Library Association (ALA) 1992, *Standards for accreditation of master's programs in library and information studies 1992*, http://www.ala.org/ala/accreditation/accredstandards/standards.htm

Atlay, M & Harris, R 2000, 'An institutional approach to developing student's "transferable" skills', *Innovations in Education and Training International*, vol.37, no.1, pp.76-84.

Australian Library and Information Association (ALIA) 2005a, *ALIA's role in education of library and information professionals*, http://www.alia.org.au/policies/education.role.html

Australian Library and Information Association (ALIA) 2005b, *Courses in library and information management*, http://www.alia.org.au/policies/courses.html

Australian Library and Information Association (ALIA) 2005c, *Library and information sector: Core knowledge, skills and attributes*, http://www.alia.org.au/policies/core.knowledge.html

Australian Library and Information Association (ALIA) 2005d, *Professional development for library and information professionals*, http://www.alia.org.au/policies/professional.development.html

Australian Library and Information Association (ALIA) 2006a, *ALIA-recognised library technician courses*, http://www.alia.org.au/education/courses/library.technician.html

Australian Library and Information Association (ALIA) 2006b, *ALIA-recognised librarianship courses*, http://www.alia.org.au/education/courses/librarianship.html

Australian Library and Information Association (ALIA) 2006c, *ALIA recognition of courses: Criteria for recognition of first award courses in library and information management at librarian and library technician level*, http://www.alia.org.au/education/courses/criteria.html

Australian Library and Information Association (ALIA) 2006d, *Employer roles and responsibilities in education and professional development*, http://www.alia.org.au/policies/information.centres.html

Berry, J 2004, 'Don't dis the LIS "crisis": Gorman is right to focus his ALA term on library education', *Library Journal*, vol.129, p.10.

Boshuizen, HPA, Bromme, R & Gruber, H 2004, *Professional learning: Gaps and transitions on the way from novice to expert*, Kluwer Academic Publishers, Dordrecht.

Bramley, G 1969, *A history of library education*, Clive Bingley, London.

Bridges, D 1993, 'Transferable skills: A philosophical perspective', *Studies in Higher Education,* vol.18, no.1, pp.43-51.

Brine, A & Feather, J 2002, 'Supporting the development of skills for information professionals', *Education for Information*, vol.20, no.3/4, pp.253-262.

Bruck, B 2002, *Taming the information tsunami*, Peachpit, Berkeley, CA.

Bundy, A 2001, 'Education, education, education', *InCite* vol.22 no.6, p.4.

Carroll, M 2002, 'The well-worn path', *Australian Library Journal*, vol.51, no.2, pp.117-125.

Carroll, M 2005, 'Profile of Australian library technician students', *LIBRES*, vol 15, no.2, http://libres.curtin.edu.au/libres15n2

Chartered Institute of Library and Information Professionals (CILIP) 2005, *Body of professional knowledge*, http://www.cilip.org.uk/qualificationschartership/bpk

Dalton, P & Levinson, K 2000, 'An investigation of LIS qualifications throughout the world', *66th IFLA Council and General Conference*, held in Jerusalem, 13-18 August 2000, http://www.ifla.org/IV/ifla66/papers/061-161e.htm

Department of Education, Science and Training (DEST) 2005, *Our universities: Backing Australia's future*, http://www.backingaustraliasfuture.gov.au/review.htm

Dillon, A & Norris, A 2005, 'Crying wolf: An examination and reconsideration of the perception of crisis in LIS education', *Journal of Education for Library and Information Science*, vol.46, no.4, pp.280-298.

Down, C, Martin, E, Hager, P & Bricknell, L 1999, 'Graduate attributes, key competence and judgements: Exploring the links', *Cornerstones: What do we value in higher education? HERDSA International Conference*, held in Melbourne, 12-15 July 1999, http://www.herdsa.org.au/branches/vic/Cornerstones/authorframeset.html

Dressel, PL & Marcus, D 1982, *On teaching and learning in college*, Jossey-Bass, San Francisco, CA.

Durrance, JC 2003, 'Crisis as opportunity: The shaping of library and information science education in the United States', *Japan Society of Library and Information Science (JSLIS)*, Tsukuba, Japan, October 2003, http://www.si.umich.edu/~durrance/infoprofedu/japan/JSLIS-50thAnniv.pdf

Feather, J 2003, 'Whatever happened to the library schools?' *Update*, vol.2, no.10, October, http://www.cilip.org.uk/publications/updatemagazine/archive/archive2003/october/update0310d.htm

Garrod, P & Sidgreaves, I 1998, *Skills for the new information professionals: The SKIP project. Part 3 Conclusions and recommendations*, http://www.ukoln.ac.uk/services/elib/papers/other/skip/finalpt3.html

Genoni, P 2005a, 'The changing face of LIS higher education in Australia, Part 1', *InCite,* vol.26, 18 July.

Genoni, P 2005b, 'The changing face of LIS higher education in Australia. Part 2', *InCite*, vol.26, 18 August.

Gibbons, M, Limoges, C, Nowotney, H, Schwarzman, S, Scott, P & Trow, M 1994, *The new production of knowledge: The dynamics of science and research in contemporary societies*, Sage, London.

Gonczi, A 2001, 'Advances in educational thinking and their implications for professional education', Research Centre for Vocational Education and Training (RCVET) Working Paper 01-04, University of Sydney, Research Centre for Vocational Education and Training, http://www.oval.uts.edu.au/working_papers/2001WP/0114gonczi.pdf

Gorman, M 2004, 'Whither library education?', *New Library World*, vol.105, no.1024/5, pp.376-380.

Gorman, M 2006, 'Confronting the crisis in LIS education: Teleconference panellist', 9 June 2006, College of Dupage Press, Library Learning Network, http://www. dupagepress.com/COD/index.php?id=1164.

Grogan, DJ 1983, 'Education for librarianship: Some persistent issues', *Education for Information*, vol.1, pp.3-23.

Haddow, G & Klobas, JE 2004, 'Communication of research to practice in library and information science: Closing the gap', *Library and Information Science Research,* vol.26, no.1, pp.29-43.

Hallam, G, Partridge, H & McAllister, L 2004, 'LIS education in changing times', *Australian Law Librarian,* vol.12, no.2, pp.11-32.

Harvey, R 2001, 'Losing the quality battle in Australian education for librarianship', *Australian Library Journal*, vol.50, no.1, pp.15-22.

Harvey, R 2004, 'Changes in the librarianship curriculum: Where are we heading?' *Australian Law Librarian,* vol.12, no.2, pp.33-36.

Harvey, R & Higgins, S 2003, 'Defining fundamentals and meeting expectations: Trends in LIS education in Australia', *Education for Information,* vol.21, no.2/3, pp.149-157.

Innovation and Business Skills Australia (IBSA) 2005, *General information on training packages: Frequently asked questions(FAQs)*, http://www.ibsa.org.au/downloads/FAQs_General_Trng_Pkgs_FINAL.pdf

International Federation of Library Associations and Institutions (IFLA) 2000, *Guidelines for professional library/information education programs, 2000*, http://www.ifla.org/VII/s23/bulletin/guidelines.htm

Irwin, R 2002, 'Characterizing the core: What catalog descriptions of mandatory courses reveal about LIS schools and librarianship', *Journal of Education for Library and Information Science,* vol.43, no.2, pp.175-184.

Jennerich, EZ 2006, 'Confronting the crisis in LIS education: Teleconference panellist', June 9 2006, College of Dupage Press. Library Learning Network, http://www.dupagepress.com/COD/index.php?id=1204

Koehler, W 2003, 'Professional values and ethics as defined by "The LIS discipline"', *Journal of Education for Library and Information Science,* vol.44, no.2, pp.99-119.

Levett, J 2001, 'A resounding silence?' *Australian Library Journal,* vol.50, no.2, p.1.

Library and Information Association of New Zealand (LIANZA) Taskforce on Professional Registration 2005, *Professional future for the New Zealand Library and Information Association: Discussion document*, http://www.lianza.org.nz/library/files/store_009/prof_reg_discussion_doc.pdf

Ling, HJ 2005, 'The points of ALA task force on library school closing', *PRISM,* vol.13, no.2, http://www.ala.org/ala/accreditation/prp/prism/prismarchive/FA05v13i2.pdf

Macauley, P 2004, 'Challenging librarians: The relevance of the doctorate in professional practice', *Challenging ideas. ALIA 2004 Biennial Conference*, Gold Coast, 21-24 September 2004.

Maceviciute, E 2002, 'Information management in the Baltic, Nordic and UK LIS schools', *Library Review,* vol.51, no.3/4, pp.190-199.

Mayer, E 1992, *Putting general education to work: The key competencies*, The Australian Education Council and Ministers for Vocational Education and Training, Melbourne, Vic.

Middleton, M 2003, 'Skills expectations of library graduates', *New Library World*, vol.104, no.1/2, pp.42-56.

Middleton, M & Hallam, G 2001, 'Generic education for specialist information professionals', *Australian Law Librarian,* vol.9, no.3, pp.181-194.

Moran, B 2001, 'Practitioners vs LIS educators: Time to reconnect', *Library Journal,* vol.126, no.18, pp.52-55.

Mulvaney, JP & O'Connor, D 2006, 'The crux of our crisis', *American Libraries,* vol.37, no.6, pp.38-40.

Munn, R & Pitt, E 1935, *Australian libraries*, Melbourne, Vic.

Myburgh, S 2003, 'Education directions for NIPs (new information professionals)', paper presented at the *11th Information Online Exhibition and Conference*, Sydney, 21-23 January 2003, http://conferences.alia.org.au/online2003/papers/myburgh.html

National Centre for Vocational Education Research (NCVER) 2005, *Students and courses 2004*, http://www.ncver.edu.au/statistic/publications/1602.html

Nelson, B 2005, 'Interview: Dr Brendan Nelson, Minister for Education, Science and Training', *ABC Four Corners*, http://www.abc.net.au/4corners/content/2005/s1399260.htm

Nicholson, J & Tattersall, N 2001, 'Issues, challenges and directions in education and training for the current and future library and information services sector: An association perspective', unpublished paper presented to the *ALIA LISEKA Ideas Forum*, Melbourne, November 16 2001.

O'Connor, A 2001, 'The graduates', unpublished paper presented to the *ALIA LISEKA Ideas Forum*, Melbourne, November 16 2001.

Oliver, R, & McLoughlin, C 2001, 'Exploring the practice and development of generic skills through web-based learning', *Journal of Educational Multimedia and Hypermedia,* vol.10, no.3, pp.207-226.

Partridge, H & Hallam, G 2004, 'The double helix: A personal account of the discovery of the structure of the Information Professional's DNA', *Challenging ideas*, *ALIA 2004 Biennial Conference*, Gold Coast, 21-24 September 2004.

Raju, J 2003, 'The "core" in library and/or information science education and training', *Education for Librarianship,* vol.21, no.4, pp.229-242.

Ray, K 2001 'The postmodern library in an age of assessment', *Crossing the divide, ACRL tenth National Conference*, Denver, 15-18 March, http://www.ala.org/ala/acrl/acrlevents/kray.pdf

Rochester, MK 1997, *Education for librarianship in Australia*, Mansell, London.

Roggema-van Heusden, M 2004, 'The challenge of developing a competence-oriented curriculum: An integrative framework', *Library Review,* vol.53, no.2, pp.98-103.

Rothstein, S 1985, 'Why people really hate library schools', *Library Journal,* vol.110, pp.42-43.

Schauder, D 2001, 'Challenges and opportunities for library and information studies education: a personal view', unpublished paper presented to the *ALIA LISEKA Ideas Forum*, Melbourne, 16 November.

Seavey, CA 2005, 'The coming crisis in LIS education', *American Libraries,* vol.36, no.9, pp.54-56.

Steig, M 1992, *Change and challenge in library and information science education*, American Library Association, Chicago, IL.

Stoffle, CJ & Leeder, K 2005, 'Practitioners and library education: A crisis of understanding', *Journal of Education for Library and Information Science*, vol.46, no.4, pp.313-320.

Swan, E 2000, 'Oh dear, you have had a poor education', *Online Currents,* vol.15, no.7, p.4.

Tedd, LA 2003, 'The what? and how? of education and training for information professionals in a changing world: Some experiences from Wales, Slovakia and the Asia-Pacific region', *Journal of Information Science,* vol.29, no.1, pp.79-86.

Tenopir, C 2002, 'Educating tomorrow's information professionals today', *Searcher,* vol.10, no.7, http://www.infotoday.com/searcher/jul02/tenopir.htm

Toohey, S 1999 'Beliefs, values and ideologies in course design', in *Designing courses for higher education*, Society for Research into Higher Education and Open University Press, Buckingham, UK, pp.44-69.

ur Rehman, S, Al-Ansari, H & Yousef, N 2002, 'Coverage of competencies in the curriculum of information studies: An international perspective', *Education for Information,* vol.20, no.3/4, pp.199-215.

US News & World Report 2006, 'Best graduate schools: Library science', http://www.usnews.com/ usnews/edu/grad/rankings/lib/libindex_brief.php

Wagner, GS 2000, 'Future of education for library and information science: Views from Australia', *Education for Information,* vol.18, no.2-3, pp.123-129.

Watson, JD 1981, *The double helix: A personal account of the discovery of the structure of DNA,* Weidenfeld & Nicholson, London.

White, HS 1989, *Librarians and the awakening from innocence: A collection of papers,* GK Hall, Boston, MA.

CONCLUSION
From people's university to information for all

Alex Byrne

It is a great time to be a librarian or information specialist. The challenge raised by many, including some in this volume, who ask whether libraries continue to have a role in the age of Google, misses the point. Libraries have continued to evolve to meet the changing needs of societies since an early Mesopotamian decided that there was some value in keeping a collection of indented clay bricks recording business transactions or a Chinese person kept some divining bones and shells.

At the outset of a new century, it is difficult to predict how society will develop and consequently how its libraries and information services will be shaped. A hundred years ago, at the beginning of the twentieth century, the optimism of the new century was expressed in the steel-frame buildings of Chicago that inspired Fritz Lang's *Metropolis* and the World's Fair which presented inventions and ideas from a host of countries. The sense of geographical, technological and social frontiers to be transcended entertained and hurried the viewing crowds into the new century and set one of its hallmarks, the intertwined beliefs in ceaseless growth and progress. Despite the century's world wars, many other conflicts and decades of major ideological divide, this twin idea carried through to the twenty-first century, implanting a secular faith in change for the better.

For libraries and information services, the twentieth century delivered the spread of the Anglo-American model of librarianship throughout the world coupled with continual innovation in techniques and technologies. The nineteenth century notion of the public library as the 'people's university', in which all – especially the labouring inhabitants of manufacturing towns – could improve themselves, has evolved to a belief in the democratising empowerment which is thought to be obtainable through unhindered access to information.

Representatives of the nations of the world, gathered at the World Summit on the Information Society at the beginning of the twenty-first century, proclaimed their belief in that potential in the declaration adopted at the December 2003 Summit meeting in Geneva. In that declaration they committed their nations to creating 'an information society for all'.

> We ... declare our common desire and commitment to build a people-centred, inclusive and development-oriented Information Society, where everyone can create, access, utilize and share information and knowledge, enabling individuals, communities and peoples to achieve their full potential in promoting their sustainable development and improving their quality of life, premised on the purposes and principles of the Charter of the United Nations and respecting fully and upholding the Universal Declaration of Human Rights (World Summit on the Information Society 2003a).

The declaration and accompanying plan of action (World Summit on the Information Society 2003b) set out the principles and priorities which it was hoped would guide the establishment of that 'information society for all'. The International Federation of Library Associations and Institutions (IFLA), which participated in the four-year long summit process on behalf of libraries and information services around the world, was well pleased with the outcomes of the summit (IFLA & Byrne 2004). The declaration and plan of action noted the issues which concerned IFLA's members, libraries and information services and their associations, and proposed strategies to address them. The library view supported the summit's inclusive vision of an information society in which everyone can create, access, use and share information and knowledge. It proposed an agenda in which the achievement of inclusivity demanded freedom of access to information and freedom of expression, respect for cultural and linguistic diversity, support for the disadvantaged and disabled, and equitable access to the internet and ICTs. It would be enabled through a number of strategies, including a focus on lifelong literacy, capacity building, the use of standards to ensure interoperability and balance in intellectual property regulation. It would also achieve open access to knowledge, including scientific and technical knowledge, and preservation of cultural heritage.

This bold project of creating a just and fair information society for all responds to the challenges identified in the United Nations Millennium Development Goals (2000) and takes its warrant from the fundamental human rights of all people. The deadline of 2015 and many of the immediate aims are consistent with the Millennium Goals, including the desire to eradicate extreme poverty and significantly reduce the disadvantage suffered by women and children. The World Summit's project, however, emphasises the aspects that relate to access to information. It provides an agenda for libraries and information services – as the premier information agencies in society – to address the challenges of the twenty-first century. In responding to that agenda, libraries and information services render themselves relevant to the big global issues that have been identified at the century's commencement by the assembled governments of the world, urged on by civil society organisations.

Focused on the Australian context, this book interrogates the preparedness of libraries and information services to address the challenges of the new century. The first part looks at the orientation and operation of the major types of library and information agencies and the environments in which they function. In the second part, the examination shifts to consider the key service domains which are central to the operation of libraries and information services. The third part deals with the information environment of the twenty-first century, a much more textured and complex tapestry of issues and challenges than would have been identified a hundred years ago.

Library and information agencies

This book opens, properly, with a consideration of one of the key agencies for social inclusion, the public library. As Chris Jones notes, the public library is there for everyone and is expected to provide a very broad range of services, 'to be all things for all people'. He argues that the public library cannot afford to be insular and needs to be both engaged and innovative. Australian public libraries display constant change as they seek to provide the extensive range of services their communities expect, and their success is displayed in significant growth in their number, range of services, collections and other indicators. Services extend from the traditional loans services to responding to passionate interest in investigating local and family history, to the very popular internet access.

Public libraries play a key role in education by helping young children to become acquainted with reading and providing resources and study space to school and higher education students. Australia is fortunate, however, that thanks to sustained lobbying by librarians and supporters of libraries most schools at both primary and secondary level have professional teacher librarians. James Herring describes the important role played in school education by school libraries – elsewhere known as library media centres or library resource centres – and the teacher librarians. The combination of professional library and teaching qualifications provides an integrative element in schools, which brings together curricular and pedagogic approaches on the one hand and the resources which even young students explore on the other. The revolution in education which has created collaborative environments that enable students to learn through interrogating resources would not be possible without the important contribution of school libraries and teacher librarians. The intersection between that change in pedagogy and the dramatically increased use of technology through e-learning and internet access has highlighted the importance of information literacy. That crucial set of skills has come to be considered a crucial component of the student's repertoire of learning skills, and the development of information literate students is a key aim for teacher librarians, as Herring notes.

Information literacy has assumed similar prominence in university and TAFE libraries. Shirley Oakley and Jennifer Vaughan indicate the role in promoting its importance which has been taken by the sector's library associations. They present the place of libraries within the institutions in the context of the political and other agendas that have driven rapid change in the student population, the amount of funding available and the degree of regulation. They point out the growing importance of quality assurance and workforce planning and the ongoing commitment to resource sharing. As was noted in relation to public and school libraries, these tertiary education libraries are refocusing and taking on new responsibilities such as e-publishing – in an attempt to recover control of scholarly communication for the academy. Behind such initiatives lies a determination to engage the library more fully with the work of the university or college. No longer just a repository, the modern tertiary education library provides resources twenty-four hours a day and is involved in a multifaceted fashion with the education of students and the pursuit of other priorities including, especially, research in universities.

Special libraries and information services, which are surveyed by Alison O'Connor, are even more engaged with the work of their parent organisation whether it is a mining company, law firm or hospital. Found in those and many other types of public and private organisations, special libraries in Australia have gone from strength to strength. But along the way some have foundered when they ceased to be considered integral to the operation of the firm, department, hospital or other organisation. Their steadily increasing number shows that they are justifying their keep through innovative services which confirm them to be essential. As for school libraries – and indeed many other types of libraries and information services – special library staff must have a combination of skills because of the multifaceted roles that they must fill. The small size of many of the agencies requires particular personal qualities and has encouraged professional solidarity that is reflected in the strength of special librarians' professional associations and conferences.

National, state and territory libraries by contrast are the colossi of library and information service within each jurisdiction. Established by statute and housed in monumental buildings, they are among the institutions that symbolise mightiness of the state or nation. By adopting 'Information for the nation' as the subtitle for their chapter, Roxanne Missingham and Jasmine Cameron signal the national role that these libraries play collectively in Australia through their collaboration in building, preserving and making available collections (print and digital), supporting libraries and information services throughout the country and delivering services directly to users. The state and territory libraries have particular responsibilities for coordinating and supporting public libraries and in some cases other types of libraries. Many of these priorities have been pursued for many years and to a great extent derive from the legislative requirements imposed on the institutions through their enabling acts. However, the last decade has seen very exciting initiatives by the national, state and territory libraries that have opened up access to a wealth of material through collaborative services such as Picture Australia. In this way, 'information for the nation' has been transformed into 'information for the individual Australian', a refocusing which enables people to explore their own interests often from their own computers – especially the treasury of personal, local and national heritage that is held in these libraries. Backed up by a concern to tackle the major challenges of digital preservation, these libraries have taken advantage of new technological opportunities to reposition themselves in new and more relevant ways, similarly to other types of library and information service in Australia.

Achieving agency

The broad picture that emerges from Part 1 is one of strong, innovative and relevant library and information agencies in Australia. Achievement of their objectives depends on effective implementation of the service strategies investigated in Part 2. The evolving approaches to service provision will position library and information services for the twenty-first century.

John Mills examines the librarian–user interaction. He considers the dimensions of that interaction and how it influences and is influenced by information-seeking behaviour. He argues that assistance to users is the most important activity performed in libraries, but that the level of assistance is conditioned by both type of library and the availability of staff. Considered in the global context of the information society, other dimensions include the challenges of multiculturalism and multilingualism which are such major features of twenty-first century pluralist societies. Even heretofore largely homogeneous populations such as those found in Scandinavia are responding to such needs because of the acceptance of refugees and the increased mobility of workers. Many societies, especially post-colonial ones, are also trying to respond adequately to the needs and concerns of indigenous peoples. It is clear that cultural and linguistic dimensions will increasingly affect the experience of libraries by users and the responses of libraries to their users.

Provocatively, Alastair Smith begins by recognising the importance of the internet and the search engines, notably at this time Google. In a short space of time they have made the internet an exceedingly powerful and ready gateway to information. He notes that a 2006 survey suggests that 38 per cent of American internet users will use a search engine on any given day. Smith surveys the wealth of information sources available online and in print and briefly discusses some of their characteristics and limitations in various formats. He highlights the ways in which the internet revolution has dramatically changed reference to information sources and led to the introduction of new sources, such as Google Earth, while maintaining the need for skill and judiciousness in their use, again reinforcing the importance of information literacy.

Collecting has of course always been at the heart of librarianship. From the earliest records of business transactions and tax receipts to the Alexandrian aspirations of the great national and university libraries, the shaping of the collection to the purposes of the library – universal or selective – has been a major focus. Except for special libraries and information services, the standing of a library has traditionally been evaluated in terms of the size of its aggregate collection. Paul Genoni tackles the changing nature of collecting including the major shift from a focus on holding to a focus on providing access. This has permitted the creation of vast 'virtual' collections which are not physically held in the library or information service but are deliverable just in time from huge datastores. But the challenges of library management continue: selection and deselection, storage, preservation. The detailed concerns have metamorphosed but the issues remain priorities for libraries both individually and in working collaboratively.

A particularly challenging area for collaborative action is information organisation which is covered by Philip Hider. The essential means of providing information access – cataloguing, classification, metadata – continue to lie at the heart of library and information practice. It is our skill in applying those techniques and in redeveloping them to meet new challenges that differentiates our curated information resources from crude computer-accessible datastores.

Our capacity to meet the challenges of managing print and digital collections, describing their elements and making them available rests on the tools we use. In addition to the intellectual tools, the library and information systems, which are discussed by Tom Denison, are crucial to the successful operation of our services. Denison identifies the phases through which systems have developed and surveys the capabilities of current systems in which progressive refinement can be discerned. The most exciting aspect, however, lies in the new frontiers that new systems are allowing us to cross, through the creation of digital repositories and portals, cross platform and resource interoperability and the growing adoption of non proprietary standards and software. These initiatives, operating separately and in combination, hold the promise of truly providing 'information for all'.

The agency of libraries and information services

It is in the application of these systems and the concepts and techniques developed in libraries, that we see the emergence of the information age. As Michael Middleton argues, the roots of information management lie in the need to address the informational needs of big government and big business. Just as the complex data and information management needs of the newer military technologies and the space race led to the development of information management and retrieval systems, the need to handle large scale record keeping, transaction processing and policy implementation led to the codification of the techniques of information and knowledge management. The recognition of the crucial relationship between information use and business performance has driven the development of both specialised tools and analytical schemas. It has taken established library methods such as description and classification and reframed them for other applications, as in the specification of metadata. These new methods have in turn informed library and information practice as we engage with digital creation, management and delivery of information. Through the application of those reframed techniques in domains far removed from traditional library services, we can see the agency of library and information concepts pervading the information economy and society.

Sharing a common origin with libraries and frequently co-located, archives have developed their own character, methods and standards to deal with unique primary sources. Karen Anderson notes their evidentiary importance, which demands reliable provenance and assurance of integrity. This is especially true in regard to the records of government and corporations which enable the organisations to operate effectively and to investigate failures when necessary. Digital technology has assisted the tasks of archives management enormously but it has also resulted in a proliferation of digital records which need to be kept and brought forward unchanged, or at least in useable form, through successive versions of software and hardware.

Information literacy, which Christine Bruce (2002) has called 'the overarching literacy essential for twenty-first century living', has been mentioned in various chapters – indicating its centrality to the information society. It is treated in some detail by Anne Lloyd and Stuart Ferguson who link it to knowledge management. That approach to understanding and managing information flows focuses on the organisation while information literacy is identified as a core set of skills for individuals. In becoming drivers of both, libraries and information services, especially those in corporate settings, have significantly enhanced their importance and power within the organisations they serve.

On the principle that there are 'lessons to be learned from the study of the history of libraries', lessons that will inform future improvements, Ross Harvey bemoans the limited interest in library history in Australia. Certainly the patterns of library provision charted in the first part of this book and the development of other information services has been shaped by history. The historical forces have included not only the history of libraries in Australia but also the broader sweep of library and information service development internationally and the social and political context of Australia, from the foundation of the British colony to the modern multicultural nation of the early twenty-first century. Today's influences extend beyond the professional and technological initiatives described in this book to include ideological tussles such as the 'history wars' which posit alternative and contrary understandings of the history of Australia.

Some of those wider dimensions are analysed by Jake Wallis in a brief survey of the social, political and cultural context of libraries in the twenty-first century. He rehearses the observations of such commentators as Machlup and Castells and suggests some of the implications for libraries. Among those implications are a stronger emphasis on legal and ethical issues which are considered by Jan Houghton and Jennifer Berryman. They note the widespread expression by library associations of 'a set of values based on the right of every individual to access information, and to enjoy intellectual freedom and freedom of expression'. Statements of these values inform ethical positions that are difficult to maintain in the face of the pressures experienced in practice. The broad sweep of issues with which librarians and other information specialists deal include restrictions on access to information and the challenge of meeting the special needs of the disadvantaged from a principled professional stance. This increased emphasis has led to the exploration of information ethics – the ethical and related issues that pertain to the information society and the institutions that characterise it.

The weight of responding to the social and other expectations and of taking advantage of new technologies, renewed techniques and novel opportunities falls on the shoulders of the managers of libraries and information services. Damian Lodge and Bob Pymm chart a long list of the issues with which the managers must engage and place those requirements in the context of the high levels of transparency and accountability that are expected of managers today.

The capacity to deal with such a broad range of issues demands effective professional education from entry level onwards. Gillian Hallam notes a decline in student numbers in undergraduate and library technician courses while postgraduate courses have maintained – but not increased – their level over the last decade. This must be a major concern since the age profile of the profession in Australia is older than for most other professions. It is even greater cause for disquiet when we consider that we are in the early stage of the development of the global information society in which the skills of library and information professionals will be extremely valuable as, for example, has been demonstrated by the employment of large numbers of librarians by Google. The tensions between educators and practitioners which are reflected in different views on the curriculum are more than just a symptom but indicate the need for serious reconsideration of professional education.

Final conclusion

In the early years of the twenty-first century, library and information services in Australia are in good shape. They have proliferated in number and type, including many which are neither labelled 'library' nor give the appearance of a traditional library. They have shown themselves to be responsive and adaptable to changed social, political and economic circumstances and expectations. They have been ready adopters of new technologies and innovative in service development and the use of staff. They are well regarded internationally through such bodies as IFLA.

Australian libraries and information services are well positioned to serve Australians and their organisations as the information society develops during the twenty-first century. Their ready adoption of the internet and associated technologies and their active engagement with the challenges of the digital information environment, including preservation in particular, has made them even more relevant to the nation and its people. But there are some areas for attention such as professional education and achieving greater levels of collaboration. The twenty-first century, like the twentieth, will be a great time for libraries and information services, a time in which they come into their own as essential gateways for the information society.

References

Bruce, C 2002, *Information literacy as a catalyst for educational change: A background paper*, White Paper prepared for UNESCO, the US National Commission on Libraries and Information Science, and the National Forum on Information Literacy for use at the Information Literacy Meeting of Experts, Prague, http://www.nclis.gov/libinter/infolitconf&meet/papers/bruce-fullpaper.pdf

IFLA & Byrne, A 2004, *Promoting the global information commons: A commentary on the library and information implications of the WSIS Declaration of Principles*, IFLA, The Hague, http://www.ifla.org

United Nations 2000, *Millennium development goals,* UN, New York, http://www.un.org/millenniumgoals/background.html

World Summit on the Information Society 2003a, *Declaration of principles*, WSIS, Geneva, http://www.itu.int/wsis/documents/doc_multi-en-1161|1160.asp

World Summit on the Information Society 2003b, *Plan of action*, WSIS, Geneva, http://www.itu.int/wsis/documents/doc_multi-en-1161|1160.asp

Appendices

Appendix 1 The NSLA libraries – some basic facts

National Library of Australia

Website	http://www.nla.gov.au/
Establishment date	1901 (Commonwealth Parliamentary Library)
Legislation	National Library Act 1960
Annual report	http://www.nla.gov.au/policy/annual.html
Strategic plan	http://www.nla.gov.au/library/directions.html
Holdings	5.4 million items http://www.nla.gov.au/collect/index.html
Collection highlights	Endeavour Journal of Captain James Cook, papers of Eddie Mabo (both listed on international Memory of the World Register), Oral History collection, national legal deposit collection, PANDORA web archive. http://www.nla.gov.au/collect/treasures/treasures.html
Govt appropriation (2004-05)	$57,936,000
Employees (at 30 June 2005)	497
Visitor numbers (2004-05)	545,000

National Library of New Zealand/Te Puna Mātauranga o Aotearoa

Website	http://www.natlib.govt.nz/index.html
Establishment date	1965
Legislation	National Library of New Zealand (Te Puna Mātauranga o Aotearoa) Act 2003
Annual report	http://www.natlib.govt.nz/en/about/1pubannual05.html
Strategic plan	http://www.natlib.govt.nz/en/about/2pubsoi06.html
Holdings	2,005,565 items
Collection highlights	Alexander Turnbull Library – national documentary heritage collections; John Milton Collection; Maori and Pacific Collection
Govt appropriation (2004-05)	$48,033,000
Employees (at June 30 2005)	353 FTE
Visitor numbers (2004-05)	140,000

State Library of New South Wales

Website	http://www.sl.nsw.gov.au/
Establishment date	1826 (predecessor the Australian Subscription Library)
Legislation	Library Act 1939
Annual report	http://www.sl.nsw.gov.au/annual/
Strategic plan	http://www.sl.nsw.gov.au/publications/pdf/shaping.pdf
Holdings	4.7 million items http://www.sl.nsw.gov.au/collections/collections.cfm
Collection highlights	Mitchell and Dixson collections, which include nine First Fleet journals, journals and letters documenting maritime and land exploration of Australia; literary manuscripts; architectural plans;18th- and 19th-century documentary artworks; Audubon's *Birds of America*.
Annual budget (2004-05)	$65,424,000
Employees (average 2004-05)	379.0
Visitor numbers (2004-05)	629,000

State Library of Queensland

Website	http://www.slq.qld.gov.au/
Establishment date	1896 (predecessor the Brisbane Public Library)
Legislation	Libraries Act 1988
Annual report	http://www.slq.qld.gov.au/about/pub/corp
Strategic plan	http://www.slq.qld.gov.au/about/pub/strat
Holdings	3.5 million items http://www.slq.qld.gov.au/about/coll
Collection highlights	Rawson Archive; Johnstone Gallery Archive; James Hardie Library of Australian Fine Arts; Lindsay Collection
Annual budget (2003-04)	$41,630,000
Employees (at June 30 2005)	* 256 (as at 30 June 2004)
Visitor numbers (2004-05)	165,000

State Library of South Australia

Website	http://www.slsa.sa.gov.au/
Establishment date	1844 (predecessor the South Australian Subscription Library)
Legislation	Libraries Act 1982
Annual report	http://www.slsa.sa.gov.au/webdata/resources/Files/LBSA_annual_report_04-05.pdf
Strategic plan	http://www.slsa.sa.gov.au/site/page.cfm?area_id=15&nav_id=688
Holdings	1,481,080 items (2004-05)
Collection highlights	Bradman collection; 13th century Antiphonal; Colonel Light's papers; Harleian Collection; Holden archive; Pitjantjatjara children's drawings
Annual budget (2004-05)	$30m (2004-05)
Employees (at June 30 2005)	148
Visitor numbers	1,021,336 (2004-05)

State Library of Tasmania

Website	http://www.statelibrary.tas.gov.au/
Establishment date	1850 (Tasmanian Public Library)
Legislation	Libraries Act 1984
Annual report	http://www3.education.tas.gov.au/annualreport/
Strategic plan	Informing Tasmanians, http://www.education.tas.gov.au/informingtasmanians/
Holdings	
Collection highlights	Allport Library and Museum of Fine Arts; WL Crowther Library, including maritime and whaling material; JWB Murphy Collection of theatre posters and programs; apple and pear case labels.
Annual budget (2004-05)	$16.05 million
Employees (at June 30 2005)	209
Visitor numbers (2004-05)	153,000

State Library of Victoria

Website	http://www.slv.vic.gov.au/
Establishment date	1856 (Melbourne Public Library)
Legislation	Libraries Act 1988
Annual report	http://www.slv.vic.gov.au/about/information/annual_reports/index.html
Strategic plan	
Holdings	http://www.slv.vic.gov.au/collections/index.html
Collection highlights	Ned Kelly's armour and Jerilderie letter; Bendigo petition; Burke and Wills material; Port Phillip Association Records, Archives of Coles Myer, Literary archives, Australian art, Albert Tucker papers, Australian Galleries archive, Ken Pound Collection of Australian Children's Literature, M.V. Anderson Chess Collection, J.K. Moir Collection of Australian Literature, S.T. Gill's Victorian goldfields watercolours, Fauchery-Daintree album
Govt appropriation (2004-05)	$72,957,000
Employees (at June 30 2005)	316.11
Visitor numbers (2004-05)	906,000

State Library of Western Australia

Website	http://www.liswa.wa.gov.au/
Establishment date	1887 (predecessor the Victoria Public Library - to celebrate the Golden Jubilee of Queens Victoria's reign)
Legislation	The Library Board of Western Australia Act 1951
Annual report	http://www.liswa.wa.gov.au/arep.html
Strategic plan	http://www.liswa.wa.gov.au/policies.html
Holdings	1.3 million items
Collection highlights	Freycinet collection; Pelseart journal; Ray Stewart collection; Billingee drawings
Govt appropriation (2004-05)	$35,207,000
Employees (at June 30 2005)	257
Visitor numbers (2004-05)	528,000

ACT Library and Information Service

Website	http://www.library.act.gov.au/index.html
Establishment date	1935 (commenced as the Lending service, National Library of Australia)
Legislation	No legislation
Annual report	http://www.urbanservices.act.gov.au/functions/aboutus/annualreports (the Library is within the Department of Urban Services)
Strategic plan	Public library services http://www.library.act.gov.au/actpl/resourcedevelopmentrtf.rtf
Holdings	627,000 items
Collection highlights	Documents on Canberra's history
Govt appropriation (2004-05)	$18.2 million
Employees (at June 30 2005)	109.7
Visitor numbers (2004-05)	1,815,000 (includes public library visits)

Northern Territory Library

Website	http://www.dcdsca.nt.gov.au/dcdsca/intranet.nsf/pages/ntl_home
Establishment date	1877 (predecessor the Palmerston Institute)
Legislation	No legislation
Annual report	
Strategic plan	http://www.dcdsca.nt.gov.au/dcdsca/intranet.nsf/Pages/ntl_orgplan
Holdings	
Collection highlights	Cyclone Tracy documents, images and website; Thea Schmitz collection of rare books; Lou Marks reports collection
Annual budget (2004-05)	
Employees (at June 30 2005)	
Visitor numbers (2004-05)	230,000

Appendix 2: Australian law – overview of legislation discussed in Chapter 16

Topic	Jurisdiction	Key legislation	Web resources
Intellectual Property			
Copyright	Commonwealth	Copyright Act 1968 (Cth) Copyright Amendment (Digital Agenda) Act 2000 (Cth) US Free Trade Agreement Implementation Act 2004 (Schedule 9) Copyright Amendment Act 2006	Australian Copyright Council http://www.copyright.org.au/ IP Australia: http://www.ipaustralia.gov.au/ip/copyright.shtml World Intellectual Property Organisation (WIPO): http://www.wipo.int/portal/index.html.en
Patents	Commonwealth	Patents Act 1990 (Cth)	IP Australia: http://www.ipaustralia.gov.au/ The Patents Guide: http://www.ipaustralia.gov.au/pdfs/patents/patentsguide.pdf
Trade Marks	Commonwealth	Trade Marks Act 1995 (Cth)	IP Australia: http://www.ipaustralia.gov.au/trademarks/index.shtml
Censorship	Commonwealth	Broadcasting Services Act 1992 (Cth) Classification (Publications, Films and Computer Games) Act 1995 (Cth)	Australian Communications and Media Authority (ACMA): http://www.acma.gov.au/ Office of Film and Literature Classification: http://www.oflc.gov.au/special.html Electronic Frontiers Australia: http://www.efa.org.au/Issues/Censor/ Libertus: http://libertus.net/
	States	Broadcasting Services Amendment (On line) Act 1999 Corresponding legislation	
Privacy	Commonwealth	Privacy Act 1988 (Cth) Privacy Amendment (Private Sector) Act 2000 (Cth)	Office of the Federal Privacy Commissioner http://www.privacy.gov.au/ Australian Law Reform Commission http://www.alrc.gov.au/inquiries/current/privacy/index.htm Australian Privacy Foundation http://www.privacy.org.au/ Privacy International http://www.privacyinternational.org/index.shtml
	NSW	Privacy and Personal Information Protection Act 1998 (NSW)	Lawlink NSW – Office of the NSW Privacy Commissioner http://www.lawlink.nsw.gov.au/lawlink/privacynsw/ll_pnsw.nsf/pages/PNSW_index
	NSW	Health Records and Information Privacy Act 2002 (NSW)	http://www.lawlink.nsw.gov.au/lawlink/privacynsw/ll_pnsw.nsf/pages/PNSW_03_hripact

	Victoria	Information Privacy Act 2000 (Vic)	Privacy Victoria http://www.privacy.vic.gov.au/dir100/priweb.nsf Victorian Law Foundation: http://www.victorialaw.org.au/Private Lives/index.htm
		Health Records Act (Victoria) 2002 (Vic)	Health Services Commissioner of Victoria Health Privacy Principles: http://www.health.vic.gov.au/hsc/downloads/hppextract.pdf
	Queensland	Information Standard 42 and Information Standard 42A (2001)	Department of Justice and Attorney General, Queensland http://www.justice.qld.gov.au/dept/privacy.htm http://www.justice.qld.gov.au/dept/factsht29.htm
	South Australia	PC012 - Information Privacy Principles Instruction 1992	http://www.premcab.sa.gov.au/pdf/circulars/Privacy.pdf
	Tasmania	Personal Information Protection Act 2004 (Tas)	
	Northern Territory	Information Act 2002 (NT)	Northern Territory Government: http://www.nt.gov.au/ntg/privacy.html
Freedom of Information	Commonwealth	Freedom of Information Act 1982 (Cth)	Attorney-General's Department: http://www.ag.gov.au/foi Privacy International http://www.privacyinternational.org/index.shtml
	NSW	Freedom of Information Act 1989 (NSW)	NSW Premier's Department http://www.premiers.nsw.gov.au/NSWCommunity/FreedomOfInformation/
	Victoria	Freedom of Information Act 1982 (Vic)	Freedom of Information On line - Victoria http://www.foi.vic.gov.au/CA256BE9002028C5/HomePage?OpenForm&1=Home~&2=~&3=~
	Queensland	Freedom of Information Act 1992 (Qld)	Department of Justice and Attorney General: http://www.justice.qld.gov.au/dept/foi.htm
	South Australia	Freedom of Information Act 1991 (SA)	State Records of South Australia: Introduction to FOI: http://www.archives.sa.gov.au/foi/intro.html
	Western Australia	Freedom of Information Act 1992 (WA)	Office of the Information Commissioner: http://www.foi.wa.gov.au/

| Anti-terrorism law | Commonwealth | Anti Terrorism Act (No 2) 2005
Criminal Code Act 1995 (Cth)(Schedule 1,Part 5.3 (Terrorism))
Crimes Act 1914 (Cth)
ASIO Legislation Amendment Act (Cth) 2003 | Attorney-General's Department http://www.nationalsecurity.gov.au/
Parliamentary Library: Terrorism Law;
http://www.aph.gov.au/library/intguide/law/terrorism.htm#2006
Australian Law Reform Commission:
http://www.alrc.gov.au/inquiries/current/sedition/about.html
http://www.alrc.gov.au/inquiries/title/alrc104/index.html |

Glossary

24/7 – term used to refer to a service that is available twenty-four hours a day, seven days a week or, in other words, without break (typically using international partnerships).

Acquisition – in libraries the activity of obtaining, usually but not always by purchase, what has been selected for inclusion in the collection. Commonly the plural form 'acquisitions' is employed, notably in phrases such as 'acquisitions department', 'acquisitions librarian' and 'acquisitions work'. Acquisition is usually regarded as a branch of collection management, but, particularly in North America, it is sometimes seen as distinct from collection management.

Aggregators – library suppliers that assemble packages of materials from various publishers (particularly electronic serials and other digital materials) and offer the packages (termed 'aggregations') to libraries, which must frequently accept or reject the package in its entirety. *See also* Publishers' packages.

Algorithms – sets of step-by-step rules, used to solve problems.

Analogue – form of data transmission in which signals are sent as continuous waves. Contrast with digital.

Approval plans – arrangements whereby a supplier provides a library with publications that meet a predetermined set of criteria, on the understanding that the library may examine the material and return a proportion of it to the supplier if it wishes to do so.

ARROW – Australian Research Repositories Online to the World.

Asknow! – a collaborative online chat reference service operated by the National, state and territory libraries, in partnership with public libraries.

ASP service – Application Service Provider

Asynchronous – (1) a form of serial data transmission in which each transmitted byte of data is preceded and/or succeeded with special start and stop bits. These start and stop bits are used to control the flow of data for the receiving device. Contrast with synchronous. (2) used in a general sense of communication that does not take place in real time, such as email and internet newsgroups.

Audiovisual materials – 'umbrella' term for library materials which are neither in print form nor accessed by computer – notably sound recordings, films, videos, slides and other items that rely primarily on sound and/or images rather than text.

Australian Libraries Gateway (ALG) – a free web-based directory service with information about more than 5,400 Australian libraries, their collections and services.

Australian National Bibliographic Database – a database of the materials held by Australian libraries.

Bandwidth – the capacity, measured in bits per second (bps), of a communications channel.

Benchmarking – measuring performance of, say, a service or system by comparing it with an equivalent service or system or by measuring it against intended performance.

Bibliographer – in general usage, people who compile bibliographies and/or specialise in the detailed physical description of books. In North American university and research libraries it is also used to designate librarians who possess expertise in the literature of a subject or group of subjects and who are responsible for collection management and the provision of assistance to clients in regard to the subject or subjects.

Bibliographic classification – *see* Classification.

Bibliographic information – information that describes a bibliographic item such as a book, including attributes such as titles, authors and publication dates.

Bibliographic organisation – *see* Information organisation.

Blanket order – request from a library to a supplier that it send to the library all publications that meet a predetermined criterion or set of criteria, as they are published. Typically this might involve all publications of a publisher or all publications on a specific subject.

Blog – short for weblog: in general terms, a web page containing brief, chronologically presented items of information; typically, it takes the form of a journal or newsletter, made publicly available and frequently updated.

Boolean operators – also known as logical operators, these are mathematical means of representing logical functions that combine search terms: for instance, AND (both terms to be present), OR (either term to be present) and NOT (omitting records or documents containing the second term).

Broken link – a web link to a website or web document that no longer provides the intended linkage.

Browser – a piece of client software used to access the web and navigate the links between web-based documents. Also called a web browser.

CARM Centre – repository for low usage material maintained by CAVAL. The acronym stands for 'Caval Archive and Research Materials'. *See also* CAVAL.

CASL – *see* NSLA.

Catalogue –form of bibliographic database that describes information resources (typically published resources) available in a specific library or in a library network, designed to helps library clients or potential clients to identify, select and locate either specific known resources (for example, works by a known author) or resources that contain information on a specified subject. Sometimes the interface used to interrogate an online catalogue is called an OPAC (online public access catalogue).

Cataloguing – the process of creating bibliographic records that contain bibliographic, physical and (generally) subject descriptions representing information resources held by a libraries or similar institution, typically adhering to agreed standards such as the Anglo-American Cataloguing Rules. Cataloguers may create new catalogue records (original cataloguing) or paraprofessional staff may download copies of existing catalogue records from bibliographic databases or networks (copy cataloguing).

Cataloguing/technical services – in its narrowest sense, the cataloguing of material for lending, but for many libraries it also includes stock selection and weeding of stock. There is a trend towards this becoming a more holistic collection management area.

CAUL – Council of Australian University Librarians.

CAVAL – regional network in the Australian state of Victoria. The acronym stands for Cooperative Action by Victorian Academic Libraries.

CD-ROM – compact disk read-only memory: a type of optical storage medium.

Chat – a form of internet mediated human communication that takes place in real time or, in other words, synchronously.

Circulation/loans services – library services geared to the loan of library resources to its clients, including handling the issue, tracking, return and request of loan material.

Claiming – requesting from a supplier or publisher an item ordered but not received within what is considered a reasonable time or an issue of a serial publication that failed to arrive within the expected timeframe.

Classification – a process that involves the subject analysis of an information resource, the selection of a 'class' into which the resource may best fit, relative to other resources, and the assignment to the resource of a notation, based on numbers and/or letters (and sometimes other symbols), that represents the class – a device typically used for shelving books and other physical information resources. In libraries this is often called bibliographic classification. Examples include Dewey Decimal Classification and the Library of Congress Classification. In the area of censorship, classification can also refer to the restriction of access to documents to specified classes of people.

Client/server architecture – the model underlying much communication on the internet, involving the linking of a client (the user's local system) with a server, a 'remote' system that handles data and files and deals with requests via clients for access to the data and files. The model requires special client software and server software in order to function.

Client-centred methods – also known as 'user-centred methods', these are approaches to collection evaluation that focus on the usefulness of the materials in the collection to people using the collection. *See also* collection-centred methods.

Collection – term often applied loosely to any assemblage of materials, but used in libraries to refer to the books, serials, pamphlets, sound recordings and so on, more or less systematically assembled by the library to serve the wants and needs of its clients. 'The collection' is generally the totality of such resources, but the word is also employed to refer to a part of the total collection – for example, the serials collection or the French literature collection. Increasingly, library collections are regarded as including materials in digital form, including materials on the internet to which the library provides access.

Collection assessment – often employed as a synonym for 'collection evaluation'.

Collection development – term used to encompass interrelated activities concerned with building and maintaining library collections of resources to serve the wants and needs of clients. Sometimes used as a synonym for 'collection management', but often considered as more appropriate to a time, now past, when the emphasis of librarians was on building up their collections rather than on managing limited resources effectively and efficiently.

Collection development policy – though some libraries might be said to have implicit collection development policies, the phrase normally refers to a publicly available document that sets out the library's collecting philosophy and goals, describes in some detail the type of materials it holds and collects, and outlines policy on other matters relating to the collection.

Collection evaluation – process of determining the worth of a collection in terms of its ability to satisfy the wants and needs of clients and fulfil the goals of the library.

Collection management – phrase which has partly replaced 'collection development' as the preferred term when referring to the set of interrelated activities involved in building and maintaining a collection of library resources to serve the wants and needs of its clients. These activities include matters relating to selection, evaluation, deselection and preservation of materials. Acquisition is frequently also considered an aspect of collection management, although sometimes regarded as distinct, particularly in North America.

Collection management policy – see collection development policy.

Collection-centred methods – approaches to collection evaluation that focus primarily on the materials in the collection (and possibly also the materials missing from the collection). *See also* client-centred methods.

Compact disk – see CD-ROM.

Compactus shelving – shelving (typically closed-access) that will hold more library resources in a given area than conventional, fixed shelving by being mounted on rails that permit the widening and narrowing of the gaps between shelves.

Conservation – the maintenance of an item is as near as possible a state to its original one. Sometimes used in the sense in which 'preservation' is used but also used by some writers in a more specific sense to refer to methods employed to arrest deterioration of library materials. *See also* Preservation and Restoration.

Consortia – formally constituted associations of libraries, joined together to achieve a specific goal or group of goals while maintaining autonomy in most respects. Consortia are concerned mainly with collection management, with a view, for instance, to sharing resources, especially digital resources, or obtaining better terms from suppliers of library materials than would otherwise be possible.

Conspectus – approach to describing collection strengths, collecting practices and collecting intentions across a wide range of subject areas, employing a standardised alpha-numeric scale designed to facilitate comparisons between libraries and cooperation. Extensively employed in collection evaluation.

Content management – procedures for managing the creation, organisation, storage and dissemination of digital documents in organisations. Often used to refer more specifically to the management of web-based documents.

Continuum model – records management model that brings together record keeping and archival processes by providing a comprehensive set of management processes from record creation though to its use as an archive. Contrast with the traditional life cycle model which is regarded as creating too sharp a distinction between current and historical record-keeping.

Controlled terms – a list of terms in which preferred terms are indicated and non-preferred terms are listed with references to the appropriate preferred terms (thus facilitating control of synonyms). In the case of thesauri, which list subject terms, hierarchical relationships among terms are also indicated (the reference structure generally including broader terms, narrower terms and related terms).

Copy cataloguing – copying existing catalogue records, for instance, by downloading them from a bibliographic network. Contrasted with original cataloguing.

Crosswalks – in the area of metadata standards, crosswalks are a means of mapping the elements in one standard to those in another: for instance, from MARC to Dublin Core.

Current awareness services – information services that involve provision of clients and organisations with regular updates of information, typically automated and based on a set of user-profiles. *See also* SDI services.

Data dictionaries – these describe the different elements of an agent that carries information. In a database management system, for instance, the data dictionary contains information such as what files are in the database and descriptions of the data contained in the files.

Databases – collections of related computer files stored in a computer system. Library catalogues and commercial journal indexes are examples of bibliographic databases that contain descriptions of specific information resources (records), including the standardised data elements or attributes (fields) used to describe those resources, such as title, author or subject descriptor.

Deaccessioning – term sometimes used instead of 'deselection' or 'weeding', probably to emphasise the need in many environments to account formally for materials removed from the collection.

Deposit libraries – libraries that are required by law to receive a free copy of each item published within a specified jurisdiction. A state library, for instance, may receive deposits of all books published in that state. Also known as legal deposit libraries.

Deselection – removal from a collection of materials judged no longer to merit a place there. Some writers use it to describe the removal of materials from the library, while others employ it to mean removal from the main collection, but not necessarily from the library's control. Synonym for 'weeding'.

Desktop – a term often used to refer to the computer workstation on an individual's desk, whether at home or at work or elsewhere, which, with the required connectivity, links the user to the online information enviornment. Libraries aiming at such users refer to the provision of the 'library at your desktop'.

Dewey Decimal Classification – a type of bibliographic classification used commonly in libraries to classify their information resources. *See* Classification.

Digital – refers to the binary format in which computers store, manipulate and transfer data. In data communication it describes the form of data transmission in which signals are sent as discrete, on/off signals. Contrast with analogue.

Digital library – library in which all the materials for use by clients can be accessed and utilised via a computer terminal. In practice most libraries continue to include both print and digital resources, and are sometimes described as 'hybrid libraries'.

Digital repositories – initially seen as e-print repositories, designed to showcase an institution's intellectual output (especially in the university sector), but extended to include collections of learning objects to support the teaching process and research repositories, to be used as tightly integrated elements of the research process. *See also* Institutional repositories.

Digital resources – information resources held in digital form or, in other words, in a form that a computer can handle.

Digitisation – process of converting a document or other information resource from a non-digital format into a digital one.

Distributed National Collection – an aggregation of Australian library collections in Australia, recorded in generally accessible databases and accessible to bona fide users.

Document delivery services – operations designed to provide materials needed to clients on request; typically photographic or electronic copies of materials, requested directly by researchers or libraries acting on behalf of specific researchers. May be a department of a library or a more or less independent commercial entity. *See also* Interlibrary loans/interlending.

Down – term used to describe a computer-based system when it is not operating. Downtime refers to periods when systems are down.

Dublin Core – a generic metadata standard for describing information resources, based on fifteen core elements (to which other, more specific standards have added).

E-mail or electronic mail – means of transmitting electronic messages, between computers or between a computer and another device, such as a fax machine.

E-repositories – *see* Digital repositories.

Electronic library – *see* Digital library.

Encumbering – practice of setting aside funds in a financial management system to pay for items ordered, in the expectation that the transaction will not be finalised for a significant period of time. The term is often employed in acquisitions work when materials ordered are unavailable for immediate delivery because they are as yet unpublished or need to come from overseas.

Environmental scanning – process by which organisations monitor the external information environment for information that can assist it meet its strategic objectives; typically conducted by a corporate library or information centre or a business intelligence unit.

Exhaustive – used to denote an index that describes in depth the information resources to which it refers.

Federated search facility – a search tool that allows the searcher to utilise for interrogation a range of information retrieval tools using the one search: for instance, software solutions that retrieve results simultaneously from library catalogues and commercial databases.

Finding aids – information retrieval tools used to access archival collections or, more typically, specific parts of an archival collection; the equivalent of a library catalogue.

Forums – virtual space on a computer server, to which members of a group can post electronic messages for other members of the group to read; similar to newsgroups on the internet.

Frequently asked questions (FAQs) – page(s) on a website used to provide answers to questions frequently asked of the owners/managers of the site; for instance, solutions to typical installation problems displayed on a software supplier's website.

Hardware – physical, 'touchable' parts of a computer system, such as keyboards and monitors. Contrast with software.

Harvesting – automated process that enables the collection of internet resources and/or metadata relating to those resources, with a view to creating a digital archive, such as the Pandora archive developed by the National Library of Australia.

Hit – term used to denote a single search result.

Home library/housebound services – selection and delivery services to homebound individuals, nursing homes and/or retirement villages; typically provided by public libraries.

HTTP – hypertext transfer protocol; a communications protocol used to move copies of hypertext files between HTTP servers and HTTP clients.

Hyperlinks – the associative links in a hypertext document that allow the user to navigate to another part of the document or to another document or website.

Hypermedia – the same as hypertext except that what is linked is not just text but also other media, such as graphics, audio and animation.

Hypertext – software used to create a textual database, in which text is stored as 'nodes' of text, links are created between nodes and users can follow associative links between nodes. Software on which the web is based.

ICTs – information and communications technologies or, in other words, those technologies that include computing and data communications.

Information architecture – study and practice of structuring shared information environments such as websites, intranets and online communities. Applied in particular to website design, including elements such as navigation features, graphic elements, labelling systems and search features.

Information organisation – the provision of access to information resources through value-added processes such as description (addition of metadata, creation of catalogue records or provision of subject headings or descriptors) and classification.

Information retrieval systems – tools, typically digital, that allow information searchers to locate information resources by means of a search interface that leads either directly to a digital resource or to a 'surrogate' record that describes an appropriate resource: for instance, a library catalogue or bibliographic database.

Institutional repositories – sometimes used synonymously with 'digital repositories' but typically used more specifically to refer to the e-print component of a digital repository, designed to showcase an institution's intellectual output (especially research in the case of the university sector). *See also* Digital repositories.

Integrated library management system (ILMS) – information system that handles a range of library applications, such as cataloguing and circulations, and in which the different applications can share the same data, most notably, bibliographic data.

Intelligent search engines – search engines that incorporate elements of artificial intelligence (AI), making inferences, for instance, based on their memory and on their previous contact with their environment, thus learning from their environment and from past inferences.

Interlibrary loans/interlending – library practice of requesting from other libraries materials required by the clients of the requesting library, and responding to such requests from other libraries. Retention of photocopies or electronic copies by clients is more common than loans, hence terms such as 'document delivery' or 'document supply' are sometimes preferred. *See also* Document delivery services.

International Internet Preservation Consortium (IIPC) – strategic alliance of national libraries and the Internet Archive in the United States, designed to address issues of long term access to digital resources.

Internet – large international network of interconnected networks.

Intranet – network internal to an organisation that employs web standards and technologies, such as HTML, HTTP and the use of a web browser client.

ISO – International Standards Organisation: an international body responsible for the development of data communications standards.

Issuing – process of recording a loan in order that a library client can borrow a resource.

JISC – Joint Information Systems Committee: organisation that aims to foster innovative use of information and communications technologies in support of education and research.

Journals – *see* Serials.

Kinetica – service provided by the National Library of Australia; replaced by Libraries Australia in December 2005. *See also* Libraries Australia.

LCSH – *see* Library of Congress Subject Headings.

Legal deposit libraries – *see* Deposit libraries.

Libraries Australia – web-based service enabling libraries and users to find and get material listed in the national database of material (Australian National Bibliographic Database) held in Australian libraries and other databases. Replaced Kinetica service.

Library management system – *see* Integrated library management system.

Library of Congress Subject Headings (LCSH) – a comprehensive list of approved descriptors, a common standard in the English speaking world.

Licence – legal agreement whereby one party grants specific rights to another in return for some form of payment. In collection management usage the term normally refers to permission granted to libraries enabling them, subject to conditions, to access electronic databases and (usually) make them available to clients of the library.

Life cycle model – traditional model used in records management and archival work to represent the stages of a record's existence. Not seen as a sustainable model in digital environments. Contrast with Continuum model.

Listserv – electronic mail server software that supports mailing lists, in which messages from members of a list are forwarded via a server to all members on the list. Used synonymously with list and discussion list.

Logins –authentication processes developed to identify users who access a computer system, typically using a formal login name and password.

Mainframe computer – large computer with greater processing capabilities and memory than a minicomputer or a microcomputer. Typically used in large organisations such as local councils and universities.

MARC – machine readable cataloguing: an exchange format used to download and upload bibliographic records (and authority records) into different library management systems.

Mark-up language – set of coded tags, embedded in a document in order to provide information about the document's structure and how the text is to be presented. HTML, for instance, indicates how a document is to be handled by a web browser. A document that has been tagged in this way is described as being marked up.

Metadata – often described as structured data about data, and used to refer to the descriptive elements required to describe internet resources and so make these resources easier to access (e.g., the Dublin Core Metadata Element Set). Fields or data elements in a library catalogue are often described as a form of metadata.

Metasearching – searching across a variety of information tools. Used typically in the context of metasearch engines, which allow users to search across several search engines using the search interface provided for the metasearch engine.

Metatags – coded tags, the purpose of which is to identify particular elements of information such as title, author, date of creation, in the case of a metadata standard such as Dublin Core.

Minicomputers – computers that are smaller than a mainframe, with less processing capabilities and memory than it, but more powerful than a microcomputer.

Mobile library services – vehicular libraries that are used to take library services to clients; provided typically by public libraries that have customers in rural and remote locations.

Monograph – a work which is not a serial, published typically in one volume and focusing on a single subject field (distinguishing it from an encyclopedia or dictionary). In everyday library usage, 'monograph' tends to be used more loosely as a synonym for 'printed book'.

Multicultural services – library services specifically targeted at communities with a high proportion of residents from diverse cultural backgrounds.

Music Australia – web based service enabling libraries and users to find and get music material held in Australian libraries and online.

National site licensing – licensing arrangement intended to develop a national licence for a core set of databases; a project led, in Australasia, by peak library bodies and existing consortia.

Natural language processing (NLP) – automated analysis of a search query from the user of an 'intelligent' search engine and translation of the user's natural language into a form and terminology that the search engine can handle.

Network – arrangement of computers, computer peripherals, communications media and a control mechanism, designed to share data, information or components of a computer system.

NSLA: National and State Libraries Australasia – a peak body representing the national libraries of Australia and New Zealand and Australian state and territory libraries, and collaborating on a range of services and projects (previously known as CASL: Council of Australian State Libraries).

OCLC – Online Computer Library Center: a US-based bibliographic network.

Online – condition in which there is a communications link between a device and a computer, e.g., a circulations terminal and a circulations control system. Data processing conducted online is said to be real-time processing.

OPAC – online public access catalogue: term often used to describe the interface used to interrogate an online catalogue. Sometimes shortened to PAC.

Open access – term used to refer to cooperative initiatives to counter high prices for commercially produced journals by making material such as refereed scholarly publications, preprints and 'works in progress' freely available to the scholarly community via the internet.

Open source software – software that includes source code and that can be downloaded free of charge via the internet, under license conditions that include rights and responsibilities such as responsibility on the part of distributors to include source code and the right on the part of licensees to develop new software by modifying the source code and distribute it under the same terms as the license of the original software.

Open Systems Interconnection (OSI) – data communications system designed by the International Standards Organisation (ISO) and underlying many of its communication protocols.

OpenURL – a type of URL that contains metadata and/or identifiers about an information resource, typically a bibliographic resource; used, for instance, to provide a link from a citation to the full text of the resource cited.

Outsourcing – practice whereby organisations elect not to undertake certain essential activities themselves, but instead to hire outside contractors to provide them for a predetermined price and according to agreed service criteria. Applied most commonly in libraries to selection and acquisition.

Pandora – national digital archive of 'born digital' Australian online publications, established initially by the National Library of Australia in 1996, and developed in collaboration with nine other Australian libraries and cultural collecting organisations.

Pathfinders – tools that guide school students towards resources that have been mediated by a teacher librarian and chosen to meet a range of student needs and abilities in particular subject areas.

PC – personal computer: a microcomputer generally for personal use; typically refers only to IBM or IBM-compatible microcomputers.

Performance indicators – statistics and other evidence that represents how an organisation such as a library is progressing: for instance, a ratio comparing a specified statistic over a set period, such as loans per year.

Performance measurement – use of measures, both quantitative and qualitative, to assess the performance of an organisation, such as the performance of a library's services or collections. It is common practice to use inputs such as the budget, outputs such as items catalogued, and outcomes such as the effectiveness of information literacy sessions.

Periodicals – *see* Serials.

PictureAustralia – web based service enabling individual to find and get images in digital form created by cultural organisations and individuals.

Platform – the operating system and hardware on which application software runs.

Portal – resource that acts as a gateway to the internet or to an organisation's intranet, often used as a starting point for users and offering them a range of resources and services such as email, information services, current awareness services and databases.

Precision – a ratio used to assess the effectiveness of a search of an information retrieval tool such as a database, by calculating the number of relevant records/documents retrieved as a proportion of the total number of records/documents retrieved.

Preservation – steps taken to maintain library materials in good physical condition and/or ensure that their content remains useable. Some writers prefer to use the term 'conservation' in this sense, and restrict 'preservation' to the employment of specific techniques to extend the survival of materials. *See also* Conservation and Restoration.

Protocol – in networking, the set of rules and conventions governing the transmission of data; in information retrieval, the term search protocol is used to refer to the detailed (and repeatable) set of steps required to complete a search.

Publishers' packages – compilations of (generally digital) materials, similar to aggregations (see Aggregator) but containing only materials emanating from a single publisher, generally responsible for making the compilation available. The term 'aggregation' is often used as an umbrella term for both kinds of compilation.

Radio Frequency Identification systems – *see* RFID.

Reader services – traditionally the section of the library that serves its clients directly, notably by performing reference work. The division between reader services and technical services has tended to diminish in an increasingly electronic information environment. *See also* Technical services.

Recall – a ratio used to assess the effectiveness of a search of an information retrieval tool such as a database, arrived at by calculating the number of relevant records/documents retrieved as a proportion of the total number of relevant records/documents stored.

Records – (1) in record keeping, records are unique, primary information sources, retained by individuals and organisations for evidential purposes; (2) in information systems management, records are regarded as sets of fields or data elements treated as a unit within a computer file: for instance, a library catalogue will contain bibliographic records made up of fields containing bibliographic and subject descriptions of information resources held by the library.

Records continuum model *see* Continuum model.

Reference interview – interchange between a library client and a librarian to answer a question and/or solve an information need. It may be a simple answer to one question or a series of questions and answers, designed to identify what the user wants both to the librarian and to the client. It could be face to face or electronic.

Reference librarian – person responsible for providing direct assistance to library clients by answering their questions, conducting classes to assist them in using the library's resources, compiling guides to the collection and so on.

Reference/information services – library services with staff dedicated to assisting customers find information. They may include exploring the online information environment and, in the case of public libraries, the development of reader services such as advising leisure readers on potentially interesting topics. *See also* Virtual reference services.

Relational operators – like boolean operators, these are a means of combining search terms that allow users to specify where the terms appear in a record or document relative to each other: for instance next to each other or near each other (within a specified number of words).

Relegation – (1) the phrase 'stock relegation' is used with a meaning similar to that of 'deselection' or 'weeding'. (2) 'relegation' is also employed to describe the removal of material from the main collection to a store where is it is still available to clients of the library but less readily accessible.

Resource discovery – term used to denote the 'discovery' of information resources by library clients or information system users. Development of a shared bibliographic database by several libraries or the use of metatags on a website, for instance, may be designed to enhance resource discovery by potential users.

Resource sharing – the provision of access to other libraries' collections for the benefit of clients. May be mediated through the client's library or unmediated (direct contact between the client and the other library).

Restoration – activity of attempting to make good damage to materials. In libraries and archives, restoration work is generally entrusted to staff specially trained in appropriate technical and chemical procedures. *See also* Preservation and Conservation.

RFID – radio frequency identification technology, used in libraries for the identification of library resources. This requires special RF tags to be embedded in resources, which are then detected by a transceiver with decoder, via an antenna.

RLG – Research Libraries Group.

SDI services – selective dissemination of information: services that supply individuals and organisations with information on requested topics at regular intervals. Typically automated and based on a set of user-profiles. *See also* Current awareness services.

Search interface – a combination of hardware and software elements that allow users of an information retrieval system to interrogate the system; the term is often used to refer specifically to elements that distinguish particular systems, such as screen documentation, search facilities, terms used for relational and other operators and so on.

Selection – branch of collection management concerned with deciding which items will be added to a library collection.

Selective dissemination of information – *see* SDI services.

Serials – publication intended to appear in successive parts, usually intended to be published at regular intervals (typically daily, weekly, monthly, quarterly or annually), and except in rare cases intended to continue to be published indefinitely. Increasingly, serials are issued in digital form as well as, or instead of, in print form. The terms 'journal' and 'periodical' are commonly used interchangeably with 'serial'.

Server – (1) a host computer that stores data and files and makes them available to clients (*see* Client/server architecture), (2) the special software required to handle data and files, and provide access to them.

SFX – abbreviation for special effects, but in this context a software product that allows for the easy embedding of hyperlinks in text: for instance, a link in a library catalogue record that provides access to the full text of the document to which the record refers.

Software – set of instructions that tell the computer what to do. Contrast with hardware.

Spamming – the use of a mailing list to send unsolicited and generally unwanted messages in bulk. Spamming occurs in a variety of media, including email, instant messaging and blogs.

Standards – sets of criteria created by a respected authority such as a government agency or professional organisation, in order to facilitate the evaluation of an entity or a service. Library standards may relate to the totality of facilities and services provided by the library or to one aspect, such as its collection.

Standing order – request from a library to a supplier that it send to the library successive items in a monograph series as they appear, or successive issues of a serial, until a request to cease doing so is received from the library or until the series or the serial ends publication.

Stemming – in information retrieval, the shortening of search terms in order to broaden a search to include all occurrences of text that share a common stem; achieved by leaving characters off the end of the term, for example, 'librar?'. A form of truncation, also known as word stemming.

Stock relegation – *see* Relegation.

Stop words – common words that are almost meaningless in search terms and are not indexed for purposes of retrieval in an information retrieval system: prepositions such as 'of' or 'with', for instance, or the articles 'a' and 'the'.

Subscription agent – library supplier that specialises in the provision of serials to libraries, generally undertaking to manage the subscriptions on behalf of the library engaging its services. Also referred to as 'subscription jobbers'.

Supplier –sometimes used loosely in libraries to refer to any individual or organisation from which a library obtains material for its collection, but often employed more specifically to refer to companies that focus their business, or a significant part of it, on meeting the needs of libraries in purchasing materials for their collections.

Synchronous – (1) used in general terms to refer to an activity or process conducted in real time, such as various forms of videoconferencing, (2) used in data communications to refer to serial transmission, in which each bit is sent one after the other until all data have been transmitted. Serial transmission relies heavily on the sender and receiver having synchronised system clocks. Contrast with asynchronous.

Taxonomies – hierarchical classifications or categorisations of information objects that attempt to reflect the actual entities represented in the taxonomy; typically a hierarchy of terms, with a reference structure (resembling a thesaurus), used to model the information and knowledge resources of an organisation.

Te Puna – search service provided by the National Library of New Zealand (Te Puna Mātauranga o Aotearoa): includes the NZ National Bibliographic Database of bibliographic records, the Index New Zealand (INNZ) article database and the Te Puna web directory of internet resources.

Technical services – traditionally the sections of library operations 'behind the scenes' and concerned with acquiring, cataloguing and other processing of materials to make them available to clients. *See also* Reader services; Collection management.

Truncation – shortening of search terms to include all occurrences of text that share common characters: 'lab?or', for instance, might locate 'labor' (US spelling) *and* 'labour' (British spelling). *See also* Stemming.

Turnkey integrated library management system –integrated library management system in which hardware and prewritten software are supplied by the one vendor.

Union catalogue – catalogue recording the holdings of several libraries and indicating locations of individual items.

URL – uniform resource locator: a unique address for internet resources, made up of the retrieval method (typically HTTP), the host server and domain name, and the directory-type address of the resource on the host server.

User-centred methods – *see* Client-centred methods.

Vendor – person or organisation offering material for sale. Often employed as a synonym for 'library supplier' or 'supplier'.

Verification – in acquisitions work, the activity of determining that the items it is proposed to obtain actually exist and that the bibliographic details to be used in ordering them are complete and correct.

Virtual library – *see* Digital library.

Virtual reference services – library-based reference/information services that provide clients with online access to resources and services, including 'ask-a' services (using internet chat, for instance), which may be available outside library hours through collaborative arrangements with institutions in other time zones.

Web – world wide web or www: often used to refer to the internet resources that can be accessed using a variety of retrieval methods, but a more precise definition might be that it comprises the large number of internet servers that use hypertext to store and link files.

Web browser – *see* Browser.

Web portal – *see* Portal.

Web server – computer device and the software required to run it that together store website files and respond to messages that have been submitted using HTTP (or an associated protocol). *See also* Server.

Weblog – *see* Blog.

Website – refers to the collection of interlinked documents published in HTML (or a variation of it) by a specific individual or organisation and accessed via HTTP.

Weeding – *see* Deselection.

Wiki – software that allows users of a website to create and edit the website's content using their own web browsers.

World wide web – *see* Web.

XML – extensible markup language: a subset of standard generalized markup language (SGML) and an extension of HTML, designed as the universal format for the exchange of structured documents and data on the web.

Z39.50 – applications layer communications protocol that provides a means for users to access information resources such as online library catalogues using a single search interface.

Biographical notes on contributors

Dr Karen Anderson is a senior lecturer in the School of Computer and Information Science at Edith Cowan University, where she developed the Archives and Records program, which had its first intake of students in 1994. In 2006, she worked at Mid Sweden University as associate professor and guest researcher with colleagues in the archival education program in the School of Information Technology and Media to develop reseBarch partnerships. Her principal research interest to date has been in the design and delivery of authentic learning via distance education for archives and records professionals. Dr Anderson is a Fellow of the Australian Society of Archivists.

Jennifer Berryman has worked in policy and planning at the State Library of New South Wales since 1992. During this period, she has also facilitated strategic and operational planning processes and conducted several research projects at the State Library, working as a member of the Research and Evaluation team. Recent research work includes studies into the implications of e-government for public libraries and assessing the contribution made by public libraries to sustainable communities. Jennifer also teaches in the Information and Knowledge Management program at the University of Technology, Sydney.

Alex Byrne is the president of the International Federation of Library Associations and Institutions. Earlier appointments included foundation chair of IFLA's Committee on Free Access to Information and Freedom of Expression, chair of the IFLA Section on University and Other Research Libraries and president of the Council of Australian University Librarians. His career has taken him to universities from Townsville to Canberra to Darwin to Sydney, where he is currently the university librarian at the University of Technology, Sydney. His publications are primarily in information management, community empowerment and human rights, especially on freedom of expression and access to information.

Jasmine Cameron is assistant director general, Executive and Coordination Support, at the National Library of Australia. She is responsible for many aspects of policy and governance within the Library, including ministerial and departmental liaison, strategic planning and services to the Library's Council. Jasmine has a technical services background, specialising in serials management. Over the past ten years she has been involved in the development of digital services, including digitisation. Jasmine is currently a committee member of the National Libraries Section of IFLA, and during 2007–2008 will serve again as secretary of the Conference of Directors of National Libraries.

Tom Denison is a research associate with the Centre for Community Networking Research within Monash University's Faculty of Information Technology. He is currently working on the DART project, investigating data management practices within the academic research environment, and undertaking research into the take-up and use of information and communications technology by community sector organisations. The latter project forms the basis of his PhD research. With a background in library automation and electronic publishing, Tom has consulted widely in Australia and Vietnam, and is currently president of VALA and chair of the VALA2008 Programme Committee.

Stuart Ferguson is a senior lecturer in Information Management and Librarianship at Charles Sturt University, Australia. Professional experience encompasses public libraries, a national library and a college library, in Scotland, South Africa and Australia. He has an academic background in politics and political theory, and has a PhD in Marxist aesthetics. Publications include books, articles and conference papers on information ethics, knowledge management, computers in libraries and education for information management. Other research interests include information politics and the knowledge society. He is a program coordinator at CSU and has been a director of its Centre for Information Studies for ten years.

Paul Genoni is a senior lecturer in the Faculty of Media, Society and Culture at Curtin University of Technology. He has published widely in a number of professional areas including collection management, reference, scholarly communication and graduate destinations. He is co-editor of *Collection professional development: Preparing for new roles in libraries* (2005). He previously worked for a number of years in the library at the University of Western Australia, including several years as law librarian. Paul has a PhD in Australian literature and also continues to research and publish in this discipline. He is the author of *Subverting the empire: Explorers and exploration in Australian fiction* (2004).

Gillian Hallam is an associate professor in the School of Information Systems at the Queensland University of Technology, coordinating the library and information management courses. She teaches in the areas of information organisation, reference and information services, collection and access management and professional practice. She has a deep interest in professional development, mentoring and continuing education for information professionals. Prior to joining QUT, she worked as a librarian in the corporate sector, managing business and legal information. Gillian was the CAVAL Visiting Scholar in 2006, coinciding with a sabbatical to research workforce planning issues in the library and information services (LIS) sector. She is also immediate past president of the Australian Library and Information Association.

Ross Harvey is professor of Library and Information Management at Charles Sturt University's School of Information Studies. He has held academic positions at Curtin University of Technology and Monash University in Australia, and in Singapore and New Zealand, and has been a visiting professor at the University of California Los Angeles. His current research and teaching interests include the preservation of library and archival material, especially in digital form. He has published widely in the fields of bibliographic organisation, library education and the preservation of library and archival material, a recent book being *Preserving digital materials* (KG Saur, 2005).

James Herring is a lecturer in Teacher Librarianship at Charles Sturt University, School of Information Studies. Prior to his appointment there he taught at Queen Margaret's College in Edinburgh. He has been researching and writing about teacher librarianship for twenty-five years, and is the author of eight books in the area of information literacy, the role of the teacher librarian and the use of ICT, particularly the web, by teacher librarians. His current interests are the teacher librarian's role in school intranets and instructional websites, and focus on the use of the 'PLUS' model in schools.

Philip Hider is a senior lecturer in the School of Information Studies at Charles Sturt University. He has previously worked as bibliographic manager of Singapore Integrated Library Automation Services, as a lecturer in Information and Library Studies at Temasek Polytechnic and as a cataloguer at the British Library. Dr Hider has conducted numerous short courses and published many articles in the area of information organisation and retrieval. He holds an honours degree in Social Anthropology from the London School of Economics, a Master of Librarianship degree from the University of Wales, Aberystwyth, and a PhD from City University, London.

Jan Houghton is a senior lecturer in the Information and Knowledge Management program, Faculty of Humanities and Social Sciences, University of Technology Sydney, where she teaches in undergraduate and graduate programs. She has a Graduate Diploma in Library Science from Kuring-gai College of Advanced Education and a Master of Arts (Communications Technology and Policy) from Macquarie University. Her teaching is mainly in the areas of information society issues, public information and communication policies and information management, including ethical professional practice. Her recent research and consulting interests focus on access to government information and e-government. She is the author and co-author of a number of publications and has presented papers at Australian and international conferences.

Chris Jones is the manager of Library Services for the Great Lakes Library Service – a position he has held since 1998. He started work in public libraries in 1987, for Parramatta City Council. Since then he has been employed at all levels in public libraries and has previously been a housebound service librarian, a branch librarian and reference librarian. He has worked in metropolitan, rural and coastal library services. This professional experience has enabled him to develop a strong appreciation of the wide range of challenges that confront modern libraries and the people who will be steering them into the twenty-first century. He is actively involved in the marketing of public libraries.

Annemaree Lloyd is a senior lecturer in the School of Information Studies at Charles Sturt University, Wagga Wagga, Australia, and has a PhD in the field of workplace information literacy. She has strong interest in theoretical and applied understandings of information literacy and her ongoing research focuses on exploring information literacy meaning in workplace contexts; the role of information literacy in embodied learning; information affordance and communities of practice; information literacy in the construction of safe working practice; and information seeking as contested practice.

Damian Lodge is a lecturer in the School of Information Studies and Director of the Centre for Information Studies at Charles Sturt University. He has worked in academic and public libraries in New South Wales, Victoria and Tasmania. Prior to his current position, Damian was the manager of Client and Information services at the Wagga Campus Library of Charles Sturt University, where he managed the areas of Information Services, Distance Education Services and Lending Services. He holds a Masters in Applied Science in Library and Information Management and a Masters in Business Administration. Damian is undertaking a PhD through Charles Sturt University on academic library managers and organisational culture.

Michael Middleton is a senior lecturer in the School of Information Systems at Queensland University of Technology. His interests include information management, information use analysis and digital libraries. His professional career has been spent in libraries and as an academic at UNSW and QUT. He has won a variety of grants for research in information management and for development of teaching and learning in the area of information services. Publications include the books *Information management*, published by the Centre for Information Studies, and with Len Asprey, *Integrative document and content management*, published by Idea Group. Michael also has extensive experience as a consultant.

John Mills has been on the lecturing staff at CSU since 1979. His main teaching interests are value-added information services, information-seeking behaviour and user-information professional relations. He has published in the latter two areas and completed his doctoral research in 2002 on the subject of information-seeking behaviour of university academics. More recently his research has concentrated upon the experiences of international students in Australia and factors affecting student retention.

Roxanne Missingham is parliamentary librarian, Australian Parliamentary Library. She is responsible for the delivery of research and information services to the Parliament, including approximately eighty staff in the Research Branch and sixty in Information Access Branch. She was formerly assistant director general, Resource Sharing Division, National Library of Australia, where she was responsible for a range of services, including Libraries Australia, which enables libraries and individuals to access more than forty million items held by Australian libraries. She has been a library educator, library manager and researcher and was president of the Australian Library and Information Association (ALIA) in 2006/07.

Shirley Oakley is executive director, Library Services at Charles Sturt University, a multi-campus university in inland New South Wales, which is a major provider of distance education in Australia and overseas. She has worked in all aspects of technical and client services in university libraries over the course of her career. She is particularly interested in organisational responses to future-proof service delivery against the environmental challenges facing higher education libraries in the twenty-first century. She chairs the Working Group for the Council of Australian University Librarians national borrowing scheme for students and staff: University Libraries Australia.

Alison O'Connor has been national library manager for law firm Blake Dawson Waldron since 2005. She was manager of the BDW Melbourne office library for the preceding five years. She is an active member of the Australian Library and Information Association, was an original member of the New Generation Policy and Advisory Group and first convenor of the New Graduates Group, as well as serving on the committee of ALIAVic.

Bob Pymm is a lecturer in Library and Information Management at Charles Sturt University, School of Information Studies. He has worked in libraries and related cultural institutions for more than twenty years. From 1993 until early 2005, he worked for the National Film and Sound Archive in Canberra, latterly as the manager of their Collection Development area. Teaching interests include: collection development, preservation of digital materials, popular culture and libraries and audio visual materials. He has a PhD in the area of Australian popular fiction and its preservation, and is interested in researching the role of popular culture materials and their place in documenting society.

Alastair Smith is a senior lecturer in the School of Information Management at Victoria University of Wellington, New Zealand. He teaches courses in reference work and information retrieval in the Master of Library and Information Studies, the basic postgraduate professional program for librarians and information managers in New Zealand. Alastair has taught library and information management at Victoria University since 1989. Prior to this, he was involved in database development at the National Library of New Zealand, and worked as a reference librarian in scientific and technical information services. His pre-library careers included school teaching, truck driving and patent examining. He has a BSc in physics, an MA on the use of expert systems in library work, and is an Fellow of LIANZA.

Jennifer Vaughan is a Charles Sturt University alumni, who studied at Wagga Wagga campus after years spent living overseas. She is currently manager of Library and Information Services for TAFE NSW Riverina Institute. Recent projects include working on the organising committee for the first TAFE NSW library conference in over a decade, and promoting use of statistics by clients, culminating in the winning of the Australian Bureau of Statistics (ABS) Library Extension Program Excellence Award 2006. She has been the NSW representative on the TAFE Libraries Australia committee, president of ALIA Riverina, and is currently the ALIA TAFE NSW representative.

Jake Wallis is a lecturer in Information Studies at Charles Sturt University. He has worked as a researcher at the Centre for Digital Library Research, University of Strathclyde, and in information systems at the University of Glasgow. His research looks at conceptualisations of the information and knowledge societies, particularly in relation to culture and sustainable development in a global context.

Index

Because the entire volume is about libraries and information, the use of these terms as entry points has been minimised in this Index. Similarly, as much of the focus of the book is Australian libraries, 'Australia' has not been used as an entry point except for proper names. Names of cited authors are included in this Index only when their work is discussed or a substantial quote is included.